GLOBALIZATION
ISSUES AT THE GRASSROOTS

About the Authors

Prof. Ganapathi Palanithurai, Chairperson, Rajiv Gandhi Chair, Chairperson, The Hunger Project of Tamil Nadu Council, Gandhigram Rural University is an academic activist working with the people in rural areas for building the capacity of the leaders and people to reinvent and strength grassroots democracy and to achieve sustainable Rural Development. He is heading the Department of Political Science and Development Administration, in Gandhigram Rural University, Tamil Nadu. His policy advocacy role at the governmental level is increasingly felt at present in all the three levels, namely sub-regional, regional and national as he does more filed work than theorisation. He has been associating himself with Central Planning Commission, State Planning Commission of Tamil Nadu, and State Finance Commission of Tamil Nadu and he carried out several research studies in decentralization for both governments. His activities are supported by Population Foundation of India, the Ford Foundation, UNICEF, Rajiv Gandhi Foundation, CAPART, Ministry of Rural Development, Ministry of Panchayati Raj, UNDP, SDC, World Bank, Action Aid, Department of Rural Development, Government of Tamil Nadu and DANIDA (Danish-Indo Development Agency) in specific areas of activities in connection with empowerment of people. He is in the network of the Non-Governmental Organisations for Panchayat activities. He involves himself in capacity building exercise for local body leaders. He has evolved training module and manual for local body leaders. He has to his credit forty two books, seventy nine articles in reputed journals, twelve working papers, seven monographs, seven review articles on three major areas, namely, Legislative Behaviour, Ethnicity and Panchayati Raj System. He was a recipient of Fellowship from Sastri Indo-Canadian Institute, New Delhi and World Academy of Art and Science, USA. He has visited the US and Canada, on academic assignments. He was a visiting fellow in the MiGill University, Canada in 1989. He is a life member of Indian Institute of Public Administration, Indian Association of Public Administration, Indian Association of Political Science, Indian Association of American Studies and Indian Association of Canadian Studies. He is a member of the expert committee constituted by the Government of Tamil Nadu, to monitor the training programme for local body leaders. He is a member of Board of Studies of seven universities. He is a member in the high level committee constituted for devolution of powers to Local Bodies in Tamil Nadu.

R. Ramesh is currently working as a Project Officer for the Terre Des Hommes — A Netherlands based organization with its India country office at Hosur. He worked as a Research Fellow on "Globalization and Decentralization" in Gandhigram Rural University for two years. He has completed his Ph.D. programme in "Community Managed Domestic Water Supply in Tamil Nadu". He is basically a recognized trainer and an action researcher. He has worked for a variety of projects with varied scope and scale for over 15 years. He also served as a Training Expert for DANIDA assisted project on Water and Sanitation. To his credit he has published several articles in international journals and has co-authored a book title *'Analyzing Community Problems – Tentacles of PRA Methodology'*.

GLOBALIZATION
ISSUES AT THE GRASSROOTS

G. Palanithurai
R. Ramesh

CONCEPT PUBLISHING COMPANY, NEW DELHI-110059

Cataloging in Publication Data--DK
Courtesy: D.K. Agencies (P) Ltd. <docinfo@dkagencies.com>

Palanithurai, G. (Ganapathy), 1953-
Globalization : issues at the grassroots / G. Palanithurai, R. Ramesh.
p. cm.
With reference to Tamil Nadu, India.
Includes bibliographical references.
Includes index.
ISBN 13: 9788180695117
ISBN 10: 8180695115

1. Globalization--Economic aspects--India-Tamil Nadu. 2. Water-supply, Rural--Government policy-India--Tamil Nadu. 3. Agriculture and state--India-Tamil Nadu. 4. Rural poor--Government policy--India-Tamil Nadu. 5. Rural development--India--Tamil Nadu. I. Title.

DDC 338.954 22

This publication emerges out of an action research on "Globalization and Decentralization" carried out in Tamil Nadu from February 2005 to August 2007 supported by the Ford Foundation, New Delhi.

ISBN-13: 978-81-8069-511-7
ISBN-10: 81-8069-511-5

First Published 2008

Published and Printed by
Ashok Kumar Mittal
Concept Publishing Company
A/15-16, Commercial Block, Mohan Garden
New Delhi-110059 (INDIA)

Phones : 25351460, 25351794
Fax : 091-11-25357103
Email : publishing@conceptpub.com

Preface

The visible output of globalization, liberalization and privatization in the Indian context, especially during the past decade is mind-boggling. Think back the wait one was to make to get a land-line phone connection about a decade ago, against the choice of services and the variety of plan-options one gets today with a mobile phone service-provider. Similarly, compare the information service an individual researcher could avail when one had to depend singly on printed media a decade ago, and the mass of information one gets through the Internet or through a digital library today. Think of the inevitable choice one was left with when it came to buying a car in India (obviously Ambassador!) about a decade or so ago, and the type of cars that ply on Indian roads today. Travelling even short distances like from Chennai to Bangalore has also become 'simply fly'. The infrastructure development in terms of airport and seaport development, expansion of national high ways etc. that are taking place in this country is astounding.

India reports a fantastic 9 per cent growth rate. Obviously, higher the growth rate reported, faster is the consumption, and higher would be the exploitation of resources – including the non-renewable ones. The current debate about development is: who does this kind of development benefit? – and do all these result in equity in development? And who does it completely neglect at all, if it did. Is there a chance for the poor in the villages, the farmers who depend on agriculture, and the artisans who depend on their skills for a living, to enjoy the benefits globalization brings about? Some activists and the Village Panchayats that are close to people as the third government are also raising these as issues. There is also unprecedented migration reported in some of the states of India that are designated as fast adopters of liberalization policies. Similarly, while rural poverty is reported to be on the decline, urban poverty is zooming. The pace of expansion of urban slums, with zero civic facilities, is staggering. As a result there are several different explanations given about the impact of globalization in India. There are highly learned persons who come out with research results supported by macro level data either admiring liberalization policies or demeaning it. There are activists, generally with NGO background, who invariably raise dissenting voices against globalization.

Studies conducted on the impact of globalization are mostly based on either macro level data or cases and instances drawn from other countries that implement liberalization policies. Few studies have been conducted so as to understand empirically the impact of globalization in India. This book is an attempt in that direction. This book contains a series of empirical studies conducted in Tamil Nadu. The basic premises or the trigger to initiate these studies have been voices, with a tinge of globalization policies, from various villages of Tamil Nadu during post-liberalization era. The focus of analysis and discussions has been if liberalization policies and the globalization process benefit the rural poor in general and rural pursuits in particular.

We must put on record our deep sense of gratitude to the Ford Foundation, New Delhi that made this empirical research possible through a funding support. When it comes to acknowledging everyone who works for the Rajiv Gandhi Chai for Panchayati Raj Studies at the Gandhigram Rural University deserve a mention. However, we wish to acknowledge with a lot of appreciation the efforts of the team of researchers especially Dr. K. Pandimuruga Chinnan, Mr. P. Selvamani and Dr. Nataraja Murthy, who worked at the field collecting data and information, and preparing the first draft of research reports. Ms. B. Punithalakshmi and Mr. S.P. Ramesh deserve mention for their neat type setting of reports, and Ms. J. Vanishree, Lecturer in the Department of Political Science and Development Administration for her patient proof reading. Several eminent scholars, senior civil servants, NGO activists, Panchayat leaders, and academicians who participated in a validation workshop contributed immensely towards enriching the validity of these papers. Prof. K.V. Palanithurai retired full time member of State Planning Commission, Government of Tamil Nadu and Prof. R. Elango, Former Dean, Faculty of Social Sciences, Annamalai University have gone through the entire manuscript and offered their comments. Since both of them are from the economic divisions, their suggestions are highly valuable for us. It would require a separate annexure to mention all of them. We thank every one of them. Finally, those in the villages pursuing various kinds of rural livelihoods — be it agriculture, handloom weaving, carpentry, black smithy, gold smithy, etc. shared their knowledge and experiences of various sectors covered in this book. We must thank every one of them from our heart of hearts.

G. Palanithurai
R. Ramesh

Contents

Preface *v*
List of Abbreviations and Acronyms ix
List of Tables xv
List of Boxes xvii
List of Figures xix

1. Global and Local: An Overview 1
2. Water Paradigms: Issues and Controversies 12
3. Public Water for Private Profit: Globalization in its Logical Minimum 23
4. Water Service Provision: Public-Private Partnership 43
5. Natural Resources at Peril: Commercial Exploitation is the Order of the Day 59
6. Changing Face of Agriculture: Culture *versus* Commerce 84
7. Food Security in Tamil Nadu: The Survival Matrices 134
8. The Plantation Crisis: Indian Tea Knocked Out of the Cup 175
9. Traditional Rural Artisans: Remaining Contemporarily Relevant 220
10. Traditional Handloom Weavers: Market Forces that Draw Caricatures 270
11. Changing Waves of Fisheries: The State of Fisheries Sector in Tamil Nadu 335
12. Globalization and Grassroots Action 354

Annexure 361
Notes and References 364
Index 374

Abbreviations and Acronyms

AAY	:	Antyodaya Anna Yojana
AD Handlooms	:	Assistant Director of Handlooms
ADB	:	Asian Development Bank
AEZs	:	Agriculture Export Zones
AMS	:	Aggregate Measure of Support
AoA	:	Agreement on Agriculture
APL	:	Above Poverty Line
APMC	:	Agriculture Produce Marketing Committee
ASI	:	Additional Sales Tax
ASIDE	:	Assistance to States for Infrastructure Development and Exports
ATC	:	Agreement on Textiles and Clothing
ATO	:	Asymmetric Trade Opportunities
BIS	:	Bureau of Indian Standards
BLF	:	Bought Leaf Factories
BPL	:	Below Poverty Line
BSM	:	Buyer Seller Meet
Bt	:	Bacillus Thruingiensis
CACP	:	Commission on Agricultural Costs and Prices
CBoI	:	Coffee Board of India
CBOs	:	Community Based Organizations
CC Facility	:	Cash Credit Facility
CF	:	Contract Farming
CGWA	:	Central Ground Water Authority
Co-optex	:	The Tamil Nadu Handloom Weavers' Cooperative Society Ltd.
CPI (M)	:	Communist Parties of India (Marxist)
CPI	:	Communist Parties of India
CSOs	:	Civil Society Organizations

CTC	:	Crush-Tear-Curl
DCCB	:	District Central Cooperative Bank
DDHPYS	:	Deen Dayal Hathkargha Protsahan Yojana Scheme
DES	:	Duty Exemption Scheme
DPC	:	Direct Purchase Centre
DRDA	:	District Rural Development Agency
ECA	:	Essential Commodities Act
EOC	:	Eight O'clock Coffee Company
EOU	:	Export Oriented Units
EPCGS	:	Export Promotion Capital Goods Scheme
EU	:	European Union
EXIM	:	Export and Import
FAO	:	Food and Agriculture Organization
FCI	:	Food Corporation of India
FDI	:	Foreign Direct Investment
FDS	:	Free Distribution of Sarees
FGD	:	Focus Group Discussion
FLD	:	Front Line Demonstration
FPS	:	Fair Price Shop
FSB	:	Food Security Box
GATS	:	General Agreement on Trade in Services
GDP	:	Gross Domestic Product
GO	:	Government Order
GoI	:	Government of India
GRI-RGC	:	Gandhigram Rural Institute-Rajiv Gandhi Chair
HACCP	:	Hazard Analysis and Critical Control Points
HEPC	:	Handloom Export Promotion Council
HL	:	Handloom
HLL	:	Hindustan Lever Limited
HSCs	:	House Service Connections
ICO	:	International Coffee Organization
IIHT	:	Indian Institute of Handloom Technology
ILO	:	International Labour Organization
IMF	:	International Monetary Fund
IP	:	Inspector of Plantations
IPM	:	Integrated Pest Management
IWCS	:	Industrial Weavers Cooperative Society
JACCTRG	:	Joint Action Committee for Conservation of Thamirabarani River and Groundwater

JD Handlooms	:	Joint Director of Handlooms
KVIC	:	Khadi and Village Industries Commission
KVK	:	Krishi Vigyan Kendra
Lpcd	:	Litre per capita per day
MCM	:	Million Cubic Metres
MDA	:	Market Development Assistance
MFA	:	Multi-fibre Agreement
MFL	:	Madras Fertilizers Limited
MMTC	:	Minerals and Metal Trading Corporation
MNCs	:	Multi-National Corporations
MoU	:	Memorandum of Understanding
MSP	:	Minimum Support Price
MSSRF	:	M.S. Swaminathan Research Foundation
MT	:	Metric Tonne
NABARD	:	National Bank for Agriculture and Rural Development
NAFED	:	National Agricultural Cooperative Marketing Federation
NAI	:	Net Area Irrigated
NAIS	:	National Agricultural Insurance Scheme
NAS	:	Net Area Sown
NCF	:	National Commission on Farmers
NEP	:	New Economic Policy
NGOs	:	Non-Governmental Organizations
NHDC	:	National Handloom Development Corporation
NID	:	National Institute of Designs
NIFT	:	National Institute of Fashion Technology
NL	:	Nepal Loom
NOC	:	No Objection Certificate
NREGA	:	National Rural Employment Guarantee Act
NSDP	:	Net State Domestic Product
NTADCL	:	New Thirupur Area Development Corporation Limited
NTC	:	National Textile Corporation
NTP	:	New Textile Policy
O&M	:	Operation and Maintenance
OAP	:	Old Age Pension
OECD	:	Organization for Economic Cooperation and Development
OGL	:	Open General License

PACS	:	Primary Agricultural Cooperative Society
PDS	:	Public Distribution System
PFs	:	Public Foundations
PL	:	Power Loom
PPP	:	Public-Private Partnership
PRA	:	Participatory Rural Appraisal
PRODIP	:	Product Development, Design Intervention and Packaging
PSF	:	Price Stabilization Fund
PWCS	:	Primary Level Weavers' Cooperative Society
R&D	:	Research and Development
RoI	:	Return of Investment
RTE	:	Registered Textile Exporter
RWH	:	Rain Water Harvesting
SAP	:	Structural Adjustment Programme
SCA	:	Speciality Coffee Association
SDT	:	Special and Differential Treatment
SEZ	:	Special Export Zone
SFURTI	:	Scheme for Regeneration of Traditional Industries
SHGs	:	Self-Help Groups
SIBCL	:	South India Bottling Company Limited
SIDCO	:	Small Industries Development Corporation
SIPCOT	:	State Industries Promotion Corporation of Tamil Nadu
SIPPO	:	Small Industries Product Promotion Organization
SLEPC	:	State Level Export Promotion Committee
SMP	:	Statutory Minimum Price
SPIC	:	Southern Petro-chemical Industries Corporation
SPS measures	:	Sanitary and Phyto-Sanitary measures
SPs	:	Special Products
SSI	:	Small Scale Industries
SSI	:	Semi- Structural Interviewing
SSM	:	Special Safeguard Mechanism
SSML	:	Super Spinning Mill Limited
SSS	:	Savings and Security Scheme
TANTEA	:	Tamil Nadu Tea Plantation Corporation Limited
TAWIDB	:	Traditional Artisans Welfare and Industrial Development Board
TBI	:	Tea Board of India
TBT	:	Technical Barriers to Trade

THDC Ltd	:	Tamil Nadu Handloom Development Corporation Ltd.
TNCs	:	Transnational Corporations
TPDS	:	Targeted Public Distribution System
TQM	:	Total Quality Management
TRIPS	:	Trade Related Intellectual Property Rights
TRQs	:	Tariff Rate Quotas
TUFS	:	Technology Up-gradation Fund Scheme
TWAD	:	Tamil Nadu Water Supply and Drainage Board
USA	:	United States of America
UNCTAD	:	United Nations Conference on Trade and Development
UNDP	:	United Nations Development Programme
UPASI	:	United Planters Association of South India
VPs	:	Village Panchayats
VRS	:	Voluntary Retirement of Service
VWSCs	:	Village and Water Sanitation Committees
WSC	:	Weavers' Service Centre
WTO	:	World Trade Organization

List of Tables

2.1	Issues and Indicators	21
3.1	Villages that Might be Affected if SIBCL Started Operating	38
3.2	Land Particulars of the Vulnerable Panchayats	39
3.3	Cattle Population of the Vulnerable Panchayats	39
3.4	Traditional Water Bodies of the Vulnerable Panchayats	40
4.1	Particulars of (Water Related) Annual Income and Expenditure in the Villages of New Thiruppur Scheme	53
5.1	Metro Water's Daily Water Sheet	67
5.2	Particulars about River Adjacent Cultivators	71
5.3	Combined Water Supply Scheme	72
5.4	Encroachment Particulars of Water Storage Structures in Velapalayam	78
5.5	Change is cropping pattern	79
5.6	Functional Status of Domestic Water Supply Facilities in Velapalayam	79
6.1	Net and Gross Area Irrigated in Thiruvarur District during 2003-04	101
6.2	Area under Paddy Cultivation in Thiruvarur District (in ha.)	102
6.3	Seasonal Employment in Agriculture	104
6.4	Increasing Input Cost per Bag	107
6.5	Minimum Support Price Announced for Paddy by Tamil Nadu Government	109
6.6	Area under Cotton Cultivation in Tamil Nadu	115
6.7	Acreage and Variety of Cotton in Selected Villages of Madukkarai Block	118
7.1	Share of Foodgrains and Non-Foodgrains in Gross Cropped Area.	138
7.2	Categories of Family Cards as on 31-1-2005	140
7.3	Method of Distribution of Essential Commodities under PDS	141

7.4	Production, Procurement, Allotment and Off-take of Rice in Tamil Nadu	142
7.5	Details of PDS Coverage and Shift in Emphasis	143
7.6	Food Subsidy of Tamil Nadu Government	144
8.1	India's Share in International Tea Trade	181
8.2	Tea Production in South Indian States (in M. kgs.).	183
8.3	Share of Orthodox Teas in Total Tea Produced and Exported	185
8.4	Details of Export in North, South and All India	188
8.5	Average Sales Price of Tea	189
8.6	Snapshot of Financial Crisis Faced by South Indian Tea	190
8.7	Comparative Statement of Tax Liability in India	191
8.8	Agricultural Income Tax on 60 per cent of the Income from Tea	192
8.9	Details of Employment Strength	197
8.10	Coffee Production by States-2005-2006*	202
8.11	No. of Holdings under Different Size Categories of Traditional Coffee Growing in Tamil Nadu - 2003-2004	202
8.12	Details of Average Daily Number of Persons Employed in Coffee Plantations in Tamil Nadu	204
8.13	Wage Rates Prevailing in the Coffee Sector	205
8.14	Coffee Production in Tamil Nadu	209
	(in metric tonnes)	209
10.1	Performance of Handloom Weavers Cooperatives in Tamil Nadu	278
10.2	Functional and Dormant Societies in the Selected Districts	290
10.3	Number of Looms in Selected Districts	291
10.4	Profit and Loss making Societies in Selected Districts	291
10.5	Average Number of Weavers per-Loom	292
10.6	Net Wage of a Handloom Weaver	293
10.7	Production, Sales and Stock of Handloom Products	293
10.8	Dues to Societies by Co-optex and Government	294
10.9	Beneficiaries under Various Government Schemes (2004-05)	294
10.10	Sector-wise Production of Fabrics in India	304
10.11	Free Dhoti - Saree Scheme - Tamil Nadu	321

List of Boxes

3.1	Coco Cola – Pepsi Cola "Quit India	25
3.2	CSE Report Creates Stir	28
3.3	JPC on Soft Drink	28
3.4	Coca Cola Suspended in US	29
3.5	Background to the Location of SIPCOT at Gangaikondan	30
3.6	Right to Water	32
3.7	Expert Panel to Study Environmental Impact	34
3.8	Panchay Union Gives Node to Soft Drink Unit	42
5.1	Water Business	61
5.2	A New Product Called "Drinking Water"	62
5.3	Illegal Bottled Water	65
5.4	Ground Water Regulation	65
5.5	Hydro-geological Report	68
5.6	Re. 1 Water Pouches	69
5.7	High Court Statement on Water Bodies	75
5.8	State to Study Encroachments	77
5.9	Penatise Land–Grabbers	81
6.1	Falling Farm Income–UNCTAD Report	107
6.2	Dimensions of the Crisis	114
6.3	G.M. Cotton Seeds	119
6.4	Imports of Cotton	121
7.1	Rural Poverty Programmes with a Food Distribution Component	139
7.2	Charcoal Making for a Livelihood	149
7.3	Recreating a Life in Unwanted Sacks	154
7.4	Micro-indicatives of Macro Perils	156
8.1	Seasonality in Coffee Cultivation	204
10.1	Earnings of a Master Weaver	280
10.2	Age–Wise Classification of Weavers in India	288
10.3	Janatha Cloth Scheme	300
10.4	Power loom Weavers in Tamil Nadu	302

10.5 The Uneconomical Handlooms 304
10.6 Procurement Price for Saree and Dhoti by Government of Tamil Nadu 322
10.7 Falling Wage Rate 326

List of Figures

7.1	Employment in a Single Crop (S. Pudukottai	158
7.2	Employment in a Multi-crop village Murugampatty	158
8.1	Area Under Tea in Nilgiris (Taluk – Wise)	

1

Global and Local: An Overview

Introduction

Two concepts have occupied development literature more than anything else in the past couple of decades. One is 'globalization' and the other is 'decentralization'. Some describe these concepts as one being complementary to the other while others describe them as being antithetical to each other. At face value, they represent two extreme poles. Neither of them is new. But both of them have taken a new incarnation in the recent decade. In the context of India, both of them, obviously, have historical routes, and they have legitimate sanctions too.

Globalization, in its primary sense, means expansion of economic transactions and the organization of economic activities across the political boundaries of nation-states. So, it is not only a matter pertaining to *market economy*, but also to *political democracy* (Deepak Nayyar, 2002). Decentralization is the process of dispersing or delegating decision-making authority relatively away from a central authority closer to the point of service or action. One of the main features of decentralization is a bottom-to-top flow of decision-effecting ideas (Wikipedia, 2001). That is devolving political, administrative, and fiscal powers and responsibilities from a higher level Central Government to the smallest institution at the grassroots level (G. Palanithurai, 2001). Globalization advocates doing away the borders and boundaries in order to ensure efficiency; decentralization advocates breaking up in order to bring things up in an effectively manageable unit.

In India, globalization of economy and decentralization of powers are the two initiatives vigorously pursued. Tamil Nadu is considered to be one of the fastest adopters of globalization ideas – be it setting up of Information Technology (IT) parks, establishment of Special Economic Zones (SEZ), or invitation for Foreign Direct Investment (FDI). Tamil Nadu is far ahead of most other Indian states in implementing globalization ideas (*The Business Line*, July 29, 2006). The State Government of Tamil Nadu is pursuing in full swing infrastructure and urban development projects, promoting Public-Private Partnership, and structural adjustment programmes etc. to be able to attract FDI, which as per the contention of the government brings in the badly needed finance, economic efficiency and employment.

The process of privatization, liberalization, and globalization has placed new players centre stage in the world economy. There are two main sets of economic players in this game: transnational corporations which dominate investment, production, and trade in the world economy, and international banks and financial intermediaries which control the world of finance. This has induced a strategic withdrawal on the part of the nation-state in some important spheres. That means the nation-states remain political players but are no longer the main economic players. This is viewed as a problem because governments are accountable to their people, whereas markets are not (Deepak Nayyar, 2002).

The concept of globalization—being promoted by the WTO and its supporting organizations – is said to be a mixed blessing. Some say it is a blessing and others say it is a curse. It is a blessing because it brings in private finance to public domain, improves efficiency and out put, enables consumers to get good quality product at the lowest possible price, opens up new employment opportunities leading to higher income and better standards of living. It is a curse because a large proportion of the population in poorer countries remain marginalized by the process of globalization (Jagdish Bhagwati, 2004). Such exclusion or marginalization has had social consequences, environmental destruction and degradation of common property resources. There is widespread impression that the subject – globalization—is divisive and the concepts spread across are contentious (Joseph E. Stiglitz, 2002).

Even within Tamil Nadu state there are dissenting voices raised by non-conformists of globalization that it is predetermined only for the knowledgeable and the moneyed and that it robs off the livelihood resources of the poor. The world is divided into pro-globalization defenders and anti-globalization protesters (Nayan Chanda, 2002). In between is there a community that has taken a pragmatic course. They put across that proper governance can accelerate benefits and lessen the chances of getting hurt by globalization processes.

Tamil Nadu Context

Tamil Nadu state's population is 62 million as per 2001 census as opposed to 55.9 million in 1991. The ratio works out to 986 in 2001 as compared to 974 in 1991 and 977 in 1981. SC and ST population constitutes 11.3 million and of them 5.6 million are women. Tamil Nadu's HDI (2001) was 0.657 as compared to 0.571 for India as a whole. Tamil Nadu is generally regarded as a socially above average state of the Indian union. Tamil Nadu Government has always been proud of its impressive performance in the field of social sector. Among the 15 major states of India, Tamil Nadu holds impressive ranks in general literacy rates, sex ratio, birth rates, infant mortality rates. In terms of the quality of life index Tamil Nadu was assessed to be the 4th among the 15 major states of India. But it is very striking that in terms of rural index, Tamil Nadu held a lowly 11th rank, lower than even low income states such as Madhya Pradesh, Rajasthan and Orissa.

There are protests organized by civil society groups within Tamil Nadu that the life of the poor in the rural areas is becoming more and more difficult as their livelihood opportunities are taken away as the globalization process is set in motion through the policies of the State and Central Governments since 1991 when the new Economic Policy was initiated. The worst affected, are the agricultural labourers, fishers, weavers, rural artisans and women. Basic services such as medical, water supply and sanitation services are turning cost-based and are provided on the basis of the charges paid by the users. Natural resources, which are the lifeline of the poor, are being exploited for producing marketable commodities by multi-national companies. Water is being bottled, sand is being lifted and blue metal is being quarried by companies. Communities at the local level are sporadically fighting against such kind of exploitation of natural resources. Panchayat leaders are widely fighting against this kind of exploitation with the support of the communities. In the coastal areas shrimp cultivation is going on a large scale, eroding the natural resources, by which several thousands of fishermen and agricultural labourers have lost their livelihood. They are fighting against these new initiatives as they affect their life and livelihood security. When silicon soil was lifted from Vanduvancheri

Gram Panchayat area in Tanjore District, it was stopped by the Panchayat with the support of the community. The matter is now in court. When water was lifted from Sivaganga for bottling of mineral water, it was stopped by the local community which said that water is not a commodity but an entitlement of the people and the mineral water company should not be allowed to make it a commodity for the market to make profits. As the State Government stopped its subsidy for khadi and handloom products, the weavers lost employment opportunity and, as a result, they started migrating to different places in search of employment.

Thus the havoc wrought by globalization processes on the livelihood security of the people in the villages can be enumerated with the distress condition it has resulted in. The unskilled workers who were being used in the construction industry and road projects have been driven away as the activities have become totally mechanized and technology-driven. As reform activities were initiated, the subsidy for electricity consumption by the small farmers has been cut and, as a result, the small farmers have had to give up their farm activities. Being a frontline state in social development activities, Tamil Nadu has now reversed its policy options to cope with new economic policy reforms.

Economic globalization has set in motion through the policies of the State Government. The problems arise only when new policy options exert pressure on the Panchayats and the Gram Sabha (Village Assembly). The Panchayat leaders are facing all these problems. Without having enough knowledge of this process every one is struggling. In Tamil Nadu, there are 12605 Gram Panchayats, 384 Block Panchayats and 28 District Panchayats. Of the 12605 Gram Panchayats, 3046 are headed by SC and ST men and women. Of the 3046 Gram Panchayats, 1107 are headed by SC/ST women. 3150 Gram Panchayats are headed by other caste Hindu women leaders. New Panchayat Act came into force in the year 1994. Basic services have been given to the Panchayat institutions despite several constraints and yet Panchayats are struggling to serve the people. Panchayat leaders in Tamil Nadu have started assuming powers and are taking responsibilities which have already set the devolution process to emerge.

The Paradox

While democracy is being deepened through decentralization of powers, the economy is globalized. It is a paradoxical situation at present that both processes work together. While globalization aims at promoting trade, decentralization aims at promoting development. The paradox is that trade and development should take place simultaneously. Decentralization of powers and globalization of the economy are institutionalized. There are opinions, views and observations about the process, the implications of the globalization of the economy and the decentralization of powers. Studies are pouring in on the implications of decentralization of powers—positive and negative—and by nature and content they are location specific. Likewise, there are innumerable studies on globalization. Yet opposition to globalization and support for decentralization are emerging all over the world offering an impression that globalization is working against the interests of the people of small means, and decentralization is working towards the prosperity of such people. The fact remains that despite the open support for decentralization, the process of decentralization is not smooth. Despite opposition to globalization the process of globalization proceeds apace through the policies of the government. It is a major question that needs to be probed whether the government is working against the interests of the people in a democracy.

There is yet another issue to be seen in this context, namely, the position taken by individuals, organizations, associations and institutions on decentralization of powers and globalization of the economy. There are a large number of institutions totally opposed to the globalization process as if globalization of the economy causes only negative effects on the life of the people. There are organizations that wholeheartedly support the globalization process as if it ushers in prosperity to everyone. On the other hand, for decentralization of powers, one can hear predominantly positive voices. It is true that both globalization and decentralization are worldwide phenomena and a historical process. The delivery and the implications of globalization and decentralization depend on how best they are understood by the policy-makers and the stakeholders. Both have positive and negative aspects to them. So the focus should be on how best both can be utilized for the advancement of society and how best people can be saved from the ill effects of the process of the globalization of the economy and the decentralization of powers. The reality can be understood by learning from one another.

Globalization works in the society through the policies and programmes of the government, both at Centre and in the States. One obvious thing we need to understand along with this fact is that globalization has limited the ability of governments to respond

(Joseph E. Stiglitz, 2006). The impact of globalization will be felt at the grassroots and especially by the marginalized, weaker and poor segments of the society. It has to be mitigated through micro action in the field and macro action through policies and decisions. Grassroots leaders who manage local affairs have to be aware of the implications of globalization and hence they have to be sensitized.

The Synergy Required

Globalization is a mix of challenges, threats and opportunities. In fact, people at the grassroots level hardly have the capacity to understand its complex process, tide over the threats and harvest the opportunities. Threats apart, even if globalization succeeds in bringing in resources such as capital, technology etc. through FDI and opening up opportunities, do we have the ability to take advantage of the new opportunities? This is a major question—a factor determining how well a country will do is the 'quality' of the public and private institutions, which in turn is related to how decisions get made and in whose interests, a subject broadly referred to as 'governance'. India is half-way down the path of globalization. India is said to be one of the major participants in implementing the ideas that promote globalization. So to say, India is appreciated globally as one of the countries that is making the best use of globalization opportunities. It is very much evident from the growth of the service and industrial sectors in the past decade. So, now the debate is, to a large extent, no longer "anti"- or "pro" - globalization. It is about managing globalization or governing globalization so that benefits do not flow only to the rich, and it does not hurt the poor (Krishna Kanat 2003; Bhagwati Jagdish 2004; Joseph E. Stiglitz, 2006).

In this context, Panchayats as people's institution of self-governance and instruments for ensuring their livelihood security, have a critical role to play in arresting the ill effects of globalization and making use of the opportunities for which decentralization provides legitimate power the people to take decisions. Nothing prevents the grassroots leaders from making use of the opportunities, if any, in globalization to achieve development. The benefits would eventually reach the poor also is not to be waited and seen. It should be made to happen at the earliest by managing globalization pro-poor and pro-development and not only pro-trade.

This requires that our leaders at the grassroots must have a clear picture about global issues also. So a link between the advocates and the adversaries of globalization and the grassroots leaders is imperative. This kind of synergy should be a continuous process. It is necessary that Panchayats should be made to look at the reality taking scientific perspective for which they need to be oriented. The most important links between globalization and poverty reduction have to be analysed seriously at the micro level. There should be proper understanding by all concerned about the implications of globalization. To look at issues realistically and scientifically, to take the initiative to protect the people from the onslaught of the potential threats and to make use of the opportunities a continuous dialogue with rural community and concerted action at the grassroots level are crucial.

Globalization of the economy, localization of development, decentralization of powers, ensuring livelihood security of the poor and the marginalized are ongoing activities. These activities cannot be carried out in an isolated way without convergence or synergy of any form. The activities are for different stakeholders and aim at achieving different goals. But the human collective is always looking for prosperity, equity, equality and peace. Institutions which have evolved for governance over a period of time to manage development have to explore all the opportunities which are emerging in the world through the efforts of human beings. At present, globalization is an endeavour to multiply prosperity in geometrical proportion. Decentralization is an endeavour to empower the powerless to decide their destiny. Human development is the major task which the government has to ensure along with economic activity. Making development sustainable is the task of everyone at this juncture as the concept of development seems to be elusive.

In the whole process of development and democracy, learning is very essential and, accordingly, individuals and collectivities can make use of the opportunities to achieve development and to protect themselves and others from the threats, if any, which stem out of these processes. Like globalization is on, economic growth, and human sufferings are also on the increase simultaneously. Mechanization of economic activities through the modern sophisticated technology has driven millions out of job. The growth of unemployment brings about acute social conflict. Aspirations for development and the desire to be in the democratic process are also on the increase in society. Panchayats are people's institution of self-governance and instruments for ensuring their livelihood security, and hence they have a critical role to play in arresting the ill-effects of globalization.

The Empirical Research

Against this background empirical enquiries were undertaken. This was felt necessary because there is a lot of rhetoric flying around about globalization which has led to all kinds of theoretical or hypothetical arguments for and against. There is hardly any empirical study conducted to understand the goings on. This series of research studies conducted with the financial assistance of the Ford Foundation aimed at studying the impact of globalization processes at the grassroots level.

All these processes including how the new dispensation provides opportunities for society to achieve prosperity, how it poses threats and how the threats are being managed have been studied empirically. This has come out with several interesting revelations including about those who control the process of globalization and about those who control the localization of development. Both seem to have strapping complementarities. Further, the grassroots institutions have earmarked roles and responsibilities and the leaders have to administer economic development and social justice. The responsibility of ensuring the livelihood security of the poor is vested with the Panchayats. The Panchayat leaders require consciousness-raising on the implications of globalization. Thus an interconnection has been established between the globals and the locals for mutual benefit and advantage. A series of empirical studies on issues raised above were conducted with the following objectives:

- Studying the implications of economic globalization on the livelihood security of the poor which have come up with the backing of the mediated policies/programmes of the State Government, and those that have sprouted as a consequence of cultural globalization.
- Initiating a dialogue among different stakeholders, especially among the local governments and the policy-makers at the state level, on the results of the empirical research.
- Identifying opportunities for the poor, if any, from globalization and to initiate an action plan for better utilization of such opportunities.
- Establishing effective models of governance for Panchayati Raj Institutions to address the challenges brought about by globalization processes, to protect livelihood security, and to promote the interests of the rural sectors.

Sectors Studied

As this study pertains to the rural sectors in Tamil Nadu which are concerned mostly with non-financial aspects of globalization, it has covered a range of themes within the non-financial sectors. They include:

- Water Resources and Services
- River Sand-mining
- Agriculture
- Food Security
- Plantation (Tea and Coffee Sectors)
- Rural Artisans
- Handloom Weavers.

The 'men' (including both men and women) behind each of these sector and their livelihoods have been paid more attention than the sector *per se*. An empirical research on the impact or implications of globalization processes in rural sectors cannot emerge from a vacuum. There must have been some intervention with the features of globalization having taken place in the areas chosen for the study; or measures advocated as part of the sector reform or structural adjustment programme must have been under implementation to be able to identify the impact they have caused. Therefore, the themes chosen were not arbitrary. In fact, each of this study starts with a premise – that which stands as the reasoning for getting down to studying that issue; that which made the research team understand that it is an issue pertaining to globalization.

In a way, each of this study commenced in order to empirically verify certain crisis which many people believed that the situation is a corollary of globalization processes. The empirical enquiry has come out with results that convey that in some places it has been completely true that globalization has resulted in such crisis, whereas in others it has been only partially true, and they point finger at developments that are domestic and long-standing as the reasons for such crisis.

Research Approach

This is in a way trying to understand the complex social problems that the globalization processes might have resulted in. It usually begins with a problem or a crisis situation in the field. The situation prompts the research team to empirically verify if the problem has been caused by liberalization efforts or deregulation and so on. In research methodology this approach is referred to as *empirico-inductive* approach. It contrasts sharply with the traditional scientific hypothesis-testing approach. It engages in an iterative process. The one main focus of the research is identifying whether the neo-liberal policies and programmes of the government affect the livelihoods of the poor or not. Variables that are malleable to rural livelihoods and globalization processes were taken up for analysis. Therefore, the research process explicitly has had a bearing on certain normative values of society such as equity, accountability and sustainability. If the research process identifies factors that really affect these values, interpretation has tended to be wary, otherwise, it has spelt out that the suspicion is unfounded.

An empirical research on issues relating to globalization and decentralization carried out with a pre-set or even pre-tested questionnaire would tend to omit several vital issues that emerge on the spot. However, the advantage of a questionnaire cannot be completely brushed aside for they usually bring out the quantitative nuances of the problem under study. Participatory methods might be useful. But, for an exploratory exercise on understanding the influence of globalization processes on rural lives and livelihoods, one method would be markedly, less than sufficient. Therefore, this series of research studies recognize the basic differences between participatory methodologies and conventional questionnaire surveys. It has gone on an emerging consensus and has taken the conjunctive use of various methods to best seize the benefits of relative strengths of both qualitative and quantitative methods of doing social research. The basic point is gaining a synergy through methodological integration rather than taking one and embracing the others.

The Micro-Macro Link

There can be two significant ways in which globalization can influence or link up with rural sectors: (a) through the policies and programmes of the government; and (b) cultural media that present themselves in various forms such as TV advertisements, newspapers, magazines, road-side hoardings of an MNC's product carrying cultures that are non-native and so on. The former is (policy changes that are macro are) visible and comes with the legitimate stamp of the government. The latter (cultural globalization) almost stealthily finds place in human mind as desires and starts giving directions to the way one thinks and acts. Understanding grassroots realities (micro-level happenings) and appraising them if they have been outcome of certain policy decisions, institutional restructuring or structural adjustment programme is one of the important aspects of this research. Establishing this micro-macro link is vital and articulating the results of the research in terms of micro-macro link is what makes this study timely and significant.

Both of these media (policy as well as culture) can activate globalization processes and influence the way rural people make a living. The difference is for those policies being sponsored by the government one can hold the government responsible whereas for those that comes through cultural media, especially triggered by the market forces nobody can hold anybody responsible. But, they do create micro-level impact. The effect of wrong policies and programmes at the micro-level are studied. This would facilitate policy advocacy and prepare the grassroots-level institutions to develop an appropriate governance system in order to face such new challenges and to hold the government responsible for answering questions of equity, accountability and sustainability.

This can also make the citizenry responsive to the policy choices of those in government. The cultural mediation needs to be understood so that the good effect or havoc the market forces can play in the lives of ordinary citizens at the villages can be demonstrated with evidences. In the process, if there is anything that the rural people can gain from and view as opportunity could be tapped as well. These research studies have precisely attempted only this.

2

Water Paradigms: Issues and Controversies

Introduction

Today, water tops the agenda on development dialogue all over the world. The problem human race faces with water is that either it is unmanageably abundant or critically scarce. However, the condition of water being plentiful is hardly for a few months in a year. Otherwise, it is 'water crisis' that India spells for the rest of the whole year. India, with 16 per cent of the world's population and 2.45 per cent of the land mass has only 4 per cent of water resources (Ramasamy R. Iyer, 2001). At least for a decade now, there is a competing demand for water amongst purposes such as drinking, irrigation, and industrial use.

Water is indeed a renewable resource. But, in any given year, it is not inexhaustible. The per capita water availability of water for India in 2001 was estimated to be half its 1947 level (Agarwal, A. and Narayan, S., 2002). The crisis of water affects the lives of millions of people today. In 15 states, the underground water levels have been falling at rates ranging between five and seven per cent and some are expected to run dry as early as 2015 because of overdraft and misuse. It is reported that every year we draw twice as much as we replenish it. By the year 2025 the demand for freshwater is expected to rise to 56 per cent above what currently available water can deliver, if current trends persist (Maude Barlow, 2003).

During the last 60 odd years, India has invested a huge amount in harnessing water resources for irrigation, domestic use and non-agricultural activities. The public sector has invested some Rs. 1000 billion in water resource development and it is reported that a whooping

Rs. 32,000 crore has been spent on Rural Water Supply since 1954 (Lennart Nilsson, 2002). Plenty of water schemes in various matrices have been implemented by Government of India and various State Governments under bilateral and multilateral arrangements as well. Despite a large investment in water resources conservation, irrigation infrastructure development, and investment in bringing about sustainability of drinking water supply sources and systems, the net result is 'inadequate water supply for various needs'.

The imminent water crisis in India is being ascribed to, (i) the growing gap between the scarcity value of water and realized value under current pattern of water use and management; (ii) weak governance and mis-governance of water resources by the state; and (iii) the absence of clear-cut property regime or ownership of water. Traditionally, water was perceived to be a free good available from nature. Existing institutional, legal and governance framework relating to acquisition, distribution and utilization of water have not helped in changing this perception. A stage has come where the sovereign right of the state on water or any natural resource for that matter is disputed, the role of a government to assume this right has become questionable and that it needs to be dispassionately defined through consensus among stakeholders (NAAS, 2005).

Although there are many reasons for not adequately meeting the challenge of delivering these basic services, such as major environmental problems due to over-exploitation of water sources and competition among different uses and users, such as the irrigation and industrial sectors, studies initiated in this direction reveal that the primary problem is the supply-driven approach taken by the state level implementing agencies (WSP-SA, 2000). In order to solve the growing water crisis and to get over the problem of finding funds to build, operate and maintain the necessary water supply and irrigation infrastructures, as part of overall sector reform measures, and taking cue from the suggestion given by the World Bank—the largest donor to India in the area of water—the Government of India, has plunged into reform activities in water sector.

The huge fiscal deficit on creating and maintaining water supply systems for various purposes necessitated several other management options and matrices to emerge. Some of them have been advocated by National Water Policy, 2002 also. These alternative models include (Ballabh, 2004):

- Roll back of the state,

- State-community Partnerships,
- Public-Private Partnership,
- NGOs seeking to take on the development functions either through imitating the state initiatives in the field or through implementing state policies and programmes (thus the status of public service contractor),
- Decentralization.

Although decentralization and community management of water sources and water services emerged as one of the models of water sector reform in India (GoI, 2000), other models with privatization as prime solution also have emerged alongside. Many of these alternatives are also visibly seen in water governance in the recent past. As a part of the roll back of the state certain arrangements such as privatization and contracting to external agencies etc. are attempted. Worldwide as 'economics' started eating into the space of 'societies' and from the time different elements of structural adjustment programmes started gaining political acceptance instead of galvanizing on a set of political strategies that could encourage and empower people to make the State more efficient and responsive or to make the people more central in planning process, the proponents of the new globalization processes argued that it made more sense to hand over reigns of power structure deciding water rights, from State to private agents. The basic assumptions being:

- Private agents are inherently more efficient and cost-effective than public service providers and are therefore supposed to imply reduced prices and better services for consumers over time; and
- Private agents are in a position to charge prices that more closely reflect true value to society of this resource, and thereby compel consumers to be less wasteful and more inclined to conserve water.

With the mainstreaming of such an ideology, markets as well as for services related to conserve, recycle, supply, storing and exploring water resources started developing (Raghav Narsalay, 2003). The most political implications of this changing perception is that access to water started being seen as a 'basic need and not a basic right'.

Water markets tend to emerge and they serve some useful purposes, but there are dangers of unsustainable extraction as also of inequitable relationships between sellers and buyers. Besides this, there are problems of pollution and contamination as well (Ramasamy R. Iyer, 2001). However, in the context of global push by the water industry and its supports—through corporate-led initiatives like the World Water Council—to sell their services as the solution to the world's water problems is gaining currency all over the world including India.

Water Policy and Sector Reform Initiatives

Speaking on 'Water Issues' at the Twelfth Session of the Commission on Sustainable Development in April 2004, Dr. Prodipto Ghosh, Secretary, Ministry of Environment and Forests mentioned *that in order to address the challenges in the field of water resources, the National Water Policy of 1987 was revised and updated as National Water Policy, 2002 to encourage participation by all stakeholders. India has taken reform initiatives in water resources aimed at greater involvement of users in cost sharing as also in operation and maintenance. Private sector participation is also encouraged wherever feasible.*

The sector reform programme of the Government of India (GoI) and Government of Tamil Nadu, has made a paradigm shift from a supply-driven to a demand-driven approach. The shift entails the government from being 'facilitator of service' rather than being the prime 'provider of service'. Two very significant moves made in the National Water Policy, 2002 are:

(1) "Private sector participation should be encouraged in planning, development and management of water resources projects for diverse uses. Private sector participation may help in introducing innovative ideas, generating financial resources and introducing corporate management. It would also improve service efficiency and accountability to users. Depending upon the specific situations, various combinations of private sector participation, in building, owning, operating, leasing and transferring water resources facilities may be considered".

(2) Water Users Associations and the local bodies such as municipalities and Gram Panchayats should particularly be involved in the operation, maintenance and management of water infrastructure/facilities at appropriate levels progressively, with a view to eventually transfer the management of such facilities to the user groups/local bodies.

Commenting on the second of the two statements drawn from the National Water Policy, 2002, one can say that despite the fact that some states like Tamil Nadu and Karnataka have proved and have taken the lead in successfully demonstrating the capabilities of local bodies in managing water resources and services, without any controversies raised about decentralization of water supply services to elected Local Bodies, privatization of water sources and water services to MNCs and private companies are promoted in several parts of Tamil Nadu. The unmindful exploitation of ground water resources with trade-orientation and government handing over water services to private operators have raised concern among community groups and Civil Society Organisations. So, on the one hand private corporate interests are allowed to extract water for commercial purposes, on the other hand water distribution services are being slowly handed over to private companies under various arrangements. Discontentment is raised that the state is washing its hands off an essential public service or letting off a vital livelihood resource that is fast depleting in the hands of corporates.

The Controversies

Regarding the statement-1 controversies have erupted and gone a bang all over Tamil Nadu that the control of water sources and water services by private companies takes away this resource from the public and puts it in private control. It is also strongly argued that privatization of water is a violation of basic rights of citizens creating disparity in access to water (Anitha Sampath *et al.*). Thus, it raises several issues including the aspect of equity and social justice in water distribution meaning 'can poor people buy water for a price at the rates dictated by the private operators?' In India most projects with private sector participation purely aim at an increase in production capacity and holding a big market share, and do not address the main factors of inefficiency of water supply networks (Mehta M., 1999). The private companies are accountable more to shareholders than to a large section of the stakeholders who are voiceless.

These controversies have come about after GATS based liberalization of Foreign Direct Investment (FDI) in services sector led to proliferation of several modes of water privatization, where water production and distribution are partially or fully assigned to private operators through franchise bidding process. It is important, however, to bear in mind that domestic water service delivery is not officially one of the sectors covered by the GATS. But the idea of trade in services has started operating cutting across sectors due to the potential it entails as business propositions. Some legal manipulations are made whereby water provisioning is viewed as a product rather than a service. This legally keeps away from the discussion of GATS – meaning water bottle or aerated beverage is a 'product' and not a resource that belongs to certain community. It does not come with a service label.

Hence, private corporations are progressively taking control of water resources and water services in several states including Tamil Nadu. They have made 'water markets' and are fast spreading a culture of defining water as a 'commodity'. This trend has been made stronger after the introduction of the revised National Water Policy, 2002 which clearly supports privatization of water sector. Although going in for private sector participation cannot be argued as completely an unwelcome proposition, which form of privatization and what roles and rights are handed over to the private sector need to be analysed. Whereas corporatization of water resources or services that would help private profiteering needs to be condemned, part-privatization that shares the responsibilities of construction, operation and maintenance may be viewed as better governance. This is discussed in detail with solid cases which are cited in the subsequent chapters.

New Concepts that have Emerged

Globalization processes are said to have made way for global corporations as well as the domestic private traders to draw ground water for a variety of commercial purposes, often taking hold of the rights of native dwellers over water resources. It also has a substantial impact on the livelihoods of the poorest people for whom land and water are the prime livelihood resources. Therefore, it has become a serious concern as a matter of citizen's rights and in terms of deprivation and environmental damage. A review of research-based literature on water resources in India brings to surface several new concepts that were not in use a decade and a half ago. These concepts are viewed as evidences of change after deregulation and liberalization of the economy which have facilitated privatization of water sources/services and commodification of water. Whether this change implies development or retrogression needs to be analyzed and empirically verified. The new concepts that have emerged in the past decade include:

- Competing demand for water
- Right – Need dichotomy in water
- Privatization (or corporatization) of water resources
- Privatization of water services
- Public-Private Partnership (PPP)
- Water markets
- Commodification of water
- Packaged water
- Commercial draft of water
- Informal suppliers of water
- Water Tanker Operators
- Environmental and ecological concerns with special reference to water.

There are also several campaigns against many of these concepts and promoters of these concepts that these are concepts that have made way into India through the globalization processes (GATS). That this would damage the culture, tradition, and our own access and control over resources and services, and so on. The MNCs and TNCs are blamed for trying to promote such concepts, exploiting our natural resources, polluting our lands and degrading our environment. They are blamed of viewing everything including water as business proposition with assured economic viability rather than taking ecological sustainability or equitable-distribution-oriented view of things.

The World Bank, IMF and the ADB are blamed of proposing and pushing water privatization concepts, and of financing research studies and experiments that are stealthily making grounds stronger to be able to argue in favour of privatization. The concern of the campaigners are that a policy to privatize water resources and services would take hold of poor people's rights over water and if everything is going to be viewed as marketable commodities, the worst affected are going to be the poor and so the globalization processes would push a large segment of poor into deeper levels of penury rather than trying to get them out of it. These are some of the concerns expressed which required empirical verification.

The Present Study

This study aims at understanding—through participatory social analysis—the changes that are taking place in the water resources and water services in Tamil Nadu as a corollary of globalization processes.

Objectives

The specific objectives of the study are to:

- Track down the influences of globalization processes in water sector at the grassroots level;
- Diagnose the impact—across regions in Tamil Nadu—of globalization processes and institutional restructuring with special reference to water resources and water services; and
- Suggest ways to contain and manage surface and ground water from the onslaught of globalization processes so as to ensure sustainability in the use of water resources, and equity in the delivery of water services.

Methodology

For an exploratory exercise on understanding the influence of globalization processes on rural lives and livelihoods one method would be, markedly, less than sufficient. Therefore, this study recognizes the basic differences between participatory methodologies and conventional questionnaire surveys. It has gone on an emerging consensus and has taken the conjunctive use of various methods to best seize the benefits of relative strengths of both qualitative and quantitative methods of doing social research. The basic point is gaining a synergy through methodological integration rather than accepting one and eliminating the others.

Unit of Analysis: Problems pertaining to water centre around various river basins in Tamil Nadu. The pressure on water — whether they are for commercial draft, or for bottling companies or for industrial use seem to be in high order on the rivers and on the villages at the banks of rivers. So, villages in river basins such as Thamiraparani, Amaravathy, Bhavani, Ponniyaru and Noiyel rivers were taken for this study. Incidentally, these were the places where problems are frequently reported on various issues such as commercial draft of water, sand mining, privatization of water resources, and privatization of water services and so on. Hence, the districts covered in Tamil Nadu are: Thirunelveli, Salem, Karur, Coimbatore, and Thiruvallur in Tamil Nadu. The villages from the selected districts were chosen based on newspaper reports, web literature and campaigns conducted by affected communities and some civil society organizations on various issues relating to water. The results of the study are presented in the subsequent chapters.

Sources of Data and Information: The study has made use of both primary and secondary sources of data and information. Primary data have been collected from selected study villages. As far as secondary data were concerned, they have been mostly collected from either government sources including websites or from research publications of reputed institutions and journals. The published literatures on globalization are available in plenty but one has to be careful in selecting and identifying which material is valid and which is opinionated. This is because globalization is a controversial subject and the views expressed fall either as pro or against globalization. Taking a stand — either pro or anti — would affect the objectivity of the research study. Therefore, published materials — both printed and on-line — have been carefully scrutinized to be able to sift valid research materials from exaggerated propaganda materials.

Selection of Methods and Tools: This exercise essentially aims at understanding and recording how (macro) policies interact with the stakeholders at the (micro) grassroots level. Methodology-wise, this study has taken several features of a 'multi-method study' where Focus Group Discussion (FGD) has taken the prime seat and several other techniques like use of a Short Questionnaire, Semi-Structured Interviewing (SSI), workshop method, and a few other PRA methods were there in the tools box used in the field. The prime considerations in the selection of research methods and tools were: (i) bringing in as many perspectives as possible, and (ii) validity of the information generated in a given village through triangulation and or cross checking. Hence, the methods used were mostly qualitative and process oriented in nature which served the purpose of exploration intended. Wherever possible quantitative data have been obtained from the villages and used in the analysis. Each issue is reported as an individual case and it is analyzed to understand if it points towards globalization as a cause.

Respondents: Key informants identified in villages and interviews held with them, focus group discussions held with community members who are affected or remain vulnerable to certain processes of globalization, chain of interviews held in various hamlets of selected Village Panchayats, chance encounters made with community members during direct observation in the field. Selected Village Panchayats and civil society organizations working in the areas of water and livelihoods security and subject specialists on water related issues, were consulted as well.

Table 2.1: Issues and Indicators

Sl. No.	*Broad Issue*	*Premise*	*Indicators*
1.	Encroachment of traditional water bodies	The Hindu December 9, 2005 (India's National News paper) reports after heavy rains and floods in Tamil Nadu that the unprecedented rain did not bring any cheer to farmers. Over 3,500 tanks need repairs in three district.	• Missing ponds, tanks and Ooranis reported. • Inadequate community water storage structure resulting in ground water depletion.
2.	Commercial Draft of water	Commodification of water in several areas of Tamil Nadu.	• Water available for sale at shops all over. • Depletion of ground water. • Lorries turned tankers.
3.	Privatization of Water Sources	GATS discussion about services liberalization. National Water Policy, 2002.	• For example: Community revolt against South India Bottling company setting up Coca Cola bottling unit at SIPCOT in Gangaikondan.
4.	Privatization of Water Services	GATS discussion about services liberalization. National Water Policy, 2002.	• Some Panchayats under BOOT water supply arrangement in Thirupur area complain of inadequate water supply.
5.	Sand mining	Construction boom in several towns. An Officer who went to prevent sand mining killed, reported newspapers.	• Construction boom in several towns. • An Officer who went to prevent sand mining killed, reported newspapers.

Scope and Limitations

This study primarily covers the problems, if any, reported especially on livelihood security at the grassroots level as a corollary of globalization processes. Corporatisation or privatization of water sources and privatization of water services have been paid special attention. It also contemplates to find out issues that are related to water supply such as sand-mining, and the status of traditional water bodies and traditional water management system. Table 2.1 gives a broad list of issues and indicators that this study covers.

Rendering water unusable due to ground and river water pollution caused by industrial effluents is an important aspect that requires a separate study in itself. Therefore, this study limits its scope to ground water depletion due to overdraft of water for activities of trade interests. It does not intend to be a report of the utilization pattern of surface and ground water in Tamil Nadu nor a report of globalization and its implications from a theoretical point of view.

Outcome of the Study

This chapter aimed at giving a broad agenda of water paradigms, issues and controversies that have erupted as a result of deregulation and liberalization of the economy, in the past decade. The results of the research study focusing specifically on each of the issues raised are presented in the subsequent chapters. Therefore, particularly this chapter (Chapter 2), has a special link to the following five chapters (viz. Chapters 3, 4, 5, 6 and 7). Each chapter starts with a premise that briefly narrates what prompted conducting the study a given chapter contains.

3

Public Water for Private Profit: Globalization in its Logical Minimum

The Premise

> "Join hands to drive away the Coke that comes to steal water from Thamiraparani – our source of life and livelihoods".

This is a wall writing that was found all over Tamil Nadu in September-October 2005, as part of a campaign against Coca Cola Company establishing a water bottling unit at Gangaikondan in Tirunelveli, Tamil Nadu.

The campaign emerged as a big movement against an MNC trying to set up business at the SIPCOT Premises in Tirunelveli. The debate about this issue generated a lot of heat across districts, and drew the attention of the entire state of Tamil Nadu. Gangaikondan Gram Panchayat was the talk of (almost) all the vernacular newspapers. On the surface, it is a dispute over extraction of Thamiraparani water for manufacturing aerated drink by South India Bottling Company, established by the Coca Cola. Going by the nature of issues the dispute brings forth; it is globalization in its logical minimum at the community level. This is an empirical account of the causes and the state of affairs.

Introduction

In search of better standards of living the race towards exploitation of (finite) natural resources by human kind is infinite. Advancement in science and technology coupled with modernization had set this trend in motion. Globalization of Indian economy and entry of MNCs and TNCs to set up production units in the past decade has geared it up to the extent that it can neither be slowed down nor be done away with. One of the resources that has become vulnerable to the onslaught of this propensity is our water resources.

Water is the life-line of rural livelihoods. Misuse of this has brought about serious concern in terms of threat to rural livelihoods. This has also raised several questions regarding ownership right to water such as: (i) to whom does the water resources belong to? (ii) if water is a 'common property' why it is the state playing only the role of a trustee; (iii) if water is a state property, can the state decide the way it deems appropriate to use it? (iv) can the local bodies assert their 'right to object' when a state decision tends to make the local stakeholders into local stake-losers? (v) or is it that the Civil Society Organizations have a tendency to attach infinite weight on the environment and zero weight on employment and income? And so on. These are some of the questions that impinge on the life and conditions of people at the grassroots when the economy is globalized.

Gangaikondan — A Case in Point

"There is no point in selling eyes in order to buy a painting" *says a community member at Gangaikondan village comparing it with having to lose land and water resources in order to get temporary employment from the Coca Cola Bottling plant to be set up in SIPCOT premises.* 'Gangaikondan' in Tirunelveli is on the news for quite sometime now.

Since July 2005 when this problem started emerging, it has taken various shapes and several turns. Local NGOs and the Communist Parties of India have played key roles in putting across to the community the repercussions of Coke's proposal citing Kerala' Plachimada as the example for the havoc the Coke company can play in the land and water resources of the villages in the vicinity. Now, the awareness level has reached to the extent that some of them are able to give details of the anti-coke slogans raised in the University campuses in the US and the UK. (Box 3.1).

Plachimada – The Eye-opener: One of the vital events is that the community leaders from Gangaikondan, in batches have visited Plachimada in Kerala to see for themselves the havoc Coke has wrought with the ground water aquifers and to the livelihoods of the people who live in about 10 km radius from Plachimada. The lesson they learnt from Kerala about Coca Cola was: *"It is stealing water, poisoning lands*

BOX 3.1
Coca Cola—Pepsi Cola "QUIT INDIA"

The severe water contamination and increasing scarcity of potable water after the commissioning of the Cola plan in Plachimada, Kerala have adversely affected these people, particularly the women. The continuous withdrawal of ground water in the Plant Site has already adversely affected the water table. Water availability in the open wells and shallow bore-wells over an extensive area has drastically fallen. The local people strongly feel that toxic chemicals from the plant waste water are contaminating the ground water. Routine agriculture is already adversely affected over a few hundred acres of adjacent paddy lands due to water scarcity. People who are forced to depend on brackish bitter water complain of a variety of illness. Women who use the water report that rice and *dhal* do not get cooked but become hard. Food prepared with such water they report is going bad quickly. Burning sensation on the facial skin and a greasy sticky fell on the hair are also mentioned by all the people who bathe in the water.

and destroying livelihoods. This is the story of Coca Cola in Kerala". Every time a batch returned from Plachimada the community disapproval and protest against commencing the Coke Unit at the SIPCOT premises in Gangaikondan seemed to have been getting stronger and more powerful.

As per the Panchayats Act, the South India Bottling Company needs to obtain a no objection certificate from the Village Panchayat. Mr. Kamsan, President of Gangainkondan Village Panchayat initially opposed the idea—then supported it—then died of jaundice, it is reported (*The Hindu*, August 31, 2005). Rumors have it that the President drinks like a fish and so the Company people gave him a lethal cocktail of drinks and bought him for a price (*Dina Malar*: January 27, 2006). The Vice-president Mr. Perumal has been allowed to serve as acting President now. The company is yet to get the No Objection Certificate (NOC) from the Panchayat.

The Divide: The new President is one among those who visited Plachimada. Some local NGOs and a few CPI activists [including an Ex-MLA of the CPI (M)] seem to be behind him and with the protesters. The new President is opposing the Coke and is an active member of the Thamiraparani and Groundwater Protection Campaign Committee, promoted by local NGOs. There is also a section of the local people who support that the Coke must start functioning in Gangaikondan. These supporters led by an Ex-MLA of the DMK Party have formed

SIPCOT Entrepreneurs Protection Committee. The Coke Company is said to be behind in setting the agenda of this Committee. So, Gangaikondan stands divided now.

The Views of the SIPCOT Entrepreneurs Protection Committee

(i) The area is known for unemployment. At least six lorry full labourers (men, women and youth) go out daily to do errands in construction works and other menial labour works in the towns and return home late in the evening. Such people can get employment in the SIPCOT;

(ii) The Coke Company has assured employment to at least ten people from each one of the 12 habitations of Gangaikondan;

(iii) The company has been allowed to take 900,000 litres of water per day from the flowing Thamiraparani river and not through drilling bore-holes. The doubts being raised that they might go in for bore-wells is unfounded;

(iv) The company has also assured to take up common developmental works for the villages in the neighbourhood, for example, they have already spent about Rs. 4 lakhs and have set right a canal that remained silted;

(v) Preventing Coke from commencing production might scare away other investors coming to the SIPCOT at Gangaikondan, which might completely defeat the very purpose (employment generation) for which the SIPCOT was set up in Gangaikondan area; and

(vi) Water requirements of companies such as Sterilight (which once was under severe controversy) and SPIC at Thoothukudi are supplied from Thamiraparani only. The quantity drawn for such companies is more than that which the Coke has proposed to draw now. What are these protestors doing about them? The opposition against Coca Cola is a trend and fashionable for those who call themselves environmentalists.

The Stand of Protestors

(i) The employment attraction the Company (SIBCL) shows is a myth and that they would provide employment to manual labourers for a short period of two-three years;

(ii) 900,000 litres per day could be on paper and that there is no mechanism to watch if they draw only 900,000 litres a day and that if they have not drilled additional bore-holes in side the

32 acres of land they have acquired from SIPCOT area, where no body, including Vandana Siva (eco-feminist), was allowed entry;

(iii) More than the water they draw it is the effluent that has damaged the lands and livelihoods in Plachimada and what is the assurance that it would not recur in Gangaikondan. Why should we refuse to learn from the sufferings of other people? Although the order given to SIBCL specifically stipulates that no solid or liquid waste be disposed of at the growth centre, the community members who visited Plachimada are not prepared to believe that the company would abide by that;

(iv) A good number of the local community in Gangaikondan and in the neighbourhood belong to *konar* community who are, by tradition, dependent on cattle rearing. Their cows, goats and sheep graze on the banks of the river Thamiraparani. They are afraid, if the land and grass fodder would be affected by the effluents let out by the Coca Cola bottling company;

(v) The campaign committee is also advocating that let the Sterilight and SPIC in Thoothukudi be told to set up desalination plants to convert sea water from the Bay of Bengal and use it for their production plants; and

(vi) Finally, *can't human species live without Coca Cola?* Let all the other industries that which do not exploit the local livelihood resources set up business in the SIPCOT premises.

State-wide Protest: There was a state-wide protest organized on September 12, 2005 and when the police denied permission, the protestors had to seek judicial intervention. The people of Rajapathi village near Gangaikondan went on a mass fast demanding withdrawal of the permission to the unit. The issue was raised in the Lok Sabha by the Communist Party of India. Intervening during the debate, the then Chief Minister of Tamil Nadu said that the bottling plant of the Coca Cola's Indian arm, Hindustan Coca Cola Company, has been granted permission to procure water only through SIPCOT and cannot directly tap ground water. SIPCOT itself will source the water from Tamirabarani river. SIPCOT has agreed to supply nine lakh litres of water a day against the company's request for 12 lakh litres (*The Hindu*, September 29, 2005).

What is significant in the case of the Gangaikondan unit is that the State Government has not only granted license to the water-intensive plan disregarding the track record of the beverage giant, but also extended to it all the benefits of an industrial estate, which include

> **BOX 3. 2**
> **CSE Report Creates Stir**
>
> On August 5, 2003, The Centre for Science and Environment, a Delhi based NGO, convened a press conference where it alleged that 12 top brands of Coca Cola and Pepsi contained poisonous pesticides. In a high-profile counter, both Coke and Pepsi fought the allegations tooth and nail, but did not help too much. Sales plummeted by around 35 per cent in the second half of 2003-04. Since then the two companies have been running into one problem after another: These include protests relating to water exploitation in Kerala (Coke's Palakkad plant in Kerala remained shut for most of 2004 and early 2005), Andhra Pradesh and Rajansthan, and other health and pollution-related problems in Tamil Nadu, Uttar Pradesh and Uttaranchal.

assured supply of a huge quantity of water through pipelines, knowing full well that in this specific case water is going to be put to commercial use as a vital input for its products. SIPCOT, a government organization established in 1972 to serve as a catalyst in the development of small, medium and large industries, has created so far 17 industrial complexes, parks and growth centres in the State and the Gangaikondan Growth Centre is one among them. For the aspiring entrepreneurs, if offers 'readymade infrastructure', project assistance, single-window clearance, grants and State incentives and marketing assistance.

> **BOX 3.3**
> **JPC on Soft Drink**
>
> The Joint Parliamentary Committee (JPC) also after examination delivered its verdict affirming that the Centre for Science and Environment (CSE) findings about the presence of pesticide residues in aerated water were correct, the panel dismissed as hot air soft drink manufacturers's claims that their products are safe.
>
> *Down to Earth, February 29, 2004*

Policy and Action at Loggerheads

The total availability of surface and ground water (46,540 MCM) in the State is less than the present demand (54,395 MCM) and much less than the projected demand. And so, there is an urgent need for both water conservation and recycling (PWD/TN: 1994). This is one of the main reasons why the government through Orders and Ordinance compels every one of the households even in obscure Village Panchayats to put up rain water harvesting structures. This is taking place one side and paradoxically, there is permission given for commercial draft of water by the same Government of Tamil Nadu.

> **BOX 3.4**
>
> **Coca Cola Suspended in US**
>
> The Coca Cola controversy resurfaced in the land of the Real Thing. Last fortnight (January 2006), 50,000 students of the University of Michigan, US, forced campus authorities to suspend the sale of all Coca Cola products. Their grouse: The soft drinks major is draining local ground water in India causing sever water crisis for local communities. Coke's Singh says we are working with local communities to clear their doubts on the issues raised against us. Despite losses, the company is planning fresh investments in India.
>
> ***Business Today, January 29, 2006***

Questions of the On-lookers

The on-lookers (who understand only partially about whatever is happening) have a few queries seeking answer. They are:

- As per Government of Tamil Nadu Reports water resources of Tamiraparani are already heavily utilized by a variety of users. The demand for water in Thamiraparani basin, 2747 MCM far exceeds the available i.e. 2069 MCM (IWS: 1998). Wouldn't the SIBCL proposal put further stress on Thamiraparani water?
- Secondly, whether SIPCOT should provide water to an industry whose 95 per cent of the input is water?
- Thirdly, the very fact that the Company is enticing with money almost everyone even at the village level stands as a proof of the quantum of profit they expect in return.
- Fourthly, given the few industries that have been started now in the SIPCOT premises, if one company is assured of 900,000 litres of water from where would other hundreds of industries, to be set up, get water for their use? Some of the community members suspect that they might do some palm greasing and go in for ground water extraction.
- Fifthly, it seems that those who oppose Coke proposal are farmers (both big farmers and small) who are fully dependent

on agriculture (e.g. *Thevar* community) or depend on cattle rearing (e.g. the *Konar* community). The supporters of Coke proposal are those who have no agriculture but are looking forward to have their wards employed in the SIPCOT premises, or they have been 'honoured in confidence'.

- Sixthly, the issue of communalism in Gangaikondan area which got subsided over a decade ago is being rekindled, so that the community would be busy fighting for nothing, while Coke does business peacefully.
- Finally and very importantly, the local body being told by the bureaucracy to cancel the Gram Sabha meeting on the pretext that a Gram Sabha meeting might flare up as a communal conflict.

BOX 3.5

Background to the Location of SIPCOT at Gangaikondan

Gangaikondan and nearby villages witnessed a three year wave of blood-spattered caste violence in the mid-1990s to end the practice of untouchability. Residents of the Manur Panchayat Unit, within which Gangaikondan falls, are predominantly pallars, a *Dalit* (former untouchable) caste. The *Dalit* uprising of the 1990s saw scores settled for centuries-old oppression primarily with the upper caste Thevars. For every Pallar that was killed, the Thevars lost two or three. The Government of Tamil Nadu appointed a committee headed by a retired judge Mr. Ratnavel Pandian to study the factors behind the caste conflicts and give a report. One of the vital findings of the Committee was many youths in that region remained unemployed and establishment of some employment generating industries would keep people busy and end caste conflicts. Thus, SIPCOT was established 15 years ago.

Thiru. Karuppiah, Ex-MLA (DMK)
Gangaikondan

Panchayat Passes Resolution Amidst Police Protection

The October 2, 2005 Gram Sabha meeting was postponed to November 20, 2005, and again it was postponed indefinitely. Amidst tight police overseeing, the January 26, 2006 Gram Sabha meeting took place in Gangaikondan. It is reported that the presence of overwhelming number of police force, and the government officials in the village kept several members of the Gram Sabha away in their houses for the fear of something untoward happening.

The Village Panchayat on the January 26, 2006 managed to pass a resolution objecting to Coca Cola opening the bottling company (*Dina Malar*: January 27, 2006). However, it was said that the meeting did not have the required quorum and so it is in doubt if the resolution would stand. Simultaneously, the members of the Entrepreneurs Protection Committee, although quite few in number, expressed their displeasure and hankered after getting the resolution revised offering support to SIBCL. It is reported that the situation was becoming repulsive and so the police took the Coke's supporters away from the scene. Finally, it happened that an emergency meeting of the Maanur Panchayat Union (the next higher level tier of the local administration set up) gave its approval (*The Hindu*, February 10, 2006) to commence operation of the bottling unit of Coca Cola, established at the Gangaikondan SIPCOT Industrial Estate.

Analysis and Discussion

What is so Attractive about Gangaikondan?: If India, or any country for that matter, has to attract foreign investment through MNCs it has to provide attractive environment. Usually, those in business do not bother how their activities affect environment. This is because they are business people and that they must survive by making profit (Raja J. Chelliah, 2006). Indeed, no corporation ever managed to survive by continually posting losses. Providing attractive environment generally implies having political stability and economic advantages such as cheap labour or exploitable natural resources (Jagdish Bhagwati, 2004). Perhaps SIPCOT at Gangaikondan was attractive to Coca Cola on the following counts:

- River Thamiraparani is a perennial source of water supply which is the first requirement for a bottling company.
- The government through SIPCOT ensured 900,000 litres of water per day (SIPCOT Allotment Order dated 21.10.2004). So, uninterrupted water supply is assured along with certain readily-built-infrastructural facilities that any SIPCOT generally provides.
- In case of short supply (of water) from SIPCOT sources the South India Bottling Company can apply for permission to sink bore-well/tube-well within the plot leased to them, which can be considered. (This is a provision that contains in-built weakness which the community members and the Civil Society

Organisations question that the company would sink bore-wells additionally.)

- The area is known for rural unemployment. So, getting unskilled workers from the vicinity for errands such as loading and unloading of crates, bottle washing etc. would not be a problem.
- The SIPCOT premises at Gangaikondan is on the National Highway and is not far away from railways either. Transport of products would not be a problem.

Tirunelveli falls in between Madurai and Kanyakumari. The Unit at Gangaikondan can deliver its products to all the southern Tamil Nadu towns in between these two important tourist centres.

An analysis of the developments in Gangaikondan Village Panchayat tells off several things that are obnoxious about globalization. It has demonstrated the crippling effect it can put on a Village Panchayat—through the bureaucracy or through the higher level tier of the Panchayat system itself. It also has the power of calling out and renewing deeply buried problems such as riots based on caste. It has the clout of stealing water, poisoning land and destroying livelihoods as reported from Kerala (Nityanand Jayaraman, 2005). Besides it has also shown that it has the money to buy at least a section of the local people who can talk in their favour.

BOX 3.6
Right to Water

V.R. Krishna Iyer correctly noted that the poor without potable water, and the rich with cola consumerism, are a pathetic, pathological human rights contradiction. A retired Chief Justice of the highest court of law in India tries to arouse our conscience by making us aware that the right to water is a fundamental right (Article 21) under the Indian Constitution. Do we have to pay the MNCs for drinking our own water?

The Hindu, January 28, 2004

The Question of Water Rights: At the outset, it is appropriate to discuss the questions pertaining to water rights. Who does the water belong to? That is, water being one of the vital livelihood resources, is it a common property resource which the local community has granted the trusteeship to the state to regulate and safeguard. Or is it a property of the state that it (the state) can decide in whatever way it deems fit to run the government? What is the space for local bodies in approving and/or regulating the use of water resources by local people for various purposes? What is expected to be the reaction of local bodies when the state decides to allocate free water resources of one village to a neighbouring village that is starving for water? So much so, what is expected to be the reaction of local bodies when the state decides to put on sale the water resources to an MNC as a gesture of promoting FDI in the state or to experiment how it would be like if India signed the GATS (General Agreement on Trade in Services) agreement?.

V.R. Krishna Iyer, a former judge of the Supreme Court quotes (from *M.C. Mehta* vs. *Kamal Nath case*) that the state is a trustee of all natural resources which by nature are meant for public use and enjoyment. Public at large is the beneficiary of the running waters. The state as a trustee is under legal duty to protect the natural resources. These resources cannot be converted into private ownership or for commercial purposes. The menace of MNCs consuming all the water, converting all the perennial springs, depriving the poor of water is to be condemned. Nobody on earth should hold the power to supersede people's right to water. Each according to his thirst is the rule of water (Justice, Krishna Iyer, 2004).

Mr. Antony Balan, Chief Engineer of the Central Water Commission in Coimbatore in an interview to our researchers team observed: like we have clear demarcation for land rights, we have never had a clear demarcation for the water rights. At the most, what we have had is usufructory right. One reason for this is that land and forestry resources can have state, district and political boundaries whereas the ground water flow cannot be demarcated. Water below the ground is a vagabond. There is no set pattern or course for its flow. The community assumes that the water below one's piece of land is his personal property. And he assumes riparian rights over the river water that flows across his village or town.

When the state makes a decision to distribute water for free to another water-starving community in the neighbourhood (through combined water supply schemes) they 'appreciated and felt elevated too'. When the State decided to provide water from Thamiraparani to some of the local companies at Thoothukudi the community 'tolerated' it. But at the same time when the state decides to put water on sale they started 'agitating'. They think that the state is interfering in their riparian rights and, that the state is grabbing their riparian rights and is making it a private property of somebody who would use it for commercial purposes. They are agitated that the community would lose one of their prime livelihood resources viz. water. They start questioning if their assumption of riparian rights over water is a myth. They take it to mean that their food security is at stake.

Employment and Income versus *Environmental Concern*: One of the prime emphasis offered by the government for bringing in FDI and promoting private enterprises is that it would generate employment

BOX 3.7

Expert Panel to Study Environmental Impact

Madurai: The Madurai Bench of the Madras High Court has directed the Tamil Nadu Pollution Control Board (TNPCB) to produce all original records pertaining to the permission granted by it to the South India Bottling Company, a subsidiary of Hindustan Coca Cola, for establishing a soft drink manufacturing unit at Gangaikondan Panchayat in Tirunelveli district.

Passing interim orders on public interest litigation against setting up the unit, the First Bench, comprising Chief Justice Ajit Prakash and Justice Kulasekaran, also directed the company to produce relevant materials to substantiate its claim that the unit had already commenced operations. Further, the TNPCB, State Industries Promotion Corporation of Tamil Nadu (SIPCOT) and other authorities were asked to file their individual counter affidavits and the matter was posted to March.

Earlier, during arguments, the Bench said that after perusing the documents, it might consider to appointing an expert committee headed by an eminent scholar from Anna University in Chennai to inspect the unit and file its independent report on the alleged environmental degradation.

According to the petitioner, R. Krishnan (63) of Palayamkottai, a former MLA attached to the Communist Party of India (Marxist), the company had proposed to set up a soft drink manufacturing unit at a cost Rs. 280 million, spread over 31.54 acres in Gangaikondan village. The SIPCOT had agreed to supply nine lakhs litres of water per day to the unit at the rate of Rs. 15 for every 1000 litres. While it had not been made clear whether the water would be drawn from the ground or the Thamiraparani River close to the unit, either way it would affect the environment, he claimed.

Protest by Locals

Even after the local people protested against the move and restored to various forms of agitation, the TNPCB on March 3, 2005, granted consent for running the unit, though the company itself had applied to the Board only on February 28, 2005.

He alleged that the TNPCB had not followed the mandatory requirements of holding a public enquiry and instead mechanically granted consent.

"It is not a matter only between the applicant and the Board. The public are vitally interested," he added.

Mohamed Imranullah S., The Hindu, February 16, 2006

and counter caste forces' activities especially in areas like Gangaikondan (*Frontline*, October 2005). The Joint Action Committee for Conservation of Thamiraparani and Groundwater (JACCTG) argues (*The Hindu*, May 10, 2005) that the Thamiraparani does not belong to Gangaikondan or Pirancherry only. It belongs to all the community groups that live in the villages on the Thamiraparani river bank for about 75 miles from Papanasam, where the river originates, to Athur, where it empties itself into the sea.

While the intension of the government to generate employment through FDI and private initiative is appreciable, the government also is obliged to ensure that the permission granted, to SIBCL or any unit of SIPCOT for that matter, would not harm the stable livelihood resources of the local community. There are thousands of families that live on both the sides of Thamiraparani in its entire stretch of 75 miles flow (Kasi S. Viswanathan, 2005). An industrial unit that would provide employment for 200 people in one Gangaikondan or Pirancherry for 2-3 years should not wipe out the land, water and other essential livelihood resources of 2000 people in several other villages down stream irrevocably. Such a unit does not deserve government approval if the argument of the Joint Action Committee for Conservation of Thamiraparani and Groundwater (JACCTG) is proved valid.

Usually those in business do not bother how their activities affect environment and people. This is true of foreigners, Indians and everybody in business (Raja Chelliah, 2006). The mantra of global trade being 'produce goods where it could be produced at the cheapest cost and sell where it would fetch the highest profit' makes the MNCs and TNCs to shift their production units to rural areas in countries like India (M.R. Rajagopalan, 2005) where land prices are cheap; regulation on ground water draft is never adhered to; pollution control norms can be bent (www.IndiaResource.org); and human labour is available at throw away prices. Knowing fully well about what happened to the land, water and the livelihoods of the people in Kerala and in Sivaganga (read full story in the annexure 3.2), the government has given approval to the SIBCL, perhaps, to somehow bring about growth in the rural economy but at an alarming social cost.

It is possible (and it has been proved beyond doubt in Plachimada, Kerala, and a pinch of the same has been demonstrated in Sivaganga in Tamil Nadu) the neglect of the environment would turn into serious environmental and social costs later on. Putting down a condition is different from adhering to it in letter and spirit. Weren't there conditions given at Plachimada, or Sivaganga? Weren't conditions given to the units at SIPCOT in Cuddalore, for example? Aren't they letting out several loads of solid and liquid waste into the sea rendering the area impassable and stinking? The environmentalists have a point there, if they express dread.

Therefore, it should be said that environmentalists are right to argue that growth rates must be adjusted for environmental damage. That is growth that devastates the environment is surely not being measured if no downside adjustment for the environmental damage is made – a growth that subtracts for environmental degradation (William Nordhaus *et al.*, 1999). Going by this measure, the employment for 200 people assured by SIBCL needs to be analysed against the cost of environmental damage, to be able to decide whether to accept that offer or oppose SIBCL from commencing production.

The environmentalists tend to value environment over income, whereas trade (and other) economists conventionally tend to value income over environment. This difference lies at the heart of their conflicts. That the local people at Gangaikondan should strike a trade off between employment and environment implying that if some people have to get profit and employment, some of the lands will have to be polluted is no logic. It is something like saying in a globalized context for an attractive enough compensation, a poor country agreeing to be the site for burying the toxic waste generated by a rich industrialized nation. Law of no land would agree to one person's use to cause another person's damage – negative externality (Soumyen Sikdar, 2005). However, small might be the person who suffers the damage naturally he would revolt.

The Wage Rate Controversy: There are some NGOs and Campaign Committees arguing that the wage rates that the Coca Cola might pay could be higher than that which is paid locally for a menial labourer. But, it would be much cheaper compared to what they would have paid in their home country or when compared with the advertisement expenses of Coca Cola. But, it is inappropriate to compare a company's advertisement budget with the wage rate or even the wage bill. It proves nothing (Jagdish Bagwathi, 2004). It is a business strategy. All that one can ask is: whether my people are getting a reasonable wage vis-à-vis the local prices or as per the ILO standards, for example. That is a social concern. Certainly, it is not exploitation under any plausible and persuasive definition.

Interactions at the Local Body Level

- *Employment and Income*: The intention of establishing SIPCOT was to generate employment in the region and so, the benefits that the Village Panchayats could think of were: employment to the people and income to Panchayats by way of professional tax etc. The Company promised to provide employment to a minimum of 200 people from the locality (e.g. Kangaikondan and Pirancherry Panchayats). There were also some canals that needed to be repaired. The SIBCL has repaired them for the community using its money.
- *After the Pandora's Box Open*: After the Civil Society Orgnizations of that area formed a Joint Action Committee for Conservation of Thamiraparani River and Groundwater (JACCTRG) and started campaigning against the SIBCL opening Coca Cola unit at Gangaikondan, all the problems relating to environmental disaster, water depletion, land pollution, livelihood threat, Plachimada story, track history of coke in several parts of India and in other countries started spreading among the community members. The Village Panchayat that had promised to give no objection certificate soon revised its stand and objected to SIBCL operating in the SIPCOT premises. Things turned tough since then to SIBCL.
- *SIBCL's Game Plans*: The SIBCL has covertly organized a small group of influential local people and made them form a forum known as 'SIPCOT Entrepreneurs Protection Committee'. It encouraged them to counter the civil society and to raise voice in the Gram Sabha meeting in favour of SIBCL. It helped the SIBCL show that the community is of divided opinion. It has also used the members of the committee to send strong messages (based on caste divisions) so that the District Administration would postpone Gram Sabha meeting where resolutions were to be passed objecting to SIBCL operating in SIPCOT premises. The Gram Sabha has been postponed twice.
- *Gram Sabha Resolution*: Gangaikondan Panchayat amidst tight police security (to guard against any untoward thing happening) has passed a resolution on January 26, 2006 objecting to SIBCL start functioning. The Gram Sabha meeting was not attended by many members of the community as they were scared after seeing the police force on duty.
- *Will this Resolution Stand*: The question whether this resolution would stand going by community unanimity and legal provisions,

remains unanswered. The response of the community members is: "We are tired of talking about it. Let them start production, ruin our lands and water we would demolish the entire thing and pack them up." Regarding the legal validity of the resolution some experts opine that the quorum was not sufficient and so the resolution may not stand. There are also other Panchayats involved such as Pirancherry whose community supports but the Panchayat President is in favour of SIBCL.

Social Externality Costs—Assessment of the Likely Damage

Pollution is a harmful or negative externality that the Gangaikondan community is afraid that SIBCL might cause. An externality is said to be present when the action of one agent, SIBCL in this case, directly affects the utility or the opportunity of another viz., the community members of Gangaikondan and the neighbourhood villages. Such effects are typically unpriced and as a result markets often fail to achieve social efficiency in their presence. Profit maximizing firms attach weight only to private benefits or costs, but externalities create divergence between private and social magnitudes. Therefore, the local body and the civil society organizations realize that there is need for intervention to bring the activities of self-seeking agents in line with the social optimum (Soumyen Sikdar, 2005).

Going by Plachimada experience in terms of the enormity of damage, if the SIBCL started operating, in the opinion of the community members in the vicinity, it might affect the following sets of villages. This is only an assessment of the likely damage that people might talk after a few years time, if uncontrolled.

Table 3.1: Villages that Might be Affected if SIBCL Started Operating

Sl. No.	*Panchayat*	*Hamlets*	*Population*		*Total*
			Male	*Female*	
1.	Gangaikondan	11	5,366	5,511	10,877
2.	Pirancherry	5	2,180	2,830	5,010
3.	Seevalaperi	4	3,125	3,525	6,650
4.	Pathinalamberi	5	1,025	1,075	2,100
5.	Kuppakurichi	2	835	855	1,690
Total	**Panchayats 5**	**27**	**12,531**	**13,796**	**26,327**

Source: Compiled from the data obtained at the respective Village Panchayats.

Although Gangaikondan is talked about much, a considerable extent of land of SIPCOT falls in Pirancherry Panchayat. The people of Pirancherry expressed mixed feelings about SIBCL getting established. It indicates that they are not fully aware of the repercussions i.e. either of the employment or the environment concern. However, the Panchayat President of Pirancherry is very clear and is very much supportive that SIBCL must start operating. He is an active member of the SIPCOT Entrepreneurs Protection Committee. He is of the view that employment to the people is a prime need. The alleged reasons stated against SIBCL are all hypothetical. If the people sense that it really affects water or land, neither the State nor the SIBCL can stop people from flattening the company.

Table 3.2: Land Particulars of the Vulnerable Panchayats

Sl. No.	*Panchayat*	*Wet Land*	*Dry Land*	*Natham Porampok*	*Porampok Land*	*Others*	*Total*
1.	Gangaikondan	93.44	2066.36	57.41	868.12	4.19	3089.52
2.	Pirancherry	183.40	2485.74	10.63	375.46	5.29	3060.52
3.	Seevalaperi	NA	NA	NA	NA	NA	NA
4.	Pathinalamberi	48.50	33.19	0.08	85.08	0.20	167.05
5.	Kuppakurichi	191.01	176.76	NA	270.68	0.45	638.90

Source: Compiled from the data obtained at the respective Village Panchayats.

Except Seevalaperi where people mostly depend on wage employment and in occupations such as brick making and charcoal making (from wild and thorny trees) in all other Panchayats, agriculture is the main stay of the people. Paddy crops are seen widespread. For irrigation, they depend on Chitharu canal. As Chitharu canal lacks maintenance the farmers at the tail end such as Alangaraperi are running short of irrigation water.

Table 3.3: Cattle Population of the Vulnerable Panchayats

Sl. No.	*Hamlet*	*Sheep*	*Goat*	*Cow*	*Buffalo*	*Total*
1.	Rajapathy (Gangaikondan)	8540	1460	750	52	10,802
2.	Kuppakurichi (Kuppakurichi)	5010	1020	1005	480	7,515
3.	Alangaraperi (Pathinalamperi)	3010	210	305	102	3,627
4.	Venkatachalapuram (Pirancherry)	750	140	410	64	1,364
5.	Chithampachadi (Pirancherry)	860	110	321	64	1,355

Source: Calculated from the Focus Group Discussion held in each Hamlet.
Note: The figures in parentheses are Panchayats each hamlet fall in.

As a considerable segment of the population in these Panchayats belong to Konar community – traditionally known for making a living by cattle rearing, and they have all kinds of cattle population. The cattle graze in the open lands all day long and come back home in the evening. One of the threats expressed is: if the open lands got polluted the cattle population would shrink in these villages. The community that depends primarily on cattle as a means of earning their living would be affected as well.

Table 3.4: Traditional Water Bodies of the Vulnerable Panchayats

Sl. No.	*Name of the Panchayat*	*Managed by PWD*	*Managed by Panchayat*	*Total*
1.	Kangaikondan	11	1	12
2.	Pirancherry	3	1	4
3.	Pathinalamperi	1	-	1
4.	Kuppakurichi	2	-	2

Thamiraparani serves as the main source of recharging the traditional water bodies in these Village Panchayats. They are too vulnerable.

Other Drinking Water Supply Schemes

In addition there are other water supply schemes that depend on Seevalaperi (Thamiraparani water). They include:

- Drinking water scheme for Vilathikulam, Kadambur, Puthur and wayside villages.
- Drinking water scheme for Kayatharu, Kalugumalai and Ettayapuram – work in progress.
- Drinking water scheme for Kovilpatti and wayside villages.
- Drinking water scheme for Kodiyankulam and Kailasapuram.

Seevalaperi is the main pumping station that serves several combined water supply schemes in this part of the state. Three districts viz., Tirunelveli, Tuticorin and Virudhunagar get water from Seevalaperi scheme only. Whenever there is water scarcity people have the practice of tapping water from the pumping stations upon request and from the leakages.

Conclusion—Tragedy of the Commons

Profit has been central to trade thinking, and nature a handmaid to mankind. Coke therefore seems to think of the Pollution Control Board and the supportive State as being in place and the local body and Civil Society Organizations as barriers that disrupt trade and distrub them. Perhaps, trade right not want power devolution to the Panchayats as local body means regulation and close watch. Whereas local bodies and CBOs suggest that they are necessary, as activities of corporate bodies impact their lives and livelihoods, especially, when they meddle with their livelihood resources. In this case, even "the principle of polluter pays" may not be welcome because the social and environmental cost would be immense.

Jagdish Bhagwathi in his popular book titled '*In Defense of Globalization*' argues that "this may happen" is surely correct. That "it must happen" is incorrect. The experiences in Plachimada and Sivaganga and in scores of other places have proved it beyond doubt that it happens. It need not happen again in Gangaikondan to relearn that fire burns finger no matter whether it is Kerala or Tamil Nadu.

Thus, the private activity of SIBCL has a social cost, which the company denies to take cognizance of. This is because SIBCL does not have to pay for this. It is the local community that will have to pay for this, and so the company is pushing its activity. The concern of the community is that their livelihood resources would be rendered unusable and polluted which might exceed the social optimum. Despite State, as it has traditionally been, it is the local community and local bodies that have done the regulation with a high degree of efficiency. This is warranted, in the wake of globalization, especially, when commercially motivated outsiders go in for mechanical means of exploitation that are highly efficient for their private interests at the expense of the local community (Soumyen Sikdar, 2005). Joseph Stiglitz's (2006) words are stronger. He argues in terms of accountability to 'shareholders' and 'stakeholders' that if there is a case for making corporate offices individually responsible, the CEOs are by training accountable to shareholders more. They are very little concerned about the stakeholders. It is not less a crime to ruin the environment stealing the heritage of the entire community. Environmental damage done by corporations is longer lasting than book adjustment made to cheat the shareholders, and those injured are innocent bystanders who were neither party to any agreement nor stood to gain from the investment.

When a company has egregiously violated locally prevailing environmental laws, the CEO, the Pollution Control Board and others who made the decisions and permitted for such devastation to take place should be held criminally liable.

BOX 3.8

Panchayat Union Gives Nod to Soft Drink Unit

The emergency meeting of the Maanur Panchayat Union on Friday the February 10, 2006 gave its nod to commence operation of the bottling unit of Coca Cola, established at Gangaikondan SIPCOT Industrial Estate near here.

Though the Chairman Vijaya and three more councillors abstained from the meeting, the Vice-Chairman Balakumar of Dravida Munnetra Kazhagam conducted the meeting, which discussed for about 10 minutes its only agenda of permitting the operation of South India Bottling Company Limited (SIBCL), the franchisee of Coca Cola, which is going to produce a range of beverages being marketed by the multi-national soft drink major in the country.

The councillor C. S. Mani, who is against the establishment of SIBCL at Gangaikondan, asked the officials to furnish the list and names of the documents submitted by the company while it applied for getting licence.

As the officials did not provide any reply to his queries, he walked out of the meeting, after which, the remaining 16 councillors passed a resolution on giving permission to SIBCL.

Source: The Hindu, February 11, 2006, p. 3.

4

Water Service Provision: Public-Private Partnership

The Premise

> "Thottipalayam Panchayat residents have resolved to go on a fasting in front of the Office of the New Thiruppur Area Development Company Limited (NTADCL)[1] until the residents are assured of adequate drinking water supply to the locality."

This is a notice found in prominent places in Thiruppur and in front of the Office of the NTADCL, the private water service provider, pressurizing the company to provide drinking water to their locality.

Introduction

In India, like in many other countries of the world, drinking water is provided by the public sector, since it is usually considered to be a typical public good. The public utility takes charge of the overall cycle of installation of the technical system, water production, distribution, and maintenance. However, the problems associated with water crisis, system operation and maintenance have always persisted. Recently, as a movement of reform these functions are partially or fully assigned to private operators through a franchise bidding process (Vishal Narain,

1. A limited liability company in Thiruppur that has taken up the role of water service provision to the eleven Village Panchayats of which Thottipalayam Panchayat is one.

2004; Kaushik Deb, 2004). There are various degrees of involvement of the private operators in terms of contract duration, public participation, revenue collection arrangement and so on.

The opposite action of nationalization can be construed as privatization. Privatization as solution to the problems associated with water distribution services is proposed and pushed by world bodies such as WTO, IMF and the World Bank through international agreements such as GATS. The pro-privatization lobby aggressively campaigns for water privatization on the grounds that, while water subsidies promote wasteful practices, commodification of water should allow market forces (supply and demand) to set the tariff, which in turn will reduce water consumption and promote water conservation. Furthermore, it is argued that opening this sector to private service providers/contractors will bring in badly needed capital for upgrading and development of infrastructure (Anitha Sampath *et al.*, 2003).

In 1998, it has been reported that water privatization to multinationals (or its subsidiaries) was initiated in the case of seven states (Dewas, Madhya Pradesh: Industrial Water; Pune, Maharashtra: Drinking Water Supply; Panjim, Goa: Drinking Water Supply; Bangalore, Karnataka: Drinking Water Supply; Tiruppur, Tamil Nadu: Industrial and General Purpose; Visakhapatnam, Andhra Pradesh: Industrial; Delhi, National Capital Territory: Drinking Water Supply) (Jishnu, 1998). Until the year 2004 about 25 such projects had commenced in India. These are examples of corporatization of water in India. Corporatization is a form of privatization where in corporate bodies are involved. There are several other instances in India and all over the world wherein the private sector participation in water governance and management is coming in vogue in varied degrees. This is considered as a corollary to the processes of globalization, liberalization and privatization which are fast gaining ground in several countries of the world. These processes have contributed to a dramatic change in the role of the state (Keith Gauntlett, 2005).

International institutions, governments and multilateral corporations are designing and implementing policies which reduce the role of the state in the provision of basic services and the free access to water resources. This is no longer seen as a responsibility of the state but as the domain of the market forces. In this context, water supply is no longer an obligation of the state to the citizens. It becomes a commodity available only to those who pay for it, even if the price is termed 'user charges'. Corporations and consortiums pressurize various countries to let them supply and sell water, either by themselves or in partnership with public bodies (DFID, 1999).

In India, the revised National Water Policy, 2002 mentions that "*Private sector participation should be encouraged in planning, development, and management of water resources projects for diverse uses, wherever feasible. Private sector participation may help in introducing innovate ideas, financial resources and introduce corporate management and improving efficiency and accountability to users. Depending upon the specific situations, various combinations of private sector participation, in building, owning, operating, leasing and transferring of water resources facilities may be considered*".

Encouraging private sector participation in delivering water services and corporate management of water resources naturally provide space to push for corporate control over water resources and services. The same water policy 2002 (item No. 12) mentions about making use of local bodies and user groups. In actuality, the tilt seems to be towards giving it to the private service providers who are in water business for long. They are from countries such as UK, Germany etc. who have come to work in partnership agreement with certain Indian business giants such as Mahindra and Mahindra.

There are Civil Society Organizations that argue that control of water by private companies takes away this resource from the public and puts it in private control for them to make profit. If the government is unable to manage, the best is to delegate it to local bodies or to the CBOs rather than leaving the community members to buy water from private companies. There is a general impression that most projects with private sector participation purely aim at an increase in production capacity and sale and do not address the main factors of inefficiency of Indian water supply networks. This study aims at understanding how the recent initiative in water provision viz. Public-Private Partnership (PPP) works in Thiruppur, Tamil Nadu. It specially focuses on the water service delivery made to the Village Panchayats reportedly covered by the PPP arrangement.

Public-Private Partnership in Thiruppur, Tamil Nadu— A Case in Point

PPP: As part of the sector reform measures and private sector participation in service provision, the Government of Tamil Nadu for the first time has gone in for Public-Private Partnership (PPP) in providing water for the industries in Thiruppur town and for a few villages in Thiruppur Block. This is called BOOT (Build-Own-Operate-Transfer) model water supply scheme. The estimated cost of the project is Rs. 1,023 crores which includes water supply and sewage systems (GoTN). This includes both debt and equity capital where USAID and the World Bank have extended financial support to execute this project. Mahindra & Mahindra, Bechtel and the United Utilities of UK are the main contractors besides Hindustan Construction Corporation and Larsen and Tourbo Limited. It is called 'Mahindra Consortium'.

NTADCL: The consortium has registered a company called New Thiruppur Area Development Corporation Limited (NTADCL). The government describes this as a Special Purpose Vehicle with the primary objective of implementing the Thiruppur Area Development Project. This is the first Water Sector related project in the country developed under the public-private partnership. It is a 30 year contract arrangement at the end of the 30th year it would be handed over to the government.

Beneficiaries: Under the project, facilities would be constructed to provide water supply access to the dyeing and bleaching industries in Thiruppur and the domestic consumers in Thiruppur Local Planning Area, comprising the Thiruppur Municipality, 15 Village Panchayats and 3 Town Panchayats. In addition, water supply is proposed to be provided to five way-side unions which lie on the way to the water transmission system corridor (Ashim Goyal, 2004). This project is expected to benefit (i) the industries, (ii) the slum dwellers, and (iii) the way-side villages.

Operation and Maintenance: NTADCL would transfer water over a 55 km long pipeline from Bhavani river and supply 185 million litres of water per day to nearly 1000 textile units and more than 1.6 million residents in Thiruppur and its surrounding area. According to the project document, United Utilities and NTADCL will run the joint venture at a fixed 'operation and maintenance fee' that will be recovered entirely from Thiruppur municipality. However, in an effort to attract further corporate capital investment in the state, the Government of Tamil Nadu has guaranteed profitability to the investors in the project by creating a hedge fund to pay the interest and operative expenses of the project in the event of a water shortage in Bhavani river (Anitha Sampath *et al.*).

'Users should pay for water on the basis of the quantity used' is one significant move the NTADCL has made. This project has become operational now. Water supplied to industries are charged Rs. 45 per 1000 litres. In addition the industries that demand water should pay a deposit of Rs. 25,000 onwards depending on the water demanded, besides this they should be able to show a bank guarantee. Water supplied to the Village Panchayats should be paid at Rs. 3.50 per 1000 litres. Village Panchayats (VPs) receive water bills from NTADCL direct.

Analysis and Discussion

Understanding what constitutes privatization what are the various forms of privatization talked about and what roles and rights are shifted from state domain to the private domain are some of the questions one has to be clear about before getting down to analyzing any privatization arrangement. This is vital because most opposition voices that come up against privatization are mainly due to lack of understanding of 'form of privatization' and 'what is privatized — is it the resource that is privatized or the service and so on' referred to and the associated obligations and rights? (Saikrishna N. and Vishwa Ballabh, 2006). Privatization is the process through which either specific tasks or activities, ownership, decision-making powers are transferred to the private enterprises. It may be argued that 'service' can be privatized but not the 'resource'. Even within contracting out service provision, an argument can flare up: would a private firm provide service without the intent of maximizing profit from that activity? Would they ensure equity of distribution and sustainability of the source? If the transfer is of the water as a resource, does the state have the right to do so— meaning allowing a private firm to sell water for a price in the name of water service provision etc.

The privatization arrangement at Thiruppur can be considered to be under a kind of concession contract where the private contractors (meaning the Mahindra Consortium/NTADCL) manage the entire utility and is required to invest in the maintenance and expansion of the system at its own commercial risk. Concessions have longer terms, to allow the operator to recoup its investment and, at the end of the contract, the assets are usually transferred to the state or a further form of concession is granted. The government has certain regulatory authority in terms of the sector to which water service is provided and at what price and so on. Different forms of concession contracts may be planned for privatization (Gleick *et al.*, 2002). The PPP arrangement in Thiruppur comes under Build-Own-Operate-Transfer system (BOOT). For thirty years the company would own, operate and maintain the assets. Within that period the company should recoup its investment and transfer the assets to the State Government at the end of the contract period. The liabilities of the company are limited. This may be considered to be a partial concession that gives the company the big responsibilities of investment and service provision for thirty years to the area specified. This is also in a way, a joint venture as rightly called Public-Private Partnership, whereby a team of private water companies form a company specially for this purpose and work with the public sector. Perhaps, this is one of the reasons why the movements initiated against NTADCL has dropped at the very early stage itself.

It is true experience with reform had clearly shown marked failure to exist along with government failure, especially in the provision of public services. Public-Private Partnership (PPP) could be a way to utilize the best of both worlds, while overcoming the specific weakness of each. But, for this to be feasible contracts and regulation have to be carefully designed. Well-designed and chosen contracts improve governance. Insights from international experience with PPP in water supply suggest how services from public utilities can be improved with cost saving through the reduction of waste (Ashim Goyal, 2004). However, there are mixed views about it. There are records failure stories as well as there are success stories.

The Need – Right Dichotomy: Access to basic services such as water can either be gained through private contractual arrangement or as entitlements by virtue of citizenship. The concept of water as a basic human right and hence the free access to it as non-negotiable has been redefined by the World Bank and the UN to mean that water is simply a human 'need'. The difference in interpretation is not merely semantic but very significant. A human need can be fulfilled through the market on the basis of the supply and demand, with no obligation on the part of the state.

On the other hand, in a democratic polity, water as a human right is the responsibility of the state and the fundamental right of the citizen. When the state neglects its duties/obligations, the concept of human right empowers the citizens to have the constitutional and legal remedies to make the state responsible for supplying water for personal consumption and livelihood activities (Keith Gauntlett, 2005). This is particularly important for women in Indian society, since women are traditionally charged with the responsibility of looking after the water needs of the family.

The Concept of Paying for Water: If the right to water is perceived as a contractual rather than a human right, water services are subject to the laws of demand and supply, which invariably, due to the nature of markets, would be unable to guarantee equality and affordability of access. From human rights angle water is a public entitlement, access to which does not depend on one's ability to pay.

Nevertheless, viewing the water/trade nexus through a human rights angle does not necessarily mean that water services need to be free of charge or state-run. Instead, such an angle implies that states, which involve private actors in the provision of basic services, are legally obliged to establish effective and flexible regulatory mechanisms that can secure the progressive realization of the right to water for all people (Lyla Mehta *et al.*, 2005). As far as paying for water in India is concerned, the stage we are in is at the bottom most line.

Different Costs: In various stages of water production and distribution there are several costs involved. They are discussed below with a comparison to the arrangement in NTADCL:

- The prime of them, and all the argument against paying for water is about attaching a price to *water as a resource*;
- Secondly, recovering over a period of time the *capital cost* incurred in constructing the water supply installations and facilities; and
- Thirdly, charging a portion of the *Operation and Maintenance* (O & M) cost of water production and distribution.

One needs to understand the difference among these three types of costs (expenses) to be able to understand and argue what cost does the private service provider or the state is trying to recover from the water-user community. Is it charging water as a resource so as to make the citizen realize the scarce nature of the resource? Is it charging so as to recover the capital cost incurred in constructing the water supply installations and facilities? Is it charging the Operation and Maintenance expenses?

Charging for water 'viewing water as a resource' raises questions such as water right. Charging for water so as to 'recover capital cost incurred in constructing the facilities' is generally viewed wrong because in a welfare state it is a state obligation. Charging the Operation and Maintenance costs is widely accepted and there are some Village Panchayats in Tamil Nadu that has the practice of collecting user charges from House Service Connection (HSC) holders. It is a responsibility the local body is supposed to carry out with the support of the user community. Reports in several village panchayats indicate that even if the user charges were collected from all HSC holders, the local bodies would not be in a position to meet the full O & M costs. One component i.e. water pumping charges (electricity bill) would eat up the entire user-charge collection in one gulp.

Water Charges in Tamil Nadu: As far as Tamil Nadu state is concerned, the policy and practice of supplying water to the households rests with the local bodies (GoTN, 1994). The Government of Tamil Nadu from the budgetary allocations made to the TWAD Board—an auxiliary of the Department of Rural Development, takes care of constructing the installations and incurring the capital cost. Operation and Maintenance (O & M) rests with the local bodies. For the purpose of operation and maintenance, the local bodies through a special Government Order (GoTN) of the Government of Tamil Nadu are permitted to collect user charges (or water tax) which they can use for meeting the expenses pertaining to O & M.

As per the G.O. and in practice, this water tax is a fixed amount of Rs. 360 per year collected only from those who hold individual House Service Connections (HSCs). The common water collection points (otherwise known as Public Fountains) are meant for the poor who cannot afford to pay for water. This positive discrimination is there in favour of the poor. This practice is already in vogue in many of the so-called way-side Village Panchayats in Thiruppur. Water is supplied by the TWAD Board from a combined water supply scheme pumped from Mettupalayam (which is locally popular as the 2nd Scheme). The Village Panchayats are paying the O & M cost to the TWAD Board. The Panchayats pay at the rate of Rs. 3.50 per 1000 litres. This is very much subsidized by the Government and it would not cover the entire O & M cost of the scheme. Given the polluted ground water and considering the essentiality of water service, the government is subsidizing water. As of now as per the condition, given to the NTADCL, they also charge on par with TWAD Board rates only (i.e. Rs. 3.50 for 1000 litres). The actual rates could be very high as Industries are charged at the rate of Rs. 45 per 1000 litres. But recently, as many of the industries found the rate to be too high, the industries started going after informal tanker operators. It has resulted in NTADCL to reduce the water price to Rs. 23 per 1000 litres.

Perhaps, we can foresee certain limitations with private sector taking up service delivery are: (i) if the community has to pay the entire O & M costs; (ii) the fixed payment system may be done away with, and a system of charging for water based on the quantity of water supplied (minus government support) could come into practice; (iii) To be able to pay the amount to the private service provider, the local body may have to levy water tax to the poor people, who out of poverty could not afford to have a house service connection (HSC), and use only the public water collection points on the streets.

To Whom is the Scheme Meant for: NTADCL project is expected to benefit: (i) the industries (about 4000 units), (ii) the slum dwellers (about 60,000), and (iii) the way-side Village Panchayats (11 VPs) in the same order as mentioned. The analysis of some of the VP functionaries is that the scheme is primarily meant for the industries in Thiruppur, secondarily for the slum dwellers most of whom are workers in those industries, and the remaining water is distributed to the way-side VPs. The reasons for the variation in the degree of importance are obvious. The industries should survive. The workers in the industries, most of them migrants from poorer rural areas of Tamil Nadu, should be relived of the water crunch so that they work for the industries. Thirdly, the way-side VPs the water passes through, if by-passed, would become a persistent headache to the TWAD Board and to Thiruppur Municipality by agitations and protests.

The apprehension of some of the VP functionaries in Thiruppur is that, going by policy and developmental ethics, water for drinking purposes should get the top most priority. But, industries have got overriding priority in the NTADCL agreement. Clearly, water as a commercial venture (as one of the factors of production with certain money value) is more likely to succeed in industries rather than giving it to the villages for drinking purposes. This proves that the basic tenet of NTADCL like any other private business venture is commercial viability or RoI (Return on Investment) which the Government of Tamil Nadu has paid heed to. They have also made a provision that if any VPs demand more water they can buy it from the company at the rates that are given to the industries (i.e. 1000 @ Rs. 45). This raises the issue of rich-poor divide among Panchayats where VPs with sufficient income can afford to buy water for any rates prescribed by the private service provider, but people in relatively poor VPs shall suffer with inadequate water supply. However, one problem that the company has started facing recently is that the industries do not want to buy water at the rate of Rs. 45 per 1000 litres. Therefore, the informal tanker operators cater to the water demands of some of the industries. This has forced the NTADCL to bring down the rates from Rs. 45 to Rs. 32 per 1000 litres.

The VP functionaries show a calculation that indicates that if the NTADCL agreed to supply (on payment of Rs. 3.50 per 1000 litres) all the water a Village Panchayat requires the VP can save a lot of money they spend on EB bill (water pumping charges) and the regular pump maintenance expenses. One of the serious problems of most Panchayats, that is 'fat EB bill', can be brought down spectacularly. But, the quantity supplied, as of now, is not even one-fourth of what is required at the Panchayat level. One of the reasons for this is that the NTADCL goes by 1991 census in the year 2006. The VPs are told to take it for granted because the project aims at catering to the water needs of about 4000 garment factories in Thiruppur in the first place.

As a strategy of the government to make industries to pollute less, it could be reasonable if the industries were asked to pay for water, especially the ones that pollute. The idea could be designed in order to make them work keeping water as a 'ruling constraint' so that they pollute less. It would make the industries calculate water also as one of the scarce resources like any other resources involved in the production of goods. If water was made available free of cost, then its use could be indiscriminate and pollution could also be more. The Village Panchayats would naturally use water only for drinking purposes. Then there is nothing wrong if, either out of corporate social responsibility or through government subsidy, VPs were supplied water at rates much less than what it is given to the industries. As of now, the costs charged by NTADCL are on par with what TWAD Board charges to the Village Panchayats.

Are the Panchayats Discontented with PPP ? One postulate of this research was that the Village Panchayats might be discontented that water services have been privatized. Response in most villages disproved it and portrayed that the Village Panchayats do not mind receiving water from private water service providers. This is especially because of the cost these Village Panchayats are incurring on operation and maintenance expenses. The Table 4.1 shows the current state of affairs pertaining to O & M expenses.

All the Village Panchayats show only a deficit budget as far as O & M expenses are concerned. Some of the Panchayats do not have any income from water at all. But all of them meet all these four items of expenses stated above. The lion's share is taken away by the Electricity Board by way of EB Bill. There are some Panchayats that are not able to pay the Tank Operator's salary regularly. The Panchayats have to await the arrival of government grant to be able to make the salary for the

Table 4.1: Particulars of (Water Related) Annual Income and Expenditure in the Villages of New Thiruppur Scheme

Sl. No.	Villages	Income from Water (Per Year)	Expenditure on Water				Total	Surplus/Deficit
			Operator's Charge (Per Year)	Electricity Bill (Per Year)	Maintenance (Per Year)	TWAD Payment (Per Year)		
1.	Thetti Palayam	8,28,000	1,08,000	18,60,000	9,00,000	3,60,000	32,28,000	24,00,000 (–)
2.	Neruperichel	15,12,000	2,16,000	14,40,000	4,20,000	3,60,000	24,36,000	9,24,000 (–)
3.	Chetti Palayam	14,40,000	4,32,000	15,00,000	6,00,000	3,60,000	28,92,000	14,52,000 (–)
4.	Iduvai	-	43,200	4,80,000	60,000	1,20,000	7,03,200	7,03,200 (–)
5.	Mutham Palayam	-	1,36,800	6,00,000	50,000	4,80,000	12,66,800	12,66,800 (–)
6.	Aandi Palayam	9,00,000	57,600	6,00,000	30,000	3,00,000	9,87,600	87,600 (–)
7.	Mangalam	-	1,08,000	12,00,000	25,000	2,76,000	16,09,000	16,09,000 (–)
8.	Puthu Palayam	1,80,000	86,400	18,00,000	84,000	1,80,000	21,50,400	19,70,400 (–)
9.	Kaniyan Poondi	90,000	14,400	3,00,000	72,000	2,40,000	6,26,400	5,36,400 (–)
10.	Muthali Palayam	-	93,600	12,00,000	50,000	50,000	13,93,600	13,93,600 (–)
11.	Murugan Palayam	-	93,600	10,50,000	30,000	1,92,000	13,65,600	13,65,600 (–)

Source: Calculated from the data obtained from the respective village panchayats.

Tank Operators. If, the NTADCL reduces the pumping charges (EB Bill) most likely the water supply related expenses of way-side Village Panchayats will be reduced. But, they are not fully contended because the NTADCL provides only one-third of their water requirements. The rest of the supply being TWAD supplied water and the locally pumped water. There are some VPs such as Thottipalayam which are pressuring that the NTADCL should provide for the complete water requirements of Thottipalayam on the grounds that the industries in Thiruppur polluted all their ground water.

In fact, this NTADCL arrangement can reduce VP level expenses on water supply, as shown through calculations by some VP functionaries. They state that they are able to save 20 to 30 per cent cost if the NTADCL argues to provide the quantum demanded by the VPs. If this is not done, they would end up paying additionally to the NTADCL. Apart from the questions of quantity, affordability and transparency, one apprehension that most VPs raise is of 'accountability'. There is no grievance redressal mechanism to the users. When a grievance is taken to the notice of the NTADCL, 'there are only cross-references given and no answers to have the grievance redressed'.

One fact that this study has confirmed is that the Civil Society Organizations have a tendency to develop a blanket type understanding of all modes of privatization and raise voice in opposition — no matter whether they are privatization of water resources or water services; no matter whether they are construction related or Operation and Maintenance related; no matter whether they are maintenance contract or part-contracting arrangement.

But the standpoints of opposition by the Civil Society Organisations in Tamil Nadu are clear. They are based on 'commodification of water' and the 'need-right dichotomy'. They have (i) a conceptual understanding, and (ii) a practical concern. The conceptual understanding is that water is a 'public good' and it should be delivered by a public sector undertaking and it should not be put in the hands of private companies who would use it for profit-making.

Privatization of water service would most probably would prevent distance the poorer Panchayats from being able to get the required quantity of water for its poor residents. In practice at Thiruppur, as of now, the NTADCL is following only the TWAD Board rates in supplying water to the Village Panchayats. Therefore, there is no discontentment among the Village Panchayats regarding the water charges, as alleged by users and Civil Social Organizations in other parts of the world (such as Bolivia, for example). In fact, contrary to the anxiety of many, privatization in Thiruppur is 'actually reducing the O & M cost' of many of the Village Panchayats, at least for now. We are not sure if this phenomenon would continue in future also.

Is this only a temporary trick or is it going to be the permanent arrangement is yet to be seen. This is because in most countries where water services were privatized, it is often the ordinary people who end up paying the increased financial cost resulting from water privatization as the companies try to recoup their investment. This is either through increased prices for water or through state subsidies of the companies. There are industries such as Tamil Nadu Small Industries Promotion Corporation Limited in Erode district that is said to be requesting NTADCL to supply water to its Perunthurai industrial estate (GoTN, 2005).

Naturally, for NTADCL providing water to industries would fetch more profits than giving it to the Village Panchayats. Unless the NTADCL has legal binding in the agreement with the Government of Tamil Nadu, they would naturally tend to prefer to supply to industries rather than to the Village Panchayats.

Therefore, the fact could be that it is taken as a corporate social responsibility for which the consortium and the industries in Thiruppur share the expenses. As of now, although the Panchayats have complained that the Company does not provide them the required quantity of water, as far as paying a price for water is concerned they do not suffer. They pay what they would otherwise pay the TWAD Board of the Government of Tamil Nadu. Nevertheless, whether the rates would continue in the days to come also or whether the Company would revise the rates after some initial months are over is unknown.

The practical concerns are 'equity' and 'accountability'. Water being a basic need it should be accessible to the poor as much as it is available to the rich. But some of the Panchayats (e.g. Kaniyanpoondi) that are unable to pay the TWAD Board (2nd Scheme) would not be in a position to pay the NTADCL's 3rd Scheme. But the fact remains that they need water to supply to the community at least through common collection points, though not through the House Service Connections (HSC).

The Least Important Consumer: The question of accountability is another vital aspect that almost all the Panchayats complain about NTADCL. The way NTADCL deals with the Village Panchayats is as if the VPs are their least important customer. The transaction is something like "we (NTADCL) would supply a certain quantity of water; you are supposed to pay for it. That's all the dealing is". There is no mechanism to find out whether the quantity of water supplied, as claimed by the NTADCL, is true or not. There is no response when Village Panchayat functionaries want to know on what basis water demand of a Panchayat is calculated (such as Total Population by 55 LPCD etc.). There is no grievance redressal mechanism. There are no discussions. The District Collector is said to have signed on behalf of the Village Panchayats. The Panchayats have to be contended with whatever quantity they are told to have been supplied.

Behind the Corporate Social Responsibility: That the NTADCL has agreed to provide water to the way-side Village Panchayats is a compulsion warranted by the situation. This is the opinion of many of the Panchayat functionaries. They have to do it in the name of corporate social responsibility, especially because the main water line from river Bhavani (from where water is pumped) to Thiruppur Municipality passes through certain Village Panchayats that are water-starving. Bringing water to the industries in Thiruppur ignoring the way-side villages would result in the community in the way-side villages get down to tamper with the waterlines to tap water illicitly.

The company needed to avoid facing such an untoward situation. That is the reason they have, in the guise of corporate social responsibility, agreed to provide a portion of water requirement of the way-side villages on payment on par with the TWAD Board. This is clear from the fact that they have taken 1991 population as the basis to work out water requirement in these way-side villages and provide only a portion even from that calculation stating that they would get full supply only at the end of the 30 year contract period the company entered into.

As the scheme has become functional only for the past two to three months, the Village Panchayats have not been able to sense it properly how the water allocation is going to be. Moreover, the recent rains and floods in the state (October-November, 2005) have, to a considerable extent, replenished the private water sources and Panchayat water sources in the so-called way-side villages. Water from Mettupalayam (TWAD Scheme II) for these way-side Village Panchayats is supplied regularly. These are some of the reasons that keep the Village Panchayats contended about the supply at the moment. During severe water crisis, if these way-side Panchayats did not get the required water, they would definitely demand and tamper with in the NTADCL water lines.

The Guise of Providing Water to the Slum Dwellers in Thiruppur: Most of the slum dwellers in Thiruppur are from poorer Tamil Nadu villages who migrate to Thiruppur, especially, during agriculturally slake seasons. If, in some year, Tamil Nadu happened to get good rains, nearly a half of the workers would have run back—either officially or unofficially—to take up agricultural pursuits in their native villages and in the neighbourhood and escape from the problems of water scarcity and textile pollution in Thiruppur. That would result in labour shortage in the hosiery industries of Thiruppur. Although there may not be field studies carried out to prove this point, the number of "Labourers wanted" placards that are hung at the gate of each of the industry in Thiruppur during peak agricultural seasons could prove this point. The reasons for keeping employment in the hosiery industry merely as a fall back proposition by many of the migrant workers are : (i) water scarcity in Thiruppur industrial area; coupled with the problems of textile chemical pollution in the ground water that is made available for bathing and other domestic uses.

The NTADCL water is expected to solve this problem, to a considerable extent, so that the workers who have double minds about staying back at Thiruppur hosieries, and taking up agriculture in their home place would decide in favour of staying back in Thiruppur. This would also serve as a reply to the allegation that people might migrate, just in case drinking water provision is completely neglected and water for industrial use is assured. All the more, this would not amount to blatant disregard for the National Water Policy, 2002 which states drinking water should be given top priority, and water for industrial use may be given third on the priority list only after irrigation.

Conclusion

Almost all the way-side Village Panchayats covered under the new PPP scheme by the NTADCL are contented about the privatization of water services on the grounds that it has reduced their expenses on O & M of water supply expenses. All the VPs depict only a deficit budget by a big margin from the income sources of water supply, which is their prime botheration as far as water distribution is concerned. But, the new privatized scheme has shown that by providing 1000 litres at the rate of Rs. 3.50, it can reduce the EB bill of the Panchayats. Although doubts are expressed that this practice might end up shortly, at the moment, it is encouraging to see Village Panchayats are able to recover from the burden of fat EB bills.

The grouse of the Village Panchayats is that the NTADCL does not commit to provide their entire water supply requirements. Similarly, the question of accountability has been neglected after the PPP arrangement. But for these two important hitches, the Village Panchayats do not find any problem in getting water under the new Public-Private Partnership arrangement in Thiruppur. Perhaps, the NTADCL might be unhappy that they are not able to sell water to the industries at the rate put down under the contractual arrangements due to local resistance, and the Municipalities' inability to control the informal tanker operators who also ply side by side.

5

Natural Resources at Peril: Commercial Exploitation is the Order of the Day

The Premise

- The culture of purchasing bottled water has become very much a common occurrence, which one did not even dream of, about a decade or so ago.
- Sale of 'branded water' is being promoted through commercial advertisements on the television channels like soap, shampoo and other consumer goods.
- 'Bottled water' is reported to be the fastest growing industry outdoing even the most advertised aerated soft drinks and colas.
- Many farmers these days opine that sale of water as a 'commodity or product' fetches more income than using it as an in-put in cultivation.
- An Officer of the government who ventured to prevent illicit sand-mining in Tamil Nadu was killed on the (sand-mining) spot.

This Chapter is divided into four sections. Section I deals with matters relating to Water Bottling; Section II deals with matters relating to Water Tanker Operations; Section III deals with River Sand-mining for commercial purposes; and Section IV deals with Traditional Water Bodies in Tamil Nadu.

WATER BOTTLING

Introduction

Athoor village[1] near Chennai is changed a lot due to factors such as commercial draft of water, and urban extension that is eating into the rural settlement and its resources—especially their water and land resources. Coca Cola, for instance, sources a bulk of its Kinley brand of bottled water through a factory in Athoor village. Besides this, there are several other local brands of bottled water, most of them run by business people from Chennai and Kancheepuram. The attraction being: the water is sweet and rich in mineral contents. Generally soil in Athoor is sandy which has the capacity of holding water for long. Athoor is located close to *Kusasthala aru* (a branch of *Cholavaram yeri*) and the popular *Puzhal yeri* is situated about 5 kilometres from Athoor. These considerations can set the mind at rest that investment in water business would prosper.

Athoor is a typical Village Panchayat for a student of urban sociology who wants to study how urbanization endanger life and livelihoods of the villages in the vicinity. That the NH by-pass to Thirupathy first ate up some portions of the land in villages close to Athoor is yet another about which this case study has not paid attention.

The story goes like this...

The Athoor Village Panchayat has granted approval (NOC) in the year 1998 to a request made by a rich farmer in Athoor village to sell water drawn from the water sources at his land. He has started bottling fresh water in the name of 'Halo'. In the year 2002, the Coca Cola entered into an agreement with 'Halo', increased production capacity, expanded the market and started selling water bottles in the name of 'Kinley'. An application to draw extra water and to sell it in the name of MVR mineral water was turned down by the Village Panchayat on the grounds that it might affect agriculture and drinking water supply. Now the factory runs three units in Athoor. There are about 20 vehicles of Kinley carrying water as much as 3.5 lakh litres of water daily. It has provided employment to about 75 families in Athoor village.

Again in 2002, a new mineral water company was set up in Athoor in the name of 'Plus'. After objection by the Village Panchayat, it had to relocate to Nagalapuram in Andhra Pradesh. Similarly, a water company

---

1. In Chozhavaram Block of Thiruvallur district— about 40 km from Chennai.

BOX 5.1
Water Business

According to market sources in India, the packaged water industry is estimated to be more than Rs. 10,000 crore and is growing at a rapid pace of about 30-35 per cent. With growing ground water pollution, large number of people particularly in the urban centres are hooked to packaged drinking water. Although it accounts for about 6 per cent of the total beverage market in India, branded bottled water is the fastest growing industry in the beverage sector. It is estimated that the single largest share in the mineral water market might still belongs to Parle's Bisleri brand, which has about 35 per cent market penetration. Multinationals such as Pepsi and Coke have been extremely successful in edging out many smaller brands. Behind this silverlining, many environmentalists have attributed depletion of groundwater in various parts of the country to over extraction of water by packaged or bottled water industry (Nityanand).

(known as Achi moru) disguised as producing and selling moru (butter milk packets) and rasna packets started drawing water for sale. The villagers objected to it and the company had to leave the village. One of the major demands for water comes from the Chennai Metro. The water requirements of the lorries that have entered into contract with Chennai Metro used to draw water in large quantities. Despite explanation that it is taken by Chennai Metro Water as an obligation to provide water to the citizenry in Chennai Corporation, the Village Panchayat stopped it. After a few days local farmers started selling water to the Metro Water lorries, not in huge quantities though. This practice continues even now.

Several business people are reported to have tried to set up water plants in Athoor (e.g. Kokulam Water). But they have been wound up by the villagers through protests. As of now, one water company (with three plants) that operates in Athoor is Kinley with the support of the local Company Halo. The owner of 'Halo' is said to be a local farmer. More over, there are about 75 families from Athoor alone who work as labourers in this Kinley water plants. Hence, the villagers are not in a position to force Kinley to quit.

One supposition, which has been proved right in several similar studies, is that overdraft of ground water leads to depletion affecting agricultural pursuits. To put it a little more clearly, when there is competing demand between 'water for agricultural operations' and 'water for commercial bottling units', the former, most probably, would

BOX 5.2
A New Product called 'Drinking Water'

There was a time in the recently liberalized past when people didn't quite know how to refer to a new product called 'drinking water'. They would say 'bottled water' and 'mineral water' to freely refer to one or the other kind of water, perhaps meaning the same one. It used to be confusing. People were not used to drinking that had to be bought. People were getting used to paying money to drink water.

2002 should be called the year of packaged water. As a December 2002 newspaper article headline puts it, "Water Biz on a Boil". The article expands on this suggestive phrase: "The Rs. 1000 crore packaged water segment outperformed beverage categories such as carbonated soft drinks, tea and coffee, and powder drinks".

Branded bottled water is the fastest growing industry in the beverage sector. Market growth rate has been an unimaginable 80 per cent plus at the beginning of the year 2000. Competition is hot; 2002 witnessed large scale consolidation, with smaller players being gradually edging out by the big contenders **(*Down to Earth*)**.

get sidelined, unless there is strong opposition and protests from the local community against commercial draft of water. This is noticeable even in Athoor.

Pursuits in Agriculture

Livelihoods Lost: As per the records of the Village Administrative Officer, cultivable lands in Athoor are owned by about 200 farmers. About 15 of them are big farmers and 185 of them are small and marginal farmers. The mineral water companies and tankers of Chennai Metro Water are continuously drawing water using hi-power submersible pumps. The water level that used to be at 20–22 feet has gone down to 120–180 feet. Besides increasing in-put prices and escalating pumping charges, the depleting water table has made agriculture unattractive and non-remunerative in Athoor area. Many of the small and marginal farmers are selling out their lands to business people (*Saettu*) from Chennai, who buy it for making house plots. Those who still keep their lands have converted their lands – either in full or in part – as brick kilns to supply to the construction works that is booming in the city.

Alternative Livelihoods: There are about 560 agricultural wage earners in Athoor. The agricultural wage earners have also found employment in agriculture non-dependable and the wages to be too meagre. They commute by lorries and tankers to Chennai to earn better wages in construction works with building contractors in Chennai. Some of them who are not very much mobile have become menial workers in local brick kilns. There are others (about 75 families) who are employed in local water bottling companies. Another peril that is taking place is sand mining in *Kusasthala aru* which is also a reason for water depletion. There are some local people of Athoor involved in sand-mining for a wage.

Drinking Water: The village has three ponds and 7 Panchayat bore-wells. They run dry during summer. Availability of even drinking water becomes scarce during summer seasons. Then, the residents start protesting against the water companies. Once, it rains and water availability becomes normal, they forget all about the water scarcity and about the water companies return to normalcy. The companies engage in their business as usual. The Pollution Control Board that tested the water for its mineral content has reported that the mineral content in the water has come down from 75 per cent to 25 per cent in the past few years. They have also warned them of water turning saline if water draft continued at the rate it is done now.

No Water Companies Any More

Private people even now approach Athoor Panchayat seeking permission to draw water for commercial purposes. The Village Panchayat in its meeting held on December 30, 2005 has passed a resolution that no water company would be allowed to set up their unit at Athoor. Some people raised their voice that a resolution should be passed to evict the Kinley bottling company also from Athoor. Considering the number of families (75 families) that earn their wages from the bottling company, and not being able to suggest an alternative employment to them, a resolution to that effect was not passed.

Halo minerals, the contract bottler for Coke's Kinley brand of water is accused of depleting the ground water in Athoor village. Disturbingly, Kinley's bottling units are located in an area that has been declared 'critical' because of the plentiful sweet water available under ground and because of the areas important to the water security of the region and the city of Chennai.

An overview of Chozhavaram Block gives a gloomy picture again. Many of the Panchayats in Chozhavaram Block has at least one mineral

BOX 5.3
Illegal Bottled Water

According to BIS, there are 1,200 bottled water factories all over India, of which 600 are in Tamil Nadu. It is estimated to be growing at a rate of 40-50 per cent annually over the past four years (2004). In Chennai alone, more than 200 legal and 400 illegal bottled water manufacturers operate. India's packaged water industry is barely a decade old and it is earning in billions. Brand names such as Coke's Kinley, Pepsi's Aquafina and the Indian bottled water giant Parle's Bisleri enjoy a Rs. 4 billion market, according to reports.

water bottling company. In some villages though not a company, water tanker operators deplete water resources. Hardly any of them bother to get Panchayat permission. Agricultural operations have shrunk in Village Panchayats such as Athoor, Alinjampakkam and Alamathy mainly due to urbanization and commercial draft of water. The *Chozhavaram yeri* being mostly used for drawing water for Chennai population by the Chennai Metro Water tankers is also a reason for the crisis.

The villages where commercial draft began in 1998 are found to be more seriously defaced, compared to the ones where water companies have started operating recently, about 2-3 years ago. The recent rains have, to a considerable extent, reduced the cry of the people for water. Otherwise, there is a vast shift in livelihood patterns seen in many of the villages (Erumaipattypalayam, Karanodai, Alinjampakkam, Chozhavaram and Alamathi): people shifting from agriculture to construction and other works in the cities. Their water has been stolen and it has made them sell out their lands, and finally it is sad to notice some people earning their wages as menial workers in the water bottling companies.

WATER TANKER OPERATION

Mathur, a village in Thiruvallur district in North Chennai, is under severe ground water stress. Under the Groundwater (Regulation) Act, it is a notified area based on the criticality of the water crisis. Mathur is located close to Manali Industrial Estate. Water tankers steal groundwater day in and day out. The area is under severe stress for water. That which started in a small way about 20 years ago has become a big business today. There are about 50-60 tanker operators taking water from Mathur and supplying to hotels, restaurants and residential areas in Chennai. The agricultural land owners have turned to selling water to tankers, as it is more remunerative than taking up agricultural pursuits. Several of them have converted to water sales already and have given up agriculture. At least 200-300 tanker loads of water is handled daily. The number more than doubles in summer when there is acute demand for water in Chennai city.

Officially, the industrial estates in Ambattur, Guindy, and Manali are supposed to buy water from Chennai Metro Water only. But, considering the deposit to be paid to Metro Water and the charges of Metro water, most of the industries and hotels choose to buy water from the Water tankers that operate from Mathur village. It works out dirt cheap to them. Another pertinent problem is some of them have illicit power lines to operate their pump sets. There are also some who use free electricity meant for agriculture to run motors that lift water.

The groundwater that was available at 20 feet (about 10 years ago) has gone down drastically to 350-400 feet. Many of them have given up agriculture and have taken up water sales as their occupation. A Mr. Palani, who calls himself an environmentalist along with a few like-minded people of Mathur, has given umpteen number of complaints to several people including the Police, Thesildar, Collector and has filed cases in the Chennai High Court that drawing water from notified area is a criminal offence. He has also formed a local committee called "Mathur Grama Kudiyiruppor Pathukappu Podhu Nala Sangam". All the protests they make and the complaints they tender are done under this auspices.

BOX 5.4
Groundwater Regulation

Taking note of declining water table in the city and its surroundings, the State Government passed the Madras Metropolitan Area Groundwater (Regulation) Act in 1987. It applied to 285 notified villages where free extraction of groundwater is permitted only for domestic use, and extraction for commercial activities requires a permit. But the Act has failed because private tanker operators were allowed to draw water without permits in 2004 in the face of the water crisis.

One-fifth of Chennai's water supply comes from private operators who form a powerful lobby. In 2002, the government amended the Act, making it applicable to 305 villages. But even the amendment has failed to check the private tankers, who have become quite influential.

Upon pressure from the Sangam members, the officials and police often get down to action. At times, they even seize equipments. But just three days after every thing returns to normalcy as if nothing had happened. A case filed by the Sangam in 1995 was taken up for hearing in 1999. In the year 2000 the judgement came in favour of the community that drawing water for commercial purposes from Mathur and 13 other villages should be stopped.

The Tamil Nadu Government Gazette dated Friday July 7, 1995 No. 3541 (Part IV, Section 18) as per the Madras Metropolitan Area Ground-water (Regulation) Amendment Act, 1995 by the order of the Governor notified that the following areas are 'over exploited' and they should be let free from the stress in terms of water draft for commercial purposes.

(1) Mathur, (2) Manjampakkam, (3) Madhavaram, (4) Thambaram, (5) Ambattur, (6) Maduravoyal, (7) Manali, (8) Chinnasekkadu, (9) Thiruvottiyur, (10) Ayapakkam, (11) Chitlapakkam, (12) Hastinapuram, (13) Alapakkam, (14) Korattur.

Subsequent to the court order prohibiting groundwater extraction for commercial purposes in the area, the bottled water companies were shut down. But illegal extraction by tanker operators continues unchecked. Thus, the efforts of the Mathur Village Residents General Welfare Association yielded fruits, although partially. Many big companies such as Polo, King, and Acqua have left Mathur and the surrounding villages. However, the 'local tank operators' continue to extract groundwater and sell it in Chennai city. The Village Panchayats are keeping quite because all those who sell water through tankers belong to the local area. They are neither MNCs nor TNCs. Being relatives and friends, they keep quite not being able to say anything. Groundwater draft goes on as ever. The groundwater that was available at 20 feet has gone down drastically to 350-400 feet in the past 10 years. Shifting from agriculture to wage employment and the agony for drinking water during summer continues as ever.

Agriculture in Mathur

Mathur, which was primarily an agricultural village about 10 years ago has come away from agriculture to sell water. Out of the 4631 households, only about 70 families are still pursuing agriculture and about 100 families still remain as agricultural wage-earner family. The local communities face severe water scarcity during summer whereas the water tanker operation goes unabated both in winter and summer.

Areas Affected

The following are the villages affected that are located around Mathur:

(1) Periyamathur, (2) Chinnamathur, (3) MMDA (Mathur), (4) Manjampakkam, (5) Nehru Nagar, (6) Masilamani Nagar, (7) Apolo Amstrong Nagar, (8) Arun Nagar.

Table 5.1: Metro Water's Daily Water Sheet

Particulars	*Nov. 2003*	*Jan. 2004*	*Mar. 2004*	*May 2004*
Amount of water transported by tankers (MLD)	38	74	140	203
Number of tankers hired	595	726	1,100	1,300
Number of daily trips	6,733	7,555	9,500	12,000
Number of fixed plastic tanks installed	10,030	10,430	11,315	13,500
Number of new bore-wells sunk	5,500	6,500	7,000	7,500
Daily expenditure (in Rs. lakh)	55	70	85	100

Reported in *Down to Earth*, December 31, 2004 *(Source cited: Metro Water).*

Unfortunately, despite acute water scarcity in many parts of India, the government is yet to legislate effectively to conserve groundwater resources. Although with limited jurisdiction, the Groundwater (Regulation) Amendment Act, 1995, is not operationalised to the extent it could be or needs to be. Soft drink and bottled water companies pay next to nothing for the water they extract. Given that the primary raw material comes free of cost, wastage in the industry is ridiculously high. Besides this, the loss of agricultural lands due to non-availability of water is another big problem.

The resultant scarcity of clean drinking water has spawned yet another water-intensive industry that exploits one community's water and sells it at a profit to consumers who can afford to buy it. The only raw material used for bottled water companies is groundwater for which the companies pay the government (by way of cess) pittance. This is another reason that has created stir all over since the community's resources are stolen for private profits.

Small-scale providers of water supply have been an important part of water service delivery, mostly in Municipalities and Metropolitan corporations and in some cases in the town Panchayats also. Although they (especially the tanker operators) are considered as 'temporary players' who want to make money during summer, they have become an integral part of water service delivery, in several apartment areas in the cities and in metropolis such as Chennai. Thus, the tanker operators and those who deliver water cans for domestic consumption make a presence all through the year, though they might say theirs is a seasonal business.

> **BOX 5.5**
> **Hydro-geological Report**
>
> Hydro-geologists of CSE report the once the dynamic groundwater reserves are exhausted and the deeper, static reserves are exploited, replenishment of groundwater levels can't happen to the previous levels. Doesn't matter if irrigation is resumed, rainfall is good, or even a flood occurs. The bore-wells have been drawing water continuously. The aquifers are so exhausted that these bore-wells now yield less than half of what they used to in 2003, while some have dried up completely.

Another feature is that they operate in a very informal business environment without much hassles from the government. Neither the government nor the officials-in-charge of water provision are unaware of the role the private water service providers play which keeps them (the government and the officials) relieved of the headache of having to ensure uninterrupted water supply to the citizenry. This could be the reason why the Groundwater (Regulation) Act is ineffective and remains on the shelf. In the bargain the rural community losses one of its important livelihood assets viz., water, which renders the agricultural lands uncultivable for want of water for irrigation.

The Changing Paradigms

There are two paradigms of water in intense contest—the paradigm of water as commons and the paradigm of water as a commodity. Water is common because its equitable allocation and sustainability depend on the cooperation between members of a community (Vandana, 2005). Access to water as a commonly shared public good prevails even today in most places of the country, whereas on the other side privatization of water resources is also gaining momentum with profit-orientation and economic motive that globalization lure people in. Athoor and Mathur in Tamil Nadu are real-life examples to prove this point. Gone are the days when the extent of land one holds and the amount of crop one harvests determined the social status of a person in Tamil Nadu society. The market and commodity orientation has redefined that 'cash in hand or cash at bank' as the prime determinants of status in the society. This is evident from the fact that they quit agriculture and turn to selling water at Mathur and in the villages nearby.

> **BOX 5.6**
> **Re. 1 Water Pouches**
>
> Besides water tankers, another common sight in the city is tempos carrying cans of drinking water. Way-side stores stock small pouches of water that people sip while on the move. The 200 millilitre pouches cost Re. 1 each.

The profitability of this business is beyond doubt. Coke's Indian operations took a beating in the first few years of operation after fizzy drinks failed to perform to company expectations. But after Kinley, Coke's water brand, was launched in mid-2000, the multinational's revenues rosed up. In fact, Coca Cola India's third quarter 2001 results mention that "its growth of 11 per cent had been led by the successful expansion of Kinley water." For companies, it is profit and to the communities it is loss of a vital livelihood resource.

Despite Groundwater (Regulation) Act the government is not in a position to curb the menace of groundwater extraction. This is because during summer season unless people turn to private water suppliers, the government machinery in charge of providing water would be in great trouble not being able to supply water. Failure to provide water for drinking might tell not only upon the performance of a given government but also upon the longevity of the government itself.

RIVERBEDS BEING CHANGED INTO SAND-MINES

The rivers and riverine population in the country and world are not only the beds of cultural evolution but also natural eco-systems. One such area in Tamil Nadu is "Mayanur", Krishnarayapuram block of Karur district where Kaveri and Amaravathi rivers join together. The river basin of both sides in this stretch (Kattalai, Mayanur, Nathammedu, Lalapettai, Ooruvanthur, Mahanaur etc.) was badly affected by devourous and greedy extraction of sand during 1989-2000 which has created havoc in the river basin. Since October 1, 2003, the quarrying of sand in the riverbeds has been entrusted to public works department (Vishwanathan S., 2003). Sand mining in the riverbeds seems a simple matter on the surface, but if we go in to analyse deeper on this issue, its enormity is so large on livelihood rights of the people who count on the river system. In spite of several rules framed by State Government, the rapacious practices adopted by the lease holders during the period of 1989-2000 have led to ecological damage, ground-water depletion, water scarcity and loss of agricultural production (See Annexure 6.1 on Government Order about Sand-Mining). Widespread quarrying of sand has also affected the flow of water from the river systems to down-stream systems (Farmers Conference, February 9, 2004).

There are 86 river adjacent farmers who do not have patta land at Kattalai panchayat in Krishnarayapuram Taluk in Karur district. They have to pay lease amount (*vaitha*) to the government. They have not paid any amount to the government for the past three years. Some of them have dug wells in their lands which was used for drawing water for cultivation. According to Mr. Arumugam, President of Amaravathi River Basin Farmer's Association, 86 river adjacent small farmers in the stretch from Mela Mayanur to Mela Kattalai were not able to cultivate due to sand mining during 1989-2000. In this area, sand has been dug upto 20 feet. This has caused grave damage to the cultivation. He adds: "We used to cultivate groundnut and *cholam* in these lands. The bank of the river has widened. So, the lands are no longer suitable for cultivation. They report that all that they could earn from the land was that income from the leasing *seemaikaruvelai* shrub grown there. Some of the farmers are collecting Rs. 5 to Rs. 10 from bullock cart sand miners for using their land as the path to take sand from the river. A few farmers are working as labourers in sand-mining operation which takes place at Sri Rama Samudhram. They make the runway on the rivers for sand-laden lorries.

Even though bullock cart sand-miners do not have permission to take sand, they take sand for their livelihoods only. Replying to a question, the bullock cart owners say: "This is our livelihood for which we had purchased bullock and cart". We do not have any other employment here. One of the affected river adjacent small farmers, Elanchiyam, 65 years old widow, rears calves nearby her land. The land has been fetching income to her in the past years. Owing to hike in diesel price, she had to quit the cultivation since there was no profit from the land after spending on irrigating the land by using diesel engine connected in a small well.

Table 5.2: Particulars about River Adjacent Cultivators

Stretch	*Name of the Hamlets*	*Distance in km.*	*Cultivation Area (in acres)*	*No. of Farmers*	*Present Position*
Mela Mayanur to Mela Kattalai (Karur District)	• Mela Mayanur • Renganathapuram • Kattalai • Malaiyappapuram • Nathammadu • Melakattalai	5	450	86	• No cultivation due to hike in diesel price. Earning income from leasing Seemai Karuvalai which is grown on land naturally.
Chinnapalli Palayam [Namakkal District to Natham, (Trichi District)]	• Chinnapalli Palayam • Periyapalli Palayam • Mahanur • Ooruvanthur • Sri Rama Samuthuram • Sheela Pillayar Puthur • Natham	13	2300	720 (ranging 10 cents to 10 acres)	• Korai, Banana and Coconut are cultivated. • Coconut trees are grown by paying Rs. 60 per tree/year.

Source: Computed from the field data.

It is observed that a number of combined water-supply-scheme wells have been put up by TWAD Board for water supply to many villages and towns.

Table 5.3: Combined Water Supply Scheme

Name of Pumping Station	*Water Supply*
Kattalai	• Vaiyapuri Kavundanur and wayside villages. • Thanthondri Municipality and wayside villages. • Uppidamangalam Town Panchayat and wayside villages.
Mayanur	• Dindigul Municipality and wayside villages.
Seelapillayar Puthur	• Kattuputhur, Balapuram and Maruthampatty.

Source: Computed from the field data.

The State Government has spent a lot of money to supply drinking water to the people by taking several efforts. At the same time, the Government is permitting sand mining in the river beds which are main sources for the above combined water supply scheme. Indiscriminate mining which is being currently practiced, if allowed to continue without check may lead to colossal damage to the combined water supply scheme. It is, therefore, essential to look at this problem with open mind to safeguard the river basins.

Even though several rules on sand mining exist, illegal quarrying of sand has become the order of the day in several rivers of Tamil Nadu. Sri Rama Samuthram and Mohanur in Musiri Block of Namakkal District exemplify this state of affairs. The places are just opposite to the river bank at *Kattalai* and *Mayanur*. Interaction with the affected people of Sri Rama Samuthram reveals that the rules on sand mining are seldom respected. It is visible from Mohanur to Sri Rama Samuthram that a lot of sand-laden lorries ply regularly. Lorries are coming all the way from Coimbatore, Salem, Namakkal etc., as fine sand is available at Sri Rama Samuthram. From Sri Rama Samuthram to Mohanur, temporary lorry operators have been appointed to regulate the traffic which shows the number of sand laden lorries are coming and going on this route. Indiscriminate sand-quarrying at these areas is a threat to the livelihoods of the local communities from this mindless commercial activity.

In Practice at Sand-Mining Spots

- Poclain (an earth moving machine) is used to take sand and also to form the road on the riverbed.
- Quarrying is done more than the permitted quantity and depth.
- Loads more than what is legally permissible is, often, allowed.
- Pools of water stagnation is created in the river bed.
- Roads that are formed within the river for sand-laden lorries to ply is left as such when the contractors move to new places for quarrying.
- Sand mining takes place beyond 6.00 p.m. which is against the norm.
- Sand is carried and deposited at places nearby for sale later on.
- Good earnings from this business are pocketed by private owners only.
- Police force is used for sand-mining against community interest.

Adverse Consequences

- Causes grave damage to the river system particularly river banks and the adjoining cultivable lands.
- Causes grave consequence on agricultural production.
- Affects the flow of water in the river systems to down stream systems.
- Affects cattle grazing.
- Erodes river banks and water depletion that would stop regular income to agriculturists.
- Affects aquatic fauna and creating imbalance in the river ecology.
- Dust emanating from the sand-laden lorries.
- Loss of income (local cess etc.) to Panchayats.
- Damage to the roads.

The PWD's nominee has diverted the direction of river flow and constructed a sand bund to stop water into the sand mining areas at Sri Rama Samuthram. Sand mining work is done day and night disregarding the rules and regulations. As the demand for fine-sand at Sri Rama Samuthram increases, haphazard sand mining has led to deepening of the riverbeds, widening of the rivers, depletion of ground water table, and degradation of groundwater quality.

Due to continuous water scarcity during the past years, *patta* land-holders took water directly from the river through PVC pipes to irrigate plantain crops, for which they used diesel engines. When the price of banana reduced drastically in the market the farmers could not get income even when they saved plantain crops with the help of water from the river pumped by using diesel engine. Many river adjacent small farmers are living at Seelapillayarputhur. They depend on coconut trees on the river-bank. If drought prevails, they are not able to get income from the coconut trees. Sand mining would affect the water flow in the riverbed which in turn affects the coconut trees on the river banks. Their condition continues to be pathetic. They are paying Rs. 60 per tree per year as leasing charge to the government. In addition to getting income from coconut trees, they are going for wage employment to earn their livelihoods. They are very poor people living in the river adjacent land. If they had any property in the main land, they would have preferred to live in the main village.

Now, sand mining takes place at Sri Rama Samuthram. Apart from quarrying more than the permitted quantity of sand, the PWD nominee is selling more than the permitted quantity of sand. Sand is collected from the riverbed by lorries and the sand is deposited at Unniyur, a five kilometer distance from the sand mining place. Interaction with drivers of the sand-laden lorries revealed that there was no limit for the quantity of sand taken and for the trips. At Sri Rama Samuthram, the road side shops and houses are exposed to the dust emanating from the sand-laden lorries. The contract sand-miners engage two labourers to water the lorry-pathways in order to prevent the dust that plying lorries emanate. People of Sri Rama Samuthram complain that police force is used by the PWD's nominee who does indiscriminate sand mining. As per the rules, income and part of lease amount must be given to the concerned village panchayat. Panchayat office functionary of Sri Rama Samuthram said that they are yet to receive 30 per cent of the royalty.

In another area, the sand mining has been permitted in the Mohanur Panchayat limit. But PWD's nominees are taking sand beyond the permitted area (Oruvanthoor) because of the availability of fine sand. So, Oruvanthoor village did not get any royalty. In the river basin of Oruvanthoor, 15 river adjacent small farmers lost their land due to indiscriminate sand mining from their lands which are no longer useful for cultivation. Hence, it is a serious problem for the livelihood of the people. Efforts should be taken to regulate sand-quarrying operations with a view to protecting livelihood of the people. Moreover, the government should make every effort to ban the removal or extraction of sand from river where the sand bed level is below the normal level.

TRADITIONAL WATER BODIES IN TAMIL NADU

India has a long tradition of using small water storage structures—man-made and natural, variously called tanks, ponds, ooranis and so on. They are also known as water course *Poramboke*, viz., *Kuttai, Kulam, Odai*. These structures were the most important and widespread traditional sources of irrigation and drinking water before the advent of water-lifting devices. Tanks and ponds were used for a variety of purposes: as a source of water for drinking, washing and bathing for humans and animals, for irrigating crops and for raising fish (Vaidyanathan A., 2001). Besides this, especially after the dependence on ground water increased, the main purpose for which the surface water-storage-structures serve is recharging the groundwater aquifers. The more the tanks and ponds, the safer is the ground water position and *vice versa*.

In Tamil Nadu maintenance of tanks with less than 40 hectares *ayacut* is vested with the panchayat unions; while tanks with more than 40 hectares *ayacut* are under the PWD's care. In addition, there are a large number of *ex-zamin* tanks which remain to be properly surveyed and classified (Vaidyanathan A., 2001). The Government of Tamil Nadu statistics show that there are 41,915 irrigation tanks, out of which 23,156 are Panchayat Union tanks, 8,903 are PWD tanks and 9,856 are *ex-zamin* tanks (GoTN, 2001-02). Where they exist, these structures serve purposes such as (a) community rain water storage for minor irrigation, (b) water for herd, and (c) groundwater recharging.

BOX 5.7

High Court Statement on Water Bodies

Calling for a "ruthless and pitiless" removal of all structures encroaching on water bodies all over the State, the Madras High Court said the time had come for the State to take definite measures to restore tanks, ponds and lakes in its territory.

It directed the Government to "identify all natural resources in different parts of the State and, wherever illegal encroachments were found, to initiate appropriate steps in accordance with the relevant provisions of law for restoring such natural water storage resources which have been classified as such in the revenue records to its original position, so that the suffering of the people of the State due to water shortage is ameliorated."

Minor irrigation tanks are the best flood moderators and drought mitigators in the villages and provide livelihood for the marginalized people in rainfed areas. Tanks contribute to almost a quarter of irrigated agriculture in Tamil Nadu. The condition of Minor Irrigation Tanks in the State is deteriorating year by year. Many of the tanks and ponds have fallen into disuse and are in urgent need of repairs. These structures generally suffer from problem of loss of storage due to silting, poor maintenance and management, encroachment etc. There are places in Tamil Nadu where common ponds and tanks have lost any mark of trace at all.

Poor maintenance and silting give an appearance that they could be used as cultivable lands (by encroachment) using groundwater sources. Or if they are close to any suburban area, they are being converted as 'plots for sale'. A silted tank in any city boundary is, often, the first place the urban development authorities lay eyes on – be it construction of a bus terminus or location of an industrial estate. The steady deterioration of traditional water bodies has resulted in depletion of groundwater, severe shortage of water for irrigation, domestic consumption and water for cattle.

Competing demand for water and consecutive failure in rainfall in several places has led to drying up of several surface water storage structures and shallow wells in Tamil Nadu. This necessitated the farmers to go in for pumping groundwater from very deep levels. Use of technologies has equipped the rural community with the option of drawing excessive groundwater to meet the peak demands of irrigation.

Thus, 'groundwater use', which was complementary to the 'surface water use' has become the main source of water in most of the places resulting in the neglect of maintenance of tanks, ponds, *nullas* and similar surface water storage structures. Silted tanks and dried up ponds, in stead of exerting a pull on maintenance and management of traditional water storage structures, have tempted the farmers for encroachment of such lands for agricultural purposes relying on groundwater sources.

This is a common phenomenon in several Tamil Nadu villages. The nostalgic memories the local community members of Velapalayam (Salem district, Tamil Nadu) narrate about their lost traditional water reservoirs in the village are fascinating and captivating to listen to. The following is a case of changes in the trend of treatment of surface water storage structures in one of the Tamil Nadu Villages (velapalayam), and the deplorable aftermath:

BOX 5.8
State to Study Encroachments

Referring to Article 51A(g) of the Constitution, the Bench said the provision made it a fundamental duty for every citizen to protect and improve the natural environment, including forests, lakes, rivers and wildlife. This duty can be enforced by the court, it said.

The judges said: "It is imperative for the State to maintain the natural resources with a view to keep the ecological balance intact, and thereby provide a healthy environment to the public at large in the State of Tamil Nadu. Having regard to the precarious water situation prevailing in the major part of the year, it is imperative such noted water storage resources such as tanks, odais, ooranis, canals, etc., are not obliterated by encroachers."

Directing the State Government to make an overall study of all encroachments in respect of land classified as land for water storage, the Bench said: "In the present-day context, such a step is required to be taken by the State to improve the water storage facility since in many parts of Tamil Nadu, people are suffering from an acute shortage of water."

The Advocate-General, N.R. Chandran, told the court that the State Government had imposed a total ban on any form of construction on any water resource in 2002.

VELAPALAYAM—A CASE IN POINT

Profile

Velapalayam is a habitation of Kalkaveri Panchayat located in Rasipuram Block of Salem district. Velapalayam comprises five tiny settlements within viz., Gandhi Nagar, Indra Nagar, Anna Nagar, MGR Nagar, and Vadakuttai. Talking from the stand points of location, facilities, population, and occupation Velapalayam characterizes a typical Tamil Nadu village. It is a mono-caste village — all the households belong to Vanniyar caste (MBC). The total population of Kalkaveri Panchayat is 10,360 and Velapalayam has 430 households with a population of 2830. There are some families engaged in powerloom weaving, and a considerable number of youth from Velapalayam village go to the nearby town (Nammakkal, 12 km away and Rasipuram, 9 km away—the near by towns known for lorry sheds) to work as lorry drivers and cleaners.

However, agriculture, cow and goat rearing are the main occupations. Most of them are either small farmers or marginal farmers. The main crops cultivated are cotton, tapioca, groundnut, maize and millets. One of the features that single out Velapalayam is that there are hardly any big farmers in the village whereas Velapalayam hamlet is encircled by a host of big farmers who own lands in the range of 5 to 15 acres with deep bore-wells. Each of these big farmers who are themselves rig-vehicle owners has more than 2 bore-wells in his farms for irrigation purposes. Rasipuram is one of the popular places for rig-vehicle operations.

Water Resources

Traditional Water Storage Structures: Velapalayam with five settlements comes under *Kalkaveri* Panchayat. *Kalkaveri* in Tamil means 'Quarter of River *Kaveri*'. This confirms the abundance of water people of Velapalayam had been enjoying in the past (about 30-35 years ago, as recollected by the people). Besides the presence of a tributary of Kaveri flowing about 3 kilometres away from Velapalayam, there were three main traditional water storage structures present in the village. They are: (1) Madhankuttai, (2) Annammakoil lake, and (3) Ayyankuttai. One of them (Ayyankuttai – about 9 acres water storage structure) is completely missing due to encroachment. It is not known as *Ayyankuttai*[2] anymore. It is called *Ayyankadu*[3]. The second one (Annammakoil lake) is progressively getting wiped out of the village map. Madhankuttai is completely silted that it cannot be recognized as a tank at all. The drainage lines were encroached long ago which eventually resulted in the storage structures drying up.

Table 5.4: Encroachment Particulars of Water Storage Structures in Velapalayam

Sl. No.	*Name of the Structure*	*Water Spread Area (Approximately)*	*The Water Spread Area Left with after Encroachments*
1.	Madhankuttai	3 acres	Silted but not encroached.
2.	Annammakoil lake	100 acres	Hardly 10 acres remain without encroachment. But they do not possess title deeds.
3.	Ayyankuttai	9 acres	Fully encroached by nine local farmers. They have obtained title deeds also.

These village common resources have become properties of individual farmers in several cases, and in others they are in the process

2. Meaning 'Water storage structure or tank'.
3. Meaning 'farm land'.

of conversion. Water Resources Map of the village, drawn by the community members.

Change in the Cropping Pattern

The encroachment phenomenon has started reflecting in the ground-water tables. The depleting ground water level has necessitated the farmers of Velapalayam to resort to less water intensive crops. The change in the cropping pattern is shown in the table below:

Table 5.5: Change in cropping pattern

Crops Cultivated Before Encroachment	*Crops Cultivated After Encroachment*
Paddy	Maize
Sugarcane	Millets
Betal leaf	Tapioca
Black gram	Groundnuts

Structures for Providing Domestic Water: Velapalayam has a few open wells, Over Head Tanks (OHT) provided by the TWAD Board of Government of Tamil Nadu and five Hand Pumps for the purpose of providing water for domestic use. The Table 5.6 gives an account of the structures along with their functional status:

Table 5.6: Functional Status of Domestic Water Supply Facilities in Velapalayam

Water Supply Facility	*Number*	*Functional Status*
OHT 60,000 litres	1	Not functioning
OHT 30,000 litres	1	Not functioning
OHT 15,000 litres	2	Not functioning
Open Wells (Common)	3	Disused
Hand Pumps (IM2)	5	Not functioning

The loss of tanks, ponds and other surface-water-storage structures in Velapalayam has started showing very deplorably on the ground-water levels. On the request of the Village Panchayat various agencies have drilled about 6 bore-wells for domestic water supply in the past eight months (between February 2005 and September 2005) one after another. Hardly any yielded water for more than a month. The last two bore holes that went upto 1300 feet completely failed and did not show any trace of water source at all. The request made to the adjacent Village Panchayat to supply water got turned down by them on the grounds that it would hike their electricity bill in terms of pumping charges.

Purchasing Water for a Price: Water is already in the monthly expenditure list of most people in many cities and some towns in Tamil Nadu. But in rural areas, although there used to be periods of severe water stress, people did not have to buy water for a price. Unfortunately, people of Velapalayam had to buy water – water for both drinking as well as domestic use – for the past one year. The price of one pot of drinking water is Re. 1 and the price of water for other domestic use is 0.70 paise. This is supplied by tanker operators from the neighbourhood. It is too expensive for most of them. Those who could not afford it are fetching water from agricultural fields about a kilometre away. This is the condition that the loss of the traditional water bodies have brought the people of Velapalayam to. A village that is close to one of canals which is still called Kalkaveri (quarter of Kaveri) has declined to the state of buying water for a price. The neglect of traditional water bodies has played havoc in their lives.

Tracking Down the Process

A causal analysis to trace the process that has made Velapalayam a water-starved village brings to light several factors that have contributed to this state of affairs, besides the declining rain fall which is a common trend all over the state in the last couple of years. The prominent among the causes are:

- Progressive *encroachment of drainage lines* by farmers in the upstream reduced the amount of water that flowed to the ponds and lakes in Velapalayam.
- Absence of maintenance resulted in widespread *silting and reduction in the water spread area and the depth.*
- Contraction of the water bodies has resulted in poor *percolation and recharge* of groundwater.
- *Digging of bore-wells deeper and deeper one after another* by big farmers in the brim of the village without taking into consideration if recharge arrangements exist to support so many bore-wells.
- Await with trust in God the arrival of rains for recharging the depleting groundwater levels.
- *Corruption* that enabled the private people to obtain title deeds for lands which are actually dried up water bodies.

BOX 5.9
Penalise Land-grabbers

Citing provisions of the Timil Nadu Land Encroachments Act, 1905, amended by the Act of 1975, the Madras High Court said the authorities had the powers to penalize land grabbers. The moment an encroachment came up in a lake, the Village Administrative Officer should invoke Sections 6 and 7 of the Act and slap eviction and show-cause notices to the culprits. The VAO should also file a police complaint so that the culprits are prosecuted, activists pointed out.

The felt that the onus was now on the various government agencies concerned.

- The Public Works Department, the Municipal Administration and the Revenue Departments and local bodies to implement the High Court's direction.

These processes have forced the people of Velapalayam village resort to purchasing water for a price. The significance of the case is that it is not unique to one village in some obscure Tamil Nadu village. It portrays a typicality most Tamil Nadu villages experience for quite some time now. This is, perhaps, one of the important reasons why governments are trying to rediscover the watershed areas in villages through projects and programmes.

Official Intervention

The more the water stress more the headache to the governments. Therefore, the State Government of Tamil Nadu has deployed the PWD Water Resources Division to conduct a survey of such encroachments and clear them up. The Annammakoil lake in Velapalayam has been covered with stone marks so as to warn the community against any encroachment attempts. However, the Ayyankuttai (about 9 acres) for which the local farmers have obtained tilted deeds long ago could not be rescued by the community for common interest until now. The recent heavy rains have filled the Madhankuttai. It has helped recharge water levels in two of the bore-wells ensuring at least partial supply.

Analysis

The main sources of irrigation in Tamil Nadu are canals, tanks, and wells – both open wells and tube-wells. In Tamil Nadu, the demand for water and sources of supply have undergone a dramatic change during the 50 odd years. The net irrigated area that was in 1950-51 has almost doubled in the year 2000 – that which was 17.88 lakhs in 1950-51 has become 30.19 lakhs in the year 2000. During the same period the use of various irrigation sources have also changed spectacularly. That is the sources such as canal irrigation, tank irrigation and wells that was 43, 30, and 24 per cent respectively have changed to 20, 17, and 60 per cent respectively (GoTN, 2003). It means the dependence on surface water has been on the decline whereas the stress on the groundwater has more than doubled. The trend is the same in meeting the drinking water requirements as well. The progressive and increasingly widespread fall in groundwater levels in many parts of Tamil Nadu is a clear indication that extraction rates are exceeding the natural rates of recharge (Vaidyanathan A., 2004). The traditional water storage structures in many places have been rendered useless because of the absence of maintenance and the prevalence of encroachments.

Tanks and canals were the oldest sources of irrigation in Tamil Nadu and the mainstay for the livelihood of many of the poor households. However, most tanks and canals are in disrepair due to rapid decline in maintenance and upkeep over time, break down of traditional management institutions, and development of alternative sources of irrigation. Introduction of new technologies for drilling tube-wells and government incentives of cheap loans and electricity have augmented other sources of irrigation, especially the tube-well sources. Water analysts report that there has been an imbalance in irrigation investments, with subsidies for private wells (both open wells and tube-wells) leading to gradual neglect of tanks and canals (SANDEE Policy Brief).

The Hindu (India's National Newspaper) reports that after heavy rains and floods in Tamil Nadu (October-November, 2005) the unprecedented rain did not bring any cheer to farmers or water managers in these water starved districts (Madurai, Dindigul and Virudhunagar). But for an appreciable improvement in the groundwater level, the dams, which supply water for drinking and irrigation, either did not get adequate inflow or were rendered incapable of retaining water. Many tanks, which received water to an unmanageable level are empty. Over 3,500 tanks need repairs in these three districts alone.

The government has had the practice of allotting lands for house sites for the eligible poor and using them for other development schemes and public purposes. Over the years, the availability of Government land has become limited. Therefore, the Government has banned assignment of all water-course porambokes like tanks, ponds, canals, streams, etc., and also mandaiveli, grazing ground porambokes and burial grounds.

Hence, encroachment on Government lands has to be curbed as a policy. Encroachments in poramboke lands like water sources/ courses, grazing grounds, temple lands, kalam etc., are considered highly objectionable and these encroachments have to be evicted, as per existing government policy. The authorities of Revenue, Public Works and Highways Departments and the local bodies including Municipalities and Corporations have been empowered to evict unauthorised encroachments after giving due notice under the Tamil Nadu Encroachment Act, 1905. There is a separate committee headed by the Commissioner of Land Administration who is supposed to review the progress made in this regard and report to the government.

The Way Out

The following are some of the suggestions of the community members to recover Velapalayam from being a water-starved village:

- The PWD Water Resources Division with the support of the Village Panchayat functionaries should take steps for immediate removal of encroachment and desilting of all the ponds and lakes in Velapalayam. This can help restore the traditional water bodies leading to improvements in the water table in the area.
- The underground pipelines of Mohanur Combined water supply scheme from Paramathiveloor to supply water to Seerapalayam runs cutting across Velapalayam. The pipeline has been laid for about 60 kms and Velapalayam is located at about 50th km. The TWAD Board authorities may consider the possibility of providing water to Velapalayam village from the combined water supply scheme.
- Bore-wells sunk for agricultural purposes and those sunk for commercial draft of water should be permitted after making sure that it would not affect any community drinking water source. The Village Panchayats may be allowed to certify this in consultation with the TWAD Board Hydro-geologists. The depth of bore-wells should be regulated. The government should announce special schemes for water recharging for areas notified as being in 'critical stage'.

6

Changing Face of Agriculture: Culture *versus* Commerce

The Premise

> The cheap food imports have depressed prices of domestic products, and the focus on export-oriented cash crop agriculture has led to concentration of land and resources in the hands of big farmers.
> The agrarian crisis in the cotton belt has driven more than 300 farmers to suicide since June 2005 in Vidarbha region, Maharashtra.

Introduction

From the perspectives of rural employment generation and rural poverty reduction agriculture is one of the vital sectors in Tamil Nadu State. The major crops cultivated in Tamil Nadu are: paddy, millets, pulses, oilseeds, cotton and sugarcane. Area and production of any crop largely depend on various factors such as fertility of land, rainfall, irrigation, application of fertilizers, weather conditions, prices etc. The gross cultivated area under all crops has slightly increased to 53,16,027 hectares in 2003-04 from 51,91,108 hectares in 2002-03. While the area under food crops accounted for 69.9 per cent and that of non-food crops formed 30.1 per cent only in the gross cultivated area during the year 2003-04 (GoTN, 2003-04). It is recognized that agriculture is a way of life and it has been the mainstay of the state economy. It employs a large proportion of the workforce. There are strong links between agriculture and economic growth. Agriculture spurs demand for inputs such as fertilizers, pesticides and machinery, and on the supply side, it provides raw materials for agro-based industries such as cotton textiles, sugar, flour mills, milk products and vegetable oils.

It may be noted that the share of primary sector in Net State Domestic Product (NSDP) at constant prices which was at 43.57 per cent in 1960-61 reduced to 15.97 per cent in 2002-03 (GoI and Academic Foundation, 2005). Though the share of primary sector is getting increasingly reduced, the workforce depending on agriculture for their livelihood is still around 60 per cent. Even in the process of structural transformation of the economy, agriculture determines the overall growth process with strong linkages to the manufacturing sector. Economic transformation that has undergone in Tamil Nadu drives home the point that the declining relative share of primary sector has been somewhat offset by the increasing relative share of tertiary sector. However, any change in this sector, positive or negative, has a multiplier effect on the state economy. The agriculture sector, therefore, acts as a bulwark in maintaining food security. Recognizing the crucial role played by the agriculture sector in enabling the widest dispersal of economic benefits, it has been rightly emphasized that agricultural development is central to economic development of the State.

Issues Related to Agricultural Economy in Tamil Nadu

A glance at the land-use pattern of Tamil Nadu State shows that the proportion of net area sown in total geographical area has been declining over the years. The net sown area stood at 48.15 per cent during the year 1979-80. It was 38.65 per cent during the year 2002-03. It may be mentioned that the net area sown has been declining over a long span of time, mainly due to conversion of agricultural land for non-agricultural uses such as housing and industries sites.

The State also witnessed the change of cropping pattern from cultivating pulses and millets to commercial crops and it was going towards low investment to high investment. Since there is no income tax for agricultural income, the rich people from industry and politicians evince keen interest in investing on land in which horticulture crops are being promoted with government support. As a result, the farmers who sold land to rich men and the agricultural labourers are migrating to semi-urban and urban areas for alternative employment. Even though the percentages of population in agriculture to State population has decreased from 71.99 in 1960-61 to 56.77 in 2000-01, the total number of people in agriculture has been increasing from 22.39 million to 35.26 during the same period (GoTN, 2002-03). Employment in agriculture was growing at the rate of 2.45 per cent in seventies at 1.48 per cent in eighties and just 0.30 per cent in nineties.

There are 144.4 lakh workers dependent upon agriculture and allied activities such as horticulture, forestry, live stock, and sericulture. Of them only 82.34 lakh are cultivators and 29.81 lakh workers are in allied activities, the balance is in the category of landless agricultural labourers—28.09 lakh persons who know only farming but have no land of their own. There is also not much land for redistribution. Therefore, they have to survive as wage earners in agriculture and seek jobs from cultivators. However most of the cultivators themselves are small land holders and use own family labour to the extent possible. Even some of the marginal and small farmers seek jobs outside their farms because they are under-employed by excess supply of workers. Consequently, the farm wages are low. The seasonality in farm operations find seasonal scarcity at times of sowing and harvesting, providing some scope for the agricultural labourers to bargain for high wages.

Area under permanent pastures and grazing lands and that under miscellaneous tree crops and groves are shrinking; it is a sign of a decline in village common land due to encroachment and neglect. However, total area under these categories is very small. Area under cultivable waste land has come down to less than half of what it was in 1960-61. It is due to the pressure on land for cultivation of crops.

To create big farms, many companies such as Sterling, Maxworth, V.G.P., Malayala Manorama, J.C. Farms collected money from people and they invested the money on lands which belonged to the marginal and small farmers. Eventually, it engenders the process of marginalization of small farmers and casualisation of agricultural labourers.

Globalization and Agriculture

The process of deregulation and liberalization of the Indian economy. got a big boost in 1991 when dramatic changes were introduced. The private sector was permitted to enter into areas hitherto reserved for the public sector. Import tariffs were drastically reduced. Many items were put on Open General Licence (OGL) which required no import licence. The rupee was devalued significantly. Above all, a commitment was openly made for further liberalization and reforms, which were till then carried out almost by stealth. In the 1990s, the process of liberalization, privatization, and globalization under WTO agreement was set rolling. During the time of significant economic structural transformation in Tamil Nadu, Agreement on Agriculture (AoA) came into force on January 1, 1995. To accelerate the process of agriculture growth, rapid and widespread adoption of modern technology backed by institutional and infrastructure development was the new mantra of government policy. Private sector participation is being promoted through contract farming and land lease arrangements to allow accelerated technology transfer, capital inflow and assured market for crop production, especially, in oilseeds, cotton and horticultural crops. The proposed reforms are likely to improve the environment for private investment, structural change and efficiency gains in agri-business. India is moving towards a more liberal regime removing restrictions and emphasizing exports.

The Research Problem

As agriculture constitutes a vital segment of the Indian economy, finding greater market access for India's agricultural products, especially, in the developed country markets is very difficult for India. During the implementation of WTO agreements in the last ten years, India has experienced certain imbalances and inequities in the WTO agreements. It is found that some developed countries have not fulfilled their obligations in letter and spirit of the WTO agreements. This was clearly mentioned in the Tenth Five Year Plan document of the Government of India (GoI, Tenth Plan). In India imports of agricultural commodities have increased by 270 per cent in terms of volume and 300 per cent in terms of value between 1996-97 and 2003-04. The cheap food imports have depressed prices of domestic products, and the focus on export-oriented cash crop agriculture has led to concentration of land and resources in the hands of big farmers. Furthermore, developed countries force developing countries to cut down subsidies for the interest of free trade, whereas they are increasing the subsidies in agriculture. Under agricultural trade liberalizations, the agricultural goods of developed countries will enter the developing countries with lower prices. This leads to demand for traditional goods to decrease which implies reduction in production and employment.

Keeping this perspective in view, the present study is conducted with the following specific objectives:

- To examine livelihood security concerns of farmers and agricultural labourers of Tamil Nadu;
- To study the recent developments in agricultural sector in Tamil Nadu with focus on livelihood security concerns of farmers and agricultural labourers; and
- To assess the domestic policy measures in compliance with WTO rules and problems faced by the farmers and agricultural labourers in the study areas of Tamil Nadu.

Approach of the Study

The present study attempts to study the recent developments after the globalization process in a limited way. Taking into consideration, the present situation, the study has been proposed to analyse the farmers' and agricultural labourers' situation at the grassroots levels in the wake of changing agricultural situation. Out of major crops being cultivated in Tamil Nadu, rice, and cotton were selected to study the globalization effects on farming community. For the purpose of the study, two districts viz., Tiruvarur, and Coimbatore were selected since it offered the issues on recent developments initiated through new agriculture policy such as contract farming system in cotton and so on.

District	*Basis for Selection*	*Crop*	*Issue*
Thiruvarur	One of the districts of Cauvery Delta	Paddy	Rising Input Costs
Coimbatore	More number of Spinning Mills	Cotton	Collapse of Cotton Economy

At first, discussions were made with Joint Directorate of Agriculture at the district level and Agricultural Office at block level to understand the recent developments which are linked with globalization process. The primary and secondary data were used in this study. Primary data were collected through Focus Group Discussion (FGD) with farmers and agricultural labourers in the field to bring as many perspectives as possible from the grassroots levels. Secondary data relating to the crop particulars were obtained from offices of Joint Directors of Agriculture, and Season and Crop Report of Tamil Nadu Government. The websites such as Tamil Nadu Government, Central Government, and World Trade Organization have been referred to obtain the latest information on Agreement on Agriculture. The present study mainly aims at investigating the livelihood concerns of the farmers and agricultural labourers in Tamil Nadu. The study limits its scope to grassroots levels aspects in the selected places of Tamil Nadu.

Agreement on Agriculture

The New Economic Policy of 1991 stressed both external sector reforms in the exchange rate, trade and foreign investment policies, and internal reforms in areas such as industrial policy, price and distribution controls, and fiscal restructuring in the financial and public sectors. In addition, India's membership and commitment to WTO in 1995 was a clear sign of India's intention to take advantage of globalization and face the challenge of accelerating its economic growth. The change in external environment for agriculture came with the setting up of the WTO on January 1, 1995 and with the inclusion of agriculture under the multilateral trade discipline for the first time. With these developments and signing of AoA, it became inevitable that India has no option but to globalize its economy including agriculture. The gains to the farmers and rural community from the liberalization of agriculture are determined by three pillars of AoA: (a) the interaction between the relatively competitive markets, (b) market-friendly reforms in domestic agriculture, and (c) subsidy reductions in developed countries.

Competitiveness of Agricultural Commodities

The question of competitiveness of Indian agriculture has assumed great importance in the light of the WTO Agreement on Agriculture. As competitiveness will increasingly play a major role in trade, it is essential to assess competitiveness of commodity. Competitiveness of countries in the long run are influenced by the three major factors viz., (a) Comparative advantage, (b) Country's ability to develop comparative advantage, (c) Country's ability to develop competitive advantage.

For many commodities, the productivity of India is much lower than the world average competitiveness of commodities. The competitive of commodities such as cholam, cotton and maize can be improved substantially by improving the productivity. Developing new technologies and their quicker adoption would be needed in order to compete effectively in the international market. Therefore, ability to develop competitive advantage will depend on the systems and institutions, which can translate market information into actions in the value chain. India will take considerable time to develop systems and institutions, which can effectively correct the problem of Asymmetric Trade Opportunities (ATOs). Till then ATOs will be a major problem for exports. If systems and institutions are not able to adjust to the new situation, ATOs could be very significantly affecting export opportunities.

Market-Friendly Reforms in Domestic Agriculture

Agriculture being the mainstay of the rural Indian economy around which socio-economic privileges and deprivations revolve, any change in its structure is likely to have a corresponding impact on the existing pattern of social and economic inequality. Agriculture is a State subject. So, land revenue, market taxes, sales tax, purchase tax and market charges are determined by the State Governments. Central Government influences in several ways through special plan schemes, fiscal incentives/concessions, direct intervention and incentives implicit in import policy, tax credit, and marketing assistance. These agricultural policy measures can be dealt in three phases. *First phase* covers pre-Green Revolution Period (1951-61); *Second phase* covers Green Revolution Period (1965-80), and *Third phase* is divided into two category viz., (a) diversified growth period (1981-90), (b) period of reforms and liberalization (1991-till date).

First Phase: In the first phase agrarian reforms and institutional changes were introduced. Major irrigation projects were implemented to avoid the severe food shortages. During the 1950s, the period of first two five-year plans, foreign trade was considered to be almost irrelevant for economic development in India. Tenant operators were given security of farming and ownership of land and intermediary landlordism was abolished.

Second Phase: Under the second phase, new agricultural strategy i.e. Green Revolution, technology, and agrarian reforms were implemented. Research, extension, input supply, credit, marketing, price support and spread of technology were the prime concerns. Food Corporation of India (FCI) and Commission on Agricultural Costs and Prices (CACP) were constituted.

Third Phase: (a) *Diversified Growth Period:* This period witnessed the diversification of rural economy. Pressure for subsidized inputs and price support and growth in non-foodgrain out put like milk, fishery, poultry, vegetables, fruits, etc. got the priority in this phase. Also, direct government intervention was expanded in major crops such as rice, wheat, cotton, sugarcane.

(b) *Period of Reforms and Liberalization:* India started liberalizing the external sector from the mid-1980s, but it was only in 1991 that external sector liberalization gathered pace. The Uruguay Round Agreements, which came into effect from January 1995, marked the beginning of India's integration with the global economy. Some adverse consequences of the new technologies were reported and mounting burden of subsidies put a pressure on the fiscal resources. After 1980-81, public investments in agriculture started declining. State Trading Corporation for imports occupied a major role. Most of the provisions of Essential Commodities Act (ECA) were removed and Agriculture Produce Marketing Committee (APMC) Act. The APMC Act grants marketing monopoly to the state and prevented the private investments in agricultural market.

Recent Policy Initiatives

- Reforms in Food Corporation of India.
- Decentralisation of procurement.
- Relaxations in restrictions on private trade.
- Emphasis on establishment of private markets.
- Contract farming.
- Forward trading allowed in several commodities.
- Emphasis on Public-Private Partnership in agricultural research and extension.
- Promotion of value added chains through consortia approach.
- Reversing trend in public sector investments.
- Emphasis on irrigation projects/watershed.

Among the policy measures introduced with or after the new economic reforms, introduction of export promotional schemes like provision of Export and Import (EXIM) scrip in 1991, abolition of cash margins for Export Oriented Units (EOUs) in 1992, granting of tax concessions to export houses in 1996-97, setting up of Special Economic Zones (SEZs) in 2000, and exchange rate measures like the partial convertibility of the Rupee in 1992-93 and full convertibility in the trade account in 1993-94 are the notable ones to mention. The removal of quantitative restrictions through the licensing procedures on exports and imports and reduction of tariff rates on imports were anyhow done in stages in the EXIM policies and their amendments. The modifications to the EXIM policy declared by the Ministry of

Commerce in April 1999, 2000 and 2001 were very much in tune with the requirements of the WTO panel's ruling about Quantitative Restrictions (QRs). The amendments of the EXIM policy made during April 2001 further gave importance to the boosting of agricultural exports. It gave special importance to the agricultural sector through the creation of the Agricultural Export Zones wherein the State Governments could identify the product-specific zones. The EXIM policy schemes like the Duty Exemption Scheme (DES) and Export Promotion Capital Goods Scheme (EPCGS) were applicable to the agricultural sector.

Between 1998-2002, several other policy recommendations related to the sugar industry, fertilizer industry, input subsidies, agricultural extension, handling, storage and transportation of foodgrains, seed policy, plant variety protection and farmer's rights, and national water policy—were officially adopted by the Government. These policy changes resulted in deregulation of the domestic agricultural trade. However, further reforms are necessary in order to reduce the control of free movement of agriculture commodities; if the current goal of national unified market for agriculture is to be achieved.

New EXIM Policy and Farm Exports

Realising the importance of Agricultural Export, Government of India announced EXIM policy periodically since liberalization. The new EXIM policy announced by the Government in April 2002 has not encouraged subsidy and only "immunized" the Indian exports from the disadvantages faced by it. The policy aims to give farm exports a prominent place by giving farmers remunerative prices.

Salient Features of the Policy

(1) The policy has simplified a number of procedures and unveiled a number or incentives for farm exports, industrial clusters and cottage industries.
(2) The new EXIM policy has freed trade from the shackles of control. It is now up-to the exporters to rise to the occasion and prove their worth.
(3) Centre has strong commitment to assisting States in overcoming their constraints in the form of imitating a series of scheme including the setting up of Special Economic Zones (SEZs) and Agri Export Zones (AEZs). Increasing of tax holidays in view of

long gestation period of Special Economic Zones (SEZs) was a step ahead for promotion of exports.

(4) Another feature was that 90 per cent of the export consignment had been freed from the requirement of physical verification.
(5) All the quantitative restrictions on export had also been removed to facilitate export.
(6) The higher interest rate for export credit has been taken care of by aligning the export credit to prime lending rate. The EXIM policy has reduced the interest rate by 2.5 per cent from current prime lending rate of 11 per cent.
(7) Rebates have been allowed and the exporting industries have been encouraged to take up captive power plants for which the government would give duty free fuel.

The EXIM Policy, 2002-07 had much to say for agriculture, especially for the exports. With the sluggish growth in exports and rising imports, liberalization of agricultural exports was an inevitable outcome. Export restrictions like registration and packaging requirements were removed on butter, pulses, wheat and wheat products, groundnut oil, cashew and coarse grains. Restrictions on export of all cultivated varieties of seed, except jute and onion were also removed.

Recent policy of launching Agriculture Export Zones (AEZs) has received good response from the State Governments. The policy links the farm to the overseas markets, agricultural universities to trade and government funds to both. Punjab is exporting vegetables, while Uttar Pradesh is interested in mangoes, flowers and meat. Tamil Nadu started a floriculture export zone at Hosur, Dharmapuri District. No financial investment is needed from the States for AEZs.

Export Subsidy

The third important pillar of AoA is "Export Subsidy". Export subsidies include four situations:

(i) Export subsidies subject to product-specific reduction commitments within the limits specified in schedule of WTO member concerned.
(ii) Any excess of budgetary outlays for export subsidies.
(iii) Export subsidies consistent with the special and differential treatment provision for developing country members.

(iv) Export subsidies other than those subject to reduction commitments provided that they are in conformity with the anti-circumvention discipline of AoA.

The agreement contains provisions regarding members' commitment to reduce export subsidies. Developed countries are required to reduce their export subsidy expenditure by 36 per cent and volume by 21 per cent in six years, in equal instalments from 1986-90 levels (www.wto.org). The percentages reductions are 24 and 14 per cent respectively in equal annual instalments over 10 years for developing countries. Besides, the agreement specifies that for products not subject to export subsidy reduction commitments, no such subsidy can be granted in the future. In India, exporters of agricultural commodities do not get direct subsidy. Only subsidies on cost of freights on export shipments of certain products like fruits, and floricultural products are being given.

Export subsidies are universally acknowledged to be the single most trade distortive impact in agriculture because of their potential of displacing developing country exports. There would be a strong demand for a complete outlawing of export subsidies. India would also press for it. However, as long as the export subsidies are permitted to be given by any country above the *deminimis limit* provided under the WTO's Subsidies and Countervailing Measures Agreement, India should also have rights to give export subsidies up to an appropriate level. Establishment of disciplines in the field of export credits, guarantee and deferred payments which have a negative effect on prices and competition in the world agricultural market would be insisted and India would like it to be also included under the disciplines of Export Subsidies.

The most important problem is, of course, the very large subsidies given by developed countries to certain products which make the exports of many commodities from developing countries non-competitive. Furthermore, the export subsidy commitments have been made on the basis of groups of products. This gives members flexibility for increasing subsidy on a product within a group of products while reducing it on a minor product.

Two important issues, namely Special and Differential Treatment (SDT) and provisions regarding the Sanitary and Phyto-Sanitary measures (SPS) have been discussed under "other provisions" of the AoA. SDT is the recognition of the inherent constraints of developing countries for availing of trading opportunities. Some of the provisions under the SDT refer to lower level of reduction of tariffs and longer time period, for reduction of domestic support and export subsidies, and exemptions under the green box, including exemption to all the input subsidies to the small and 'resource poor' farmers. These are no doubts about the important provisions that need strengthening. But these are more than negated because of huge domestic and export subsidies given by the developed countries. Regarding the SPS, these are important provisions meant to safeguard the sanitary and health interests of trading partners. But the main problem is the provision that allows the developed countries to set up standards that are higher than set by the recognized international organizations. The developed countries have been using this as a subtle device for denying market access to exports from developing countries. The introduction of the Farm Bill, 2002 in the United States, for instance, providing an additional support of US $180 billion in the next ten years to a miniscule population of farmers, is an indication of how serious the industrialized countries are towards meeting the obligations of the Agreement on Agriculture. This also includes US $15 million to be spent every year on promoting genetically modified foods. With the OECD countries (Organization for Economic Co-operation and Development) already providing a support of US $311 billion a year to its agriculture, the addition of US $180 billion raises the total budgetary support to agriculture in the rich countries to US $491 billion.

Impact of WTO Agreement on Agriculture

The likely impact of these agreements on Indian Agriculture reported from various sources (www.dsharma.org) is expected to be on the following:

(i) Influence the size, composition, competitiveness and direction of India's Agricultural Exports;
(ii) Influence the cropping pattern and productivity of Indian agriculture; the country's food security position, cost of inputs and their use rates are likely to be affected;
(iii) The shift towards export-oriented production may lead to certain environmental problems;
(iv) Domestic prices of agricultural commodities may change; and
(v) Issues of Trade Related Intellectual Property Rights will have considerable implications on agriculture especially on export and import of seeds, pesticides, cost and so on.

Opportunities

Economic reforms introduced in India since mid-1991 have opened ways to increase productivity and competitive efficiency. India has a large potential to increase its agricultural exports in a liberalized world, provided it can diversify a significant part of its agriculture into high value crops and in agro-processing. This would depend first on undertaking large infrastructure investment in agriculture and agro-processing as also in rural infrastructure, and research and development. Globalizing agriculture through liberalization has the potential of commercialization of agriculture and export of value added farm products. However, agriculture and allied sectors have slightly been touched by the reform measures and this needs immediate correction to realise the full potential of agriculture in Tamil Nadu. Very concerted efforts are necessary because the constraints are many. Estimates revealed that India has comparative advantage in growing rice, cotton, groundnut, gingely, tomato, banana, onion, and potato. In Tamil Nadu competitiveness exist, for cashewnut, banana, mango, grapes, onion, gherkins, turmeric, chillies and medicinal plants. Based on this estimate, it was found that banana, mango and grapes among fruits, sugarcane, turmeric and tea were in surplus indicating that there exists potential for export of these commodities in the coming years. Having estimated the exportable surplus in the years to come, it is imperative to explore the markets for the absorption of these surpluses. In terms of proximity and comparative advantage enjoyed, Gulf States and Pacific Region countries excluding Japan offer excellent scope for exports from Tamil Nadu. Development of facilities for quick and reliable market information and quality control for export of value added farm products, are urgent needs in the context of globalization of agriculture.

Challenges

Globalization offers both opportunities and challenges. The opportunities consist of availing of the benefits of the world trade and growth. The challenges lie in enabling the sharing of these benefits not by a small minority of elite population but by the majority of working people in rural and urban India. It is important to realize the globalization process poses many challenges to a developing country like India, which had relied on a State directed and regulated policy regime for more than four decades. In moving to a more open market-based economy, there are many transitional problems that the country has to manage.

In India, agricultural tariffs are much lower compared to U.S.A., Canada, E.U., Japan and Korea. The peak tariff on agricultural commodities in countries like U.S.A., Canada, E.U., Japan, Korea and the Cairns group continues to prevail at very high rates. Developing countries face highest tariff rates for the major agricultural staple foods, cereals, meat, sugar, milk, butter and cheese as well as tobacco products and cotton. The tariff wedges will continue to be significantly high on account of tariff escalation which is a major factor preventing developing countries from diversifying and increasing their share of processed agricultural exports. There is an issue of import access rights by agricultural exporters of developing countries who are restricted on grounds of Sanitary and Phyoto-Sanitary (SPS) regulations in developed countries. Taking advantage of the exception clauses provided in the WTO, most industrialized countries are still enforcing various regulations on foreign producers and suppliers.

India has not only to create export surplus but has also to become competitive through increased efficiency of production in agriculture. The potential for exports would also depend on freeing of agricultural markets by the developed countries. Indeed, hopes for fairer markets have been dashed by the strategic protection given by the developed countries to their agriculture through export subsidies, tariffs, quotas and other restrictions on commodity imports from developing countries.

It is the neglect of public investment in agriculture during the last two decades which is primarily responsible for the steep deceleration in agricultural growth in the post-liberalization period. The problem of fiscal deficit continues to remain formidable both at the Centre and in the States, making it difficult for the governments to increase the outlay on agriculture.

In Tamil Nadu, farms classified as semi-medium size group are 6.33 lakhs in number and have 17.29 lakh hectares. The average size of farm is 2.73 hectares. Thus 96 per cent of land holdings are smaller than 4 hectares each (GoI & Academic Foundation, 2005). These farms are too small to operate and their credit worthiness is rated very poor. That sets the limit for investment in farm assets and modern inputs that are essential for intensive farming.

The lack or slow pace of internal or domestic liberalization is also seen to hinder the possible gains from external or trade liberalization.

For example, although central zoning restrictions have been abolished, State Government restrictions on marketing and movement of goods still exist in many cases. This interferes with the benefits from crop specialization and economies.

Capital formation in agriculture of Tamil Nadu is mostly by private sector, the public sector contribution to capital formation in agriculture is only about one-fourth of the total capital formation. However, there is need to substantially invest in infrastructural facilities for storage, distribution and processing.

Further, a market driven liberalization process in agriculture is invariably biased towards rich farmers and prosperous regions. Positive policy interventions are necessary to assure that the interests of small farmers and of disadvantaged regions are also protected and that they are enabled to share the benefits of trade liberalization.

Hong-Kong Ministerial Level Meeting

Indian agriculture policy is still hesitant to govern its agriculture with WTO clauses and global policy environment on the grounds that the agricultural sector of developed countries are highly protected by subsidies. In the recent WTO's Ministerial Level Meeting held in Hong-Kong from December 13th-17th, 2005, the developed countries have agreed to eliminate export subsidies by 2013. The agreement hardly provides any protection or gains to millions of Indian farmers. The commitment by the advanced countries to ease out export subsidies by 2013 was no achievement since they constitute a small part received by agriculture. In the coming days, more pressures and trade distorting tactics can be expected which will adversely affect farmers and Indian agriculture. The special products and special safeguard mechanism proposed will not help India, since it has already agreed to further cuts in agriculture tariff.

Apprehensions of Developing Countries

The major apprehension of the developing countries is that the developed countries did not implement the commitments made in the agreement on market access, provision of subsidies for export and production of agricultural commodities. Instead of implementation, the developed countries are continuing their subsidies and reducing the market access to developing countries thereby affecting the competitiveness of agriculture of developing countries.

At the implementation stage also the developed country market access to developing countries has been limited due to high trade distorting domestic support, high tariff, tariff peaks, tariff escalation and a number of non-tariff barriers. UNCTAD study (1997) revealed that some countries, tariff peaks reach as high as 350 per cent. One-fifth of the peak tariffs of the US, a quarter of those of EU, about 30 per cent of those of Japan and about one-seventh of those of Canada exceed 30 per cent. Highest tariff rates include the major agricultural staple foods, cereals, meat, sugar, milk, butter and cheese, tobacco and cotton. In EU, the out-of-quota tariff for banana is 180 per cent, in Japan the tariffs range from 460 to 600 per cent for dried beans, peas and lentils, and recently 1000 per cent on rice and in the US groundnuts in shell attract a tariff of 164 per cent. Tariff escalation prevailing in these countries also prevents imports of processed foods from the developing countries.

Imports have increased in the developing countries which has resulted in marginalization of small producers and added to unemployment and poverty. Many developing countries are also dissatisfied with inadequate implementation of the Marrakesh decision on measures concerning the possible negative effects of the reform programme on least developed countries and food importing developing countries. The United States and the European Union in particular that their heavy subsidization of agricultural exports have created a serious challenge to the goal of economic up-lift of farmers in the rest of the world.

Demand from WTO

To protect the farmers out of poor condition, several concerted steps are to be taken internally and externally by the developing countries. So, the developing countries demand more concessions to their farmers in the negotiations of Agreement on Agriculture. These are:

(a) substantial reduction in agricultural tariffs in rich countries while Uruguay Round mandated ratification, many countries set their bound tariffs obscenely high,
(b) the end of agricultural export subsidies,
(c) reducing domestic support and an end to questionable bailouts in rich countries to compensate for low prices,
(d) fair implementation of agreements on Sanitary and Phyto-Sanitary measures and trade related aspects of intellectual property.

RISING INPUT COSTS – A CASE IN POINT

Characterised by low and stagnating yields, a very large proportion of marginal, small and semi-medium holdings, a high proportion of landless labour households, highly concentrated and food-oriented cropping system, Indian agriculture would therefore be facing serious challenges, both internal and external, in the process of fulfilling WTO commitments. Opening up of agriculture would lead to diversification of cropping patterns away from cereals. As India opens up externally, it is also expected to face vulnerability in the wider international price fluctuations. Food prices will increase with the opening up of exports of agriculture, and the poor would suffer, at least in the short run. Over stress on export of agricultural produce will change the cropping pattern in favour of cash crops and against food crops. This will further aggravate the severity of food problem (Batra, G.S. and Dangwal, R.C., 2004). On account of falling investment and capital formation in agriculture and transfer of subsidies from agriculture to export-oriented and profit making industries, an upshot of the economic reforms, it is difficult to produce foodgrains for domestic purpose in near future.

Farming as a way of life is disappearing and is giving way to agri-business. Increased commercialization of agriculture is taking place as a result of trade liberalization and this affects the farmers and agricultural labourers adversely. Cheap food imports is expected to depress the prices of domestic products and the focus on export-oriented cash crop agriculture has led to concentration of land and resources in the hands of big farmers. Marginal and small farmers and landless agricultural labourers are increasingly becoming part of the most food insecure group due to agricultural trade policies. Structural adjustments under globalization have already started affecting the procurement system and public distribution system. Though these schemes have serious implementation problems, their role as safety nets for the poor can not be denied.

Increasing proportion of area under non-food crops in the gross cropped area is taken as a measure *albeit* simplistic of commercialisation of agriculture, on the basis of simple logic that non-food crops add more value per hectare than food crops. Area under foodgrain crops, in Tamil Nadu was 56.51 lakh ha. in 1970-71; it has steadily decreased to 36.33 lakh hectare in 1999-2000. It marked a fall in the share of food-grain crops in the gross cropped area from 76.3 per cent to 55.7 per cent between 1970-71 and 1999-2000. Correspondingly the share of non-food crops increased from 23.7 per cent to 44.3 per cent (i.e.) nearly doubled during the same period. *Thus, agriculture in Tamil Nadu is progressively commercialised.* The growth rate of area under food crops is negative for every decade since 1961 and for the whole period (1961-2000). Consequently the growth rates of area put under non-food crops is positive and larger than unity for all the decades and 1.37 per cent for 1960-2000. Commercialization of agriculture and impact of technology on productivity of major crops were made possible only by increasing use of chemical fertilizers, and groundwater. This was helped by extension education on use of fertilizers and energisation of more and more of pump sets and supply of power to them at subsidized rates in the earlier decades, and free of cost since eighties.

Premise

Rising cost of inputs, non-availability of cheap rural credit, and exposure to volatile global market price trends have squeezed the peasantry. The paradigm of the WTO's Agreement on Agriculture is biased in favour of capital intensive and corporate agri-business-driven agriculture. It threatens the livelihood of the vast masses of the marginal and small farmers and agricultural labourers. The peasantry will be compelled to accept the entry of corporate agri-business on its terms. Big farmers are going in for more and more mechanization. Further more, the role of modern mills has increased, as uniformity and polishing of grains have become quality parameters in the market. Modern rice mills are replacing hullers and have displaced labourers and have eaten into the profit margins of the small traders, producers, labourers and even the consumers. As a result, today, agricultural labourers are getting not even 100 days work in a year. Due to massive rural unemployment

Table 6.1: Net and Gross Area Irrigated in Thiruvarur District during 2003-04

Particulars	*Area in ha.*
Net Area Irrigated	118275.00
Net Area Sown	123853.00
Percentage of Net Area Sown to Net Area Irrigated	95.50
Gross Area Irrigated	128843.00
Percentage of Gross Area Sown to Gross Area Irrigated	79.44

Source: Statistical Hand Book 2004, Department of Economics and Statistics, Chennai.

that has been accentuated by serious drought conditions, there is widespread migration of agricultural workers to urban areas. Many farmers have already sent members of their family to distant cities to earn wages during the drought situation.

Thiruvarur is one of the Cauvery Delta regions. Paddy is the principal crop in the district and the source of water for the paddy cultivation is mainly from the government canals. The farmers in the district cannot go for alternative crops other than paddy because of the nature of soil suited for paddy cultivation. It is cultivated in three seasons viz., Kuruvai, Samba and Thaladi. In some pockets of the district, summer season crop is also cultivated. Cropping intensity for Thiruvarur district was 1.310 during 2003-04. Paddy varieties such as A 36, A 42, A 43, TKM 9, MDU 5, and CO 47 are cultivated during Kuruvai season. Paddy varieties such as CR 1009, BPT 5204, A 38, A 39, A 44, and CO 43 are cultivated during Samba season. Paddy varieties such as CR 1009, A 44, A 36, A 42, CO 47, TKM 9, and MDU 5 are cultivated during Thaladi season.

Fluctuating Area under Paddy Cultivation

It is reported that area under cultivation varies from season to season. The district is prone to natural disasters such as flood, cyclone and drought. There is no uniformity of area under cultivation. Hence, income from the cultivation can not be expected correctly. Profit from agriculture is not ensured because of natural calamities influencing the cultivation practices. Likewise, agricultural labourers do not find employment opportunities due to gambling of monsoon and Mettur dam water level.

Table 6.2: Area under Paddy Cultivation in Thiruvarur District (in ha.)

Year	*Kar/Karuvai/ Sarnavari*	*Samba/Thaladi/ Pishanam*	*Navarai/Kodai*	*Total*
2001-02	35,837	1,36,622	2,263	1,74,722
2002-03	8,111	1,22,021	923	1,31,055
2003-04	6,383	1,14,195	859	1,21,437

Source: Season and Crop Reports of Tamil Nadu, Department of Economics and Statistics, Chennai.

The total area under paddy cultivation has come down from 1,74,722 hectares in 2001-02 to 1,21,437 hectares in 2003-04. A good monsoon during 2005-06 would bring more area under cultivation. It is noticed from the Table 6.2 that area under paddy cultivation was not uniform even in a season. For instance, area under paddy cultivation was 35,837 hectares in Kuruvai season during 2001-02 while it was 8,111 hectares during 2002-03. It clearly indicates that there was no uniform area under paddy cultivation. As a result, marginal and small farmers and agricultural labourers are in distress to face the fluctuating area under cultivation.

Employment Opportunities

Ploughing of land is done by help of tractors. Manual ploughing is seldom used in the district. Transplantation and harvesting would give more employment to male and female agricultural workers. Weeding is normally done by female agricultural workers in the paddy field. Prominent feature of the district is the cultivation of pulse crop which is sown ten days before the harvest of paddy. It would provide at least a little bit of earnings to the farmers. Big farmers prefer to use machineries owing to quick completion of work. In case of manual thrashing, it will take more than a week. Though paddy harvest machines and thrashing machines have come in handy for farmers, who have cultivated paddy, it has deprived landless labourers of their chances of getting seasonal employment in delta regions. The heavy harvesting machines would spoil black gram and green gram seeds sown on the fields. It would destroy paddy stalks and no haystack would be left.

Agricultural labourers are not only working in their villages but also working in nearby villages. It is noticed from the Melathirumathi Gunnam village in Thiruvarur Block that agricultural labourers were coming from the villages such as Thalagudi, Karuppur and Ammaiyappan. Landlords (Mirasuthares) do not work in the agricultural fields and they will supervise the agricultural activities only. Male agricultural labourers start working at 7.00 a.m. and finish at 4.30 p.m. with lunch interval. They are paid Rs. 100 while female agricultural labourers start working at 9.00 a.m. and finish at 4.30 p.m. without lunch break. They are paid Rs. 60 each per day. In general, they receive more than the minimum wage rate fixed by the Tamil Nadu Government in case of male agricultural labourers. Although it is true that the wages in agriculture has crossed well beyond the minimum wages prescribed, the per capita earning of agricultural labourers have increased only marginally in real terms, on account of decline in the number of days a worker gets employment.

There is a practice of contract basis instead of daily wages in paddy transplantation and harvesting. On the contract basis, agricultural labourers are in a position to get more than the minimum wage-amount because they work for more time in the field. The labour-contracting system gives the agricultural labourers a better deal, in the sense, they are able to complete the work swiftly, and get on with another work the same day doubling their income for the day. Although the land-owners have a feeling that they are paying more, farmers are relieved of watching the work being carried out every minute more than under the daily wage payment system. This is mutually convenient. Actually, the agricultural activity had supposed to be done by ten persons, but under the labour-contracting system, the work would have been completed by four or five persons. The ten members' wage amount will be shared by four or five members. The agricultural labourers are keen on going for harvesting the paddy because they would keep the paddy for consumption purposes. They will be paid four *marakka* of paddy per bag (one *marakka* is equal to 4 kgs). When talking with farmers about agricultural labourers, they categorically said: "As harvest is time-bound, it has become difficult to mobilize such a large number of workers at a given point of time. So, they pay more amount than ordinary days.

Table 6.3 : Seasonal Employment in Agriculture

Sl. No.	*Employment Opportunities*	*Name of the Months*
1.	High Demand	January, July, August and November.
2.	Moderate Demand	June, September, October and December.
3.	Low Demand	February, March, April and May.

Source: Computed from the Seasonality Analysis done in the field.
Note: Employment opportunity is subject to change.

The number of days a labourer gets employment in agriculture has come down due to mechanization and introduction of short-term crops. Many of the wage earners watch out for, and prefer to get employed in building construction works that provides employment almost throughout the year these days. Agricultural labourers do not get employment opportunities more than 80 days for male and 100 days for female in a year because of mechanization and labour saving techniques during 2004-05. Female agricultural labourers are wanted by the farmers because of low wages given to female agricultural labourers. According to report on Agricultural labourers, the number of days they employed in a year for Thiruvarur was 150 days in case of male agricultural labourers and 120 days in case of female agricultural labourers during the year 1997 (GoTN, 1998). Within eight years, "employed in a year" has reduced from 150 days to 100 days for male agricultural labourers whereas 120 days to 100 days for female agricultural labourers. As there is no continuous employment opportunity, agricultural labourers are forced to send their male children to other states such as Kerala, and Gujarat. During the lean season, the family migrates to another district especially Tiruppur where they work in hosiery companies. Those who live in the villages as they do not have road access, they depend on agricultural activities only. They do not go for alternative employment opportunities. Those who live in and around the cities, go for construction works in the absence of agricultural works. They get good wages in construction work. In Thiruvarur town, modern rice mill has come up and it has displaced labour force.

Relationship between Cost and Price

A clear picture of profitability and income of farms can be had from a close study of cost-price relationship. The cost of production of a kg of rice has increased from Rs. 3.46 in 1990-91 to Rs. 7.28 in 1999-2000. The price received by farmers is not uniform. They are getting different prices for different variety in areas where scheme of procurement is in operation and in rest of the area where private traders buy paddy from the farmers either directly or through brokers or commission agents. The price paid by the traders less the cost of selling incurred by the farmers by way of packaging, transporting and other payments is called farm harvest price (i.e.) the actual price received by farmers. If paddy is sold at the farm gate to the village traders there is no cost of transport, brokerage or commission but traders incur such costs and so offer a lower price. If the farmers deliver the grains to a Mandi, they incur the cost of packaging, transport, commissions and other costs such as deductions for quality variations etc. Actual price paid by the commission agents less these costs constitute what is called farm harvest price or farm gate price. This price minus the cost of production is the net income per kg received by the farmers. The cost-price relationship is yet another factor that influences the farming decisions of the farmers.

If the gap between the cost and price is wide, the farmers would treat that crop cultivation as a profitable one. If it is other way, farmers get discouraged. The very fine paddy has not been cultivated since 1998 in Thiruvarur district. While discussing with farmers in the same district, they said that merchants from Kerala State used to buy TK9 variety of paddy. Now, they are going to Karnataka State where TK9 variety is being cultivated in extended areas of cultivation. So, the price for this variety has reduced sharply from Rs. 350 per quintal to Rs. 230 quintal during the year 2005. The farmers who cultivated TK9 variety did not get returns from what they invested on their land. Probably, the non-remunerative prices may be the reason why invariably many farmers in the district are looking for better alternative opportunities to exit the farm activity once for all. The farmers are discontented with the non-remunerative prices. They attempt to compare with their counterparts in the manufacturing industry who reap in general a minimum of 20 per cent or more profit margins for their finished products. They also demand for remunerative prices for farm products. The small and marginal farmers, who often, engage in agriculture with borrowed funds, find agriculture non-remunerative and have a tendency to give up agriculture and become wage earners or go in search of employment elsewhere.

Increasing Input Costs

Farm income has come down resulting in suffering by the agrarian families because the cost of production is invariably higher than the minimum support price. Farm families are in a mood of despair. They do not know what the future holds for them. Some of the farmers in the district have given up agriculture because agriculture is no more a profitable occupation. Expressing serious concern on decreasing farm income, the farmers said that they did not get income from ten *Ma* as much as we received it from one *Ma* (Three *Ma* is equal to 1 acre) just a few years ago. Today, growers would find it hard to get income. So, they leave agriculture and settle in urban areas. It was also reflected in the recent survey of the National Sample Survey Organization that 40 per cent of the farmers would quit farming given the choice.

The basic input cost of production has been increasing especially for Urea and DAP. The farmers believe that they would get good yield if they apply fertilizers. Even today the farmers are ignorant and adopt unwise application of fertilizers, which is not at all required at a

BOX 6.1

Falling Farm Income – UNCTAD Report

A recent United Nations Conference on Trade and Development (UNCTAD) report shows that the farmers are getting today is the same at which they were selling their produce 20 years ago. The UNCTAD report not any substantiates but also goes much beyond the computation done by the Union Ministry of Agriculture. A recent study by the Ministry had demonstrated that farm incomes have fallen in the past five years. Rice farmers in West Bengal, for instance, in 2002-03 earned 28 per cent less than what they earned in 1996-97. Incomes of sugarcane farmers decreased in Uttar Pradesh by 32 per cent and in Maharashtra by 40 per cent during the same period.

The Hindu, October 10, 2005, p. 10.

given point of time. It also brings the pest attack in the crops. This information was shared by the Agriculture Officer of Thiruvarur district, confirmed through his frequent field visits.

Table 6.4 : Increasing Input Cost per Bag

Year	*Urea (Rs.)*	*DAP (Rs.)*
1999	203.00	431.00
2000	234.00	462.00
2001	238.00	485.00
2002	251.00	487.00

Source: Tamil Nadu Government Price List.

It is seen from Table 6.4 that there is an upward trend in the price list of Urea and DAP. In case of Urea, the price per bag was Rs. 203 in 1999 and it increased to Rs. 251 in 2002. Similarly DAP per bag stood at Rs. 431 in 1999 and rose to Rs. 487 in 2002. The increase is only per bag but farmers are using more quantity of fertilizers in an acre hoping that they would get good yield. Even though, they have spent on agricultural inputs for the cultivation, the average yield per acre was 30 bags (1 bag contains 60 kgs). The farmers said that the cost of cultivation would be Rs. 7000. When one kilogram is procured at Rs. 5, they would get Rs. 9000. The net income is only Rs. 2000 to farmers, who worked in the field for 3 to 4 months. They have to repay the amount which they bought for the cultivation from this amount only. They fail to pay the interest amount to PACS when they did not get adequate yield. This was the economics of paddy cultivation narrated by the farmers at Mangudi and Melathirumathigunnam villages in Thiruvarur Block of Thiruvarur District. That is why the Prime Minister of India (Dr. Manmohan Singh) has been frequently hinting at withdrawal of free power supply would seriously escalate input costs of cultivation.

Profitability

In general, farmers calculate their net income without taking farmer's own inputs used in production such as farm produced manures, own bullock power and equipments and family labour, the value of depreciation of farm assets, an interest on working capital and fixed capital costs into account. Therefore their calculation can be said to be based on actually paid out cost or accountant's cost. *In all the years farm harvest price is larger than MSP, showing that MSP has helped farmers more by pushing up the farm harvest price to some extent but not enough to fully cover cost 'C' assuring positive net income.*

Wholesale and retail prices are market-determined and cover the marketing cost and margin of the traders. Therefore, they are larger than farm harvest price, showing that the marketing cost and margin (called price-spread in the literature) is as high as cost of production or even higher. This indicates that the market for farm products (as judged by the price spread of rice) is not that efficient and leaves scope for improvement by efforts to reduce price spread (i.e.) by way of reducing both marketing costs and marketing margin. These efforts are necessary to protect the interest of consumers because demand for rice being inelastic, any rise in retail price of rice directly increases the cost of living and the government has to come to their help.

Direct Purchasing Centre (DPC)

The farmers express that they do not get a good price from the government. Processing industries cannot buy directly from the farmers except through the notified markets where intermediaries take away a sizable share from the price of the producer. Government opens the Direct Purchasing Centre (DPC) in the district particularly in samba season. Tamil Nadu Government gives incentive bonus to farmers, which ranges from Rs. 20 to Rs. 50 per quintal of paddy taking into account of the non-remunerative price received by the farmers.

DPC is opened only after the several requisitions made by the farmers. There was a complaint made by the farmers that DPC would not be opened in correct time of harvesting. The delay in opening up of DPC causes several hardships to the farmers.

Table 6.5 : Minimum Support Price Announced for Paddy by Tamil Nadu Government

Year	*Fine Variety*	*Coarse Variety*
2001	520	490
2002	560	530
2003	560	530
2004	590	560
2005	600	570

Source: Tamil Nadu Consumer Civil Supply Corporation, Chennai.

The DPC would not take all paddy harvested by the farmers and it has a ceiling amount of procuring Rs. 1 lakh worth of paddy. One bag is filled up with 70 kg. Officials from DPC would charge grading fees of Rs. 25/bag. Farmers are expected to bring two labourers to help in the process of selling paddy to DPC. They are promptly paid at the rate of Rs. 600/quintal to the 'A' grade paddy while Rs. 570/quintal to *motta* (coarse) variety. DPC officials are accepting paddy with moisture content up to 20 per cent with a cut in price. The farmers in the district urge the government to increase the procurement price to Rs. 1000 per quintal considering the high cost of cultivation.

Co-operatives are in Deep Distress

Agricultural credit is vital for ensuring food security. Co-operatives are in the forefront in extending credit to the agricultural sector. But co-operatives are in deep distress with mounting arrears, administrative and financial problems. Co-operatives have a large number of borrowers in the small and marginal farmers category compared to the commercial or regional rural banks. The contribution of Co-operatives to farm credit has dropped sharply from 70 per cent to about 30 per cent leading to distress in the farming community (*The Hindu*, September 10, 2005). In the absence of institutional credit, poor and marginal farmers would have to borrow at usurious rates from money-lenders. But finance remains the core issue for most farmers owing to high wages to the agricultural labourers, hike in price of fertilizers and pesticides etc. With the virtual collapse of the cooperative system, both on account of mismanagement and the continuing cycle of draughts and floods, farmers are unable to pay back their loans and co-operatives become ineligible for "recycling" advances from either the Reserve Bank of India or the National Bank for Agriculture and Rural Development (NABARD). Consequently, the commercial or scheduled banks are asked to step into the market. But the defaulting farmers become ineligible for bank loans because they cannot secure a "No Objection Certificate" from the cooperative banks. This vicious cycle forces the farmers into the clutches of private money-lenders who advance funds at usurious rates.

Institutional credit is provided only for those who have *pucca* land documents. Leasers of temple land and other type of land-holders do not get institutional credit because the credit institutions demand *pucca* land documents which were not provided by them. They are forced to get loan from money-lenders. Furthermore, loan amount is not sufficient to the needs of agricultural activities. Even if the credit is given, it is not given at the appropriate time. The reach of institutional credit is still restricted to the relatively better-off farmers. It is revealed from the field that those who did not have membership by virtue of changing the patta, were not provided loan from Primary Agricultural Co-operatives Society (PACS). PACS staff members were readily booking the insurance amount to the farmers who have borrowed the loan from PACS. Others do not know the deadline of insurance. Information about insurance is not disseminated promptly to the farmers by PACS. Farmers in the Cauvery delta region were under the misconception that only those who have taken loans from the societies benefited from the schemes. It is worth mentioning here that the farmers are unable to pay even the interest amount because of crop failure. They ended their lives in Maharashtra, Kerala and Andhra Pradesh.

No Storage Facilities

Farmers are supposed to sell the entire harvested paddy immediately to the Direct Procurement Centre (DPC). They are also required to pay the amount which was borrowed from the societies. And also, there is no storage facility for the paddy produced. The cost involved in transporting the products causes unwanted expenditure to the farmers. Any delay in opening of DPC will cause severe blow to the condition of the farmers. *Badhiyam* (Traditional paddy storage system) is no longer used in the houses of farmers. It is implied that farmers are forced to sell their products immediately, so that they can repay the amount to the banks or to private of money-lenders.

Subsidy

Agricultural subsidy is an important instrument for the growth of agricultural production in Tamil Nadu. The utilization of agricultural subsidies has increased over the period. Central Government provides fertilizers on subsidized rates. Tamil Nadu Government supplies free electricity to farmers. It also provides water for irrigation purposes at a highly subsidized rate. Apart from these, the Department of Agriculture in Tamil Nadu offers subsidies on different items such as seeds, plant protection, bio-fertilizer, micronutrient, gypsum, weedicide, agricultural implements and machineries.

Paddy cultivation in Thiruvarur district is completely dependent on the irrigation system provided government canals. It is quite difficult to estimate the value of this subsidy. Many irrigation systems are multipurpose systems and the cost of water for irrigation cannot be calculated easily. Electricity subsidy is another farm input subsidy provided to all farmers in the State. The State Government as a policy decision helps farmers by supplying electricity to farm use absolutely free of charge. The amount of electricity energy consumed is not metered. The sale of power to agriculture sector had increased from 2804 million units in 1985-86 to a much higher level of 9,181 million units during 2000-01 (Salam, Abdul A., 2004). Since power is supplied free of cost by the State Government, almost all farmers invariably have utilized the facility and converted their diesel motors into electric motors.

Seeds are supplied to farmers at subsidized rates by the Department of Agriculture, Government of Tamil Nadu under Intensive Cereal Development Programme (ICDP), National Pulses Development Programme (NPDP), Intensive Cotton Development Programme (ICDP) and Oilseeds Production Programme (OPP). Seed subsidies are relatively minor. The rates of subsidy per kilogram of paddy certified seed, millet certified seed, pulses seed, cotton seed were Rs. 2, Rs. 4, Rs. 3 and Rs. 4 respectively. Bio-fertilizers such as asospyrillum, phosphobacteria are supplied to the farmers under 50 per cent subsidy under ICDP cereal, ICDP cotton and OPP.

Modernization of agriculture requires the use of agricultural machinery for various agricultural operations. Tractor, power tiller, power thrasher etc., are some of the machinery for which subsidies are given by the Government of Tamil Nadu. The subsidy amount of Rs. 30,000 on tractor and power tiller induced and enabled the small and marginalized farmers of the State to buy and use these agricultural machineries. A subsidy amount of Rs. 12,000 on power thrasher is given to the farmers under ICDP cereal and Small and Marginal Farmers Scheme in Tamil Nadu.

Authors in the edited book on *Agricultural Incentives in India* have pointed out that the level of Indian farming subsidies is much below to those in the U.S. or in EU (Dorin Bruno *et al.*, 2005). Further, it is because of these subsidies that the Indian households are now well secured in rice, wheat and sugar since these food stuffs are provided to them in sufficient quantity at a rather low price. The developed countries, which are heavily subsidizing their agricultural products, are allowed to retain up to 80 per cent of their subsidies, while developing countries can subsidize their farmers not more than 10 per cent of the total value of agricultural production. The aim of any reform should not be to reduce subsidies but to better manage them for the greater benefit of farming communities with an active involvement of the concerned communities.

Farmers' Social Security Scheme

All the marginal/small farmers and agricultural labourers (1 crore and 37 lakhs in Tamil Nadu/between 18 and 65 years are eligible to enroll under the Farmers' Social Security Scheme. There are 86 lakhs of agricultural labourers and 51 lakhs of marginal and small farmers in Tamil Nadu who will be benefited from this scheme. The members subscription of Rs. 10 will be borne by the Government itself. The beneficiaries should be engaged in agricultural activities for at least six months in a year. Agricultural labourers who are not engaged in farm activities owing to illness also are eligible for benefits such as accident death assistance, marriage assistance, education assistance, maternity assistance. There seems to be no takers for the education scholarships granted under the Farmers' Social Security Scheme. Students prefer scholarships under the BC/SC/ST schemes which offer more money. Students doubt whether the scheme will continue in the event of a change in the State Government. Another deterrent is that unlike other schemes, the demand draft is drawn in the name of the student's father. Recently, eligible marginal and small farmers and agricultural labourers have been given identity cards throughout the State. Most of the agricultural labourers are not aware of the existence of the Minimum Wages Act.

Monopoly Ownership over Seed

The farmers' capital are his land, seed and water. Since the beginning of farming, farmers have sown seeds, harvested crops, saved part of the harvest for seeds and exchanged seeds with neighbours. Multinational Companies (MNCs) are promoting genetically modified seeds. It is the inevitability of farmer's dependence on MNCs for seeds due to trade liberalization and its impact on agriculture. In compliance with implementing WTO norms, farmers do not have seed right in future—says Mangudi village president, Mr. Masilamani. He adds that one terminated seed can produce many seeds which may not be capable of producing even a single paddy. The introduction of genetically modified seeds will replace the small farmer and farmer-based agricultural economy of India with agricultural-business controlled industrial agriculture. This shift is associated with a transformation of farmers as breeders and reproducers of their own seed supply into farmers as consumers of propriety seed from the seed industry. Farmers are pushed into dependency on corporate monopoly of patented seed. In compliance with agreement on agriculture, the Central Government has proposed two laws in 2004 viz., Seed Act and Patent Ordinance. According to the famous environmentalist Mrs. Vandana Shiva (2005), the 2004 Seed Act has nothing positive to offers to farmers of India but offer a promise of a monopoly to private seed industries (Bunsha Dionne, 2006). So, there should not be any restriction on farmers' saving and exchanging seeds. It is observed from the field that only a very low percentages of farmers had any knowledge of the World Trade Organization, Agreement on Agriculture, Seed Act, Kisan Card and Crop Insurance Scheme.

Impact of Globalization

As India opens up externally, it is also expected to face vulnerability in the wider international price fluctuations. For example, Indonesia provides 100 per cent of export subsidy to rice only. This clearly suggests that it is difficult for India to compete with Indonesia in the global trade of the food item. Procurement price especially for rice has been increasing faster than the general price level. Such high price along with guaranteed purchases by the Food Corporation of India has pushed up market price. This higher price is partly responsible for the large buffer stocks with the Food Corporation of India. If this trend continues, India's comparative advantage will be eroded.

COTTON CRISIS – A CASE IN POINT

Premise

An unfortunate consequence of the hardships faced by small farm families is the growing number of suicides. The situation is particularly alarming in Maharashtra's Vidarbha Region. In cotton territory, fake and costly inputs have placed lakhs of farmers in grave danger. Further, despair has led many to embrace costly Bt Cotton as some kind of magic bullet. Meanwhile, Bt Cotton has not only been attacked by other pests, it has been struck by the bollworm itself. Bloated claims of performance have sold many pockets, but ground realities are grim in Maharashtra's Vidarbha Region. Major newspapers in Vidarbha have begun reporting more bollworm attacks on Bt Cotton in the region. The cotton economy has collapsed and most fear that there is worse to follow.

The agrarian crisis in the cotton belt has driven more than 300 farmers to suicide since June 2005 in the Vidarbha Region. This once-prosperous cotton belt in eastern Maharashtra has faced the brunt of 15 years of liberalization (Bunsha Dionne, 2005). Production cost of cotton has multiplied three to five times, but its market price has fallen from Rs. 2,500 a quintal in 1991 to Rs. 1,785 now. Prices of other crops have also fallen. Most farmers are running up huge losses and have to borrow heavily to keep afloat. Since most of them have defaulted on loan repayments the banks are unwilling to extend fresh loans. Their only recourse is to borrow from the trade-moneylender at 60 to 120 per cent interest. This has ensured that the farmers are trapped in debt.

BOX 6.2
Dimensions of the Crisis

- More than 300 farmers have committed suicide since June, 2005.
- Cotton price has dipped from Rs. 2,500 a quintal in 1991 to Rs. 1,785.
- Government reduces procurement price this year by Rs. 500.
- Procurement this season: 6.25 lakh quintals; last season: 185 lakh quintals.
- Number of procurement centres this year: 160; last year: 410.

Frontline, March 11-24, 2006, p. 43.

Once cotton was considered 'white gold', and Vidarbha's black soil was perfect for its cultivation. There are 2.5 million cotton producers in eight districts in Vidarbha. With liberalization, the 'white gold' became worthless. The government has withdrawn market controls, tariffs and subsidies for agriculture, leaving Indian farmers to compete with farmers in the United States and the European Union who are protected by trade restrictions and provided with billions of dollars as subsidy.

Contract Farming in Tamil Nadu

In Tamil Nadu, area under cotton cultivation has come down from 3,96,000 hectares in 1960-61 to 1,78,000 hectares in 1999-2000. Similarly, percentages of cotton cultivation to the gross cropped area has come down from 5.41 in 1960-61 to 2.73 in 1999-2000. The cotton is cultivated in Tamil Nadu in an area of 2 lakh hectares in the normal years and the State production is around 4-5 lakh bales. More than 60 per cent of the textile mills in the country are located in Tamil Nadu, which annually consumes nearly 50 lakh bales of cotton. The State production meets only 10 per cent of the requirement. This huge gap between demand and supply has forced the mills to get their requirement from other states. Since there is a huge demand for cotton within Tamil Nadu, linking farmers with the assured marketing and protecting the interests of both the farmers and the industry, contract farming is promoted by the State Government through Department of Agriculture. The main objective is to provide farmers assured remunerative prices and increasing area of cotton cultivation. The farmer is provided support in diverse areas such as input, technical assistance, credit, production management, insurance coverage, marketing, etc., under contract farming.

Table 6.6 : Area under Cotton Cultivation in Tamil Nadu

Year	*Area in Hectare*
1960-61	3,96,000 (5.41)
1970-71	3,11,000 (4.21)
1980-81	2,22,000 (3.43)
1990-91	2,39,000 (3.61)
1999-2000	1,78,000 (2.73)

Source: Season and Crop Reports, Government of Tamil Nadu.
Note: Figures within parentheses are percentages to the Gross cropped area.

Tripartite Contract Farming in Coimbatore District

There are three recent developments happening in Coimbatore district pertaining to agricultural sector in addition to the normal cultivation pattern. These are as follows:

(1) Contract farming in cotton cultivation.
(2) Contract farming in maize cultivation.
(3) Increasing awareness on natural farming.

In Coimbatore district alone cotton area under cultivation has decreased from 22000 ha. in 1992-93 to nearly 6000 ha. in 2004-05. In order to increase the cotton area under cultivation, contract farming is being promoted by the government. In Coimbatore district, some of the farmers have recently joined contract farming system hoping that they would get higher prices. It is unfortunate that everyone talks about higher prices as if higher prices would automatically translate into higher incomes for cotton growers. There is no guarantee that higher prices mean higher incomes.

The Government of India's National Agriculture Policy too envisages that private sector participation will be promoted through contract farming and land leasing arrangements to allow accelerated technology transfer, capital inflow and assured market for crop production, especially of oilseeds, cotton and horticulture crops. During 2004-05, the Department of Agriculture, Tamil Nadu has organized a 'Cotton Stakeholders Meet' to promote contract farming at Coimbatore on 20.11.2004 involving officials from Government of India, Mills, Cotton farmers, Credit Institutions, Insurance Agencies, Marketing sector, Input suppliers, Tamil Nadu Agricultural University and Central Institute for Cotton Research, Coimbatore. The Commissionerate of Agriculture formulated a tripartite contract farming model for enhancing cotton production in the State. The main objectives of the model developed by the Commissionerate of Agriculture are as follows:

- Focus on cluster of villages.
- Viable price mechanism.
- Credit linked inputs supply.
- Insurance coverage.
- Ensuring quality as per mill specifications.
- Extension support by the department.

Under this model, the Department of Agriculture acts as the chief co-ordinator of the programme and Tamil Nadu Agricultural University renders R & D support. Coimbatore based Super Spinning Mill Limited (SSML) has come forward and entered into the Tripartite model of contract farming covering various districts in Tamil Nadu such as Coimbatore, Madurai, Salem, Vellore, Namakkal, Theni. The Commissionerate of Agriculture's prime responsibility is networking all stakeholders in the project. It provides extension support as well as training to the farmers. Apart from identifying the progressive farmers, government extends pre- and post-harvesting extension. Awareness campaigns are conducted at village level. In case private mill company fails to procure the agreed quantity of cotton as per norms and conditions of the MoU, Cotton Corporation of India shall purchase the balance cotton at the actual prevailing market price with a premium depending on the quality of cotton. It also gives waiver of 1 per cent market less to private mills for three months.

Contract Farmers in Cotton

A group consisting 15 to 20 cotton farmers was formed to cultivate the cotton crop in an integrated manner. The group organizer was selected among the group. He acted as the linking person between the SSML and the farmers. All the group organizers from the project areas were invited to fix the price before procurement. Crop loan (Rs. 7000 per acre) was arranged to the farmers who were in need of money to meet the expenses of the cultivation. They were given free cotton cloth bags to pack cotton without contamination. Though the entirely hand-picked cotton is supposed to be the cleanest in the world, the contamination starts from storage, transport and processing upwards. However, there is a chance for contamination in storing the picked cotton at the collection centre. All the quantity of the cotton was procured at the prevailing market price which was higher than the minimum support price announced by the Government for the first quality of cotton. The measurement in procurement of cotton was correct. The procured cotton was transported from the identified centres by the SSML to their ginning units. A cheque for the procurement was sent to the designated bank within two days in the name of the farmer after deducting the amount for the loan. The main intention of the company was very clear that it wanted to purchase good-quality cotton for which it was spending one part of the amount on quality control.

Acreage and Variety of Cotton under Contract Farming

Cultivation of cotton under the contract farming was done in 741 acres at Vazhukkuparai project area. Of the 741 acres, the area of 385.5 acres was cultivated by the variety of 'Sara II' while the area of 347.5 acres was cultivated by the variety of 'Bunny'. Area of 8 acres was cultivated by the variety of 'Super Bunny'. This variety caused allergy in hands and body of the farmers. So much so, labourers were hesitant to pick cotton where the variety was grown. The cotton varieties used by the farmers were not uniform in each village. The farmers selected the variety on their own expecting good yield and price for the cotton variety. Some of the selected villages where farmers cultivated the variety are given in Table 6.7:

Table 6.7 : Acreage and Variety of Cotton in Selected Villages of Madukkarai Block

Name of the Village	*Super Bunny*	*Sara II*	*Bunny*	*Total*
Vazhukkuparai	8.00 (2)	67.00 (27)	23.50 (12)	98.50 (41)
Appatchi Goundanpathy	-	26 (10)	81 (29)	107.00 (39)
Marichettypathy	-	113 (42)	7 (3)	120 (45)
Pachappalayam	-	14 (8)	33.50 (24)	47.50 (32)
Meenachipuaram	-	18 (4)	31.50 (14)	49.50 (18)

Source: Agriculture Department, Madukkarai.
Note: Figures in parentheses are number of farmers who cultivated the variety.

Seeds were supplied by the SSML at 10 per cent discounted rate to the contract farmers. Mainly, hybrid varieties viz., Bunny and Sara II were sown in the above villages. Sowings of seeds started from the first week of May, 2004 onwards. Supply of agro inputs was given directly to the contract farmers by the SSML. The contract farmers got the price which was more than Minimum Support Price (MSP) announced by the Government for the first quality of cotton variety. For the second quality of cotton, they got almost the price of MSP.

Farmers Covered under Contract Farming

Madukkarai is one of the blocks in Coimbatore district covered under the contract farming system. Among the different project areas set up by the SSML covering 12 villages in Madukkarai Block, Vazhukkuparai has been selected as a project area in which 308 farmers were involved in contract farming system during the season of May 2004 – May 2005.

Technology Mission on Cotton

The SSML identified the villages such as Vazhukkuparai, Appachigoundanpathi, Marichettipathy, Meenatchipuram, Palathurai, Patchapalayam in Madukkarai Block covering 304 acres during 2005-06 registering Front Line Demonstration (FLD) plots under the guidance of Technology Mission on Cotton (Mini Mission II) for Integrated Pest Management (IPM) and Production Technologies. There were about 100 farmers involved under the FLD programme from six selected villages of Madukkarai Block in Coimbatore district.

BOX 6.3

G.M. Cotton Seeds

Cotton seeds are modified genetically to contain a common bacterium, Bt (Bacillus thuringiensis), that is potent enough to resist one of the most dreaded pests of cotton: the bollworm. The Genetic Engineering Approval Committee (GEAC) cleared the commercial cultivation of Bt Cotton on March 26, 2002.

According to Union Government estimates, Genetically Modified (GM) cotton seeds are expected to yield Rs. 10,000 per hectare more than traditional varieties. The fact that India is the largest grower of cotton underscores the relevance of this amount.

Down to Earth, April 30, 2002.

Under the Technology Mission on Cotton Programme, awareness camps were organized to teach techniques involved in cotton cultivation for the benefit of farmers. Srinithi Bt Cotton variety of seed was distributed to the contract farmers. The yield was not up to the expectation level of the farmers because improper season of selection for sowing, continuous rainfall during bursting time and incidence of pink boll worm. Moreover, the quality of cotton was not the desired level of expectation and market price for Bt Cotton Kapa was very low. It was reported that the farmers did not follow the technical advice completely during the period of Bt Cotton cultivation.

It is obvious from the field that the SSML has done its role correctly in the manner in which all the aspects were provided to the contract farmers as per the tripartite contract farming model. The farmers were provided support in diverse areas such as inputs, technical assistance, credit, production management and marketing under contract farming. Even though contract farming sounds beneficial to farmers, some of the farmers were not satisfied with the yield, and fluctuations of price.

In addition, they had to spend more on wages for the agricultural activities such as weeding, harvesting, and grading. A few farmers have sold their cotton directly to agencies other than the SSML due to urgent financial needs of the family. They are slowly repaying the bank loan which they obtained for growing cotton. Since they did not get price, yield, and exorbitant labour charge in cotton production, they could not increase the area of cotton cultivation. They simply switched over to cultivate 'Tomato' which was considered as preferable crop by the farmers in the villages.

Under the guidance of Technology Mission on Cotton, Srinithi Bt Cotton has been cultivated in Front Line Demonstration (FLD) plots in collaboration with the SSML at Vazhukkuparai, Meenatchipuram, Pachapalayam, Masthigoundanpathy, Marichettipatti in Madukkarai block during the kharif season of July to December, 2005. It has been reported from the FLD plots that the yield from Bt Cotton was less (only 2½ quintals per acre at Vazhukkuparai) compared to Sara II variety which yielded 4 quintals per acre in the same area. The procurement price for Bt Cotton was only Rs. 2700 per quintal for the first quality. The farmers who cultivated Bt Cotton under contract farming did not benefit because of high cost of seed, low yield, low price and the same expenditure like the other cotton seed variety.

New Management Model in Contract Farming

A technological change brings along with it a new management model. It helps for the private mill (The SSML), contract farmers, and government.

(a) *For the Private Mill*: The mill advises the farmers on what seeds to sow under which agro-climatic condition, what fertilizer and pesticide to use. It also educates the growers when to apply the fertilizer and particular pesticide for the pest attack. The farmers are supported well in terms of price and ready market in the form of company procurement. The price at which cotton procured is higher than the minimum support price fixed by the government. The mill employs seed specialists, and technological assistants for farm management. This provides technical know-how to the cotton farmers. In turn, the mill gets desired quality cotton for their mills. Thus, it helps to construct a high quality institutional environment, flow of technical efficiency, productivity of land, and increasing production. The Contract Farming (CF) provides good opportunities to increase cotton area under cultivation without spending more on transport charges by the company. It makes arrangements to allow accelerated technology transfer, capital inflow and assured market. The main intention of the company is very clear that it wants to purchase good quality of cotton for which it spends one part of the amount on quality control.

BOX 6.4

Imports of Cotton

Post WTO Period	*Quantity (Lakh bags of 170 kgs)*
1997-98	85.00
1998-99	57.40
1999-2000	237.40
2000-2001	212.30

C. Ramaswamy, K.N. Selvaraj and N. Aijan, Implications of WTO Agreement on Agriculture in Tamil Nadu, TNAU, Coimbatore

For the Cotton Farmers: The farmer is provided support in diverse areas such as input, technical assistance, credit, production management, insurance coverage, marketing, etc., under contract farming. Supply of agro-inputs is given directly to the contract farmers by the mill. They are assured the price for cotton in the agreement. They are given free cotton cloth bag to plug cotton without contamination. The measurement in procurement of cotton is correct. The procured cotton is transported from the identified centres by the mill. Money is promptly paid. Even though contract farming sounds beneficial to farmers, some of the farmers are not satisfied with the yield, fluctuations in price and the increasing input costs.

For the Government: The Contract Farming (CF) may be encouraged in commercial crop like cotton. It would be to increase the efficiency of production and to create institutional mechanisms to enable the small and marginal farmers to share the benefits of agricultural diversification. In case private mill company fails to procure the agreed quantity of cotton as per norms and conditions of the MoU, Cotton Corporation of India shall purchase the balance cotton at the actual prevailing market price with a premium depending on the quality of cotton. It also gives waiver of 1 per cent market less to private mills for three months. The system could help to reduce the import from other countries. The mills and farmers would be benefited from this new management model. It is accepted by even staff members of Agriculture Department of the State Government that regular visit and technical guidance given by the private company are not possible with limited man-power resources with Agriculture Department.

To Sum Up

India's production, consumption and export of textiles and garments are still heavily weighed in favour of cotton-based products. Cotton industry is not known to have involved in cotton development and extension the way sugar industry did for sugarcane cultivation. To sustain the competitive edge of cotton industry, the raw cotton production has to be cost effective and of high quality standards. CF could be taken up in the context of market imperfections and distortions in prices arising due to various factors. With the pre-decided prices and availability of technical know-how, it is felt that this farming can help in sorting out a few tangles due to market imperfections. The system could be one of the best solutions which may decrease the polarization of the rich and the poor and thus encourage the farmers to compete with the very large, rich and highly indirectly subsidized western farmers. It would be helpful to reduce the import from the other countries. This innovative system helps the farmer to get assured price and the company to get quality products at a specified time. There is an urgent need to work towards developing technologies that are labour intensive and at the same time efficient in both farm and non-farm activities. The Central Government can protect its producers from imports and crashing international prices by hiking the import duty on cotton. At present it is only 10 per cent import duty on other products such as sugar (60 per cent), rice (80 per cent) and second-hand cars (180 per cent) are much higher. India has to be vigilant on not being caught on the wrong foot in terms of labour, human rights, phyto-sanitary and environmental standards fixed in the Agreement on Agriculture.

SUMMARY OF THE FINDINGS

In Tamil Nadu, nearly 72 per cent of the human population was dependent on agriculture in 1960-61 and it was 56.77 per cent in 1999-2000. Significant decline in the relative share of agriculture in NSDP and a very small decline in percentages of population dependent on agriculture allowed very little increase in real per capita income in agricultural sector. Area under foodgrain crops in Tamil Nadu was

56.51 lakh hectares in 1970-71; it has steadily decreased to 36.33 lakh hectares in 1999-2000. It marked a fall in the share of foodgrain crops in the gross cropped area from 76.3 per cent to 55.7 per cent between 1970-71 and 1999-2000. Correspondingly, the share of non-food crops increased from 23.7 per cent to 44.3 per cent (i.e.) nearly doubled during the same period. Thus, Tamil Nadu agriculture is progressively commercialized. After five decades of planned development, agriculture in Tamil Nadu has shown significant changes. Farming as a way of life is disappearing and agri-business is taking place as a result of liberalized policies through the new agriculture policy. Globalizing agriculture through liberalization has the potential of commercialization of agriculture and export of value added farm products. The agriculture sector in Tamil Nadu has recently been touched by the reform activities in a sporadic way. Even though Central Government has initiated many liberalized policy measures towards commercial agriculture, the outcome slowly penetrates in the State Government. The reason for slowness may be due to agriculture coming under the 'state list'. In the context of globalization of economy, a top priority for export-led growth is given, thereby, some of the crops have the prospect of coming to prominence by their potential contribution to exports such as turmic, trophical fruits, sugarcane, flowers, medicinal plants, onion, pepper and cardamom.

Rising Input Costs of Cultivation

- Thiruvarur is one of the Cauvery delta regions. Paddy is the principal crop in the district and the source of water for the paddy cultivation is mainly from the government canals. The farmers in the district can not go for alternative crops other than paddy because the nature of soil is suitable for paddy cultivation. The paddy is mainly cultivated in three seasons viz., Kuruvai, Samba and Thaladi.
- Prominent feature of the district is the cultivation of pulse crop which is sown ten days before the harvest of paddy. The money farmers get from this.cultivation is a useful supplement to their ordinary income.
- The cost of production has increased in paddy cultivation. The price received by the farmers differs for the variety of paddy. The farmers deliver the grains to procurement centre; they incur cost of packaging, transport and labour charges. Net income

per kg received by the farmers is very low due to various factors involved in cultivation. In general, farmers calculate their net income without taking into account the input costs. The cost of human labour constitutes a major part of the total variable input cost in the case of paddy cultivation. The farmers have a feeling that in all the years' farm harvest price is larger than MSP, showing that MSP has helped farmers more by pushing up the farm harvest price to some extent but not enough to fully cover all the costs assuring positive net income.

- The small and marginal farmers, who often, engage in agriculture with borrowed funds, find agriculture non-remunerative and have a tendency to give up agriculture and become wage earners or go in search of employment in the town.
- Modern rice mills in Thiruvarur replacing hullers have displaced labourers and eaten into the profit margins of the small traders, producers and labourers. As a result, today, agricultural labourers are getting only minimum days work in a year. Due to massive rural unemployment that has been accentuated by serious drought conditions, there is widespread migration of agricultural workers to urban areas. Many farmers and agricultural labourers have already sent the members of their family to distant cities to earn wages during the drought situation.
- In the district, area under cultivation varies from season to season as the district is prone to natural disasters such as flood, cyclone and drought. As there is no uniform area under paddy cultivation, margin and small farmers and agricultural labourers are in distress to face the fluctuating area under cultivation. So, profit from the agriculture is not ensured because of natural calamities influencing the cultivation practices.
- Big farmers prefer to use machineries owing to quick completion of agricultural works. Though paddy harvest machine and thrashing machine have come in handy for farmers, it has deprived landless labourers of their chances of getting seasonal employment in the delta regions.
- The number of days a labourer gets employment in agriculture has come down due to mechanization, shrinking agriculture and introduction of short-term crops. Many of the wage-earners watch out for, and prefer to get employed in building construction works that provides employment almost throughout the year these days. Within eight years period (1997-2005), employed in a year has reduced from 150 days to

100 days for male agricultural labourers whereas 120 days to 100 days for female agricultural labourers.

- The labour-contracting system is followed in paddy transplantation and harvesting. This system gives the agricultural labourers a better deal, in the sense, they are able to complete the work swiftly, and get on with another work the same day doubling their income for the day.
- Although it is true that the wages in agriculture for various activities have, in several parts of the district, crossed well beyond the minimum wages prescribed, the per capita earning of agricultural labourers have increased only marginally in real terms on account of the decline in the number of days a worker gets employment.
- Merchants from Kerala used to buy TK 9 coarse variety of paddy. Now, they are going to Karnataka where TK 9 variety is being cultivated in extended area of cultivation. So, the price for this variety has reduced sharply from Rs. 350 per quintal to Rs. 230 per quintal during the year 2005. The farmers who cultivated TK 9 variety did not get return from what they spent on their land.
- The State Government opens Direct Purchasing Centre (DPC) particularly in the Samba season. DPC is opened only after the several requisitions made by the farmers. The delay in opening up of DPC causes several hardships to the farmers. Farmers have been paid Rs. 600 per quintal to fine variety while Rs. 570 per quintal to motta variety. Farmers urge the government to increase the procurement price to Rs. 1000 per quintal considering the high cost of cultivation.
- With the virtual collapse of the cooperative system, both on account of mismanagement and the continuing cycle of draughts and floods, farmers are unable to pay back their loans. The reach of institutional credit is still restricted to the relatively better-off farmers. Information about insurance was not disseminated to the farmers by Primary Agricultural Co-operative Societies. Farmers in the Cauvery delta region were under the misconception that only those who have taken loans from the societies benefited from the schemes.
- Farmers want to sell the entire harvested paddy immediately to DPC. They are in need of money to repay the amount which was borrowed from the PACS/Commercial Banks/Money-lenders/ Private seed and fertilizer stall. Further more, *Badhayam*

(Traditional paddy storage system) is no longer used in the houses of the farmers. It is meant that the farmers are forced to sell their products immediately so that they can repay the amount.

- Modernization of agriculture requires the use of agricultural machinery for various agricultural operations. Tractor, power tiller, power thrasher etc., are some of the machineries for which subsidies are given by the Government of Tamil Nadu. Electricity subsidy is another farm input subsidy provided to all farmers in the State supplying electricity to farm use is absolutely free of charge. Similarly, seeds are supplied to farmers at subsidized rate by the department of agriculture. Paddy cultivation in Thiruvarur district is completely dependent on government canals and it is quite difficult to estimate the value of this subsidy. Government should take efforts to increase the productivity of land for which subsidy may be provided to marginal and small farmers.
- Recently, eligible marginal and small farmers and agricultural labourers have been given identity cards under Farmers' Social Security Scheme through out the State. Most of the agricultural labourers are not aware of the existence of the Minimum Wages Act. Only a very low percentages of farmers have any knowledge of farmers on WTO, AoA, Seed Act, Kisan Card and Crop Insurance Scheme.
- It is the inevitability of farmers' dependence on multinational companies which promote genetically modified seeds due to trade liberalization. Mangudi village president says that farmers do not have seed right in future and it would offer a promise of a monopoly to private seed industries.
- The biggest challenge of globalization is that the procurement price especially for rice has been increasing faster than the general price level. Such high price along with guaranteed purchases by the Food Corporation of India (FCI) has pushed up market prices. This higher price is partly responsible for the large buffer stocks with the FCI. If this trend continues, India's comparative advantage will be eroded.
- Rising cost of inputs, non-availability of cheap rural credit and exposure to volatile global market price trends have started squeezing the peasantry. The paradigm of the WTO's agreement on agriculture is biased in favour of capital intensive and corporate agri-business driven agriculture.

COTTON CRISIS

In Tamil Nadu, area under cotton cultivation has come down from 3,96,000 hectares in 1960-61 to 1,78,000 hectares in 1999-2000. Similarly, percentages of cotton cultivation to the gross cropped area has come down from 5.41 in 1960-61 to 2.73 in 1999-2000. Cotton is cultivated in Tamil Nadu in an area of 2 lakh hectares in normal years and the State production is around 4-5 lakh bales. More than 60 per cent of the textile mills in the country are located in Tamil Nadu, which annually consume nearly 50 lakh bales of cotton. The State production meets only 10 per cent of the requirement. This huge gap between demand and supply has forced the mills to get their requirement from other states. Since there is a huge demand for cotton within Tamil Nadu, linking farmers with the assured marketing and protecting the interests of both the farmers and the industry, contract farming is promoted by the State Government through the department of agriculture.

- The contract farming provides good opportunities to increase cotton area under cultivation without spending more on transport charges incurred by the company. This system could be taken up in the context of market imperfections and distortions in prices arising due to various factors. With the pre-decided prices and availability of technical know-how, it was felt that this farming can help in sorting out a few tangles due to market imperfections. This system could be one of the best solutions which may decrease the polarization of the rich and the poor and thus encourage the farmers to compete with the very large, rich and highly indirectly subsidized western farmers. The innovative system helps the farmer to get assured price and the company to get quality products at a specified time.
- In Coimbatore district alone cotton area under cultivation has decreased from 22,000 hectares in 1992-93 to nearly 6,000 hectares in 2004-05. In order to increase the cotton area under cultivation has been promoted by the State Government in compliance with the new agricultural policy. Even though the contract farming sounds beneficial, the farmers did not get more in terms of net profit. Input costs especially, labour cost component consumes a lot of expense in cotton cultivation.
- Under the tripartite contract farming system for enhancing cotton production in the district, Department of Agriculture,

Coimbatore based Super Spinning Mill Limited (SSML) and cotton farmers have entered into the Tripartite model of contract farming system for enhancing cotton production in the district. In this connection, the SSML has signed Memorandum of Understanding (MoU) with Tamil Nadu Government. So, it fulfilled all the facilities to the farmers. The SSML has done its role correctly in the manner in which all the aspects were provided to the contract farmers as per the tripartite contract farming system.

- Madukkarai is one of the blocks in Coimbatore district covered under the tripartite contract farming system. Among the different project areas by the SSML in Madukkarai block, Vazhukkuparai has been selected as a project area in which 308 farmers from 12 villages have been benefited under the system during the season of May, 2004 – May, 2005.
- A group consisting 15 to 20 cotton farmers was formed to cultivate the cotton crop in an integrated manner. The group organizer was selected among the group. He acted as the link between the SSML and the other farmers. All the group organizers from that project areas were invited to fix the price before procurement.
- Hybrid seeds such as Bunny, Sara II, and Super Bunny were supplied by the SSML at 10 per cent discounted rate to the contract farmers. Sowing of seeds was started in the first week of May, 2004. Supply of agro-inputs was given directly to the contract farmers by the SSML. The farmers, who got good yield under contract farming system, have undertaken again cotton cultivation.
- Vazhukkuparai project area, covered by 308 farmers, had 741 acres. Out of 741 acres, the area of 385.5 acres was cultivated by the variety of 'Sara II' while the area of 347.5 acres was cultivated by the variety of 'Bunny'. Area of eight acres only was cultivated by the variety of 'Super Bunny'. 'Super Bunny' variety caused allergy in hands and body of the farmers. Agricultural labourers were hesitant to pick cotton from these fields. Selection of the variety by the farmers was based on yield and price for the particular cotton variety.
- During the period of May, 2004 – May, 2005, the contract farmers got the price for the first quality cotton which was more than the Minimum Support Price (MSP) signed by the contract system

between the mill and farmers. For the second quality of cotton, they got the price of MSP. However, the farmers did not get more net profit due to increase in input costs and average yield of cotton. As this contract system in cotton is a new one, it may take some time to get popularized. As a result, the farmers can voluntarily come forward to cultivate cotton crop.

- The private mill advised the farmers on what seeds to sow under which agro-climatic condition, what fertilizer and pesticide to use. It also educated the growers when to apply the fertilizer and particular pesticide for the pest attack. The farmers were supported well in terms of price and ready market in the form of company's procurement.
- The farmers were provided support in diverse areas such as inputs, technical assistance, credit, production management and marketing under contract farming system. Crop loan (Rs. 7000 per acre) was arranged to the farmers who were in need of money to meet the expenses of the cultivation.
- The farmers were given free cotton cloth bags to pack cotton without contamination. Though the entirely hand-picked cotton is supposed to be the cleanest in the world, the contamination starts from storage at farmers' houses, transport and processing upwards.
- All the quantity of the cotton was procured at the prevailing market price. The measurement in procurement of cotton was correct. The procured cotton was transported from the identified centres by the SSML to their ginning units. A cheque for the procurement was sent to the designated bank within two days in the name of the farmer after deducting the loan amount.
- Due to liberalized policies, private mills can import quality cotton easily. Suddenly, when the price of cotton gets down, the cotton farmers would be severely affected. But, in this system, the farmers are assured of prices. However, the price of cotton is not matching with the production cost of farmers in the recent years.
- Even though contract farming system sounds beneficial to farmers, some of the farmers were not satisfied with the yield, and the fluctuations of price. In addition, they had to spend more on wages for the agricultural activities such as weeding, harvesting, and grading. A few farmers have sold their cotton

directly to agencies other than the SSML due to urgent financial needs of the family. They are slowly repaying the bank loan which they obtained for growing cotton.

- Since the farmers did not get the expected price, yield and exorbitant labour charge in cotton production, they could not increase the area of cotton cultivation. They simply switched over to cultivate 'Tomato' which is considered to be the preferable crop by the farmers in the villages.
- Three factors viz., input costs, price, and yield influence the farmers' decision on cotton cultivation. At the grassroots level, the input cost can not be reduced. Giving higher price than the market price is not profitable to the mills point of view. The third factor i.e. yield influences almost the farmers' decision on cotton cultivation in their field. It is clear from the field that the farmer is satisfied if he gets good yield.
- The SSML identified the villages such as Vazhukkuparai, Appachi Gounanpathi, Marichettipathy, Meenatchipuram, Palathurai, Patchapalayam in Madukkarai block covering 304 acres during 2005-06 registering Front Line Demonstration (FLD) plots under the guidance of Technology Mission on Cotton. In these areas, soil is suitable for cotton cultivation and it is cultivated under rainfed condition.
- Under the Technology Mission on Cotton, awareness camps were conducted by the Department of Agriculture to involve in Bt Cotton cultivation which are expected to yield Rs. 10,000 per hectare more than traditional varieties. Srinithi Bt Cotton variety of seed was given to the contract farmers. The yield was not up to the expectation levels of the farmers because improper season of selection for sowing, continuous rainfall during bursting time and incidence of pink boll worm. The quality of cotton was not upto the desired level of expectation. Moreover, the market price for Bt Cotton was very low.
- The yield from Bt Cotton in FLD plots was less (only 2.5 quintals per acre at Vazhukkuparai) compared to Sara II variety which yielded four quintals per acre in the same area. The procurement price for Bt Cotton was only Rs. 2,700 per quintal for the first quality. The farmers who cultivated Bt Cotton under contract farming did not benefit because of high cost of seed, low yield, low price and the same expenditure like other cotton seed variety.
- It may be accepted that the cotton industry is not known to have involved in cotton development and extension the way the sugar

industry did for sugarcane cultivation. To sustain the competitive edge of cotton industry, the raw cotton production has to be cost effective and of high quality standards. Farm production strategies should be income-focused than price, which can be achieved only by higher productivity and reduction in cost of production.

- Ground reality shows that Bt Cotton did not yield as farmers-expected level. Quality of cotton was not exceptionally good. Price of Bt Cotton was high. The farmers who cultivated Bt Cotton got the amount what they spent for the cultivation. Any way, they did not lose because of minimum yield and moderate price given by the mill.
- Bt Cotton is Genetically Modified (GM) seeds which are invented and innovated by rich Multinational Companies (MNCs)/Trans National Companies (TNCs) for their profit. The government has permitted these companies to sell the GM seeds which snatches the farmers' seed right. Bt Cotton has not only been attacked by other pests, it has been struck by the bollworm itself. Hence, farmers' traditional wisdom must be safeguarded at any cost.
- With liberalization, the white gold became worthless due to fall of price in domestic market. In this scenario, farmers can not think for export of cotton. It is very difficult to compete with farmers in the United States and the European Union who are protected by trade restrictions and provided with billions of dollars as subsidy. Therefore, the Central Government can protect cotton farmers from imports and crashing international prices by hiking the import duty on cotton.

Conclusion

In Tamil Nadu, the agriculture sector is generally more vulnerable to external shocks of nature. The farmers in Tamil Nadu have no insurance mechanisms for responding to the shocks, despite the fact that agriculture remains an important source of livelihood to the large percentages of the population. The profit from the agriculture is not assured because of natural calamities influencing the cultivation practices. The root cause of the farmer distress is the sharp decline in the prices of agricultural commodities through abundant supply of products in a particular area and sharp increase in the input costs. It can be witnessed from the agriculture economy in Tamil Nadu that a significant deceleration in the growth of crop output and yields have adversely affected the farmers by reducing their income and profitability.

Clearly, farm income has come down resulting in suffering by the agrarian families because the cost of production is invariably higher than the minimum support price. The number of days a labourer gets employment in agriculture has come down due to mechanization, shrinking agriculture and introduction of short-term crops. Although it is true that the wages in agriculture has crossed well beyond the minimum wages prescribed, the per capita earning of agricultural labourers have increased only marginally in real terms on account of the decline in the number of days a worker gets employment. To mitigate the problems of marginal and small farmers (51 lakhs) and agricultural labourers (86 lakhs) in Tamil Nadu, Farmers' Social Security Scheme is being implemented through the Village Administrative Offices. The challenge in the case of landless agricultural labour is enhancing the economic value of their time and labour by bringing about a paradigm shift from unskilled to skilled work.

The establishment of the WTO in 1995 promised to give a big push to trade liberalization in agriculture. The commitments which members are to undertake the WTO's AoA fall under three main areas namely market access, export subsidy and domestic support. Globalization of Agriculture can be welcomed in the context of improvement of productive efficiency by ensuring the convergence of potential and realized out put, and increase in agricultural exports and value added activities. Export promotion via the development of export and trading houses as well as effective liberalizing export promotion zone schemes for agriculture are fairly recent measures. It may be known as to how effective these measures are. Other possibilities such as agro-industry parks for promoting exports are also in the pipeline. Positive policy interventions are necessary to assure that the interests of small farmers and marginal farmers of disadvantaged regions are also protected and that they are enabled to share the benefits of trade liberalization. India should not only try to improve its bargaining position in on-going negotiations on agriculture, it should also try to improve its competitiveness in many agricultural commodities through increase in their productivity.

To accelerate the process of agricultural growth, rapid and widespread adoption of modern technology backed by institutional and infrastructure developments are the main areas which are given priority in the government policy. The proposed reforms are likely to improve the environment for private investment, structural change and efficiency gains in agro-business. At the grassroots levels, Technology Mission on cotton with contract farming system has provided support in diverse areas such as inputs, technical assistance, credit, production, management and marketing arrangements. Even though contract farming sounds beneficial to farmers, some of the farmers are not satisfied with the yield and fluctuations in the price of cotton.

In particular, it has been tried to examine in what way the establishment of a free and liberalized trade regime under Agreement on Agriculture would affect the fortunes of the farmers. WTO provisions on 'domestic' support also have some important ramifications for India. A great deal of concern has been expressed regarding the very high levels of 'domestic support' given to agricultural products by the developed countries. This has not only distorted world prices, but has also resulted in harming exports from the developing countries. More importantly, huge domestic and export subsidies given by the developed countries inhibits exports from developing world. India has a large potential to increase its agricultural exports in a liberalized world once the developed countries agree to eliminate their subsidies. There is no level playing field in the agriculture sector in the world today between capital, subsidy and technology-driven agriculture, and small farmers struggling to survive without such support. It must be accepted that this is mainly due to internal problems, apart from the fears have been voiced that removing Quantitative Restrictions would dramatically increase agricultural imports from other countries and vulnerability in the wider international price fluctuations.

It is quite apparent that at this relatively early stage, there is little observable evidence of gains to India's agricultural performance. However, there could easily be benefits that have not yet surfaced, or are yet to be identified and perhaps too difficult or intangible to measure. Whatever the case, it is too soon to assess the full impact of globalization and economic reforms. Further more, the process of liberalization has been gradual and remains incomplete. As agriculture is the bone of contention for developed and developing countries, WTO-watchers feel that the negotiations are likely to continue for a few years as there are serious differences amongst the major players. Urgent measures are, therefore, needed to make agriculture a profitable activity at the earliest, not only to benefit farmers and a large section of the rural poor but also to give a boost to the economy through backward and forward linkages of agriculture with the rest of the economy.

7

Food Security in Tamil Nadu: The Survival Matrices

The Premise

> There are starvation deaths reported from Orissa and several other states of India. That Tamil Nadu has been able to refrain from starvation deaths is—a reality or a myth? If it is real what has contributed to Tamil Nadu for being able to prevent starvation deaths?

Introduction

As far as food security is concerned there are two different scenarios described of India. One scenario is shining while the other is grim. The shining scenario which is more often used by those in power is: Agriculture is the means of livelihood of about 2/3 of the workforce in the country. From a nation dependent on food imports to feed its population, India today is not only self-sufficient in grain production, but also has a substantial reserve. The second scenario is: Poor rural people in the State of Bihar unable to find food are reported to have been eating mango kernel. People in some interior areas of Tamil Nadu have eaten rats to relieve themselves of starvation.

The Problem Statement

There are Civil Society Organizations (CSOs) and political parties with leftist leaning that shout WTO is extinguishing agriculture and rural livelihoods and, therefore, the food security, especially, of the rural people, has come under threat. On the other hand, the State Government of Tamil Nadu claims that the successful functioning of Public Distribution System (PDS) in the state as the prime reason for the people to have been able to avoid hunger related deaths/suicides in Tamil Nadu.

These statements – apart from the fundamental questions of the state ensuring food security as a constitutional obligation and as a way of obliging to the Universal Declaration of Human Rights – seem to pose issues such as: Food security is not merely a question of food production or food availability; rather it includes vital issues such as the system in place to provide essential commodities that effectively caters to the food related cultural practices of communities. If PDS is said to be such a system, the role played by PDS for the poor people to have been able to avoid starvation deaths is yet to be ascertained, despite the State Government's claim that it has substantially helped.

If PDS is a vital source of food security in villages, urban slums and in the tribal settlements, why are there reports that state International Organizations such as the World Bank advice the government that the State Government should make efforts to contract the food subsidy bill and phase it out in stead of thinking of further expansion? So much so, when such organizations call for a contraction in the food subsidy bill of the State, why is it that the State Government takes a stand that runs directly in the opposite direction – expanding the food subsidy bill? Finally and most importantly, what are the sources that uphold food security in Tamil Nadu villages to have been able to avoid starvation deaths that was reported from several other states, and none in Tamil Nadu? These issues require an in-depth empirical study in the context of Tamil Nadu with the following objectives:

- Studying the food security status of the rural people in Tamil Nadu and identifying the sources that have contributed to preventing starvation related deaths in Tamil Nadu;
- Analyzing the place of Public Distribution System (PDS) in ensuring household food security;
- Understanding the seasonal dimensions of food security management and coping strategies of the poor households during the slack years.

Research Approach

This is an exploratory exercise on understanding the Food Security problems of the rural people and the impact of globalization processes, if any, on food security. Both participatory methods such as FGD and the conventional questionnaire survey have been used for data collection. Twenty four villages in five districts of Tamil Nadu viz., Dindigul, Ramanathapuram, Dharmapuri, Krishnakiri, and Pudukottai were taken up for this study. The Unit of analysis, sources of data and the methods of data analysis are presented below:

Unit of Analysis: Village Panchayat has been taken up as unit of analysis. The rationale for this is that one significant aspect of this research study is to find out if there is any role played by Village Panchayats in mitigating food insecurity at the villages level; combating corruption, if any in Fair Price Shops; and ascertain if there is any role the VP plays in ensuring effective reach of essential commodities in the village.

Data Sources: The study has made use of both primary and secondary sources of data and information. Primary data were collected from common people in the villages – men, women, young, old, the landed class, and the working class, – who use PDS, and the sales persons of Fair Price Shops. Secondary data have been mostly collected from either government sources including websites or from research publications of reputed institutions and journals. The studies conducted on hunger-free programme have also been a useful source of reference material.

Data Analysis: This exercise essentially aims at understanding and recording how (macro) policies interact with the stakeholders at the (micro) grassroots level. Methodology-wise, this study has taken several features of a multi-method study where Focus Group Discussion (FGD) has taken the prime seat and several other techniques like use of a Short Questionnaire. Semi-Structured Interviewing (SSI), workshop method, and a few other PRA methods were there in the tools box used in the field.

The prime considerations in the selection of research methods and tools were (i) bringing in as many perspectives as possible, and (ii) validity of the information generated in a given village through triangulation and or cross checking. Hence, the methods used were mostly qualitative and process oriented in nature which served the purpose of exploration intended. Wherever possible quantitative data have been obtained from the villages and used in the analysis.

Scope and Limitations: The term food security as used in this study means access to adequate stocks and flows of food and income earning activities including reserves and assets to offset risk, ease shocks, and meet contingencies. It is a little more than mere survival (hand-to-mouth), but it falls short of nutritional angle or biological measures that some studies focus on.

The coverage intended is studying the household and community food security of rural people in Tamil Nadu. Food security to prevent from starvation deaths has been the orientation of this study and so it does not intend to gauge the nutritional intake or the biological aspects of food security that some studies dwell upon. Similarly, the inter-household food security (between the 'landed class' and the 'working class' households) has been analyzed, whereas intra-household variations in food security such as food availability and accessibility for women and children are not given exclusive treatment, like it has been done about seasonal dimension relating to food security. Although a considerable section of people living in urban slums also get food security mainly through PDS, urban slums have not been in the coverage of this study.

THE MACRO PERSPECTIVES

Food is one of the most basic human rights—achieving it should not be seen as 'charity' but as an obligation of the state (Stephen Jackson, 2002). Going by the Constitution of India as well as by the Universal Declaration of Human Rights, food security is vital. Indian policy planners have treated food security as a national priority. The country's total output of foodgrains, which was merely 50 million tonnes in 1950-51, has shot up over eight folds to cross 212 million tonnes mark, according to latest estimates. The per capita food availability has risen during the same period from nearly 395 grams to nearly 500 grams per day despite unabated rise in population. Considering that the normative annual demand for food under the current scenario is only between 195 and 200 million tonnes and the actual demand is even less than that, the country appears to be not only self-sufficient in foodgrains but marginally surplus as well (Surinder Sud, 2004).

Increasing proportion of area under non-food crops in the gross cropped area is taken as a measure of agriculture growth, on the basis of the simple logic that non-food crops add more value per hectare than food crops. Sugarcane compared to paddy, cotton and groundnut compared to *jowar* and *bajra* are the cases to cite. Area under foodgrain crops, Tamil Nadu was 56.51 lakh hectare in 1970-71; it has steadily decreased to 28.37 lakh hectare in 2003-04. It marked a fall in the share of foodgrain in the gross cropped area from 76.3 per cent to 53.3 per cent between 1970-71 and 1999-2000. Correspondingly, the share of non-food crops increased from 23.7 per cent to 46.7 per cent (i.e.) nearly doubled during the same period. Thus, Tamil Nadu agriculture is progressively commercialized (GoI & Foundation, 2005).

Table 7.1 : Share of Foodgrains and Non-Foodgrains in Gross Cropped Area.

('000 hectares)

Year	*Foodgrains*		*Non-Foodgrains*		*Gross Cropped Area*
	Area	*%*	*Area*	*%*	
1960-61	5651	76.3	1752	23.7	7403
1970-71	5196	70.4	2188	29.6	7384
1980-81	4109	63.5	2360	36.5	6470
1990-91	3901	58.8	2731	41.2	6632
1999-2000	3633	55.7	2884	44.3	6517
2003-2004	2837	53.3	2479	46.7	5316

Source: Season and Crop Reports, Government of Tamil Nadu.

However, food self-sufficiency does not automatically reflect food security for the entire population at all the times. To be effective food security needs to manifest covering all regions and all economic strata of society. In fact the real issue today is not the availability of food but of its affordability by the poor. As per plan, the food security system does not remain confined to mere food self-sufficiency—which had, of course, been the prime objective—but goes beyond it to take care of buffer stacking and distribution as well. This holds good at the national level as well as at the household level.

The Public Distribution System (PDS)

Public Distribution System (PDS) was first started in 1939 as a war-time rationing measure. The Government of Tamil Nadu has been implementing PDS since the year 1964. Tamil Nadu has a vast network of Fair Price Shops (popularly known as 'Ration Shops') most of them run by cooperatives and some through Civil Supplies Corporation and SHGs etc. The scheme Village Shop Programme was introduced by the

State with the intention to have one shop for one village in order to feed essential articles to rural population. Subsequently, the scheme was converted into PDS with the intention of providing essential commodities to the public both in rural and urban areas at concession rates. Although the PDS is a national policy, the exact entitlement varies across states, and the responsibility for implementing, monitoring and enforcing legal provisions relating to public delivery rests with the State Governments. Since the introduction of TPDS from 1-6-1997, the universal PDS is in operation in Tamil Nadu with the Antyodaya Anna Yojana and the expanded Antyodaya Anna Yojana schemes. Under the universal PDS there is no discrimination of families on APL and BPL lines based on income (Nakkiran S, 2004).

BOX 7.1

Rural Poverty Programmes with a Food Distribution Component

In addition to the PDS and AAY, the government operates a number of rural poverty alleviation programmes, most of which have a food distribution component. These include:

- Sampoorna Grameen Rozgar Yojana (SGRY) (2001) provides 5 million tonnes of foodgrains annually to State, free of cost, for undertaking work programmes and covers women, Scheduled Castes, Scheduled Tribes and parents of children withdrawn from hazardous jobs.
- Food for Work Programme (2001) supplies foodgrains in States/areas affected by natural calamities. This scheme has been integrated with SGRY.
- Annapurna Scheme (2002) provides 10 kg of foodgrains per person per month free of cost to indigent senior citizens or persons above the age of 65 who do not receive pension under the National OAP Scheme.
- Pradhan Mantri Gramodaya Yojana (2000) promotes village-level development in the areas of health care, primary education, drinking water, housing and roads.
- Jawahar Gram Samriddhi Yojana (1999) develops community infrastructure and provides rural employment, paying wages in both food and money. This scheme has been integrated with SGRY.
- Swarna Jayanti Gram Swarozgar Yojana (1999) promotes micro-enterprises and Self-Help Groups among the rural poor.
- Employment Assurance Scheme (1993) provides lean season employment for assetless rural poor, paying wages in both food and money. This Scheme has been integrated with SGRY.

Public Distribution System in Tamil Nadu is a unique system as it is not based on income criterion of the people. Universal Public Distribution is in operation. It covers all the needy families by supplying rice at a price much lower than the BPL price fixed by the Government of India under Targeted Public Distribution System. In Tamil Nadu, there is no classification of families as Above Poverty Line/Below Poverty Line as done by the Government of India and by other states in PDS.

Commodities Handled

Generally, rice, sugar, wheat, kerosene, maida, and iodinated salt are the commonly distributed items in FPS in Tamil Nadu. Also, State Government distributes Ooty tea through FPS so as to protect the interests of the small tea growers of Ooty. Rice (staple food of the people), Wheat, Sugar and Kerosene are the commodities being supplied to the public in specified quantities at the prices fixed by the Government from time-to-time under the PDS.

Details of Cards

PDS is considered as principal instrument in the hands of State Governments for providing safety net to the poor against the spiraling rise in prices of essential commodities. In the case of rural Tamil Nadu, though the share of rural population has come down over the years from 73.31 in 1961 to 56.14 per cent in 2000-01, the size of rural population is at 3.49 crores out of the State population 6.21 crores in 2000-01. In this regard, Tamil Nadu sets a model in implementing the PDS as universal system for the cause of eradicating poverty and improving standard of living of the people living below the poverty line.

Table 7.2 : Categories of Family Cards as on 31-1-2005

Sl. No.	*Particulars*	*No. of Cards*	*Percentage*
1.	Rice Cards	16087090	86.80
2.	Sugar Cards	1105451	5.96
3.	Kerosene Cards	1309552	7.07
4.	Police Cards	312171	0.17
	Total Cards	**18533310**	**100.00**

Source: Policy Note 2005-06, Demand No. 12, Department of Cooperation, Food and Consumer Protection, Government of Tamil Nadu, Chennai, p. 3.

Light green colour family cards have been issued to those who opt for rice as well as all other essential commodities, and white colour family cards to those who opt for commodities other than rice. These white colour cardholders can have additional sugar in lieu of rice. This scheme was followed in the case of new family cards issued recently (GoTN, 2005-06).

Method of Distribution of Essential Commodities

The aim of the Government is to have at least one fair price shop in each Revenue Village. The District Collectors have been empowered to open Fair Price Shops as per the guidelines prescribed. No cardholder should walk more than 2 kilometres distance and maximum number of cards attached to a shop should not exceed 800 in the case of urban areas and 500 in the case of rural areas. However, with the objective of reaching the essential commodities to the cardholders in remote and far-flung areas, more than 20,000 shops are run with less than this number of cards each. 36 mobile Fair Price Shops are functioning to cater to the needs of cardholders in remote areas.

Table 7.3 : Method of Distribution of Essential Commodities under PDS

Sl. No.	*Agency*	*Full Time*	*Part Time*	*Total*
1.	Tamil Nadu Civil Supplies Corporation	1091	58	1149
2.	Co-operatives (Under the Registrar of Co-operative Societies)	21656	4634	26290
3.	Other Co-operatives (Fisheries, Plantations etc.)	149	9	158
4.	Women Fair Price Shops	367	174	541
5.	Mobile fair price shops run by co-operatives	36	—	36
	Total	**23299**	**4875**	**28174**

Source: Policy Note 2005-06, Demand No. 12, *Department of Cooperation, Food and Consumer Protection*, Government of Tamil Nadu, p. 8.

More than 93 per cent of the fair price shops of Tamil Nadu are managed by co-operatives. It shows the extensive involvement of the Co-operative Societies in serving the rural people by taking steps to supply essential commodities in the right time at affordable prices. In addition to the regular and full-time FPS, the Department of

Co-operation has established part-time FPS in villages. It enables the villagers to purchase the essential commodities in the nearby places.

Off-Take of Rice

The supply and off-take of rice in PDS are shown in Table 7.4:

Table 7.4 : Production, Procurement, Allotment and Off-take of Rice in Tamil Nadu

Sl. No.	*Particulars*	*1990-91*	*1995-96*	*1999-2000*
1.	Production	57.82	52.90	75.32
2.	Procurement	13.86	03.40	13.72
3.	Percentage of Procurement to Production	23.97	06.43	18.22
4.	Allotment*	9.20	14.55	18.15
5.	Total Supply to the PDS	23.06	17.95	31.87
6.	Off-take in PDS	12.33	15.04	22.11
7.	Percentage of Off-take to Supply	53.47	83.79	69.38

Note: *Allotment from Central Pool.

The procurement by government varies year to year. The allotment from the central pool is around 9-18 lakh tonnes showing that this allotment is crucial to sustain distribution through PDS. It shows that the state is not self-reliant for the supply of rice required for PDS distribution.

Secondly, in the short period of 10 years, off-take in PDS has increased from 12.33 lakh tonnes to 22.11 lakh tonnes, and it may not be entirely due to increase in number of cardholders. Therefore, at least a part of the increase in off-take may be due to the benefit passing on to the not really poor families (GoI & Academic Foundation, 2005).

The total requirement of rice including AAY under PDS is about 2,17,222 MTs. per month. Government of India monthly allotment of rice is 1,31,050 MTs for BPL 3,05,665 MTs for APL and 39,148 MTs for AAY. The present off-take of rice including AAY is around 2,06,473 MTs (GoTN FCPD-Policy Note, 2005-06). The State Government lifts the entire BPL allotment of rice, out of the Government of India allotment and whenever required, the State Government lifts the required quantity of rice under APL allotment. There is no problem in the distribution of rice under PDS in the State.

Under Targeted Public Distribution System the Government of India issue rice at the rate of Rs. 830 per quintal for APL allotment and Rs. 565

per quintal for BPL allotment and Rs. 300 per quintal for AAY allotment. Except the Antyodaya Anna Yojana Cardholders, all other rice-option cardholders are supplied with rice at a uniform price of Rs. 3.50 per kg. The State Government subsidises the difference between the actual cost of rice obtained through procurement of paddy under Decentralised Procurement System and the economic cost of the same fixed by the Government of India and also subsidises the difference between the central issue price of rice and the State issue price. Rice is supplied to that Antyodaya Anna Yojana cardholders at Rs. 3 per kg as fixed by the Government of India.

Table 7.5 : Details of PDS Coverage and Shift in Emphasis

Five Year Plan	*PDS Coverage and Shift in Emphasis*
I.	Distribution of foodgrains through statutory rationing system in cities and towns having above 50,000 population and highly-deficit areas.
II.	Besides foodgrains, coverage of other essential commodities.
III.	Public procurement and distribution system for price stabilization and introduction of institutional changes in private trade through inclusion of consumer co-operatives.
IV.	Extension of PDS to rural areas and distribution of other goods of mass consumption with the help of co-operatives.
V.	Focus on the poor and PDS was linked to prices, income and wage-policy.
VI.	Distribution of foodgrains to the disadvantaged groups.
VII.	Inclusion of PDS as one of the Minimum Needs Programmes.
VIII.	Intensification of PDS in rural/disadvantaged areas covering several mass-consumption articles (salt, pulses, soaps, tea, etc.) besides the mandatory commodities (rice, wheat, sugar, edible oil, kerosene and soft-coke) and development of infrastructure.
IX.	Inclusion of nutrition security as one of food securities.
X.	Transparency and Management of PDS by ensuring proper supply, computerized billing and maintenance of records for inspection.

Source: Government of Tamil Nadu, *Tamil Nadu an Economic Appraisal,* 2001-02, p. 146.

Food Subsidy

The difference between procurement price (MPS) and the issue price is the subsidy to be met by the government. In the procurement and distribution, and there are three varieties of rice viz., common (or coarse), fine, and superfine.

It may be seen that procurement prices have gone up nearly three-folds by 1997-98, while the issue prices were allowed to rise only marginally. As a result, food subsidy has reached a high of Rs. 1500 crore in 2006-07. Annual Dialogue on Hunger Free Programme conducted by the MSSRF in April 2006 records that except for 1993-94, the food subsidy was less than three per cent of total government expenditures in the early 1990s. From 1997-98 onwards, the share has been above three per cent. Estimated from GDP point of view, share of food subsidy was around 0.48 at the beginning of the decade, it was 0.7 in 1993-94, and has been a little over 0.5 after the introduction of the TPDS. So, the food subsidy accounts for roughly half per cent of GDP (Madhura Swaminathan, 2003).

Table 7.6 : Food Subsidy of Tamil Nadu Government

Sl. No.	*Year*	*Amount (in crores)*
1.	1990-1991	219.31
2.	1995-1996	615.00
3.	2000-2001	1540.00
4.	2001-2002	1240.00
5.	2002-2003	1240.00
6.	2003-2004	800.00
7.	2004-2005	835.00
8.	2005-2006	1200.00

Source: Government of Tamil Nadu, *Statistical Hand Book,* 2005, Department of Economics and Statistics, Chennai.

An Outline of Reform Measures

One of the central concerns of the economic reform process that was initiated in 1991 was to limit the quantum of explicit and implicit subsidies as well as other forms of non-plan expenditures (Singh L.P., 2004). The Tenth Plan (2002-07) Documents point out that the level of government subsidies granted on food rose from Rs. 24.5 billion to Rs. 212 billion between 1990-91 and 2002-03. And in 2004-05, it again rose to Rs. 277.5 billion. Most of the increase are said to have been spent on administration rather than on productive purposes. To check mismanagement of funds, while guaranteeing food security, the Tenth Plan Documents put across the government to explore the effectiveness of the Food Security Programme (FSP), and proposed that each eligible household should be given documents specifying the number of household members, their age and entitlement which would determine the number of stamps given to them per month. The target households would then collect stamps each month from prescribed distribution centres and use them at the retail outlets to buy rice and wheat, and the State Governments would subsequently reimburse the retailers (Debshis Chakraborthy, 2005). Although this idea initially received appreciation, after finding out similar schemes have failed in other countries, it started being viewed with skepticism.

Targeted Food Stamp Programme is a dangerous path to tread argues Ms. Madhura Swaminthan of the MSSRF on the grounds that such a scheme will exclude a large number of needy persons from the food distribution system, erode the value of the subsidy to those who receive benefits and undermine the existing network of fair price shops. Moreover, food stamps entitle a household to a fixed value of purchase, not a fixed quantity of grain, and there is no assurance if retailers would participate in the programme to make it a success (Madhura Swaminthan, 2004). It is also quoted that in Andhra Pradesh following people's protests against the food coupons, the scheme was withdrawn.

In recent years, there are several moves made by the Central Government to restructure FCI or to completely hand over the operations to private sector. Different Committees have recommended varied measures—some dismantling FCI based on the premise that it has become unwieldy, others recommending of strengthening FCI on the grounds that FCI has performed remarkably well in the task assigned to it for the past 40 years. Any reform attempt should only aim at improving its performance rather than dismantling it. In the present situation of the country, particularly the uneven development of markets, any dismantling or privatization of the FCI is likely to adversely affect the goal of food security. Similarly, the Essential Commodities Act was found to be a distortion to private trade and as part of the reform and liberalization measures, it has been abolished on the grounds that ECA is required as an emergency measure during war time or during a tsunami, and it need not be operational all the time.

The Agreement on Agriculture has indicated ceiling and reduction on government subsidies and other forms of domestic support to agriculture. India has played only defensive interests here and has, in fact, suggested a Food Security Box as well. The WTO prescribes an Aggregate Measure of Support (AMS) to be 10 per cent of the total value of production. However, it permits for providing cheap food to poor consumers, and public stock holding to ensure food security.

The Food Security Box

Food security consequent to trade liberalization in agriculture is one of the important issues that have come to the fore in India. The shift of emphasis from subsistence-farming to cash-crops is very much visible from the declining foodgrains production and upsurge in commercial crops. Many argue that this is a mind-set brought about by globalization – the shift from 'food-first to export-first policies'.

Another alarm raised is that WTO through AoA negotiations threatens food security of the poor in India, and that it is making moves to close down the Food Corporation of India (FCI). They also state that the World Bank and other international organizations advise gradual phasing out of PDS because of the high food subsidy bill the government has to foot every year.

The way negotiations are made India seems to be cautious with regard to safeguarding agriculture and food security from being affected by trade negotiations. Even the WTO Chief has given statements very recently that India plays fast when it comes to services-negations, especially the Information Sector opening up, whereas it wants to take only defensive interests when it comes to agriculture. It is reported that India officially proposed a Food Security Box along the lines of the Green, Blue and Amber Boxes relating to subsidies in its submission to the AoA negotiations. The Food Security Box asks that measures for poverty alleviation, rural development and diversification of agriculture, should be exempt from reductions. The Indian submission has also asked for continuation of the safeguard mechanism allowed under Article 5 of the AoA, to introduce quantitative restrictions in the event of import surges so as to protect domestic markets and domestic producers. These are good steps. The Civil Society Orgnizations in India need to keep an eye on that and that the negotiators stand by this position.

Another provision mentioned about food subsidy and poverty as far as WTO is concerned is that there are legitimate provisions such as Special and Differential Treatment (SDT) on food security that provides safeguards on a regular basis at subsidized prices for meeting the food requirement of the poor. However, provisions of the AoA are still under negotiation and it plays unfavourable role only to certain extent. What makes food insecurity predictable is the trade-oriented-culture that the AoA emanates in Tamil Nadu agriculture – many of them sponsored by the government – either at the centre or at the state.

Therefore, the fear with regard to food insecurity in India or specifically in Tamil Nadu stems from aspects such as:

(i) Globalization permits entry of MNCs for setting up production organizations in the villages that are close to cities/towns. They exploit the livelihood resources such as ground water, land, river, etc. of the people who are already resource-poor. In other words, allowing the livelihood resources being used for commercial purposes, and thereby depriving the local people's traditional rights on the use of such resources for making a living might eventually lead to problems of food insecurity.

(ii) Globalization might accelerate the general trend of declining area under food crops because of high in-put costs and the growing suspicion that (because of opening up) the Minimum Support Price (MSP) might be withdrawn by the government.

(iii) In the recent past, the encouragement shown by the Department of Agriculture is mainly towards commercial and horticultural crops (with export orientation). This might lead to neglect of food crops and consequently it might lead to food insecurity. In other words, neglect of food crops in order to promote commercial and horticultural crops does not augur well for India in terms of food security.

(iv) The declining water table in many parts of the state encourages many farmers to go in for tree crops or fruit-bearing tree crops or as a coping strategy cultivate only a portion of the land. It might consequently lead to food insecurity.

(v) The talk about privatization of power sector (which would halt free electricity for agriculture) sends shock waves that if electricity for agriculture was charged agriculture would be completely non-remunerative. It might further reduce area under cultivation.

(vi) The general culture that is spreading even among agriculturists is that 'cash-income-first', and food is a commodity that can be purchased at markets. These are some speculations that even availability of food might turn out to be a problem unless timely interventions are made to improve area under food crop cultivation. Farmers involved in food crop production are encouraged and protected.

MICRO-LEVEL ANALYSIS

Residents Vulnerable to Starvation

People in cities and towns are generally involved in some kind of assured employment in industries or in the service sector. No matter whether they are permanent employees or casual labourers they gain access to cash income and thereby, they gain access to food security. In fact, for many of them food security is no big deal. The kind of poverty statements they make are: *'owners pride neighbours envy'*. 'My neighbour has a motor bike and I have only a moped' is the kind of poverty such people are in, which is called relative poverty*.

People who live in abject poverty and those who really suffer from starvation are in rural areas, in urban slums and in tribal villages. Those who live in remote villages are worse than those who live in road-side villages or in villages that are close to urban centres; even in villages dry-land holders are more vulnerable to food insecurity than those who own wet lands. One irony found in many of the villages, and which has been proved in some of the studies also is that the working class seem to be in a better position than the landed-class, due to factors such as indebtedness associated with crop failure.

There are also seasonal dimensions to food security issue. There are some months of a year people feel secure about food and during the other months, by and large, they need to be completely dependent on the food aid programme of the government. This again can be applied to areas that are rain-fed and those that are well-irrigated. In a spell of four-five years, there are good years and lean years in terms of harvest which in turn determines the state of food security.

Chain of Interviews and a series of Focus Group Discussions held with 24 rural and tribal villages of varied nature in five districts of Tamil Nadu viz. Pudukottai, Ramnathapuram, Dharmapuri, Krishnakiri and Dindigul, revealed several interesting information on rural food security, coping strategies of the poor in surviving food insecurity, the role of PDS in ensuring food security, and other local practices that traditionally exist for ensuring food security.

---

*Although this is generally true of urban areas, one segment of urban population who should be excluded from this description is the urban-slum dwellers. Those who live in urban slums, often, suffer conditions which are very bad.

Rural Livelihoods—The Base that Ensures Food Security

Before analyzing why people have to starve or how people manage food security, it is appropriate to understand the livelihood base of the people who are supposed to be vulnerable to food insecurity. Livelihood is the means to earn one's living. Livelihood in turn comprises three important elements viz., Assets, Capabilities, and Activities. Although it sounds as simple as that, essentially any rural livelihood hinges on these three elements only. Therefore, an analysis of these three elements (livelihood analysis) assumes significance in order to understand the potential of each of the livelihood source in ensuring food security of the people who depend on such livelihood ventures.

Assuming that Tamil Nadu villages have principally the landed class, the working class, and the traditional artisans spread across in small proportion, this study has focused its analysis into these categories of rural population, viz., (1) the Landed Class, (2) the Working Class, and (3) the Rural Artisans. Studying the 'asset categories' plus the 'capabilities' of various categories of rural population and how they perform 'activities' in order to make a living would answer several of the questions relating to food security. This is based on the premise that all the livelihood activities necessarily have to lead to earning either cash income or food income. This serves as the basic intent of putting to use assets and capabilities into activities.

BOX 7.2

Charcoal Making for a Livelihood

Some people in Ramanathapuram and Pudukottai live by making charcoal from karuvel trees. Where there are matured karuvel trees they take the land on contract, fell the trees and split into woodlots for charcoal making. The land owner would just walk off with the money agreed upon. It is upto the charcoal maker to cut trees down and transport them to place where he would make charcoal. Somebody who buys wood for Rs. 3000 can sell them off for Rs. 5000 converting the woodlots into charcoal. It requires men for cutting trees, transporting the wood pieces, being close-by watching and watering day-and-night so that woods don't burn out on fire. The entire process would require about 12–15 days and about 20 person-days. One big source of employment and earning in Ramanathapuram district, especially during dry season is cutting karuvel trees and charcoal making.

Asset Categories: The asset categories of the landed class usually includes physical resources like land, well, pump sets, cattle, etc., natural resources like water, sun shine, etc., financial resources although could be weak, they have local banks or money-lenders they can borrow from. In addition, they have their human capital to work in the farm or supervise farm operations. One important drawback with those in dry regions is that they lack some of the assets like well, pump sets, and water, which, often, deprives them of gaining access to institutional sources of credit. This becomes a hurdle in carrying out livelihood activities, thereby crumbling the flow of cash income and food security. Those who live in wet regions have an edge over the others in this regard.

The artisans or working class have their own assets such as agricultural implements, and tools meant to carry out their works. For artisans, although the physical assets they possess (meaning the tools they work with) are vital, more than anything else, their capabilities assume paramount importance. Cattle population is seen as a common physical asset in many of the dry regions. One social asset generally seen in many of the villages is Self-Help Groups (SHGs). It serves as a constant source of money for farm-related investments and to be able to meet unexpected (contingent) expenses.

Capabilities: The capabilities associated with the rural population we refer to, although are special, cannot be banked upon as one can do with the skill of a person in the industries or in the service sector. Moreover, even the villagers who possess such skills do not consider it a specialized livelihood, skill because they acquired it by traditional practice and handed-down experience and not through any formal training. The capabilities of some of the artisans such as handloom weavers, blacksmiths, and goldsmiths etc. are fast being replaced by mechanized processes. In the economies of scale, often, the activities carried out with local capabilities are found to be economically unviable. Therefore, while on the one hand the livelihood resources of the poor are reportedly shrinking, the capabilities of those in villages are becoming not very much sought after. Hence the value attached to such capabilities is fading. Consequently their food security is at stake, unless they find alternative avenues of making use of their skills.

Activities: Owing to problems such as water scarcity, increasing in-put-cost in agriculture and unassured prices for agricultural commodities in the market, the marginal addition of employment force into agriculture is, year after year, heading towards almost zero. It could be seen in the villages that those who are above 35-40 years of age and who inherited agriculture from their parents carry it on, by and large, in half of the land area they possess, with grumblings though. Whereas many of the youngsters have a tendency to move towards the urban centres in search of casual employment in construction works, mills, brick-kilns, as fast-food centres, and in all kinds of errands.

Talking about livelihood activities in the villages, milch animal rearing, goat and sheep rearing retain the same place it possessed years ago, despite the fact that their number has come down drastically over the years. Although considered as an activity allied to agriculture (or secondary occupation), milch animal rearing, goats and sheep rearing activity is retaining many of the marginal and small farmers in the villages still—meaning it serves as an explanation for not migrating. It gives the solace and salvation to absorb seasonal shocks and trends, these people are vulnerable to.

Surviving Food Insecurity

In almost all the study villages (24 villages covering five districts) one prime source of supply of essential commodities for both the *landed class* and the *working class* is PDS. PDS apart, the sources that effectively ensure food security for the landed class and working class are subtly different. For the 'landed class' the other sources that ensure food security are: (i) the paddy harvested in their land, and (ii) the cash income they earn after selling the agricultural produces. With cash income, they go for exchange, of essential commodities required, from (a) the Fair Price Shops (on ration basis), and (b) obtain the rest from the informal open markets/merchants who deal in rice. These informal, open markets are one of the main players in meeting the essential commodity requirements when the PDS delays providing rationed items, and in filling the gap between what the PDS offers and the actual need of any given community.

For the 'working class' the sources that effectively ensure food security are essentially two: (i) the cash income one earns as wages; and (ii) wages received in kind. The practice of paying in kind especially by farmers who harvest paddy is widely prevalent in many districts of the state. An average worker gets about 10 kg of paddy in exchange of one full day's work. The wages received in kind (paddy) is considered significant because in one harvesting season an average family earns 4-5 bags of paddy which is the second source of food security – the first being PDS. Whatever may be the occupation one is involved in, during paddy harvesting season, many a rural family have the practice of going for paddy harvest, especially, to earn wages in terms of paddy which sustains life of the entire family for 2- 3 months in a year. This is true of remote dry villages also where, in place of paddy, they get *ragi*, as most of them cultivate only *ragi* as a rain-fed crop.

The third source is the 'informal markets' (Rice merchants or grocers who deal in rice) that operate. These are small traders who sell essential commodities such as rice, groceries and vegetables for a price. This is, of course the last resort that the rural poor approach, but it is unavoidable to buy from informal merchants as the supply of essential commodities a given community get from the earlier two sources (i.e, PDS and kind-component of wages) are always insufficient to ensure food security of the family for an entire year.

The description given above relates only to a normal year. During slack seasons and during a year of dry spell, the 'kind-income' component (paddy in wet regions and *ragi* in dry regions) fail to find place in their food basket. Nor would they have cash income to buy rice or *ragi* from informal markets. This is the time they become indebted or sell off assets such as goat or sheep to ensure the food security of the family. This is the time they tend to migrate in search of alternative employments in the town. All the three sources put together, coupled with the coping strategies indicated at the end, is what surviving food insecurity in Tamil Nadu means.

Community Grain Banks: At this juncture, it would be appropriate to mention about 'traditional grain banks' and 'traditional grain storage system'. In some villages, both on the plains and in some fishermen villages, there have been common grain banks in existence, to be used during rough months/lean seasons. Such arrangements have been supported by governmental assistance and aid agencies (such as MSSRF/World Food Programme initiatives in Orissa) as well. They are exceptions that can make special case studies, but they are not in vogue widely for coverage with the idea of generalization.

Household Grain Storage System: Similarly, there used to be grain storage system (made of mud or wood – called *granary*) at the household level in many land-owners, houses, with capacities to contain 4-5 bags of grains, to 40-50 bags. Now, they only serve the purpose of offering a nostalgic memory of agricultural families as to how they used to harvest paddy and other grains in plenty those days. Those that were made of mud (small in size) are hardly anywhere to be found now. The one in wood (bigger one) serves purely for the nostalgia. The reduction in the yield of foodgrains, and reduction in foodgrain crops in general have made such granaries irrelevant today. Moreover, the practice of cashing paddy/grains immediately after harvest has made granaries unwanted.

Livestock and Small-Stock — As Buffer against Starvation

Although agriculture has assumed a prime place in providing the means of living for majority of the rural population in Tamil Nadu, the irony is that it has been one of the most undependable livelihood activities known to human kind. The undependable nature of agriculture does not need elaboration or substantiation. The rural people are often displeased that agriculture failed due to: failure of the monsoon, pest attack, cyclone, and so on. No matter season cared or uncared; no matter it rained or shined, the cows, buffalos, goats and sheep have cared and rendered food security to majority of the rural population – ALWAYS. Rearing livestock (milch animals) and small-stock (sheep, goat, hens etc.) although are considered as secondary occupation or 'allied occupation', as it may be called by Questionnaire Survey Managers, they, indeed, render the solace, support and food security to many a rural household especially during slack seasons and at times of lean harvests.

If PDS is one of the reasons for non-occurrence of farmers' suicides in Tamil Nadu, the practice of rearing milch animals, goats and sheep can definitely be attributed as another factor that has helped prevent farmers' suicide in Tamil Nadu State. In districts like Dindigul, Pudukottai, and Dharmapuri there are families that earn Rs. 500–Rs. 750 per week selling milk, with little expenditure on fodder. As many of the milk producers cooperative societies are declining towards dormancy, the private milk procurement centres (for manufacturing 'pocket milk') procure milk from villages, and make weekly disbursal of sale proceeds. The money thus received helps them buy their ration from the Fair Price Shops.

BOX 7.3

Recreating a Life in Unwanted Sacks

Mootampatty village at Andakulam Block is a small village in Pudukottai district of Tamil Nadu. A section of the people in this village makes a living by peeling off old cement/fertilizer sacks thread-by-thread and, recreating it as rope for various utilities. They enumerate a shopping list of utilities the different types of ropes can be put to. Out of the thread, they get from two sacks they are able to make seven metres of rope. The process involved is similar to coir-making. They have a wheel-shaped tool which stands installed on the ground. When one person rotates the wheel, another person walks backwards carefully feeding the assorted threads to get one rope done. But the material used is not coir but unwanted sack threads.

It requires, generally three persons to carry out this work. They earn a minimum of Rs. 300 a day which means each person earns Rs. 100 a day. Reportedly, the ropes they make are in good demand in the village markets. They sell the ropes either in the rural grocery shops or directly like an itinerant seller of ropes wandering on village streets. They also send their products to places like Thanjavur, Kumbakonam and Mannarkudi etc. The money they earn enables them to buy ration from the Fair Price Shop. They have some small-stock such as goat, sheep, and hens as buffer during rainy days.

These livestock and small-stock (cow, buffalo, sheep, goat, and hen) serve as rescue and sustenance during seasonal trends and shocks. So, if each milch animal is a source of steady and stable flow of income to a poor household; each one of the small-stock—be it a goat or a sheep or a hen—is a kitty to cash in on when the family is in financial crunch, such as meeting the unexpected medical expenses, marriage of a close relative, expenses that come with sudden death of a family member, replacing the worn-out thatches and so on. Hence, livestock and small-stock provide buffering effects providing milk or cash at otherwise lean times. It also puts off the need to migrate.

There are farmers in Gujiliamparai Block of Dindigul who are settling their crop (failure) loan by the income they earn from the milch animals. The FGDs conducted in several villages in Dindigul and Pudukottai districts reveal that as sanctioned by custom, agriculture could be primary. But when it comes to actual living, it is these assets that offer practical sanction and assume primacy to sustain rural life. They provide silent salvation to food security problems that the rural households face any time of the year—irrespective of seasons and trends. Given this revelation it becomes imperative for the Village Panchayats to safeguard the common grassing grounds and pasture development to be able to ensure household food security at the village level. This is important in the sense that food security of the cattle population needs to be ensured as well to be able to sustain the food security of a section of rural population.

Food Security for the Cattle Population

Three important problems they face with regard to rearing animals are:

(i) Fodder during drought season;
(ii) Medical expenses of the cattle, especially when the family is in distress; and
(iii) Availability of pasture land. With regard to availability of fodder there are seasonal variations – such as green-fodder and dry-fodder.

During a drought year, like men starve for food, the animals also starve for food and water. Animals do not get green-fodder. They get only dry-fodder such as *seethakai (pods of Juliflora)** and not green grass or green leaves. It revealed that villagers have learnt to laugh their agony out, when they said: "*Sir, during drought seasons: ration rice for the man and seethakai for the goat*". It is as much pathetic as it is interesting when the villagers draw a parallel between 'ration rice' (rice supplied under PDS) and *seethakai*. So, during a good monsoon, the animals get green-fodder and man gets fresh rice (often, earned as kind component of wages) and during a lean harvest the man is dependent more on the PDS, and the animals look up for to feed on *seethakai*.

The goats, it is reported, fall ill if they continuously feed on *seethakai* for a few days. The villagers could hold themselves back from going to a doctor, if they fell ill. But they would not dare keep the goat without immediately taking it to a veterinary doctor, as it is his important asset. It is reported that the veterinary doctors would not attend to the case

---

*A kind of beans-like dry yellow pods that grow from a wild and thorny drought-prone plant (*prosofis Juliflora*), often called "introduced weed". It grows and multiplies on its own in degraded soil all over Tamil Nadu. The wood and stems are used for making charcoal in dry regions. Goats feed on the pods during drought seasons.

unless they are assured of an immediate payment of fees. In such situations and for purchasing the medicines required, the villagers sell a goat to be able to save the lives of the remaining cattle. It happens for purchasing fortified (or prepared) fodder for milch animals purchased on loan. That is, to be able to feed the animals, especially milch animals, during a drought season, the rural people have to sell off one or two of their goats or sheep.

BOX 7.4
Micro-indicatives of Macro Perils

Water is at once an essential element and a prime determinant of food security. A case in point that proves this could be widely noticed in Ramanathapuram and Pudukottai districts, especially during drought years. Lands with fertile soil being put to cultivate – or rather allowed bushy growth of – Prosofis Juliflora (Karuvel maram as it is called in Tamil) is commonly found in several places.

The story goes like this. In some parts of Ramanathapuram and Pudukottai districts (Kamuthakudi village in Paramakudi Block, of Ramanathapuram, and in some of the villages in Kundandarkoil Block of Pudukottai for example) due to water scarcity, some farmers cultivate a portion of the land and deliberately allow natural growth of prosofis Juliflora (Karuvel maram in Tamil) in the rest of the area. The reason stated is: 'no water to cultivate foodgrains and cultivating Juliflora does not require water'. Their contention is that in stead of keeping the land uncultivated for want of water, cultivating Karuvel maram in one acre of land gives yield upto Rs. 10,000 to Rs. 15,000 within a period of 3-4 years. They are able to sell it off to people who make a living by making charcoal. It requires no watering, no fertilizer, and no supervision. From a Panchayat called Parthibanoor in Paramakudi Block charcoal is transported by goods train to cater to the demands in north Indian towns as well. Practically speaking, cultivating Juliflora and making a living through charcoal making can be taken as indicators of 'drought proneness'. Living in drought-prone conditions and choosing to cultivate Juliflora does not auger well in terms of food security.

Talking from a macro perspective and from the angle of 'national food security' this is dangerous – giving up foodgrains cultivation for want of water for irrigation. But from the micro 'household food security' point of view – that is the household to which such lands belong – it is practically an intelligent idea to earn upto Rs. 15,000 within a period of 3 years with almost zero-production costs. Nor are there any risks involved. Communities understand the household food security matters fairly

(Contd.)

(Contd.)

clearer rather than the national food security. Their point of view seems to be: 'think micro and de-link macro'. For them, household food security matters more. When irrigation infrastructures are not taken care of by the state or community governance systems, individual households tend to take to recourse of this kind. This suggests that irrigation infrastructure and water storage structures play an important role in ensuring food security – at the household level, community level, and at the national level. And the neglect of irrigation infrastructure or agriculture for that matter might end up in the farming community losing faith in agriculture leading to large scale dangers in terms of food security.

Providing rice at Rs. 2.00 a kg is viewed as an expenditure proposal. It is true that it is an expenditure proposal. But, budgetary allocation for creating and reconstructing irrigation infrastructures should be viewed as an investment proposal and not as an expenditure proposal.

All common lands, not necessarily the pasture land, in the villages serve for the purpose of grassing by animal population in most villages. Some of them being classified as 'waste-land'. The government planning to take them away for commercial purposes and for the cultivation of plants such *'jetropha'* is not welcome. The Village Panchayats might be made use of, in removing encroachments and in developing pasture lands.

Employment and Wages

As most Tamil Nadu villages are agrarian, rural employment is chancy and is determined by, whether it rains or shines. There are months in a year of good rain fall when it would be difficult to get labour for employment due to the fact that immediately after rains, every farmer wants to initiate agricultural operations. This simultaneousness in availability of employment all over and *vice versa* is one serious problem that sustains rural unemployment. Another interesting revelation is where varied cropping patterns (multiple crops such as fruits, flower, some variety of foodgrains – Muruganpatty, Athoor Block, in Dindigul district) are practiced, employment seems to be available for more than 200 days per year. But where people depend on cultivation of a single crop (S. Pudukottai, Gujiliamparai Block in Dindigul district), employment availability is much less (about 115-135 days/year).

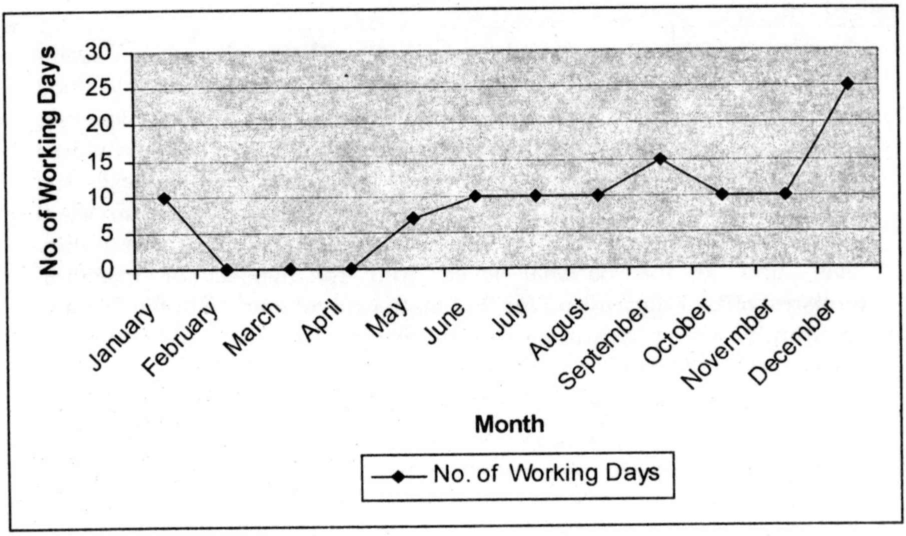

Fig. 7.1: Employment in a Single Crop Village (S. Pudukottai)

During bad years (and dry seasons within a year) when labour supply is abundant, it becomes far more serious, prompting migration. It shows that availability of employment in rural areas is not stable and it reflects in wages and purchasing power also, which determines food security. This undependability is one of the reasons why people do not trust agriculture and start looking for employment in other sectors.

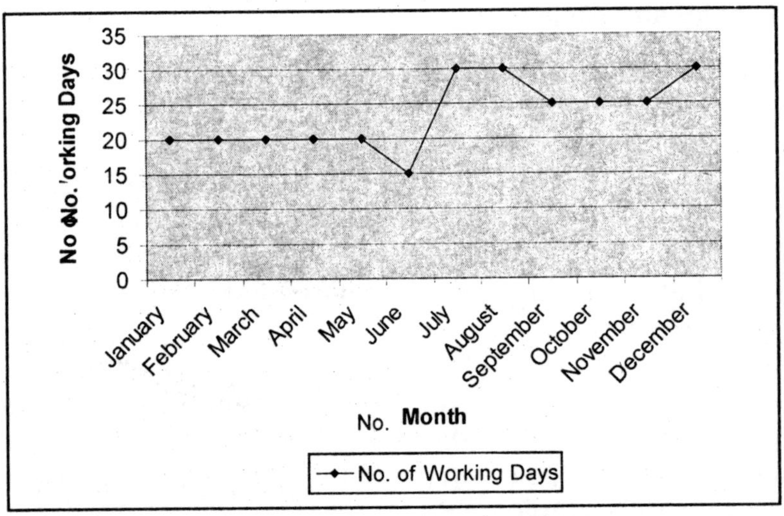

Fig. 7.2 : Employment in a Multi-crop Village (Murugampatty)

Another gut-feeling that this study has come out with, which requires further verification is that mechanization of agriculture has replaced mostly men's employment in agriculture rather than women's. It is not only the non-remunerative nature of agriculture that has brought about the phenomenon of feminization of agriculture, but also mechanization. The number of days people get employment in two of the study villages is presented in Fig. 7.2.

The Migration Factor

Migration from rural to urban centres is widely prevalent all over Tamil Nadu. The tempo of migration is becoming faster year after year. Several questions linger here, they include: Is it that agriculture is often a failure and more a drudgery, so the villagers have lost faith in agriculture and as a result are they migrating? The modern agriculture and mechanization in agriculture have left little scope for the human labour in agriculture and as a result they are migrating. The shift from subsistence farming to commercial cultivation has made the in-put costs of cultivation more and so agriculture has become non-remunerative and so are they migrating. Tamil Nadu in general is fast on the urbanization track and so is the attraction to urban centres. Then again, which segment of rural population is migrating?

Migratory Patterns : The last question assumes overriding importance to be able to answer several of the questions. That is, which segment (age group) of population migrates? Where do they migrate? What is the basic intent behind this migration—is it food security or things beyond food security?

During the discussions held in several villages regarding the migration factor, from rural areas to urban centres, there are two segments noticed and two patterns noticed. The two segments are: (a) those between 30-45 years of age; and (b) those between 15-30 years of age. The people of the former segment (30-45 years) are usually either unlettered or have had only little education and migrate to places like Kerala or Karnataka in search of unskilled manual labour in farms and for cutting woods in hilly terrains. This kind of migration takes place only when there is no employment available locally or in the vicinity. The basic intent is food security of the family. Either the head of the household or the entire family migrates. Though not in a massive scale this kind of migration takes place to a considerable extent. This is what is, perhaps called, transient migration—migration for a brief period in a year. They would return home once it starts raining in their native

BOX 7.5

Thatch-makers of Pudukottai

Although urban areas are flooded with concrete and tiled houses, the thatches made of coconut leaves are still in high demand in rural areas. They are used primarily as roofing materials and in some cases as sidewalls of houses also. Thatches have several uses from making a cowshed to putting up a pandal for a political party meeting. One community group in Themmandampatty village (Andanur), Pudukottai district make a living making thatches. They procure coconut leaves from places like Killukottai, clean and shape them up in the coconut farm itself, transport them as lorry loads, make thatches and sell them. In their opinion, the demand for thatches is not crumbling. They sell 100 pieces of thatches for Rs. 150. They are able to make 100 thatches from 50 pieces of coconut leaves, which they buy at Re. 1 each. The main expenses involved are cleaning and shaping up, lorry hire and the number of days the family spends in making the thatches. During paddy harvesting season they go for harvesting in order to get the kind-component of wages as paddy which serves as food security for a few months. Otherwise, they buy their daily ration from the PDS shops.

villages/districts. This takes place when all local livelihood options are closed due to drought and absence of agricultural operations. *So, the urge or the basic instinct is food security of the family especially during bad months.* The aged persons in the family take care of the goats or sheep in the house and all able-bodied ones in the family migrate in search of making a means of living.

The people of the latter segment (15-30 years) usually have had at least school education and have picked up informal training in some specific skills such as the ones required for a hosiery industry, for varied jobs in construction works (helpers, masons, rod benders), to work in bus tinkering workshops etc. Many of them often join as unskilled labourers or helpers in a semi-skilled kind of work and pick up the tricks of the trade by associating themselves with running errands.

Under this segment, there is at least one person (mostly a male youth) from several of the villages in Tamil Nadu who has migrated to either Thiruppur or Chennai. Other places on the second stair are Coimbatore, Erode, Karur and Sivakasi. He ensures food security for his parents in the village, especially during drought season. With money he sends or brings home, the family is able to buy rice at the Fair Price

Shop or from the informal open markets. If there is any improvement in the standard of living of that family, it is because of his efforts from the town. This kind of migration facilitates cash-inflow into the family—into the village and thereby food security of the family is guaranteed. For migrant labourers Thiruppur, and Chennai are the most preferred places in Tamil Nadu.

Many of the youths who migrate this way, do not want to return home and settle down, except financially supporting the family in the village. Whatever precarious may be the condition, many of them prefer to stay on in the urban slums and earn cash income unlike their parents who are involved in subsistence farming contented with food security. These youngsters do not mind frequently changing their work place (company or the industry they work for) in their attempt to get better income/wages. Their prime intent is earning cash income and thereby secure food and other comforts of life that the city introduced them to. As far as the employers who employ them are concerned, they are almost nomads or drifters. They might be living in urban slums, but in the opinion of these youngsters, change in the culture, and urban life style they are introduced to require them to strongly feel cash income an imperative if one has to move in the ladder of life with stairs such as Survival—Security—Respect—Improved Standard of Living.

There is a third segment that belongs to almost the same age group (25-35 year) who have employment in the town as a fall back proposition and agriculture as the permanent proposition. They are partly transient and partly permanent migrants. It need not be Thiruppur or Chennai. It can be any town close-by. During agriculturally off-season, they become casual labourers in non-agricultural sector in the town. In other words, they are in their native place when agricultural works are its peak in the village, and on employment at Thiruppur/Chennai during non-season/drought seasons.

Another pattern noticed is that almost all the urban centres, say the district headquarters or the town that is fast developing becomes a place for absorbing the rural youth who spill out or opt out of agriculture in villages. This basic instinct is earning cash income and a spotless understanding that agriculture is undependable to improve one's standard of living. They claim cash income can ensure both food security as well as better standards of living whereas food-crop cultivation can ensure only food security at the most, if at all it really did. Although urban centres have been attractive and made way for the rural folks to come in; increasing in-put costs in agriculture, deployment of machineries have served as repellent factors to get out of the village and migrate.

Migration in varied forms – transient, permanent etc. – as a strategy of ensuring food security is prevalent in almost all the study villages. All said and done, many a village on the fringe of towns generally depends on the town for casual employment during slack seasons and for selling off agricultural produces such as fruits, vegetables, flowers etc. during peak seasons. So, villages on the rim of towns benefit in a big way earning cash income through employment and sale of agricultural produces. It ensures cash flow into the village and food security to the poor.

Extinction of an Occupation

It is a logical argument if someone puts across that mechanization in agriculture has rendered a handful of agricultural wage earners jobless. That the agricultural wage earners are rendered jobless as a result of mechanization in agriculture is perceptible. It only reflects a consequence of what should happen to agricultural wage earners when machineries are introduced. A visit to Madhanayakanur in Gujiliamparai Block of Dindigul district showed a ring beyond what usually is perceptibly noticed – meaning the next ring of the ripple effect of mechanization in agriculture.

Black-smithy is a traditional-livelihood option that offered a means of living to a particular community. There are 73 households in Madhanayakanur that depended completely on black-smithy. They are dwindling due to mechanization in agriculture. They were mainly making: (1) plough, (2) sickle, (3) horse shoe nail, and (4) sabre. What modernization had in store for them was: *'you are out of date'*. Tractors tailed with ploughshares have contracted the demand for 'animal pulled plough' in the market. Harvesting machine has thrown sickles away; and the considerable reduction in the use of animals (bullocks) for agricultural purposes has reduced the demand for horseshoe nails as well. It is well known that modernization of agriculture as a stimulant for globalization is widespread. That the black-smiths are also joining agricultural wage earners looking for alternative employment as a result of modernization of agriculture needs to be recorded.

Globalization has been a powerful mechanism for spreading new technologies. That it makes occupation of a certain community group obsolete is dismal. The 73 families in this village are fully aware that black-smithy is dying. They are able to narrate what makes their occupation obsolete as well.

Plough and sickle are cheap tools that require simple maintenance. There was no need for fuel to operate them. The hi-tech agriculture, besides increasing the cost of operation in terms of capital investment and fuel, affects the livelihoods of community groups – in this case the black-smiths. This is not the fate of a handful of black-smiths in one village. Provisionally, if we estimate on an average there are at least two black-smiths families in each of the Village Panchayat in Tamil Nadu, this is the fate of not less than 25,000 black-smiths households in the State, with a population that could well cross one lakh.

As a blessing in disguise, the younger generation from this community does not want to take up black-smithy for two distinct reasons: (i) it holds no future, and (ii) it involves a lot of drudgery. Although none of them is educated beyond school level, many of them go to work as casual labourers with bus-body building workshops in *Karur* town. Some of them have learnt carpentry by experience and have joined in wood works involved in bus building. They have learnt by hands-on-experience welding, tinkering, and carpentry and so on. This new skill and mobility has become the life-line of this village now.

PDS, no doubt, has played a vital role in ensuring food security and preventing starvation deaths during all droughts if we consider the years before November last year when torrential rains slashed all over Tamil Nadu. Somebody could argue that the share of PDS in meeting the total food requirements, especially, of the rural poor and those in urban slums, is not even 35-40 per cent. The truth of the fact is PDS, by definition, is one stable and steady source of essential commodities to the rural poor, whereas all the other means of food security are not reliable.

The Place of PDS in the Poor Man's Life

Asked: *"what do you think is the alternative suppose the Government makes a decision to close down PDS"*, one elderly woman at Kallikudi village in Ramanathapuram stated: "With what we should be washing our back, we will have to choose to fill in the front". This clearly conveys the place of PDS in the lives of poor households in Tamil Nadu. FGDs conducted in several villages across four districts in Tamil Nadu put across that in a normal year a poor rural family in Tamil Nadu depends on PDS for about 90-120 days (spread across a year); wages received in kind (usually paddy in wet regions, and *cholam* or *ragi* in dry regions) ensures food security for 75-90 days; and the 'informal markets' (local private merchants who deal in essential commodities) cater to the rest of the 120-150 days in a year.

There is a general impression and it is possible also some earlier studies on PDS had come out with results such as: "*when poor people purchase rice from Fair Price Shops, it is for their own use they buy it. But when they buy sugar it is for selling it in the open market*". This is not true any more. In all the study villages people report, of using sugar for making tea and coffee at home. Even if they don't make milk coffee, they make black coffee and use sugar. If at all they sell, they sell wheat only.

However, it is also true that except in a very few places, diversion of PDS articles to private shops (to open-informal markets) do take place. The alleged reasons found are: (i) as Ration Cards in Tamil Nadu are said to be one basic document of Identity Proof, almost every family—whether one has any intension of using the FPS or not—manages to get a Ration Card. But, often, they do not buy essential commodities, especially rice, wheat and kerosene from FPS. If at all they buy, they buy sugar. That helps the salesman of FPS divert the unsold stock to the private traders who again sell it to the poor people at open-market rates.

The poor people are aware to which private traders are these unsold stock from FPS are diverted. They again buy the same articles at open-market rates from the private trader. On the contrary, there are places like T Keelaiyur Panchayat in Pudukottai district where local youths are used for weighing and measuring the commodities to be distributed to the cardholders. Although there is nothing official about it helps avoid incorrect measurement and corrupt practices.

After witnessing the distress state agriculture is in vis-à-vis the queue in the Fair Price Shops (FPS) in Tamil Nadu, as a non-participant observer and after holding chain of interviews in several different rural villages, this research team is sufficiently convinced to put across categorically that dismantling PDS in the pretext of the exchequer it claims in the government revenue is simply impossible. But one possibility is the price of articles may slightly be enhanced which might, to some extent, reduce the food subsidy bill of the state. But, the political parties in their attempt to exert a pull on votes, announce further reduction in the price of essential commodities. This is a sensitive issue to be investigated.

Footing the Food Subsidy Bill

There are two options, one can think of when it comes to reducing food subsidy bill. Option one is: An effective targeting of the poor instead of making PDS universal. It is this idea of universality that makes food subsidy bill high and helps diversion to open market. One practical suggestion in this regard is the practice of Ration Card being required as a Basic Identity Proof should be done away with. This makes every family hold a card and inadvertently helps diversion, resulting in hefty food subsidy bill. Instead, the Election Identity Card should be made to serve as the basic proof of identity. It can make everyone hold an Election Identity Card which many people do not bother to obtain. Option two is to launch programmes to raise the income levels of the poor in the villages, which eventually would make the people feel standing in queue at the ration shops below their dignity and gradually reduce the number of families that depend on PDS.

As far as India is concerned while the percentages of people living below poverty line is falling, concerns over food security are increasing. One positive thing about Tamil Nadu State is that while hunger deaths are reported from several other states, fortunately Tamil Nadu has not deteriorated to that extent. Public Distribution System (PDS) in Tamil Nadu can be attributed as one of the main reasons for non-occurrence of hungry deaths in Tamil Nadu, notwithstanding the corrupt practices PDS is known for. This is more so during slack seasons and at times of a lean harvest. Focus group discussion conducted in several poorer villages in Tamil Nadu also has endorsed this statement. Be that as it may in terms of nutritive value, with regard to making food articles physically available, the fact remains that PDS meets 25-40 per cent of the food requirements of the 'poor people in the State'. Thus, PDS is one permanent and stable source of rice, wheat, sugar and kerosene at prices that are affordable vis-à-vis the incomes the ultra-poor in the villages and urban slums earn. So, PDS is one necessary scheme for ensuring essential food articles to the rural and urban poor. Despite complaints, majority of the poor still depend on PDS to meet at least ten days' food requirements (in a month) of the family.

The Political Economy of Food Subsidy

As on January 31, 2005, there are 1,85,33,310 family cardholders in Tamil Nadu. There are 27,619 PDS shops in the State, most of them (26,477) run by the co-operatives. The annual State subsidy on PDS articles is Rs. 1870 crores. The subsidy on PDS rice alone is about Rs. 800 crores at the moment. Taking into consideration the heavy food subsidy bill, the government has to foot every year, the government, until before the election, was seriously considering the need to reduce the loss to the exchequer caused by the food subsidy bill.

Things have changed upside down after dates for elections were announced. In the game of political one-upmanship, almost all the political parties in Tamil Nadu are committing themselves to further increase the food subsidy burden of the State. Governments have frequently lost elections on the basis of their action or inaction, actual or alleged, in relation to food. Rice in Tamil Nadu in 1967 and in Andhra Pradesh in 1983, Sugar all over India in 1979, and onions in the North in 1998 have all been credited, rightly or wrongly, with changing political fortunes.

The politics of food is as risky as economics is. And so, the very first item in the political manifesto of various parties in Tamil Nadu in Election 2006 targets 'food security' in variegated forms. With rice at Rs. 2.00 a kg it would cost additional Rs. 560 crore food subsidy bill to the government. Moreover, this goes against the recommendation of the World Bank, and the WTO who keep on saying, "reduce subsidies". The learned and articulate Finance Minister who is a strong supporter of economic reforms and World Bank suggestions, when it comes to election has to face the ordinary people, and so has to flatly says that reducing the price of PDS rice to Rs. 2.00 a kg is feasible.

It all shows that they need us more than we need them. So, with a view to entering the heart of the people (via stomach!), subsidization of PDS articles sits pretty nicely on the election manifesto of various political parties during electioneering; but the 'food subsidy bill' is believed to be a pain in the neck of any political party that forms the government and assumes the office of power.

The inference could be that things that touch upon the life of the ordinary poor man in the society cannot be changed by pressure of the WTO provisions, because, after all, more than anything else, remaining in power and running the government is more important than pushing reforms through satisfy the macro indicators of development and economic growth rate. Development should be shown in a language the ordinary poor man understands. When a government offers PDS rice at affordable price, the ordinary man understands it and not the macro growth indicators. So, from the political dimension of things, for reformers the areas to touch upon are not the essential commodities and the PDS.

As of now, as far as 'food availability' is concerned, there is no problem, there are PDS functioning and people have their own ways of sustaining themselves as food-secure through local practices. So, availability of food is not a problem, but accessibility is. By accessibility means not being able to access food articles/essential commodities unless certain coping strategies are adopted. That is during monsoon failure and lean harvests people undergo food insecurity and have to adopt different coping strategies to be able to remain food secure during those periods. If this can be called being under transitory food insecurity, unless measures were not taken up on matters relating to 'domestic preparedness' to improve agriculture, and repairing and revamping FCI and the PDS, it might end up in chronic food insecurity.

Summary of Findings

The study primarily aims at finding out if poor rural families secure adequate flow of food and cash to meet basic and emergent needs round the whole year. Hence understanding the ways in which rural households gain food security; how do they cope when food stocks and cash flow are inadequate; what is the role of Public Distribution System (PDS) in ensuring food security, and what else bear a part in preventing starvation among the poor; and finding out if economic reform measures of the government have a bearing on the food security status of the poor.

Sources that Ensure Food Security

FGDs conducted in several villages across five districts in Tamil Nadu put across that in a normal year a poor rural family in Tamil Nadu depends on PDS for about 90-120 days (spread across a year); wages received in kind (usually paddy in wet regions, and *cholam* or *ragi* in dry regions) ensures food security for 75-90 days; and the 'informal markets' (local private merchants who deal in essential commodities) cater to the rest of the 120-150 days in a year.

Public Distribution System (PDS) in Tamil Nadu can be attributed as one of the main reasons for non-occurrence of hungry deaths in Tamil Nadu, notwithstanding the corrupt practices PDS is known for. This is more so during slack seasons and at times of a lean harvest. Be that as it may in terms of nutritive value, with regard to making food articles physically available, the fact remains that PDS meets 25-40 per cent of the food requirements of the 'poor people in the State'. Thus, PDS is one permanent and stable source of rice, wheat, sugar and kerosene at prices that are affordable vis-à-vis the incomes the ultra-poor in the villages and urban slums earn. So, PDS is one necessary scheme for ensuring essential food articles to the rural and urban poor. Despite complaints, majority of the poor still depend on PDS to meet at least ten days' food requirements (in a month) of the family.

PDS, no doubt has played a vital role in ensuring food security and preventing starvation deaths during all droughts, if we consider the years before November last year when torrential rains slashed all over Tamil Nadu, as put across by poor families across study villages. Somebody could argue that the share of PDS in meeting the total food requirements, especially of the rural poor and those in urban slums, is not even 35-40 per cent. The truth of the fact is PDS, by definition, is one stable and steady source of essential commodities to the rural poor, whereas all the other means of food security are not dependable by nature.

One prime source of supply of essential commodities for both the *landed class* and the *working class* is PDS. PDS apart, the sources that effectively ensure food security for the landed class and working class are subtly different. For the 'landed class' the other sources that ensure food security are: (i) the paddy harvested in their land, and (ii) the cash income they earn after selling the agricultural produces. With cash income they go for exchange, of essential commodities required, from (a) the Fair Price Shops (on ration basis), and (b) obtain the rest from the informal open markets/merchants who deal in rice.

For the 'working class' the sources that effectively ensure food security are essentially two: (i) the cash income one earns as wages; and (ii) wages received in kind. The practice of paying in kind especially by farmers who harvest paddy is widely prevalent in many districts of the state. An average worker gets about 10 kg of paddy in exchange of one full day's work. The wages received in kind (paddy) is considered significant because in one harvesting season an average family earns 4-5 bags of paddy which is the second source of food security— the first being PDS. Whatever may be the occupation one is involved in, during paddy harvesting season, many a rural family has the practice of going for paddy harvest especially to earn wages in terms of paddy which sustains life of the entire family for 2- 3 months in a year.

The third source is the 'informal markets' (Rice merchants) that operate. These are small traders who sell essential commodities such as rice, groceries and vegetables for a profit. This is, of course the last resort that the rural poor approach, but it is unavoidable to buy from the informal merchants as the supply of essential commodities a given community get from the earlier two sources (i.e, PDS and kind component of wages) are often insufficient to ensure the food security of the family for an entire year. So, people buy rice and other essential articles from open markets at open market rates making use of the cash income they earn. Another matter noticed is food articles, especially the rice diverted from PDS, is available for sale at almost double the price, at local grocery shops. So, although food articles are diverted from PDS, they are again used only by the poor who are not entitled to get more than 20 kg or 35 kg of the rationed item (esp. rice) from the PDS.

The description given above relates only to a normal year. During slack seasons and during a year of dry spell, the 'kind income component' (paddy in wet regions and *ragi* in dry regions) fail to find a place in their food basket. Nor would they have cash income to buy rice or *ragi* from informal markets. This is the time they become indebted or sell off assets such as goat or sheep to ensure the food security of the family. This is the time they tend to migrate in search of alternative employment in the town. All the three sources put together, coupled with the coping strategies indicated at the end, is what surviving food insecurity in Tamil Nadu means.

Coping Strategies Identified

Livestock and Small-Stocks: Rearing livestock (milch animals) and small-stock (sheep, goat, hens etc.) although are considered as secondary occupation or 'allied occupation', in deed, render the solace, support and food security to many a rural households especially during slack seasons and at times of lean harvests. If PDS is one of the reasons for non-occurrence of farmers' suicides in Tamil Nadu, the practice of rearing milch animals, goats and sheep can definitely be attributed as another factor that has helped prevent farmers' suicide in Tamil Nadu State.

These livestock and small-stock (cow, buffalo, sheep, goat and hen) serve as safety and sustenance during seasonal trends and shocks. So, if each milch animal is a source of steady and stable flow of income to a poor household; each one of the small-stock — be it a goat or a sheep or a hen—is a kitty to cash in on when the family is in financial crunch such as meeting the unexpected medical expenses, marriage of a close relative, expenses that come with sudden death of a family member, replacing the worn-out thatches and so on. Hence, livestock and small-stock provide buffering effects providing milk or cash at otherwise lean times. It also puts off the need to migrate.

Although considered as an activity allied to agriculture (or secondary occupation), milch animal rearing, goats and sheep rearing activity is retaining many of the marginal and small farmers in the villages still. It serves as an explanation for not migrating by some of the poor. It gives the solace and salvation to absorb seasonal shocks and trends these people are vulnerable to.

All common lands, not necessarily the pasture land, in the villages serve for the purpose of grazing by animal population in most villages. Some of them being classified as 'waste-land' and planning to take them away for commercial purposes and for the cultivation of plants such '*jetropha*' is not welcome. The Village Panchayats might be made use of, in removing encroachments and in developing pasturelands.

Indebtedness: The practice of borrowing from money-lenders even for consumption purposes is still prevalent. During scarce months or years, some borrow from money-lenders with an agreement that they would repay during next harvesting season. Mostly, the landed class has this practice and the landless borrow small amounts locally and settle it once they earn some wages. One social asset generally seen in many of the villages is Self-Help Groups (SHGs). It serves as a constant source of money for farm-related investments and to be able to meet unexpected (contingent) expenses. The SHGs have played a commendable role in some of the study villages and have enabled the poor to keep away from money-lenders, by providing credit for both production as well as consumption purposes. In many places, they seem to have the practice of woman borrowing for the family requirements, with the understanding that the man would help her repay it to the group.

Migration: During the discussions held in several villages regarding the migration factor, from rural areas to urban centres, the following have been noted. They are: (i) two segments, and (ii) two patterns. The two segments are: (a) those between 30-45 years of age; and (b) those between 15-30 years of age. The former segment (30-45 years) are usually either unlettered or have had only a little education and migrate to places like Kerala or Karnataka in search of unskilled manual labour in farms and for cutting woods in hilly terrains. This kind of migration takes place only when there is no employment available locally or in the vicinity. The basic instinct is food security of the family. Either the head of the household or the entire family migrates. Though not in a massive scale, this kind of migration takes place to a considerable extent. This is what is, perhaps called, transient migration—migration for a brief period in a year. They would return home once it starts raining in their native villages/districts. This takes place when all local livelihood options are closed due to drought and the absence of agricultural operations. The basic instinct found among them is food security of the family. The aged persons in the family take care of the goats or sheep in the house and all able-bodied ones in the house migrate in search of a means of living.

Another pattern noticed is that almost all the urban centres, say the district headquarters or the town that is fast developing becomes a place for absorbing the rural youth who spill out or opt out of agriculture in villagers. This basic instinct is earning cash income and a spotless understanding that agriculture is undependable to improve one's standard of living. They realize that cash income can ensure both food security as well as better standards of living where as food crop cultivation can ensure only food security at the most, if at all it really did. Although the urban centres have been attractive and made way for the rural folks to come in; increasing in-put costs in agriculture, deployment of machineries have served as repellent factors to get out of the village and migrate.

Observed a little more closely, there is a third segment that belongs to almost the same age group (25-35 year) who has employment in the town as a fallback proposition, and agriculture as the permanent intention. They are partly transient and partly permanent migrants. It need not be Thiruppur or Chennai. It can be any town close-by. During agriculturally off-season, they become casual labourers in non-agricultural sector in the town. In other words, they are in their native place when agricultural works are in its peak at the village, and on employment at Thiruppur/Chennai during non-season/drought seasons.

Migration in varied forms—transient, permanent etc.—as a strategy of ensuring food security is prevalent in almost all the villages of Tamil Nadu. All said and done, many a village on the fringe of towns generally depends on the town for casual employment during slack seasons and for selling off agricultural produces such as fruits, vegetables, flowers etc. during peak seasons. So, villages on the rim of towns benefit the rural poor in a big way by helping them earn cash income through employment and the sale of agricultural produces. It ensures cash flow into the village and provides food security for the poor.

The Reform Measures and the External Drive for Reform Measures

The governmental measures such as shifting of FCI operations mostly to State Governments, abolition of Essential Commodities Act on the grounds that it is distorting trade, proposal to introduce Food Stamp Programme where private retailers would play the main role in place of PDS and, continuous mention of making food aid as a targeted programme instead of making it a universal one make critics of globalization state that these are thrust upon us by the WTO and the World Bank. Another alarm raised is that WTO through AoA negotiations threatens food security of the poor in India, and that it is making moves to close down the Food Corporation of India (FCI). They also state that the World Bank and other international organizations advise gradual phasing out of PDS because of the high food subsidy bill the government has to foot every year.

This comes up despite the fact that India has initiated with the WTO the need for a Food Security Box to be able to protect the food security of the poor in developing countries. Statements that come from WTO also indicate that India plays only a defensive interest when it comes to issues such as agriculture, food security and poverty reduction. The way negotiations are made, India seems to be cautious with regard to safeguarding agriculture and food security from being affected by trade negotiations. The food security box asks that measures for poverty alleviation, rural development and diversification of agriculture, should be exempt from reductions. The problems with FCI and PDS are well known. They are high administration costs, unwanted transportation costs, storage loss, theft, and so on. These are things India need to repair and revamp at the domestic level. They way FCI operates and PDS functions cannot be allowed to function it has been doing.

Another provision mentioned about food subsidy and poverty as far as WTO is concerned that there are legitimate provisions such as Special and Differential Treatment (SDT) on food security that provides safeguards on a regular basis at subsidized prices for meeting the food requirements of the poor. However, provisions of the AoA are still under negotiation and it plays unfavourable role only to certain extent. What makes food insecurity predictable is the trade-oriented-culture that the AoA emanates in Tamil Nadu agriculture—many of them sponsored by the governments—either at the centre or at the State.

The general trend of neglect of foodgrain crops and promotion of commercial crops is a dangerous sign. It signals food insecurity. Neglect of irrigation infrastructure, water bodies, absence of management practices and rising in-put costs make agriculturists develop a tendency not to engage the younger generation in agriculture. The tendency to go for cash income rather than food security through subsistence farming is catching up in several places. That cash can buy food articles and trying to grow foodgrains might end up as a futile exercise is a general impression spreading across.

This might require or has already made India to go in for import of wheat again after six years. There is domestic preparedness required in terms of building irrigation infrastructure, ensuring minimum support price etc. to be able to sustain self-sufficiency in foodgrains production and to ensure food security to the mass of this country.

The Political Dimension of Food Security

When the government is accountable to the people through contesting election to public office, a programme such as PDS cannot be dismantled simply. That very action would pull the government down either immediately or in the very next election. All the political parties in Tamil Nadu have once again proved in the recent general election 2006 that 'PDS Rice' must be on the top of their political manifesto. While the Central Government and World Bank proposes to reduce the food subsidy bill, all the political parties in Tamil Nadu that contested in the election 2006 chose to run a race towards the bottom line announcing further subsidy. It happened with Andhra Pradesh also, that the government had to withdraw the Food Stamp Programme (FSP) following protests by the people a little before the election 2004. We can infer that whatever might be the pressure the globalization processes exert; popular programmes upon which a large mass of rural population depend, cannot be dismantled without any socially acceptable alternative.

Suggestions for Reduction in Food Subsidy Bill

After witnessing the distress State agriculture is in vis-à-vis the queue in the Fair Price Shops (FPS) in Tamil Nadu as a non-participant observer and after holding chain of interviews in several different remote villages, this research team is sufficiently convinced to put across categorically that dismantling PDS in the pretext of the exchequer it claims in the government revenue is simply impossible. But one possibility is that the price of articles may slightly be enhanced which might, to some extent, reduce the food subsidy bill of the State. But, the political parties in their attempt to exert a pull on votes, announce further reduction in the price of essential commodities. This is sensitive again.

There are two options, one can think of when it comes to reducing food subsidy bill. Option one is: An effective targeting of the poor instead of making PDS universal. It is this idea of universality that makes food subsidy bill high and helps diversion of food articles to the open market. One practical suggestion in this regard is the practice of Ration Card being required as a Basic Identity Proof should be done away with. This makes every family hold a card and inadvertently helps diversion, resulting in hefty food subsidy bill. Instead, the Election Identity Card should be made to serve as the basic proof. It can make everyone hold an Election Identify Card, which many people do not bother to obtain. Option two is to launch programmes to raise the income levels of the poor in the villages, which eventually would make the people feel standing in queues at the ration shops below their dignity and gradually reduce the number of families that depend on PDS.

8

The Plantation Crisis: Indian Tea Knocked Out of the Cup

The Premise

"Planters Associations in Tamil Nadu unilaterally decided to defer the application of formula for adjustment of variable DA from the quarter beginning October, 2000, with an assurance to the estate labourers that their dues would be paid when the situation improved".

"Plantations are working-*cum*-living units with a large workforce with families residing in plantations. Their closure might lead to law and order problems", says Mr. D.P. Maheswari, Chairperson, Planters Association of Tamil Nadu to *The Hindu*, citing reasons for not closing down the plantations.

"A meeting of the Planters Association held at Coimbatore on December 1, 2000 decided that the estate managements should resort to agitations, besides refusing to pay taxes and other duties to the government, unless the Government abolished the excise duty and suspend import of tea with immediate effect".

According to the manager of one nationalized bank in Valparai, "many savings account-holders are closing their accounts and are moving out of this scenic town. During the last one year alone, nearly 400 accounts were closed".

"Coffee Board of Government of India shrinks. Marketing function closed down. Employees sent on VRS".

Introduction

The culture pertaining to food in Tamil Nadu is such that not a single day passes without the use of tea, coffee and spices. It is a known fact that by nature, these crops grow only in certain climatic conditions and beyond certain altitudes. The hilly regions in the Nilgiris, Coimbatore, Salem, Dindigul and Thirunelveli are the few districts where plantation corps — especially tea and coffee — are cultivated in Tamil Nadu. North Indian states such as Assam and West Bengal are also popular for plantation crops. In fact, the popular Darjeeling tea has been a subject-matter of controversy on 'patenting' grounds. The Nilgiris Tea also has its popularity and special aroma. Tea and coffee from South Indian states have certain unique qualities; and tea from North Indian states also is unique in taste, colour and flavour. India is one of the major exporters of tea, whereas our coffee exports are comparatively much less.

One of the distinctive characters of plantation crops such as tea and coffee is that unlike paddy or sugarcane which require planting every time a crop is to be cultivated. Plantation crops require only one-time investment in terms of planting materials. The crop stands for almost one full century. All that is required is only maintenance and harvest. The sector is labour-intensive.

The Problem Statement

Financial crisis constrained many tea estates in Tamil Nadu to delay disbursing wages and provident fund dues. Tales of woes about plantation companies and plantation labourers keep appearing on regional news coverage in the media. Over 30 tea estates in Kerala are reported to have been closed down not being able to manage the financial crisis created by emerging market conditions. The unprecedented crisis in the tea industry has assumed alarming proportions with prices crashing at the auction centres, week after week. In one of the auctions, certain grades of tea were said to have been sold at an all-time low of Rs. 20 a kg. Planters in Tamil Nadu decide to 'temporarily' defer application of the formula to adjust the Variable DA of the wage settlement they agreed upon.

Similarly, in the coffee front, the Coffee Board of Government of India close down its marketing wing. Employees are sent on VRS. Indian coffee is let open to compete in the international market. The small growers who form the major chunk (98%) of the coffee growers have to survive this competition. Given this background, this is an emprico-inductive analysis to find out what caused the situation tea and coffee plantations are in, at Tamil Nadu. The specific objectives of the study are :

- Track down the policy changes that have taken place in tea and coffee sectors as an aftermath of reform measures/globalization processes.
- Analyse the impact and find out the nature and extent of such impact on the tea and coffee sectors at the grassroots level, disaggregated as plantation companies, small growers, and the plantation labourers.
- Identify the direction, if any, the plantation companies, the small growers and the plantation labourers are taking to be able to manage/tide over the situation.

Research Approach

This is primarily an empirical enquiry of what led to the crisis being faced by the plantation sector, especially the tea and coffee industries. Snow-ball sampling technique has been adopted in selecting the districts, and the respondents. A variety of quantitative and qualitative methods of data collection has been employed.

Sample Districts: In order to have a thorough understanding of the problems, those districts of Tamil Nadu that are popularly known for cultivation of plantation crops viz. the Nilgiri, Coimbatore, Dindigul, Salem and Kanyakumari were chosen for this study. As planters in Kanyakumari are largely cultivators of rubber, and this study aims at covering only coffee and tea sectors, excluding Kanyakumari all the other four major plantation districts (Nilgiris, Coimbatore, Salem, and Dindigul)—and Tirunelveli district especially for the rueful Manjolai estate incident—were selected for this study.

Sources of Data and Information: The study has made use of both primary and secondary sources of data. Secondary data have been collected from published literature of the plantation companies, planters associations, traders associations, journals and websites. Primary data have been collected through conducting Focus Group Discussions, Individual Interviews, and Chain of Interviews with the planters, planters associations, small growers, plantation labour unions, managerial level staff at plantation companies and plantation labourers.

Data Analysis: Data analysis was made from the field notes by culling categories, patterns, similarities, contrasts etc. and by going for additional probe on certain oddities.

Scope of the Study: Plantation for a general definition implies tea, coffee and rubber. This study has concentrated only on tea and coffee sectors and rubber is not in the purview of discussion here. Rubber sector would be taken up later in a separate report, or incorporated along with this report later. Wherever a simple comparison would get across message in the way it is interpreted, references are made to Kerala, Assam, and West Bengal. But, it does not intend to cover the status of plantation sector in those states. The outcome presented relate only to the plantation sector in Tamil Nadu State.

One of the important agenda of this study was to find out if there is any impact of globalization processes in the changes that are taking place in the plantation sector. The general problems, which have always been there, of labour or labour unions are not taken into account.

Limitations: That rubber—one of the vital elements of plantation sector—is not in the purview of the discussion and so the discussion does not make this report a comprehensive one about the plantation sector in Tamil Nadu. Non-availability of certain data which are supposed to be with the Inspector of Plantations (IP) or the disorderly manner in which those data are kept at the IP Office could not be used. Some of the quantifications that this study aimed at could not be done due to non-availability of such data, therefore, at some points, estimates had to be made in consultation with the plantation companies or the labour unions.

MACRO-LEVEL CHANGES IN THE TEA SECTOR

This section aims at tracking down the macro-level changes that have taken place in the tea sector after liberalization of Indian economy. Only those changes that have transpired from the moves of the WTO, or as a result of the reform measures of the Government of India have been covered here.

Collapse of the USSR

One of the very prominent macro-level changes that emanated from outside India is the collapse of the USSR. This is considered as one of the major factors because USSR was one prominent buyer of Indian teas before the collapse of USSR in the mid-1990s. Indian Tea Industry was heavily reliant on the erstwhile Soviet market. This was facilitated by very favourable terms of trade between India and the Soviet Union. The cost of capital items and equipments received from the Soviet Union was paid for in commodities like tea and other agro products, based on rupee-rouble agreement. South Indian tea had a very secure market, until the disintegration of the USSR in the mid-1990s, resulting in a free market economy there also. Russian buyers stated sourcing their teas from different markets other than India, in order to achieve the maximum cost advantage.

Liberalization Policy

Liberalization policies resulted in new players like Vietnam, Indonesia and Kenya to name a few, emerging in the international tea trade. A situation arose where teas from those competing countries started being off-loaded in the Indian domestic market. This created a glut in the domestic tea market and price crashed to unsustainable levels.

Demand-Supply Imbalance

Many countries of the world have started cultivating tea. Thus, world supplies of tea are on the increase. A projection made by CommodityIndia.com in October 2005 indicated an increasing imbalance between supply and demand of 98,000 tonnes.

Price Competitiveness

The inability of Indian tea, particularly the South Indian tea to match price competitiveness in the export market and consequent fall in exports have led to a glut in the domestic market. The import of tea through various permitted channels, under the trade liberalization policies further deteriorated the situation.

Indo-Sri Lanka Agreement

Sri Lankan teas come into India under preferential arrangement. Sri Lanka, the second largest tea exporting country in the world, is expected to increase exports by 1.2 per cent annually to account for 25 per cent of the global total in the year 2014.

Opening up of Tea Market

The earlier legal requirement was that atleast 70 per cent of the tea produced by planters should be necessarily sold through the auction centres. With the advent of globalization and free-market economy, this restriction became irrelevant, as the producers demanded removal of the restriction so that teas could be sold privately at the best available price rather than the price realized at the auction centres which was driven more by market sentiment. Subsequently, this legal restriction of compulsory sale in the auction has been removed by the Government. Any buyer/trader can source his producer privately. This has made the e-auction a failure which was already suffering from certain technical snags. This has enabled the business of tea outside the auction system to thrive.

The system of electronic auction or e-auction is a recent development initiated by the Tea Board of India to provide an on-line link to all tea auction centres in the country. This will ultimately enable traders to bid for teas from remote locations and would do away with the requirement of being physically present at the auction centre. The system will also provide more accurate and timely transaction details, besides greater transparency, when compared with the manual system. The system is however yet to be fully implemented at all the auction centres.

Additional Sales Tax (AST)

Teas worth more than Rs. 10 crores sold through e-auction centres are charged Additional Sales Tax (AST). This has become one of the factors that discourages sale through e-auction and to opt for private sale of tea.

Excise Duty on Tea Withdrawn

The Union Budget for 2005-06 of the Government of India has withdrawn excise duty on tea. After the duty free import of tea for re-export started, net Indian tea export has fallen from a minimum required level of 200+ million kgs to 160 to 170 million kgs.

Import for Export Policy

Import of tea from other countries for re-export is legal in India. Import duty for tea has been brought down. This enables many traders to import tea on the pretext of re-exporting, after the purported value addition, replacing and reducing the net volume of exports of Indian tea.

Pepsi Cola

In the global beverages marketplace the competition is large. The youth are being lured to think that taking Pepsi and Coke products are fashionable, rather than taking tea or coffee. This is the cultural aspect of globalization that spreads through media especially the TV and the magazines.

FDI

Even though Foreign Direct Investment (FDI) has been permitted, there are not takers because of the bleak prospects of the Tea Industry.

India's Business Share in World Tea

In absolute figures, the share of Indian tea business to total tea is on the increase, whereas the percentages of share of Indian tea to the world's share is declining.

Table 8.1 : India's Share in International Tea Trade

(in MT)

Year	*World*	*India's Share*	*Contribution in Percentage*
1995-1996	1095	168	15.34
1996-1997	1129	162	14.35
1997-1998	1206	203	16.83
1998-1999	1307	210	16.07
1999-2000	1263	192	15.20
2000-2001	1331	207	15.56
2001-2002	1391	183	13.16
2002-2003	1439	201	13.97
2003-2004	1390	174	12.52
2004-2005	1501	184	12.26

Source: Plant Hort. Tech (Bi-monthly), Bangalore.

Domestic Preparedness and Relief Measures

No Level-Playing Field

Plantation sector in India is regulated by the Plantation Labour Act, 1951. In addition to the wages paid based on periodical wage settlements arrived at between labour unions and planters association, there is a host of other social security benefits the planters have to offer to the plantation labourers, which planters in many of the competing countries such as Kenya or Sri Lanka either do not offer or are provided by the government. Their costs, and wages are reportedly much less. This increases the cost of production of Indian tea when compared to the competitor countries.

Agricultural Income Tax

Levy of agricultural income tax of 65 per cent was in existence in India. Planters protested paying it, indicating the crisis the industry is undergoing. The government has withdrawn the agricultural income tax for plantation crops now.

Special Purpose Tea Fund

In order to step up the productivity of tea and to hold the competitiveness of the Indian tea industry given the high-age profile of tea bushes, a Special Purpose Tea Fund of Rs. 100 crore has been earmarked in the Union Budget 2006-07.

World Tea Expo

Planters have started preparing themselves to face international competitions by introducing Specialty Tea Show, Tea Golden Leaf Awards and World Tea Expo etc. The Tea Board has proposed to make the tea-cupping contest as an annual event and to hold it abroad during major fairs. India has also started participating in the International Tea and Coffee Fairs.

Quality Up-gradation

The Indian tea, especially most of the tea manufactured in South India are of CTC type — the variety made using coarse leaves. The world trend now is towards orthodox variety of teas which are of premium quality. The company-run estates would recognize the market trends and would shift to making the orthodox variety. But, the small growers and the Bought Leaf Factories would continue to produce the same old

CTC variety. In order to set right this situation the Tea Board joining hands with KVKs is implementing Quality Up-gradation Programme where small growers get subsidy and the other technical support for producing the orthodox tea.

TEA SECTOR – THE MICRO-MACRO LINK

Size of the Sector

On an average India produces 950 million kgs of tea every year, out of which we consume about 650 million kgs. and the rest go for export. The share of south Indian tea to the total tea production in the country is only 200 million kgs. India is one of the largest producers and consumers of tea in the world. India accounts for 27 per cent of the world production and 13 per cent of the world tea trade. The other major tea producing countries are Sri Lanka, Kenya, and Vietnam.

In Tamil Nadu tea is grown mainly in the Nilgiris and in the Anamalai hills. Area-wise, 70-80 per cent of the tea estates in Tamil Nadu are large estates and the remaining 20-30 per cent are managed by small growers. Estates in Anamalais are fairly bigger. The small growers are mostly concentrated in the Nilgiris, whereas their number is thin in Anamalai. An estimate is that the Nilgiris has over 65,000 small growers of tea and the number is growing due to sub-division and fragmentation of holdings amongst the family members of small growers. The Nilgiris, Valparai (Coimbatore), Yercaud (Salem), and some parts of Dindigul and Tirunelveli are the major tea and coffee producing areas in Tamil Nadu.

Table 8.2 : Tea Production in South Indian States (in M. kgs.).

Year	*Tamil Nadu*	*Kerala*	*Karnataka*	*South India*
2000	131.8	68.9	5.5	206.2
2001	132.4	65.2	5.5	203.1
2002	129.0	59.7	5.7	194.4
2003	166.6	58.0	5.3	229.9
2004	163.0	62.2	5.6	230.8
2005	154.6	67.0	5.4	227.0

Source: The UPASI, Tea Situation, May, 2006, p. 2.

The Players in the Tea Sector

In both coffee and tea sectors, the number of players involved is more than one can possibly think of. For example, in tea, we have company-run-estates, small growers, Bought Leaf Factories (BLF), warehouses, auction centres, brokers, blenders, packers, wholesalers (or distributors), retailers and then the consumers. The title these players are known by, suggests the kind of job they are involved in, except perhaps the small growers and the BLFs. Small growers by Government of Tamil Nadu definition are those who own less than 25 acres of tea garden. Bought Leaf Factories buy green tea leaves from the small growers and process the leaves into tea dust, to be sold either as 'commodities' or as 'branded tea products'. Big company-run estates have their own factories to process green leaves into dust tea. All the others are middlemen involved in the handling and distribution.

Like in most other sectors of Indian economy, in Tamil Nadu the tea sector also we have private limited companies, public limited companies (TANTEA), cooperative tea factories and small growers. Unlike employment in agriculture, plantations are usually living-cum-working places where the planters provide housing, water, medical facility, primary education, provident fund contribution, gratuity etc. to the workers as per the Plantation Labour Act. The employer employee-relationship is fairly clear. In addition there are small growers, about 65000 of them in the Nilgiris alone.

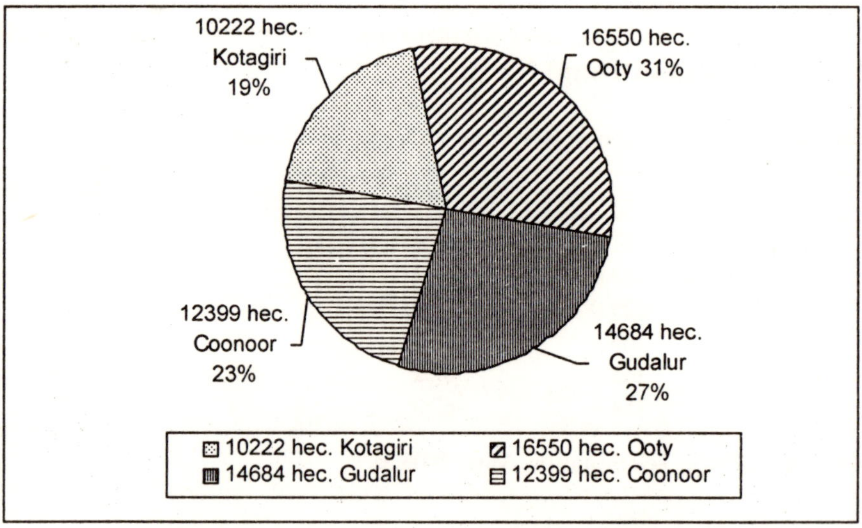

Fig. 8.1: Area under Tea in Nilgiris (Taluk-wise)

The Promoters-*cum*-Rule Setters

The Tea Board of the Government of India – both directly and through KVKs–implements programmes, especially to promote productivity and quality. These come in addition to the actions taken by the planters and the planters associations. Many of the schemes of the Tea Board and the KVKs mainly concentrate on the small growers. Quality up-gradation in order to promote orthodox tea is one of the areas of concentration that the KVK is striving for the past 5-6 years.

Variety of Tea

Two major varieties of tea available are: (i) Orthodox tea, and (ii) CTC tea. Orthodox teas are made from selected leaf (*two leaves and one bud* formula) and CTC teas are made from coarse leaves. In Tamil Nadu, most of the teas manufactured belong to CTC type only, whereas the world trend now is towards orthodox teas. In other words, orthodox and CTC are two available methods for processing green tea leaf into black tea. For both, the raw material (that is, green tea leaf) and the basic stages of processing (that is, withering, rolling, fermentation, drying and sorting) remain the same. The major difference lies in the number of cups of tea we get per kilogram of made-tea. While orthodox tea yields nearly 200 cups per kg in the case of CTC it is more than doubled.

Table 8.3 : Share of Orthodox Teas in Total Tea Produced and Exported

Decade	*Percentage Share of Orthodox Teas in Total Tea Produced*	*Percentage Share of Orthodox Teas in Total Tea Exported*
1951-60	59	79
1961-70	43	76
1971-80	35	71
1981-90	19	57

Source: The Hindu Survey of Agriculture 2006, Tea Board, Kolkata, p. 213.

The Orthodox method requires more fine leaf and longer withering period than the CTC and, therefore, it is more time-consuming and expensive. CTC processing requires less time and labour. Orthodox process is the oldest method and the CTC process was adopted in India only in the early 50s mainly to meet the growing domestic demand. The domestic demand growth rate between 50s and 80s was in the range of 6.73 per cent to 5 per cent whereas the production growth rate during this period was far less at around 2.19 to 2.55 per cent.

Wide Gap

Because of this wide gap between demand growth and production, most of the producers have switched over to CTC method. Currently, the orthodox production in India is only 10 per cent of the total production. However, it constitutes 32 per cent of the exports from India since the domestic market demands mostly CTC teas. The volume of CTC teas currently consumed within the country is around 700 million kgs. Had the industry continued to rely only upon orthodox processing, the total production needed just to fulfil the domestic demand alone should have gone up to more than 1400 million kgs. In other words, but for the CTC processing, India would have become net importer of tea.

Marketing of Tea

As far as marketing of tea is concerned small growers generally sell green tea leaves to the Bought Leaf Factories and their business ends there. There are a total of 165 factories apart from large corporate and estate factories in the Nilgiris. If only the quality leaves are to be plucked, particularly of the much hyped 'a bud and two leaves' formula, many of the BLFs were to be closed for want of raw materials. But company-run estates have their factories where they process the green tea leaves into dust-tea and sell them as commodities in the e-auction centres or to any buyer (trader/broker/agent). There are some planters who sell tea as 'branded products' through established market channels using advertisements.

Tea trade generally involves a large number of middlemen, including those involved in blending and pocketing, which results in unbelievable hike up in the market price of tea, compared to the cost the growers get for the green tea leaves. There are bought leaf factories run by private traders who buy green tea leaves from small growers and manufacture especially CTC type tea, which is said to be inferior in quality compared to the orthodox type of tea manufactured by many company-run estates.

The Crisis

Indian tea industry in India is undergoing a severe market crisis for the past 6-8 years. There are reports that state the crisis Kerala tea industry undergoing is grave, causing shut-down of several (24 as reported by Plantation Chronicle) of the plantation companies. Tamil Nadu does not seem to be far away from this sliding-business trend. Focus Group Discussions and chain of interviews held with planters, plantation labourers and tea traders across Nilgiri and Coimbatore districts confirmed that the tea industry in Tamil Nadu is no better. It is in a critical position. The general indications of tea sliding down the elevation are: (i) Plantation labour unions consent to have downward revision of wages and social benefits offered to the labourers; (ii) many labourers are leaving the plantations and are moving downhill in search of employment in the plains; (iii) the unhealthy business trend reflected by the Profit and Loss Account of plantation companies has necessitated rewriting and overhauling of the estate management systems; and (iv) the price of green tea leaf does not touch even half of what it was about 6- 8 years ago.

Although during the current year (2006) the industry seems to be able to breath again, business analysts opine that it is actually a breather caused by an unprecedented drought in Kenya and so it cannot be construed as having infused a fresh life into the sector. They mean the countries that depended on Kenya for tea (e.g. Pakistan) have approached India to supply tea to them in the year 2006. Once Kenya received good rains next year, the demand would fall again in India. Therefore, it cannot be taken as a recovery stage for Indian tea industry.

Initially, in the opinion of many planters, it looked as if it was a general recession in the business cycle that any industry undergoes cyclically—and that it would recover. It was much later that they realized that most of it was due to the liberalization policy of the government and that recovery is nowhere near sight. Several interesting revelations crop up in the analysis of what has happened to the sector.

One thing that is very clear and understandable is that India had depended mainly on Russian tea market until internal political problems erupted in the USSR causing collapses of USSR in 1994. Then it had become the story of the one who suffered due to the strategy of having put all the eggs in one basket. India, having been carried away by the USSR tea market, did not concentrate sufficiently on retaining the customers it served before. When India woke up to the reality of having lost the USSR-market, with the need to fall back on the customers it had earlier, all the earlier customers of Indian tea had changed place.

Table 8.4 : Details of Export in North, South and All India

Year	North India			South India			All India		
	Qty. M. kgs.	*Value Rs. Crs.*	*Price Rs./kg.*	*Qty. M. kgs.*	*Value Rs. Crs.*	*Price Rs./kg.*	*Qty. M. kgs.*	*Value Rs. Crs.*	*Price Rs./kg.*
2000	95.7	1160.4	121.25	111.1	738.2	66.44	206.8	1898.6	91.81
2001	85.4	1021.9	119.63	97.2	660.2	67.95	182.6	1682.1	92.13
2002	94.4	1055.8	111.84	106.6	697.6	65.44	201.0	1753.4	87.23
2003	92.2	1064.9	115.50	81.5	525.3	64.45	173.7	1590.2	91.55
2004	100.8	1203.9	119.43	96.8	637.3	65.84	197.6	1841.2	93.14
2005	91.9	1068.8	116.27	99.9	668.9	66.94	191.8	1737.7	90.58
Jan./Mar. 2005	19.3	224.6	116.57	28.1	190.2	67.75	47.4	414.8	87.62
2006	14.2	168.6	119.07	22.4	140.0	62.53	36.6	308.6	84.43

Source: The UPASI, Tea Situation, May, 2006, p. 3.

Another immediate-plausible reason for the critical situation Indian tea industry is in, is attributed to liberalization of the economy. Better quality tea at cheaper prices enters Indian market from countries such as Sri Lanka, Kenya, and Vietnam etc. It is possible that the tea from such countries are better in quality because of the fact that the plantations in such countries are young, whereas our tea shrubs are anywhere between 80 and 120 years old. However, more than the quality, it is the price at which such countries offer that is attractive especially to the traders, buyers (who buy for packaging and re-sale) and the middlemen who deal in tea.

On the surface of it, these two developments are said to have caused the set back to Indian tea industry. The way in which these developments, especially the one stated latter, present and reveal itself in the Indian tea market is what is quite interesting to a student of market studies. In other words, the ramifications of these developments are as much puzzling as it is interesting to an average student of economics.

One of the puzzles is that the price of tea leaf has tremendously fallen (from Rs. 18 to a rock bottom of Rs. 3 per kg). This fall should have benefited the consumers by causing a fall in price of tea in the market. But, the tea price in the market has not fallen. It is either the same that prevailed earlier or rather it has slightly increased. We can infer that consumers do not benefit. Nor do the planters (the producers) benefit. Therefore, the common saying that globalization can bring in competition which consequently enables the consumers get a better quality product for a cheaper price has become a myth in the tea sector. The question still remains. If the fall in the price of tea leaf does not benefit the consumers, but it has severely affected the tea planters—who does it benefit? It shows that there are several slips between the cup and the lip.

Tea business is one where plenty of middlemen are involved. Auction centres, agents, brokers (broking houses), buyers, packers, traders etc. The competition and the fall in price have benefited only these segments. One of the strategies they adopt is blending cheap priced tea from other countries with the tea locally made, pack them up in brand names and sell them in the domestic market, or outside India. Or buy Kenyan tea or Sri Lankan tea at cheap price, stamp them as: 'INDIAN TEA' and re-export it to other countries. *Business Today* (July 2, 2006) endorses these statements. It reports that last year, Darjeeling produced 11 million kgs of tea, but total volume of *Darjeeling tea* sold world-wide was more than 20 million kgs. The strategy of: '*manufacture where it can be manufactured at the cheapest and sell where it would fetch the highest economic value*'. That it affects the primary producers or the ultimate consumers is not for the traders to bother about.

The Indian Tea Industry, particularly the South Indian Tea Industry has been undergoing a severe financial crisis for the sixth year in succession. The crisis in tea plantations in Valparai started reflecting in the general business of Valparai town for the past 3-4 years. The general economy — meaning business and financial transactions — of the entire Valparai area has become disgraceful. Mr. Jebaraj, President of the General Merchants Association in Valparai laments that many merchants from Valparai area are leaving for Dubai and the Middle East countries as a result of very poor business prospects at Valparai.

Table 8.5 : Average Sales Price of Tea

Year	*Average Sales Price (Per kg.) in Rs.*
1998	74.51
1999	68.84
2000	56.59
2001	60.66
2002	54.05
2003	55.67

Source: Parry Group of Estates, Valparai.

Causal Analysis

Global developments specifically on tea trade and its impact on Indian tea industry made it clear that they have been a direct fallout of the policies of liberalization and globalization of trade. Traditional industries like plantations have been the hardest hit by this process. Upto the year 1999, the South Indian Tea Industry was heavily reliant on the erstwhile Soviet market. This was mainly facilitated by very favourable terms of trade between India and the Soviet Union. The cost of capital items and equipments received from the Soviet Union was paid for in commodities like tea and other agro-products, based on the rupee-rouble agreement. South Indian tea had a very secure market, until the disintegration of the USSR in the mid-1990s, resulting in a free-market economy there also. Russian buyers started sourcing their teas from different markets other than India, in order to achieve the maximum cost advantage. As a result, new players like Vietnam, Indonesia and Kenya to name a few, emerged in the international tea trade. Besides eating away into India's share of exports of tea, a situation arose where teas from those competing countries started being off-loaded in the Indian domestic market. This created a glut in the Indian domestic tea market and prices crashed to unsustainable levels. The following is a snapshot of the extent of financial crisis faced by the South Indian Tea Industry:

Table 8.6 : Snapshot of Financial Crisis Faced by South Indian Tea

(in Rupees)

Year	*Average Auction Price Per Kg. of Tea (South India)*	*All Inclusive Cost of Production Per Kg. of Tea*	*Profit or Loss*
1999	57.10	57.00	(+) 0.10
2000	44.63	60.00	(-) 15.37
2001	46.02	62.00	(-) 15.98
2002	41.62	55 to 58*	(-) 14.88 (Avg)
2003	42.27	55 to 58*	(-) 14.23 (Avg)
2004	47.01	55 to 58*	(-) 9.49 (Avg)
2005	42.69	58 to 60*	(-) 16.31 (Avg)

* Depending on region-wise wage settlements.

Source: Planters Association of Tamil Nadu, Coimbatore, July 2006.

The liberalization of economy is said to have caused a demand-supply imbalance in tea trade. The arrival of tea from countries such as

Sri Lanka, Kenya, Vietnam and Bangladesh have caused further set back to the domestic tea market in India. Sri Lanka the second largest producer of teas, under Indo-Sri Lankan agreement is bringing tea into India also at cheaper price. This attracts the traders and buyers causing Indian tea to remain on the shelves.

It is widely reported in the plantation circles that considering the geographical position of South India and Sri Lanka, there is not much of a qualitative difference in the teas produced by the two regions. However, where the Sri Lankans have scored better, is in terms of value addition and branding, which has enabled them to command a better premium than South Indian teas, over the past one and a half decade. Sri Lanka has managed to capture the high end of the overseas market. Their efforts over the years have been towards product-orientation, rather than the commodity-orientation followed by us. That is the reason why the Sri Lankan tea industry is more resilient to international competition when compared with the South Indian industry which suffers from a high cost economy and is highly commoditized. A comparative statement of tax liability in India and other countries is given in Table 8.7:

Table 8.7 : Comparative Statement of Tax Liability in India

Sl. No.	*Country*	*Corporate Tax (%)*
1.	Indonesia	30.0
2.	Sri Lanka	35.0
3.	Vietnam	32.5
4.	Thailand	30.0
5.	Malaysia	28.0
6.	Bangladesh	35.0
7.	China	19.0

Source: Planters Association of Tamil Nadu, Coimbatore.

The fundamental problem with South Indian tea industry as uniformly reported by Planters Associations in Tamil Nadu is that nearly 60 per cent of the cost of production goes for labour as wages and welfare amenities. The planters opine that with such a high component of labour cost, it is extremely difficult to compete with the emerging countries like Vietnam, Indonesia or Malawi, where the labour cost is around 25 to 30 per cent of what Tamil Nadu plantations incur. Under the Plantations Labour Act, 1951, employers are required to provide cradle-to-grave welfare schemes like free housing, free medical facilities, free water supply and sanitation, free crèche facilities, education facilities etc., which in the normal course are governmental functions. Plantation employers in other competing countries mentioned above are not burdened with these responsibilities. Apart from this, the rates of corporate taxes are higher in India compared to other countries.

Table 8.8 : Agricultural Income Tax on 60 per cent of the Income from Tea

Sl. No.	*State*	*Tax (%)*
1.	Tamil Nadu	65.0 (now abolished)
2.	Kerala	60.0
3.	Karnataka	35.0
4.	West Bengal	45.0
5.	Assam	45.0
Central IT on 40 per cent of Tea income		36.75

Source: Planters Association of Tamil Nadu, Coimbatore.

The Small-Grower Sector

An estimate is that apart from some big companies, there are about 80,000 small growers in Tamil Nadu who are involved in tea leaf cultivation for a livelihood. There are about 65,000 small growers in the Nilgiris alone. The definition that the Government of Tamil Nadu adopts is: 'anybody who owns less than 25 acres of tea garden is a small grower'. Practically, many small growers, especially in the Nilgiris, would fall in the class interval of owning 0.5 acre to 5 acres only.

Because the foundation for the tea industry was laid by entrepreneurs a long time ago in an organized manner, more than 80 per cent of the production in India is now accounted for by the corporate sector of the industry. Growers holding tea area up to 10.12 hectares (that is, 25 acres) are considered as small tea growers. Although small farmers, to begin with, started cultivating tea in certain pockets in Nilgiris in the 1920s, their contribution remained insignificant till the late 1980s. Currently the small sector has gained prominence and accounts for nearly 20 per cent of the all India tea production.

The small tea growers, because of their scattered (small size) holdings are, by and large, unorganized. The growers find it difficult to obtain proper technical help on good crop husbandry practices. Therefore, despite technological advancement in tea science, the productivity of small holdings is way behind that of the organized sector.

Steps Initiated by Tea Board

Keeping this in view, several steps have been initiated by the Tea Board for augmenting the productivity of the small holdings. These include imparting training on modern aspects of tea growing, creation of awareness amongst the small tea growers and manufacturers of the need to upgrade the quality of their produce; organizing study tours to visit various tea growing regions within the country and also abroad, setting up of nurseries for the supply of good quality planting materials to the growers.

The small growers are being motivated to set up self-help groups amongst themselves so that it becomes easier not only for obtaining technical support but also for disposal of their green tea directly to the factories and get a reasonable price.

Financial assistance is given to the self-help groups by way of a 100 per cent grant towards setting up of leaf collection centres in close vicinity of the growers fields, purchase of weighing balances and leaf carry bags/plastic crates and the like. Assistance is also given at the rate of 50 per cent of the actual cost towards purchase of transport vehicle required for the haulage of the leaf from the leaf collection centres to the processing factories. These interventions by the Board have helped the small growers in increasing their productivity from 800 kgs./hectare in 1982 to 1711 kg./hectare in 2005 in the Nilgiris District of Tamil Nadu where the small growers account for 40 per cent of the production.

In order to bridge the extension gap and effectively meet the development needs of the small growers, it is proposed to set up a Small Growers Development wing within the Tea Development Directorate of Tea Board, which will be responsible for the development and regulation of the small sector.

Quality of Indian Tea

When it comes to competing at the international tea market, one of the factors that come to question is quality. Quality and price are the two factors that determine a product's existence in the market. India was used to producing cheap quality CTC variety tea for over a decade for the USSR market. When India has to look out for exporting tea to other countries such as the US, premium tea or the orthodox variety is in great demand for which our factories are not equipped nor are the growers (especially the small growers) prepared.

The government through Tea Boards and Farm Science Centres (KVK) assist—technically and financially — all the small growers to pluck good quality green leaves. The large-sized company-owned estates are left to themselves—or to organizations like UPASI, PAT etc. The small growers depend on Bought Leaf Factories (BLF) to sell tea leaves, where tea leaves are crushed. The bought leaf factories mostly run with the financial assistance offered by local banks. In many places in between the Small Growers and the BLFs there are 'agents' involved. In addition to over 150 BLF in the Nilgiris, there are at least a dozen of them run by INDCOSERVE—a quasi-government organization run on cooperative lines. Big company-owned estates have their own machineries for processing tea leaves.

One of the concerns expressed regarding the made tea brought about by the Bought Leaf Factories making use of the 'coarse type of leaves' supplied by the small growers is that the quality of 'made tea' is inferior. It is not fit for manufacturing orthodox variety (superior quality) that high-end consumers in the Western countries ask for. It is meant either for the low-end consumers or for mixing up in some proportion with a slightly better quality tea. The small growers are not unaware of it. They seem to be doing it after careful calculations. If they should go for supplying leaves for orthodox variety of tea, their yield comes down by 1st/5th. That is all the harvest, the formula of 'two leaves and one bud' offers them. Where they would harvest 100 kgs of coarse leaves, they can harvest only about 20 kgs of tender leaves for orthodox variety, although they would get a slightly higher price if they abide by: 'two leaves and one bud' formula.

The small growers tend to go only for a blanket type harvest. The reasons are: (i) what they cannot make up by supplying quality leaves, they can make up by supplying a large quantity of coarse leaves. It means 'more the leaves; more the income' is the formula the small growers adopt. So they tend to harvest even the coarse leaves; (ii) the Bought Leaf Factories are very much scattered, and so small growers are not in a position to take tea leaves to the factory within 2-3 hours of their harvest; (iii) as the tea products of BLF are not sold in the market in any brand name, the BLF managers are not bothered about the quality of the output. The mechanism to regulate or offer prescriptions regarding the quality of output, and the way the BLFs deal with small growers is grossly inadequate. One good news is that some of the BLFs in the Nilgiris have been closed down upon inspection.

The large-sized companies such as Tatas, and AVT have to maintain hygienic manufacturing practices and certain quality standards to be able to sustain the market, mainly because it goes in their respective brand names. The Tea Board (Government of India) is taking efforts to encourage the small growers to convert to supplying tea leaves for making orthodox tea. Their prescription is that at least 65 per cent should be two leaves and one bud, and the remaining 35 per cent can be coarse variety. There is a compelling economic logic behind the argument of Small Growers that they produce only for the low-end consumers and it works out profitable to them. They are not prepared to buy the: 'two leaves and one bud' formula of the Tea Board and the KVK.

The KVK seems to think that superior quality tea (orthodox variety) would fetch a good price in the market. Perhaps, the Quality Up-gradation Scheme that they are implementing makes them think so. But the Small Growers tend to ask: *forget about the 'high price, where is the market, after all'*? Because of the entry of cheap tea from countries such as Sri Lanka and Bangladesh even the cheaply priced Indian tea for low-end consumers is not moving, and which high-end consumers are we talking about, is the question raised by the Small Tea Growers. We cannot be producing without a market in mind. It is the contention of many of the Small Growers. All said and done, a bulk of the tea produced both in the Nilgiris as well as in the Anamalais is CTC variety only.

Marketing through E-Auction

The main business of BLF is with the small growers. This is the first stage of processing before 'made tea' goes to the auction centres at Coonoor or Coimbatore. The price is determined only by the market trends and not by growers or the government. The present auction system is reported to be placed in a great financial burden on BLFs as they have to wait almost three weeks to receive their payments. This delay causes unwanted burden to the BLFs and to the small tea growers. Often, in the auction centres, collusion-of-buyers takes place and they all get into a kind of syndicating so that price of tea does not go beyond what they mentally fix up, and are willing to pay for. Thus, the buyers tend to have a grip over the markets and clandestinely determine the price of tea. This is detrimental to the interests of the planters/producers.

One of the reasons for the auction system to have become less attractive is that it takes almost 30 days to make payment to the producers. The producers' view it as money getting locked. But the advantages are that because going through auction system is legal it involves no risk with regard to receiving payments, and accountability to the government in terms of tax payments. Credit transactions are not allowed under the auction system. The possibility for competition is more. Possibility for better prices to the producers is more. Selling out-side the auction system is risky, in the sense, often it is done with no papers for having carried out the transaction so as to evade tax. But still producers prefer to sell outside the auction system, because payment is made either immediately or the buyer gets credit based on the trustworthiness demonstrated earlier. The working capital requirement is less for the buyers who deal outside-auction system. The auction system gives the private traders a base price to transact the deal.

The other reasons for the auction system to have become less attractive are: the government has withdrawn export concessions and excise duty reimbursement, which served as motivating factors to go through the auction system. Recently, AST (Additional Sales Tax) is imposed on turn over that exceed worth Rs. 10 crores. These factors encourage the parties to finalise the deal outside the auction system without any legal formalities. The situation is business outside auction system flourishes. Private business remains private. No transparency. No accountability.

In a nutshell, first of all, USSR got divided and so the tea market of USSR which was in Indian hands slipped away, causing tea stock pile up. Secondly, arrival of better quality tea at a cheaper price from Sri Lanka and Kenya flooded Indian market which traders used for blending with Indian tea so as to increase their profit margin. It resulted in Indian tea losing a good portion of domestic market as well. Thirdly, tea traders who wanted to make use of the situation to their advantage purchased tea from Sri Lanka and Kenya at cheaper rate, stamped it: INDIAN TEA, and started re-exporting them from India. All these together have caused a very serious set back to Indian tea industry. The main sufferers are the plantation labourers and the planters including the small growers.

The current state of affairs is that big and long time players in the tea industry such as HLL (broke-bond), and Mahaveer plantations are selling off estates to small growers and smaller companies and are leaving the sector. Tata tea—another giant and a long time player in tea industry—is making strategic plans by putting to use concepts such as worker management of industry by seeking only a share in the profit from the workers who would own the estates. The plantation labourers who lost hope are climbing down to the plains in search of employment in hosiery and construction industries.

Coping Strategies

Soon after the year 2000, when the full impact of the financial crisis was felt, it was evident that the industry had to adopt a few unpleasant structural adjustments to face the new economic situation and to ensure the long-term survival of the industry. Elements of costs like power and fuel, fertilizers, insecticides, taxes etc., were beyond the control of the employers. The only cost element which could be rationalized was the labour cost which formed the largest chunk of the cost of production. Planters state that experts they consulted suggested that the wage cost should be reduced at least by 10 to 15 per cent.

As the tea price in auction centres fell down drastically, the plantation companies resorted to cost reduction strategies in all possible ways. It has almost stopped recruiting new labourers in place of the ones who retire. The companies seek extra task from the existing labourers and resort to recruiting casual labourers so that the company does not have to take responsibilities such as PF, gratuity, medical allowance, housing and so on. On Sundays and on week-days after extracting the legitimate amount of work, labourers are transported to other plantations of the same Group of Company to work for an additional payment of Rs. 2 per kg. of leaves plucked. Employment is shrinking in the estates.

Table 8.9 : Details of Employment Strength

Name of the Estates	*Employment Strength*		
	01-01-1979	*31-12-1985*	*2005 (Approximately)*
Kil-Kotagiri	1004	1094	600
Kothari Industrial Corporation	1346	1114	650
Craigmore	1905	1904	1200
Total	**4255**	**4112**	**2450**

Sources: (1) Joint Commissioner of Labour, Coimbatore, 1986.
(2) Assessment made during field level interactions.

The Planters Associations have entered into an agreement with labour unions for a downward revision of wages—both in Valparai as well as in the Nilgiris. It has led to almost a riot-like condition in the Nilgiris and Valparai in the year 2000-02. Employment in plantations is not lucrative for the wards of labourers of plantations. Many of them have learnt certain technical skills. They earn upto Rs. 800-1500 per week in Coimbatore and Thiruppur. The parents who toiled in the plantations life-long tend to give voluntary retirement and settle down in Coimbatore or in Thiruppur. Tea estates are not attractive any more as a place for employment. There is shortage of labourers in the plantations. The Plantation Companies think it is not wise to recruit new labourers on permanent basis, as it would warrant payment of all kinds of social benefits as per the Plantation Labour Act, Industrial Dispute Act, Bonus Act and so on.

Due to the pragmatic approach of the trade unions in Tamil Nadu, a marginal reduction of the labour wages has been effected, as opined by the experts, through various negotiated settlements. In Kerala, since the predominant plantation crop is Rubber which is an industrial raw material fetching better prices than Tea and Coffee, the wage levels for workers in all the crops are often fixed using the Rubber wages as the benchmark. More workers are employed in Rubber in Kerala than in Tea and Coffee. However, the high wage levels and the inability to rationalize such high wages have spelled doom for the industry in Kerala. Precedents are available in the State of Kerala where more than 30 estates had to be closed down and abandoned by the employers who were unable to withstand the financial burden.

Simultaneously, employers in Tamil Nadu were forced to cut down cost to the bone by reduced fertilizer application, rationalization of staff and executives strength through voluntary retirement schemes, re-grouping of estates, postponing replanting schedules etc. However, all these have only provided marginal relief on the cost front and the mismatch between price realization and cost of production still continues.

Employers in India are constrained by rigid labour legislations, prohibiting retrenchment or rationalization of productivity norms or the size of labour force. Faced with insurmountable problems, employers are left with no option but to allow the rot to set in and finally abandon their business. Moreover, there is a very wide gap in the wages paid to the estate labourers and the salary paid to those on management positions (employed). The salaries and other benefits given to those on management positions are several times more than the wages paid to the workers. This is precisely what has happened in some of the Kerala estates. When the return on investment is negative, no sane businessman would want to continue with it. If the situation remains as such over a long period of time, the expectation is that it could lead to the disintegration of the organized sector of plantations run by corporate houses. In the bargain, whatever is left of the industry would be highly fragmented. In such a situation, ultimately it is the workers who will suffer the most and large-scale unemployment could lead to undesirable social consequences.

The planters are in a situation where they have to produce the maximum out of the minimum, if they are to achieve at least some marginal cost reduction. The need for increase in productivity all-round has now been realized in the industry. Settlements have been reached with unions on increase in productivity levels of labour, with corresponding increase in the incentive amounts payable to workers, in order to motivate them to put in their best efforts. For instance, the plucking output of a plantation worker in the African state of Malawi is on an average at 70 kgs of green leaf per day; whereas the average plucking output of the South Indian worker is around 35 to 40 kgs of green leaf per day, even with a much higher daily wages than the Malawian worker. This is the level of cost advantage that our competitor-countries have over us.

Efforts are also on for greater level of private marketing of tea by the producers. Currently, there is a wide gap between the price realization of the producer and the retail price of tea. This is mainly because of the cost addition incurred at each stage of the supply chain, namely, brokers, wholesalers, distributors, retailers and so on, besides the cost involved in blending, packing and promotion of the product. If producers by themselves are able to gain a market share of the retail trade, it would be of great economic advantage to them. However, the reality is that the investment for promotion and the kind of volumes required for a sustainable and consistent supply of a standardized product is beyond the reach of many tea producers.

One of the options left for the plantation companies was to go in for 'mechanization'. But, technically, the topography of Nilgiris and the Anamalais, is said to be unsuitable for mechanization. This is one of the reasons why plantations are still employment-abundant industries. Therefore, either they employ casual labourers from the plains, or make use of the local tribals who have not hither to sought employment in the plantation sector.

Different employment models need to be explored in order to face the reality of globalization. Guaranteed payment to workers without linkage to productivity and price realization may not be sustainable in the long run. Alternatively, at least a rudimentary form of outsourcing of planting operations, either involving the existing workers or though 'out workers' is badly required to control cost. However, these ideas may not be feasible unless the present laws are made flexible.

MACRO-LEVEL CHANGES – COFFEE SECTOR

The following are the major macro-level changes that have taken place, as far as coffee sector is concerned:

- Until 1995, the Coffee Board of Ministry of Commerce, Government of India, had the monopolistic control over the marketing of coffee in India. After 1995, as part of liberalization measures, the marketing of coffee was made a private sector activity. The Coffee Board went through a massive down-sizing and two-thirds of its employees were retired under Voluntary Retirement Scheme. This is one significant change that has taken place in the Indian Coffee sector which has given way to the emergence of several other constraints as well as opportunities.
- As of now, marketing is a private affair. The Coffee Board involves only in basic and applied research, and in promotion of coffee consumption in India and abroad. The extension set up provides the day-to-day link with grower community and this wing facilitates transfer of technology from lab-to-land.
- The price of coffee is determined at international levels by International Coffee Organization (ICO) in New York and London. The growers are supposed to browse the web to find out the day's coffee price for Robusta and Arabica.
- Since the Coffee Board does not involve in marketing, there is no procurement or storing taking place by the Coffee Board. Therefore, the financial support the coffee growers were enjoying (through periodical payments from the Coffee Board) got done away with.
- The excise duty for import of coffee has not been reduced and so the import is under control.

- The Government of India has established a Price Stabilization Fund (PSF) Scheme for the benefit of coffee, tobacco, tea and rubber growers with effect from the year 2003-04 to bring in stability in terms of income for the small growers.
- After several representations by Planters' Association regarding rationalization of AIT (Agricultural Income Tax), the Government of Tamil Nadu took the decision to abolish the AIT with effect from 1-4-2004 which is considered as a major breakthrough in the coffee industry. However, sales tax, purchase tax and central sales tax on coffee seeds are still levied on coffee which are considered as burden faced by the coffee producers.
- The proposed levy of VAT (Value Added Tax) at 12.5 per cent on coffee with effect from 1-4-2005 is likely to affect the coffee industry.
- Agriculture cess is collected at the port of shipment by the customs authority for coffee exported out of India which is yet another burden on the coffee plantations. Coffee growers are optimistic that the package meant for the coffee industry announced by the Central Government would provide much-needed financial relief to the coffee growers.
- Sales tax, purchase tax and central sales tax are also levied on coffee which add to the burden of taxes suffered by the coffee producers.
- Agricultural Cess (Customs Duty) is collected at the port of shipment by the Customs Authority for coffee exported out of India.
- Local-body taxes land revenue on land and house-tax on building and plantation areas. Some estates have never paid these taxes to the Local bodies, while many of the estates have stopped paying after the crisis.

COFFEE SECTOR—THE MICRO-MACRO LINK

Introduction

Tamil Nadu is the third major coffee producing State of the country. As on 2000-01, coffee is grown in an area of 30,681 ha. of which Arabica occupies major (25,018 ha.) while remaining area is planted with Robusta coffee (5,663 ha.). The State contributes nearly 16,500 tonnes to the country's coffee production with an average productivity of 503 kg. per ha. which is less than the national average of 954 kg. per ha. (Coffee

Board, 2001). In India, there are 1.75 lakh growers, owning 3.50 lakh hectare of area, producing 3.00 lakh MT of coffee, employing, 5.00 lakh labourers, earning 1200 crores. In Tamil Nadu, Coffee is mainly grown in four regions viz. Pulneys, the Nilgiris, Shevroys (Yercaud/Salem), and Anamalais (Valparai/Coimbatore).

Table 8.10 : Coffee Production by States – 2005-2006*

(*in MT*)

Sl. No.	*State*	*Arabica*	*%*	*Robusta*	*%*	*Total*	*% to India*
1.	Karnataka	79175	28.1	120050	42.6	199225	70.7
2.	Kerala	1375	0.5	58800	20.9	60175	21.3
3.	Tamil Nadu	15150	5.4	4400	1.6	19550	6.9
4.	Non-Traditional Area	2850	1.0	100	0.0	2950	1.0
	Total	**98550**	**35.0**	**183350**	**65.00**	**281900**	**100.0**

Source: Economic and Market Intelligence Unit, Coffee Board, Bangalore.
* Post-Monsoon Estimate.

Pulney hills form the major coffee area of Tamil Nadu (15,000 ha.) produced about 7,000 tonnes. In the Nilgiris coffee is cultivated in 7,785 ha. out of which Robusta occupies 4,175 ha. and the remaining area by Arabica coffee. In Shevaroys coffee is planted over an area of 5,020 ha. of which 5,000 ha. is under Arabica, while only a few hectares is under

Table 8.11 : No. of Holdings under Different Size Categories of Traditional Coffee Growing in Tamil Nadu – 2003-2004

(*in M. kgs.*)

Ha.	*Arabica*	*Robusta*	*Total*
< 2	8241	3247	11488
2-4	1296	498	1794
4-10	645	152	797
10-20	189	25	214
20-40	49	2	51
40-60	25	5	30
60-80	10	1	11
80-100	1	2	3
> 100	7	4	11
Grand Total	**10463**	**3936**	**14399**

Source: ICO and Coffee Board.

Robusta. So, Arabica and Robusta are the two major varieties of coffee grown. Small growers form a majority (98%) with only 25 per cent area, while the 2 per cent large holdings occupy the remaining 75 per cent of the area. Productivity in small grower sector is only 300 kg./ha. while in large holdings it is 450 kg./ha. with an average of 400 kg./ha. for the entire zone.

In Tamil Nadu those who own less than 2 hectares are the vast majority. Hardly 11 holdings are more than 100 hectares size. Arabica and Robusta are the two varieties of coffee grown in India, and in most countries of the world. Arabica is grown in more area than the Robusta variety.

Employment

Many of the coffee planters grow coffee along with pepper, banana, orange, and beans. This fetches additional income or a cushion that can save the planters during drought. Almost everyday bananas from coffee plantation areas such as Perumbarai go to Chennai as lorry loads. Coffee sector gives a lot of employment opportunities through growing, curing, manufacturing and trade. Coffee cultivation is one of the occupations where employment prevails almost throughout the year, although generally October to March is said to be the high-season time. The Economic & Market Intelligence Unit of the Coffee Board, Government of India reports that the coffee plantations in Tamil Nadu employ about 26,900 workers (2003-04). Employment in coffee estates would be at its peak during October-March, and so, the big estates-owners have a tendency not to keep many permanent workers. The ratio of permanent workers to casual workers is 1:5. They employ a handful of permanent workers, and hire casual labourers either locally or from the plains during peak seasons. The employers think:

(i) this is economical for them, and
(ii) they can keep away from paying the statutory benefits they need to pay several permanent labourers whom otherwise they would have employed.

The number of people dependent on coffee cultivation in Tamil Nadu is presented in Table 8.12:

BOX 8.1
Seasonality in Coffee Cultivation

Employment opportunities are plenty during harvesting season as far as coffee is concerned. However, the private estate management does not consider coffee cultivation as a full-time occupation. The seasonality estate management talks about the following: Stripping (February); cleaning and pruning (March); weeding, pre-blossom manuring; borer control, boundry clearing; nursery work (April and May); shade lopping, removing suckers, handling and spraying (June); weeding, post-blossom manuring and planting (July and August); and spraying, lime application, borer control and fly picking (September and October). During the plucking season (November to January), the causal labourers are brought from the plains.

Table 8.12 : Details of Average Daily Number of Persons Employed in Coffee Plantations in Tamil Nadu

Districts	*1996-97*	*1997-98*	*1998-99*	*1999-00*	*2000-01*	*2001-02*	*2002-03*	*2003-04**
Pulneys	19940	19820	19940	19940	19940	17946	18029	18159
Nilgiris	3640	3640	3630	3630	3630	3267	3291	3281
Salem (Shevroys)	3830	3830	3830	3830	3830	3447	3466	3471
Coimbatore (Anamalais)	2260	2260	2260	2260	2260	2034	2044	2049
Total	**29670**	**29550**	**29660**	**29660**	**29660**	**26694**	**26830**	**26960**

*Provisional.

Source: Economic & Market Intelligence Unit, Coffee Board, Bangalore.

Wages

As far as wage rates are concerned, it is not uniform in all the states. The smallness of the holding does not require many labourers. Many of the small coffee growers work in their farms. Again the smallness of the holdings does not provide the required number of labourers to form labour unions. So, coffee still remains a sector where the lowest wages are paid. It is strange to note that marginal and small coffee growers work as labourers (Yercaud area) in private coffee estates. The permanent workers in estates get Rs. 59.58 a day and temporary workers get Rs. 45 a day. Although women are predominantly employed in coffee estates, there is no gender-based discrimination noticed in wage payments. Many of the small coffee growers and almost all of the plantation workers have a tendency to borrow from the private money-lenders, and pawn brokers who often commute from the plains. Weekly shandy (market) is their usual meeting point to get further loan or to redeem a part of the loan received already or to pay the interest alone.

Table 8.13 : Wage Rates Prevailing in the Coffee Sector

States	*Wages (Rs./day)*
Karnataka	71.00
Kerala	86.18
Tamil Nadu	58.00
Andhra Pradesh	73.45

Source: Economic and Market Intelligence Unit, Coffee Board, Bangalore, August 2005.

Role of the Government

Until the year 1993 the Coffee Board, under the Ministry of Commerce and Industry of the Government, had the monopoly of handling coffee market in India single-handedly. Marketing was a major activity of the Coffee Board. The Board used to get about Rs. 400 crores from the RBI as over draft for marketing related operations and used to redistribute sale-proceeds to the growers. After the free-trade policy came into being, the growers were allowed to sell upto 70 per cent of their harvest in any open-market they chose to. It means it was enough if they sold about 30 per cent through the Coffee Board. After a couple of years, this was made 90:10 per cent and after 1995, it is completely free. There is always conflict of statements made regarding the civic facilities to be provided to those who reside in plantation areas: if estate management should provide them or the Panchayats should provide them.

The government (i.e. Coffee Board) is not in the marketing scene anymore. It has been made completely private, free and open. The marketing wing has been closed down and to that extent VRS has been implemented to reduce staff at the Coffee Board. The Coffee Board is now involved in research, extension services and campaigns for promotion of coffee drinking habits among the public. It helps organize and participate in trade-fairs and international coffee melas.

BOX. 8.2

Availing Government Benefits

There are 8 revenue villages in Kodaikanal Union under Coffee Board. The following is a case of how small farmers formed into SHGs were able to avail Coffee Board Schemes.

Sl. No.	*Name of the Revenue Village*	*No. of Growers*
1.	Adukkam	248
2.	Vilpatty	418
3.	Vellakavi	120
4.	Vadakavunji	850
5.	Kookul	15
6.	Poondi	25
7.	Manavanur	20
8.	Poomparai	59
	Total	**1755**

Out of 1755 small coffee growers, 1446 are having less than two acres. The Coffee Board renders on-farm and off-farm services to small growers of coffee. Apart from these facilities, encouragement for replanting and quality up-gradation are done by the Coffee Board. To be able to avail some of the government schemes, the small growers are asked to surrender land patta to the Coffee Board. This is not possible for many of them because many of them have joint pattas or they have not transferred the name while sub-dividing among sons and daughters etc. This was a constraint in availing government benefits. This facilitated the big farmers only to avail Coffee Board Schemes. Recently, 25 small coffee growers from Adukkam Panchayat have formed SHG to avail benefits from the Coffee Board. It has been registered to receive Rs. two lakhs from the Coffee Board to construct a room, drying-yard, purchase of machineries etc.

After the market system became open, no buyer needs to reveal for whom a buyer is purchasing and to whom he would sell. There are international prices that get uploaded on the Internet. You get coffee price at New York, and London at the click of a mouse. An Inter-governmental organization, which speaks for both producers and consumers, called ICO (International Coffee Organization), does this function. This organization develops political solutions and coffee policy for several governments world over. If a farmer wanted to know the day's coffee price (of any variety) at Thandikudi in Dindigul, he is expected to browse the web and find out the price uploaded by the ICO.

Demand-Supply Disparity

One of the major problems with coffee or any product for that matter is over production, creating a wide demand-supply disparity. For example, the world's coffee production was 130 million bags and the world's consumption was 100 million bags. In that scenario naturally the growers must get a fair return. The prices would be sustainable to the growers. Suppose many farmers become over-ambitious and start producing coffee, taking into consideration the fact that coffee is a marketable commodity and it has export potentials as well, then it creates a glut in the market. It has sometimes become global glut as well. The market conditions pull down the prices so badly that it becomes completely non-remunerative. In the past 10-15 years every country started growing coffee. Even Chinese, who until a few years ago have not tasted coffee at all, have started cultivating coffee. Brazil and Vietnam, big players in coffee business, have expanded the area and have gone very vigorously. While India is going very slowly, not doubling up the production. India has never been a major player on coffee front. Our share to the world coffee trade is hardly 4 per cent.

Analysis of Causes and Influences

Most of the (about 98%) coffee plantations in India, or in Tamil Nadu for that matter belong to small growers only. By small growers it is meant those who own less than 10 acres. One of the major changes that the coffee industry in India underwent was in 1995, when Coffee Board got its marketing function wound up. The market became open to the coffee producers. It was good news for big players in coffee business such as the Hindustan Lever Ltd., and the Tatas. But for many of the small growers, it was sweepingly drastic for they did not know any other mode of marketing. Until then the small growers were being spoon-fed by the Coffee Board. So, for them it was something like they were left high and dry. However, the years that followed—that is until

2002—proved that open market prices could give them better prices. The prices touched as high as Rs. 150 a kg.

But, in the year 2003, Vietnam coffee flooded Indian markets causing a glut in the local coffee market. The prices fell to a rock bottom of Rs. 40 a kg. This fall was reported as 'drastic fall' which the previous 100 years never experienced. This fall was not exclusive for India, it was a glut experienced world over. Now, the prices that rule are moderate and reasonable – between Rs. 70 and Rs. 90. The price of coffee is determined in New York and in London. That is the universal price applicable all over the globe after free market came into being. This free market policy and the act of browsing the web to find out the day's prices are all for the knowledge society, or for the so-called company estates. Some of the growers have access to such facilities, whereas many of the small and marginal coffee growers only 'come to know the price as a hearsay'. One interesting thing about globalization is that even the tribals who grow coffee talk in terms of British pounds and cents, because prices for *arabica* and *robusta* variety of coffee are fixed in London.

After globalization the medium and large sized planters as well as the company estates participate in trade fairs and in regional quality coffee awards such as 'Fine Cup of India Award' etc. The trend in some parts of the world now is for 'estate branded coffee' that fetches a premium price. Participation in trade fairs and exhibitions enable them to penetrate the market and be able to position the coffee as a branded product, whereas small growers of coffee are still trying to sell coffee as a commodity. Globalization has made this market penetration possible for those who are knowledgeable and moneyed. Despite the fact that India is not a major coffee producing country, we export coffee to 30-40 countries. But, only after globalization and after participating in many trade fairs, many countries of the world have come to know that India is also producing coffee.

The small growers are still contented selling their produce at the farm-gate price, whereas those growers who are enterprising, question: *'why should somebody else (be it the Coffee Board or anybody for that matter) do the marketing for me? When I present my produce to the market, I am able to see for myself why I get this price and how my neighbour is able to get a better price. I would find ways to improve the quality to be able to stand in the market and fetch a better price? I also understand the market mantras rather than blindly dumping my produce to the Coffee Board who would make payments in bits and pieces,* says a small grower of coffee who has his coffee farm in Pattiveeranpatty (Dindigul) and lives in Salem. If this guts should develop the planters must be knowledgeable and prudent to decide when to sell and when to retain his produce. The planters need to be alert to the market trends, and be familiar to put information technology to the best possible use.

Coffee Production: Tamil Nadu is the third major coffee producing State of the country, next to Karnataka and Kerala. We produce approximately 20,000 metric tonnes a year, whereas we consume nearly 25,000 metric tonnes. Coffee consumption is much less compared to tea consumption in Tamil Nadu, especially because of the relative price difference—tea is slightly cheaper. Nestle India Ltd. and Hindustan Lever Ltd. are the two companies that rule the coffee market in Tamil Nadu. In addition to these companies that have their factories in Karnataka, we have several regional brands that come in various brand names such as: Narasu's Coffee, Leo Coffee, Joseph's Coffee, Pandian Coffee, Gemini Coffee and so on. The market tends to lean towards that producer who responds to consumer tastes and preferences and so, regional brands such as the Narasu's Coffee which was known for making pure filter coffee and blended coffee, have recently started manufacturing instant coffee also. Narasu's Coffee is opening up foreign trade in coffee. It all suggests that growing coffee for a business is welcome and not a subsistence proposition.

Table 8.14 : Coffee Production in Tamil Nadu

(in metric tonnes)

Sl. No.		*2005-2006**			*2005-2006#*		
		Arabica	*Robusta*	*Total*	*Arabica*	*Robusta*	*Total*
1.	Pulneys	7875	300	8175	7975	275	8250
2.	Nilgiris	1575	3625	5200	1675	3650	5325
3.	Shevroys (Salems)	4175	0	4175	4300	0	4300
4.	Anamalais (Covai)	1525	475	2000	1600	500	2100
	Total	**15150**	**4400**	**19550**	**15550**	**4425**	**19975**

Source : Economic & Market Intelligence Unit, Coffee Board, Bangalore.
* Post-Monsoon Estimate. # Post-Blossom Forecast.

Coffee Marketing

Brazil is one of the major coffee producing countries in the world, and Brazil is the main competitor to many coffee producing countries across. In 1993-94, Brazil's coffee plantation was affected by frost. At that time, coffee growers in Tamil Nadu got a price up to Rs. 160/kg. Incidentally, it was a little before the marketing wing of the Coffee Board was removed.

In 2005, coffee price became normal with Rs. 90-95/kg. due to average coffee production in Brazil. When production becomes abundant in Brazil the price falls to Rs. 65-70/kg. However, 'A' grade and premium coffee varieties are given slightly higher price in the market. The liberalized policies taken by the government paved way for anybody to involve in coffee business. Permit license from coffee board for doing coffee business is no longer required. Traders who involved in the business know coffee prices over phone from coffee exporting traders who are mostly operating from Bangalore.

After liberalized policies taken by the government, private traders are allowed in coffee business. They powder coffee seeds even through rice mill. There are no quality control measures followed by such private traders. They dry the seeds on road; they don't maintain quality; they don't control the moisture content; and they don't adhere to any of the quality standards. The marketing practice is that the agents are given advance money by the big companies like Joseph, Leo, Eswari and Pandiyan. The agents buy coffee seeds from the marginal and small farmers. They grade the quality and give them to the company located in different places with a marginal profit of 25-50 paise. Apart from these agents, there are middlemen involved in buying coffee seeds and giving them to the local coffee power selling stalls. Many growers sell coffee seeds at farm itself to the agents of big coffee curing companies. Similarly, the growers who borrowed from private coffee curers are also not in a position to choose where they would sell. Often, they have to sell it to the businessman who lent money during cultivation. The LAMPS (cooperative) is not very much functional to support the small growers financially.

Instead of bid auction, private traders are engaged in open-market of coffee. The private traders purchase through agents and they sell it to the big companies such as Joseph, Leo, Pandiyan which export coffee to various countries from Tuticorin, Kochin, and Bangalore. Some of the private traders are also exporting coffee to various countries directly. Small traders are not able to export coffee directly because of the largeness of the volume required for export (one container is said to contain 18 tonnes of coffee). So, only big companies are involved in coffee export. Samples of coffee from farm or from local brokers are sent to Bangalore where exporters are doing the coffee business.

Similarly, particular grade and quantity may be required from Bangalore which can be communicated over phone or by fax.

Previously curing was controlled by the Coffee Board. Private curing companies were also controlled by the Coffee Board. The companies had to devote certain time for curing only. Now, they are engaged in curing-*cum*-trading. For example, there were three curing works at Pattiveeranpatty (Pulneys). Now, only one curing works (Joseph) is functioning. Other two (Justin Leoanard and Pattiveeranpatty Coffee-*cum*-Cardamom Growers Co-operative Ltd.) have become bankrupt and are dormant now.

Some of the Coffee growers who visited trade fairs in countries such as Vietnam report that coffee growers in such countries participate in exhibitions and trade fairs in large numbers and try to obtain orders. They show samples and canvass orders speaking broken English such as: "*See this coffee sample, sir. Best Quality sir. You buy our coffee, sir.*" The contrast is that the small growers in Tamil Nadu sell at the nearest coffee procurement centre and walk off. The practice of intercrop-cultivation and cultivation of silver oak trees act as cushion during financial crisis. The trees are also useful for supporting creepers like pepper.

You provide options the growers can choose from. This is a concept favoured by the open-market policy. Secondly, some of the studies conducted by the Government have shown that the marketing expenditure is so much with the Coffee Board. For many of the MNCs in the Coffee Sector, Nestle for example, their marketing expenditures are about 3 per cent of their turn over. But for the Coffee Board it was upto 20 per cent of the turn over. But then you must understand that if you are aiming at small growers, your marketing expenditures are bound to increase. When we discuss marketing you need to add upto the cost of procurement as well. Thirdly, the produce comes for 3 months and we need to structure the distribution for 12 months. It means the commodity remains in your hands for quite a few months before being converted into cash. In the process, the money is locked in the form of inventory where the producer loses on the interest he would, otherwise, be earning. All these add upto the total marketing cost. Now the Board is not involved in marketing.

Growers like Tata Coffee, Hindustan Levers, and Manjushree Coffee have realized and have the knowledge of the world trade and world's trends. For example, the Tata Coffee has acquired the EOC (Eight O'clock Coffee Company) in the US recently. EOC has about 60 per cent of the US population as his customers. So, Tata's coffee production from India would find a confirmed market in the US. There are certain sectors called Specialty Coffee Association (SCA). We have SCA America, SCA India etc. who have established tie-ups and commodity/product flows. In such arrangements transparency is completely absent. It all takes place under a veil. So, the big players are safe. Only the small growers are helpless and the fact is that they make the major chunk of Indian Coffee Industry. One option left for our small growers is that they can try to catch hold of the customers that the big coffee producers such as the Tata's might not be able to cater to, because of their concentration in making a presence in the foreign market.

Limitations to Stretching too Far: One of the serious limitations with regard to small growers in Tamil Nadu or in India for that matter is the size of landholdings. Most of the holdings are small, that is, less than 2 acres. Sub-division and fragmentation render it smaller again year after year making it economically unviable. They do not get into grips with the market trends. This smallness of the holdings is one of the factors that is holding Tamil Nadu coffee sector back. The government is trying to see that we measure upto the international standards supporting the small growers, especially, through extension and research. Grants are made available for infrastructure development like construction of godowns, purchase of machineries, technology up-gradation, training in quality up-gradation, etc. Geographical Indication System is another patent type of thing, the government is doing for protecting the uniqueness of some of our coffee varieties such as *monsoon malabar coffee, coorg coffee, Nilgiris tea,* etc. These are domestic preparedness the government is attempting. However, the inconsistencies in offering support and lack of continuity of support, especially, to small growers remain problems.

The way out suggested by many experts in the sector is that the growers have to unite. They need to be exposed to international standards. There is a need to emphasize that if they want to make their presence in the world market, they need to adhere to those standards, sanitary and phyto-sanitary measures before going for competition in the international markets. The management models might also require certain changes such as going for contract farming, collective farming, cooperative farming, etc.

If the small growers are happy with the price, they are getting at the farm-gate, nobody can help them. All other countries view India as a very good marketplace taking into account the magnitude of the population. Our small growers do not know how to cash in on their produce. Without preparing the growers to the level of producing quality coffee to compete in open and international markets when we open up, it might collapse. Those who are knowledgeable and alert make use of liberalization, and they are, in fact, happy about open-market policy. But to make all the small growers associate and work in a united manner is the real challenge. First of all, we need to teach our small grower to look beyond his farm-gate.

Summary of Findings

A researcher who undertakes to study the plantation sector cannot view the sector as one or two distinct entities (as coffee sector or tea sector). Rather, a disaggregated analysis of the goings-on in the sector for large sized-company estates, the small growers and the labourers involved in these sectors are considered in order to have a clear picture of the status of the sector.

The study aimed at understanding the reasons for the crisis in tea and coffee industries in Tami Nadu, and to find out if the policy changes of the government caused the crisis. It has also pointed out the impact of the crisis on the planters and the plantation workers in Tamil Nadu. The following are the summary of major findings.

This empirical enquiry conducted by the RGC-GRI reveals that globalization processes affect not only the small growers, but also the big players — the company-managed estates. The difference is one of degree and not of nature. In other words, the brunt can vary based on the capacity to bear, but the nature is the same.

Reasons for the Crisis

Adoption of liberalization policy by the Government of India is attributed as one of the main reasons for the crisis tea and coffee industries, especially the tea industry, is undergoing today. The reason why the government had been supporting coffee sector more than the tea sector is obvious. About 95 per cent of those involved in coffee sector are small growers with landholdings not exceeding 10 acres. The tea sector, although it has considerable number of small growers, the sector has several big players, who can manage on their own.

The planters are at a loss. The plantation labourers are quitting the sector. The Government of India—as it adopts a policy of making omelette without breaking eggs—is not in a position to pitch in for rescue. Several factors – both internal and external – have contributed to this state of affairs. By internal factors is meant problems which were very much within the hold of the tea industry, they did not take any action about it though. By external means the corollary of liberalization. The internal factors include:

- Age of Indian tea shrubs are anywhere between 80 and 120 years. They are too old to provide a good quality orthodox tea as demanded by black tea consumers of the west.
- Cost of production of Indian tea is comparatively higher which works out disadvantageous at the market place.
- After India got huge orders from the erstwhile USSR, India did not concentrate sufficiently on retaining the customers it served before. When India woke up to the reality of having lost the USSR market, with the need to fall back on the customers it had earlier, all the earlier customers of Indian tea had changed place.
- When the supply was only to the USSR, the quality was not a big deal. USSR needed only CTC variety. After losing the USSR market, India had to approach a whole range of customers including those who seek orthodox tea (pure and superior quality) for which neither our cultivation practices nor the machineries were malleable.
- Absence of quality consciousness especially among the Bought Leaf Factories who generally do not have a brand name.
- The practice of CTC tea (inferior quality) production in the past years rendering conversion to orthodox tea (better quality) very difficult.
- The scattered settlement of Bought Leaf Factories (BLF) is not within the easy reach of small growers. It renders late reach of green leaves to the BLF resulting in the production of poor quality of tea.
- Inability to cope with the market trends and fashions such as not being able to cater to the demand for ice tea, lemon tea, cold tea etc.
- The hazard of selling adulterated tea (with mere colourants) is widely prevalent all over Tamil Nadu. Sellers of such adulterated tea materials target especially the tea shops that calculate only in terms of cuppage per kilo.

- The youth today think it is fashionable to take Coke or Pepsi instead of taking tea/coffee, and this has caused general reduction in the demand for tea. This is another view expressed for the insufficient demand for tea.

So much so, several external factors can also be pointed out as reasons for the set back the Indian tea industry is undergoing for the past few years. The principal of them which point at liberalization as the cause are the following:

- The tea shrubs in Sri Lanka and Kenya are not more than 30-40 years old. So, green leaf growth is more and quality is also definitely higher.
- Several countries such as Indonesia, Myanmar, Malaysia which did not cultivate tea earlier (or cultivated in a small area) started concentrating on manufacturing tea, and marketing world-wide.
- Another interesting aspect is, statistics show that India sells more than what it produces. It means, there is much adulteration material going in, or sale of tea from other countries being blended with Indian tea etc.
- Tea from countries such as Kenya, Sri Lanka, and Vietnam are arriving in India. Tea traders buy them, especially for blending with local tea variety in a bid to pep up the profit margin.
- Tea traders buy foreign made-tea, stamp them as INDIA TEA and re-export to countries such as Pakistan who buy from India.
- Planters in the Nilgiris and Anamalais report that one of the main reasons for the cost of production in countries such as Sri Lanka and Kenya to be less compared to India is, especially, because of absence of statutory social benefits rendered to plantation labour in such countries, whereas India has to abide by all labour laws.
- To be able to capture the Indian market, Sri Lanka sells its tea with a meagre profit margin, which it might increase once they hold the market in hand.

The situation affected not only the small growers of tea but also giant players in tea industry such as the Hindustan Lever Limited and the Tatas. The situation in Tamil Nadu is not one of recovering, but of preventing from falling further down. Plantation companies these days do not make profit-planning exercises. Rather they make plans only for reducing the cost of production, bringing down administrative overheads, getting into agreements with labour unions to increasing the task an average worker performs (augmenting labour productivity), retrenchment and economizing on staff at supervisory and managerial levels, mergre of plantations, putting to use concepts such as 'worker management of plantation industry', and leasing out of estates to SHGs, and small growers and so on.

The Government of India has clearly shown – by winding up the marketing function of the Coffee Board, and making e-auction not an exclusive place to sell tea – that doing business or being in business is none of government's business. If at all the government showed some interest in the plantation sector, it might be for two distinct reasons: (i) tea and coffee are labour intensive sectors. In Tamil Nadu alone there are about 2.5 lakh labourers and their families, who depend on tea and coffee gardens for a living; (ii) serving tea and coffee is a culture related activity in India, and so for the quantum of tea and coffee required for India's consumption, importing them would cost a handsome foreign exchange.

Perhaps, these are the prime reasons why the government still supports activities like extension and research in these sectors. Otherwise, it is for anybody to do the tea/coffee business and not the government's. By making the market for tea and coffee open and free, the government has put across clearly that marketing is for the enterprising and that the government would not play protectionism any longer. Whether one sells his tea and coffee at the auction system or outside the auction system it is for the producers and buyers to decide. There is no compulsion that the transaction should take place in designated auction centres only. The modified role that the government has assumed is that it comes out with schemes for quality up-gradation and other kinds of domestic preparedness so as to enable the Indian tea and coffee industries face the global competition.

One of the challenges that globalization has brought about, especially, in the tea sector, and to some extent in the coffee sector, after the government took the back-seat allowing the private players to operate in full swing is that bulk tea and coffee from other countries arriving Indian market. The guise is that it comes especially for re-export, which is permissible as per law. This has turned favourable to the traders and brokers. They dictate terms to the local producers that they do not have to depend on domestic production. This is especially so in tea, though not in coffee where the import duties are a little higher. The fortune of producers who actually toil in the process of bringing out tea to the market is at the mercy of the traders and brokers/agents. In a market that has surplus production, when there is an accumulation caused from outside the country, it creates unfavourable situation to the producers. The WTO provisions of Quantitative Restrictions and Anti-dumping do not seem to be in place, especially in tea sector. Or a portion of imported tea meant for re-export goes for local consumption camouflaged as Indian tea. The situation is that it has completely become traders' and brokers' arena rather than producers'.

The second aspect is that the market has been made free and open, in the sense, for example tea producers do not have to sell tea through the e-auction centres. They are allowed to sell outside the auction system, if they desire so. This has made possible for the producers not to maintain any meticulous accounts as to how much they sold to which buyer at what price etc., making sales tax and excise duty evasion possible. Buyers can directly source their requirements from the factories known to them. Every transaction being accounted for sales tax and excise-duty purposes are by passed. Private sales mostly become illegal with no returns filed. *The government had only rules earlier, which were very stringent. After it was made free and open certain rules have been made flexible. Now, only the flexibility works and rules do not work any more,* opines a tea trader. Although it involves risk especially to the producer, business outside the auction system is on the fast track.

Auction system has become less attractive. The producers think that sale under auction system causes undue delay in receiving payment from the auction centre. Sales out-side auction system also enable evading sales tax and AST etc.

Coffee in Tamil Nadu is generally a small growers' arena. About 98 per cent of the coffee planters are small growers, who are satisfied at farm-gate price. They are unaware of what international coffee standards are. Coffee Board has wound up its marketing function. Coffee prices are determined at international levels by the International Coffee Organisation (ICO). Knowledgeable big players like the Tata Coffee make use of this, while small planters are contented selling it locally. Intercrops in coffee plantations have enabled them to sustain their income levels.

One of the major changes that the coffee industry in India underwent was in 1995 when Coffee Board got its marketing function wound up. The market became open to the coffee producers. It was good news for big players in coffee business such as the Hindustan Lever Ltd. and the Tatas. But for many of the small growers it was sweepingly drastic, for they did not know any other mode of marketing. Many of the coffee planters grow along with pepper, banana, orange, and beans. This fetches additional income or a cushion that can save the planters during drought.

The big estates owners have a tendency not to keep many permanent workers. They employ a handful of permanent workers, and hire casual labourers either locally or from the plains during peak seasons. The employers think: (i) this is economical for them, and (ii) they can keep away from paying the statutory benefits they need to pay several permanent labourers whom otherwise they would have employed.

Coffee still remains a sector where the lowest wages are paid. Although women are predominantly employed in coffee estates, there is no gender-based discrimination noticed in wage payments.

One of the major problems with coffee is over-production, creating a wide demand-supply disparity. Many farmers become over-ambitious and start producing coffee taking into consideration the fact that coffee is a marketable commodity and it has export potentials as well, then it creates a glut in the market. It has sometimes become global glut as well. The market conditions pull down the prices so badly that it becomes completely non-remunerative. In the past 10-15 years every country started growing coffee. Even Chinese, who until a few years ago have not tasted coffee at all, are also starting to cultivate coffee. Brazil and Vietnam, big players in coffee business, have expanded the area and have gone very vigorously. Whereas India is going very slowly, not doubling up the production.

After globalization the medium and large-sized planters as well as the company estates participate in trade fairs and in regional quality coffee awards etc. The trend in some parts of the world now is for 'estate branded coffee' that fetches a premium price. One of the obvious benefits of globalization and after participating in many trade fairs, many countries of the world come to know that India is also producing coffee. Participation in trade fairs and exhibitions enable them to penetrate the market and be able to position the coffee as a branded product, whereas small growers of coffee are still trying to sell coffee as a commodity. Globalization has made this market penetration possible for those who are knowledgeable and moneyed. The small growers are still contented selling their produce at the farm-gate price.

One of the serious limitations with regard to small growers in Tamil Nadu or in India for that matter is the size of landholdings. Most of the holdings are small say, less than 2 acres. Sub-division and fragmentation render it smaller again year after year making it economically unviable. They do not get into grips with the market trends. This smallness of the holdings is one of the factors that is holding Tamil Nadu coffee sector back. The government is trying to see that we measure upto the international standards supporting the small growers especially through extension and research. Grants are made available for infrastructure development like construction of godowns, purchase of machineries, technology up-gradation, training in quality up-gradation etc. Geographical indication system is another patent type of thing, the government is doing for protecting the uniqueness of some of our coffee varieties such as *monsoon malabar coffee, coorg coffee, Nilgiris tea* etc. These are domestic preparedness the government is attempting.

ANNEXURE – I
PATTIVEERANPATTI COFFEE-*CUM*-CARDAMOM GROWERS CO-OPERATIVE LTD. (A CASE)

It is called 'PCC' for short. It was started in 1940. It provided employment opportunities to women who came from Pattiveeranpatti and nearby villages. Now, it is dormant. It was making profit until 1988-89. It met with loss since 1989-90. The net profit was Rs. 2,19,141 during the year of 1987-88.

Particulars	*Up to 1995*	*As of now (18-08-2006)*
Membership	6000	3000
Curing works done	20 lakhs/year	Nil
Machineries holding	20 lakhs, operational	Idle
Paying Central Excise Duty	Yes	Nil
Usage of 1000 tonnes capacity godowns	Three	Nil
Drying yard	Used	Used partially
Salary to staff	Regular	One year pending of salary
No. of employees working	65	13 including six members who have quit their jobs.
Land area coverage	5 acres	Idle
Sales tax payment	Yes	Nil
Short-term loan to members	Regular	Irregular

Field Pulse

- Those working for this society and those benefit from this society have a feeling that like TANTEA, Tamil Nadu Government should undertake the control over the society. Tamil Nadu Government can procure coffee from the coffee growers and sell it to the government-approved traders.

9

Traditional Rural Artisans: Remaining Contemporarily Relevant

The Premise

Pursuits in agriculture have proved time and again that it is non-remunerative, and so distress departure from agriculture is commonplace in Tamil Nadu. This is evident from the fact that the proportion of population involved in agriculture has come down considerably in the last few years. One pertinent question at this juncture is: what is happening about the occupations (especially traditional rural artisans) that are dependent on agriculture? It could be carpenters who used to make the bullock cart and other agricultural implements to the farmers; it could be blacksmiths who used to make spades, and ploughshares; it could be potters who made pots and household utensils for the community in general; and the traditional stone carvers who made temple idols making use of stones. If agriculturists themselves are in grief, what is happening to the rural artisans who, most often, depended on agriculturists? This is relevant in the sense, among the 93 per cent of the workforce that is unorganized in India, most of them either belong to agricultural sector or work as artisans. In other words, artisans are a major chunk of people who are unorganized next to those in agriculture.

The dynamic nature of the society is on high-gear after India started adopting policies that further the concepts and models of globalization and liberalization. Although earning one's livelihoods, making use of assets such as land, tools such as spade, and capabilities such as farming existed even during the primitive age, there is a need to talk about livelihood of the poor and the traditional artisans in the changing socio-political and economic environment. This is required, especially, because the digital divide has clearly brought about two Indias—the India of the poor and the India of the rich. Our concern is about the India of the poor, where marginal and small farmers, agricultural labourers, farm women, and traditional rural artisans live.

The globalization policy of 'one size fits all' and viewing everything with a market mind-set, naming it efficiency, has become a culture all over, without taking into account the human factor behind it. For the rural artisans, who were once addressed as native engineers, the toughest thing today, perhaps, is remaining contemporarily relevant. There are new machines, fresh knowledge, new technologies, and capsule courses being introduced one after another in all spheres of work. It is quite understandable that for our traditional artisans keeping the tools-box dusted and the tools periodically sharpened would not be sufficient to remain relevant in the market.

Are our rural artisans, the tools they work with, and the capabilities they put to work keep changing to remain contemporarily relevant? It is a vital question in the context of globalization. This is pertinent because these days trade zooms; trade-oriented capacities and skills thrive; and traditional capabilities with primitive kind of tools that used to provide livelihoods to a section of population are generally at peril. It is in this context, we analyse the livelihood aspects of traditional rural artisans of Tamil Nadu.

Who Do We Call: 'Traditional Rural Artisans', After All?

Who do we mean when we generally say: 'Traditional Rural Artisans'? The dictionary definition is safe but escapist. It says: 'skilled workman or craftsperson'. Only when one attempts to understand and explain the expression empirically, one comes to know that by tradition and convention it has acquired certain definition; and the agencies of the Government and NGOs that came to promote artisans welfare expanded the scope of the definition to be of help to an array of artisans. There is no one confirmed definition to explain who all form rural artisans.

Getting down to documenting the societally accepted definition of rural artisans is one unplanned outcome of the research on Globalization and Decentralization at the Rajiv Gandhi Chair for Panchayati Raj Studies of the Gandhigram Rural University. *Viswakarmas*, also referred to as *panchalas* consists of the age-old five primary disciplines dealing in iron, wood, gold, all other metals such as bronze and copper and *Silpi* (stone carving, making statues and building temples etc.). Therefore, traditional artisans by definition included five occupationally related sections of the community mentioned above. Potters should have been there even before metal workers came in. Viewed from that angle one needs to start the definition all over again with potters to begin with. Hence, one conventionally acceptable definition of traditional rural artisans should include: Potters, carpenters, blacksmiths, goldsmiths, and other workers in metals (brass-vessel makers) and stonesmiths (or stone carvers). Other rural artisans such as those involved in *cora* mat weaving, those involved in basketry etc. are later additions, perhaps after the setting up of the Khadi and Village Industries Commission (KVIC), Handicrafts Board etc.

The five traditional artisans (known as *Viswakarma* or *Kammalar*), apart from the claim they make of the references being made about them in *Vedas*, in fact, as occupational groups and native engineers have gone into scientific and sociological documentation way back in 1805 itself (Abbe J.A. Dubois, 1805), whereas all the other crafts have only followed them. Although they were known for their engineering precision and meticulous workmanship in several jobs such as stone carving, wood carving, gold-jewellery making and so on, technological intervention and introduction of machineries have, lately, been a challenge to them.

As social groups or caste groups, each one is recognized by a different name although one common noun used to refer to all of them is: '*Asari*'. Separately, those involved in making gold ornaments are known as '*perunthachar*'; those involved in carpentry are known as '*thatchar*'; those involved in pottery are known as '*kulalar* or '*velar*'; and so on.

The new class of rural artisans as defined recently by voluntary organizations and officials of the Khadi and Village Industries Commission (KVIC), and Handicrafts Board do not necessarily belong to traditional artisans by community identity. They include the new breed of craft-persons who were signed up to do artisans' work out of training and as a means of livelihood. This has diluted the conventional distinctiveness or the traditionalistic identity of rural artisans. There are several classes of rural artisans involved in cane-baskets and furniture-making, mat-weaving, coir-making, woollen-weaving, *Oil-ghani* industry, bee-keeping, palm-gur making and so on. They are also supported by banks and other institutional agencies of the government through various schemes, often, recognizing them as rural artisans. Although there is nothing wrong in the list of rural artisans expanding, historically when one talks about traditional rural artisans of Tamil Nadu still only those five categories mentioned earlier are recognized all over Tamil Nadu.

Key Research Questions

- What is happening to the traditional rural artisans in the changing techno-economic and political environment?
- Is there any influence of globalization processes in the changes that are taking place in the lives and livelihoods of the traditional rural artisans?
- What is the likely future of the traditional rural artisans, and what is required to be done by the State and the local bodies in order to bring about desirable changes in the way the artisans work and earn a living?

Research Approach

As this intends to be an empirical account of the lives and livelihoods of traditional rural artisans of Tamil Nadu, primary data has taken prime-place. However, to be able to track down if any of the policy changes of the government led to such situations – whether they are for better or for worse – the schemes of the government, especially, those of the KVIC and the Handicrafts Board have been perused as well. Selection of districts (and the villages) and the respondents for interview were made based on snowball sampling method.

When we started the exercise we came to know from the secondary data available in which of the districts of Tamil Nadu what type of artisanal work is practised in good number so as to hold a meaningful discussion. Artisans in districts such as Sivagangai, Madurai, Thirunelveli, Coimbatore, and Pudukottai have been interviewed for this purpose. Individual interviews and Focus Group Discussions (FGDs) were held with the aid of a check-list. Interviews and FGDs were held not only with traditional rural artisans who are practicing but also with the *sangam* members who often take the political route to get things done for the *viswakarma* community as they are called. The data for this study were collected during September and October, 2006.

Scope and Limitations of this Study

As it was defined at the outset, this study covers only those who are conventionally accepted as traditional rural artisans viz. goldsmiths, blacksmiths, carpenters, potters, vessel makers and stone carvers. It has not taken the government definition which then should include a whole array of artisans and crafts persons.

Obtaining quantitative data on the category-wise number of traditional rural artisans in Tamil Nadu was not available. Even the Tamil Nadu Viswakarma Sangam that is working to further the interests of the traditional rural artisans do not have any authentic figures in this regard. The State Backward Community Welfare Board in the year 2003 has asked the Tamil Nadu Viswakarma Artisans' Sangam to provide the data regarding the artisans in Tamil Nadu, for which the Sangam has responded in the negative stating reasons such as manpower and resource constraints. Therefore, their living and working environment and the changes that are taking place due to changes in the society are qualitatively captured. Several rounds of conversations with individual artisans and FGDs helped obtain these data and information. But, getting down to arriving at a figure was extremely difficult. In order not to be incorrect, figures have been reduced to the minimum.

1. Traditional Goldsmiths of Tamil Nadu

Introduction

Gold in India serves many functions and wearing it has several implications. As a concept it is ornamental for the rich, saviour for the poor and capital for business persons. Purchasing gold is, most often, considered as an investment. Especially for women in Tamil Nadu, being exhibitive of all one's jewellery during festive and ceremonial occasions is a matter of pride and pleasure. One estimate is that about 10,000 to 15,000 tonnes of "above the ground gold" is available in India. The global stock of gold being estimated as around 1,45,000 tonnes, the share of gold held in India would be something like 10 per cent (Rhona O' Connell www.gold.org). India is said to be the biggest consumer of gold in the world. As far as Tamil Nadu is concerned, there are places like Chennai, Coimbatore, Madurai, Salem, and Villupuram, where the number of jewellery shops are in large numbers. In each of the district of Tamil Nadu, we can count at least 500-700 families that belong to goldsmiths, and about 100-150 of them actually involved in making jewellery.

Gold Artifact—As It was

A goldsmith is generally a pious person, doing his arty work with gold as a cottage industry, making gold and silver ornaments by hand at the sit-out of his house or in a tiny shop. The ornaments which are popular in Tamil Nadu are *mangal suthra* (*thali* chain), *oddiyaanam* (gold-waist belt), *jimikki* (eardrop), and *Mookkuthi* (nose-petal) and gold bangles etc. They were traditionally crafted and finished with great dexterity. Ornaments worth several thousand rupees are handed over to goldsmith just out of trust for making, with no acknowledgement for the transaction taking place. It is based on mutual trust and long-standing relationship. Their skill can be recognized from the jewelleries adorning the statues of various Gods in Hindu temples. Goldsmiths are generally located in a row of tiny shops one after another in specific streets – whether they are towns or cities. The deal (if we can call this 'stage-one') is generally like this:

- Gold is given by the client, meaning the goldsmith does not have to invest his money in gold.
- The client is supposed to: (a) pay the making charges; (b) pay for the stones if it is a stone-encrusted jewellery; and (c) allow for the wastage of gold while making.
- The goldsmith normally takes one-week to ten days time to deliver the finished gold ornaments.

There used to be a small jewellery shop near the goldsmiths working place, which later or the working place of the goldsmiths is adjacent to the small jewellery shops. In either way, the goldsmith had a place. In the former case, goldsmiths assumed significance and in the later case it is the jewellery shop that assumed significance. This is stage-two. After liberalization we should say we are in stage-three, where jewellery showrooms have assumed the prime-place, where traditional goldsmiths go seeking employment.

Recent Trends

Jewellery business or the way gold is purchased and sold has undergone a sea change in the past 10-12 years.

(i) The number of customers approaching who approach the goldsmiths for making jewellery has drastically come down, and the trend to select ready-to-wear jewellery from showrooms is fast catching up. This is sending shock waves in the spinal cord of the goldsmiths.

(ii) Small and medium-size jewellery-shop owners needed either investment or finance to showcase ready-to-wear jewellery items, and so, they have started holding new business deals with gold traders and financiers from north India. In the bargain, the goldsmith who depended on the local jewellery shops got sidelined.

(iii) The goldsmiths as artisans who have hitherto been making a livelihood out of their capabilities suffer as they need money to invest in gold to supply to the customers or to the small-jewellery shop owners.

(iv) Business giants (such as the Tatas for example) who have never been in jewellery business are opening gigantic jewellery showrooms and showcase machine-cut designs, fashion jewellery and branded jewellery which sell like hot-cakes. The goldsmiths are mute spectators to these developments.

(v) There are also jewellery complexes opened in places like Chennai and Coimbatore which has, in reality, confirmed that goldsmiths have to find employment in such complexes and they are no more the main players in making jewellery items.

(vi) And the vigorous advertisement coupled with business tactics (often said to be deceiving) lure customers to go in for purchasing ready-to-wear jewellery from giant showrooms, rather than getting them made by a local goldsmith.

(vii) The popular jewellery shops have their display windows for branded jewellery to be displayed. That is somebody else's product upon which you have made no investment being displayed in your showroom. The strategy of: '*doing business with others money*' is catching up even among the middleclass jewellery shop-owners. You get a percentages of the profit. This is out and out trade mentality which dispenses with the local artisan.

The recent trend of jewellery buyers preferring to buy from jewellery showrooms rather than getting it made by a local goldsmith has necessitated the goldsmith to be employed for wages by jewellery shop-owners instead of being self-employed, as he was earlier. Another option is that the goldsmith himself has to invest money in gold and keep them ready for sale, for which he needs huge capital investment. If he does this he moves from the stage of being an artisan to the stage of running it as a business venture. Again, the current trend is towards branded jewellery, where big players from North India, especially Jaipur and West Bengal and abroad showcase their jewellery designs in the showcases of our showrooms. The local artisans should be equipped in terms of designs and variety to be able to compete with the business giants who beat the artisan at his own game with money.

Jewellery trade benefits those who can invest money, and sometimes benefits consumers, and it never benefits the producers or artisans who sell their artistic skills and acquired talents. It pressurizes the artisans to give the best at the least possible cost, otherwise the market would not be in favour of him. The trend today is better being a trader rather than being a producer or an artisan.

Challenges that have Become Commonplace

The goldsmith is the only artisan who has survived among all the six categories of artisans (including the potters). But he is now facing the industrial giants who are pumping millions of rupees, purchasing tonnes of gold, flooding the market with the machine-made jewels with modern and ever-changing designs. Even the middle-class shop-owners have to oblige the industrial giants because without any effort, the modern jewels occupy his showroom and he can pay for them when they are sold and retain his share of the profit. Another aspect is that rich showroom-owners by procuring from other states ready-made ornaments in large quantity deprive the local goldsmiths of Tamil Nadu from getting work orders. Next to the goldsmiths, the small and middle-level gold shop-owners (merchants) are also losing their business because of the rich showrooms and losing their deceptive advertisement of 'No making charges' etc.

Thus far it is clear that the gold-jewellery work has slipped from the hands of the artisans (goldsmiths) into the hands of business persons and industrial giants who run jewellery showrooms with machine-cut designs and fashion jewellery. They also advertise that they have installed machinery worth of a million rupees for instant testing of the quality of gold as against the traditional checking by hand i.e. by rubbing on the touch stone. The faith of the business persons is more on the advertisements than on the goldsmiths. So, as of now, this trade mentality has occupied many of the jewellery showrooms in important cities of Tamil Nadu such as Chennai, Coimbatore, Trichy, Madurai, and Salem. However, it is slowly percolating down to the smaller towns such as Karaikudi, and Dindigul that they invest crores of rupees in jewellery business and send across advertisements as high-way hoardings, on the TV and in the print media that they sell jewellery items: (a) Rs. 43 or so less per gram of gold; (b) No making charges; (c) No wastages charges; (d) No cost for stones incrust on jewellery items and so on. Hence, all other jewellery showrooms are forced to fall in line to remain in the business. Many of these showrooms claim to be selling Hallmark jewellery items, whereas the fact could be that only a part of what they keep as stock may be Hallmark items (Himadri Bhattacharya, 2005).

Aren't these Unfair Trade Practices?

The traditional goldsmiths have a pertinent question here. When an ornament is made from the metal, the charges have to be paid or incurred as making charges. Similarly, when an ornament is made from a piece of metal, wastages are bound to be there. A better procedure may reduce the quantity of wastages but no procedure can completely rule out the wastage. Similarly, the claim about giving stones free of cost, as if stones have no sale or purchase value is another deception in the opinion of the traditional goldsmith. These can be termed as 'unfair trade practices' in the context of globalization. Paying for the making charges, paying for the stones, and paying for the wastage – do all these expenses go from the showrooms owner's pocket, without accommodating them in the sale price of ornaments, still giving the hallmark quality gold for Rs. 43 less per gram—is a question raised by the traditional goldsmiths. The contention of many of the goldsmiths is that it is impossible to sell gold like that without compromising on quality.

A recent study (Amar Kothari, 2002) estimates gold adulteration at 16 per cent of Indian retail consumption amounting to $ 2 billion per year in the domestic market. The confidence of the domestic consumers in purity is shaken. A press report in *Dinkaran* (Tamil daily) dated 9-10-2006 reveals that out of 162 jewels picked up in 16 cities for testing, 147 are found to be sub-standard. In other words 90 per cent of the jewels sold with attractive advertisements, the quality of gold suffered from 13 to 45 per cent. However, the Indian export sector it has very strong hallmarkng norms, with very sophisticated equipment ensuring that the required quality standards are met.

Quality Standards

Another dimension that has come along with several showrooms—with no certification for quality—is the purity or the fineness of gold being sold. In the market for ornaments and jewellery, consumer protection is still not assured. Those in cities who consider purchasing gold as an investment only think in terms of quality, caratage etc. Those in middle class towns buy gold, especially, to meet ceremonial requirements such as marriage. Their fond wish is also to buy good quality gold only. But they are unaware of KDM or Hallmark and so on. It is a well-known fact that cheating on caratage (fineness) is widespread. The practice of hard bargaining in price that is still prevalent in middle class towns, and the business tactic of reducing the price in order to ensure that customers continue to come to one's jewellery shops make the jewellers reduce the price and compensate on quality. The customers are calculative of the financial savings they have made after bargaining. They hardly think of nor are they technically competent enough to test the quality of the gold they are carrying home. This enables the traders to adopt unfair trade practices.

In April 2000, the government introduced voluntary hallmarking of gold jewellery through Bureau of Indian Standards. However, the progress in this regard has been very slow, with only about 154 jewellers having accepted the necessary certification with most of them having only partial stocks of their jewellery hallmarked. The Government of India has decided to implement jewellery-hallmarking mandatory in phases (Himadri Bhattacharya, 2005). Hallmarking comprises stringent checks and controls for ensuring the quality and purity of gold that should be judiciously adhered to. The government has announced to make gold hallmarking mandatory from January 1, 2008. At present, the Bureau of Indian Standards (BIS), a government agency, grants hallmark for gold as demanded on a voluntary basis. This is a step appreciated by the goldsmiths whereas the jewellery shop-owners express apprehension about it because they consider it a trade barrier.

Technology Gap and Capital Crunch

Of late, another development that one witnesses is that hand-made ornaments are being replaced by machine-made articles. With the introduction of machineries, dies and machine-cut designs one stark reality we need to understand is when one jewel-making machinery goes for production, it carries out the jobs of almost 500 goldsmiths a day. The wristwatch makers such as the Titan at Hosur have started making fashion jewellery of machine-cut design, which is fast emerging as a challenge to the workmanship of the traditional artisans. Jewellery items in one-gram and half-a gram are also possible when technology is put to use, which is not possible in hand-made process of the goldsmith. This gets an edge over the artisans. But, the longevity of the machine-cut designs is very poor, which does not occur to the customers when they see the elegant designs. Computer-aided design is a state-of-the art technology that is creating ripples through the jewellery industry. From the poor artisans' point of view, he along with his family members will starve when he is deprived of his wages, as a result of technology intervention. The investors are happy about the Return on Investment (RoI) that is why the sale of jewellery items is on the increase. There is also on-line gambling of gold being talked about now, which creates artificial hike in the price of gold.

In big cities such as Coimbatore, there are Jewellery Complexes opened where plenty of jewellery items are made, making use of computers, dies, machines and the latest technologies. There are also small jewellers from all over Tamil Nadu purchasing fashion jewellery from Coimbatore Jewellery Complexes. The establishment of jewellery complexes is a development after globalization, where in addition to goldsmiths, young girls are also employed on daily wage basis, which is altogether a new trend in jewel making viewed as a male artisan's work. Similarly, there are also employment-seeking young boys and girls who have no previous experience in gold jewellery making or about the gold business enter for a job. This is a new trend zooming that 'members of non-artisans community' coming into take up jewellery business, viewing it either as employment opportunity or as an investment proposition. This started in 1992 when V.P. Singh government did away with the Gold Control (Rhona O' Connell). This is becoming very common in cities like Coimbatore and Chennai now.

It was in the past that the customers wanted to select designs from a catalogue. Now, the trend and the demand is to show them the made-jewellery in original for which the goldsmith and small jewellers require finance. In moderate towns like Karaikudi in Tamil Nadu, computer-aided designs and machine-cut designs have not become popular as yet. Reportedly, there are about 600 goldsmiths in Karaikudi alone. Business challenge comes to them in the form of gold traders from other states. Their role-visibly sidelines the need for goldsmiths, as they deal in gold bar and a variety of made-jewellery items. One of the indications of dealing with goldsmiths is that where the tea stall located close-by their shop continually supplied about 50-100 cups of tea a day, is hardly supplying 5-6 cups of tea today, says a goldsmith in Coimbatore.

The competition has become hectic that the goldsmiths are also required to get in to the fray. The winner is determined mostly by factors such as: (a) amount of capital investment made; (b) the varieties kept on the showcase as ready-made; and (c) the attraction of the advertisement. The longevity or the sturdiness of the ornament made, the trust in terms of caratage (fineness) and the relationships have all been pushed to the back-seat. The market is such that the goldsmiths cannot sit with his capabilities and tools to make deliveries to the orders placed with him. He has to invest capital to buy gold and deliver products to the consumers and to the jewellery shops. Mobilizing the capital required is a big challenge to many of the goldsmiths who have always viewed theirs as a wage-earning occupation (livelihood) and not as a business proposition that would require funds for investment, and the technology to stand on a par with the competitors. Converting to sale of gold jewellery would require a minimum of Rs. 10 lakhs. Even those goldsmiths who have got down to doing it as a business, express grouse that the percentages of profit has drastically come down from 15 per cent to 5 per cent due to the competition prevailing in the jewellery business.

In June 2006, on the request of the Visvakarma Sangam in Karaikudi, Thiru P. Chidambaram, Finance Minister (GoI) announced about the starting of the Jewellers Consortium Development Service. It has helped about 300 goldsmiths in this area receive gold worth Rs. 1 lakh to Rs. 1.5 lakh each through Minerals and Metal Trading Corporation (MMTC) and SIDCO. The Bank of India and Indian Bank have lend their helping hand to carry it out. This has been given as loan to be repaid within a period of five years. This has, to some extent, saved the small jewellers and goldsmiths from the onslaught of gold traders from north India. With this investment, the hands of local goldsmiths have now been strengthened to supply made-jewellery items to jewellery shops and to take it up as a business venture. In the opinion of jewellers this is also a temporary solution only, and it is not sustainable. This has come not as a scheme. Mr. Chidambaram has been able to do it for the goldsmiths in Karaikudi area only, which is his constituency. This is not applicable to other goldsmiths in other districts of Tamil Nadu or elsewhere.

What can be Done?

They also suggest certain measures, which in their opinion would help further the interests of the goldsmiths. They are:

- The branded-jewellery items are taxed 2 per cent extra as excise tax. The goldsmiths appreciate this step of the government. Similarly, the machine-cut jewellery items may be levied upto 16 per cent by way of excise duty.
- The gold that comes from other states may be taxed (special sales tax) as well.
- The customs duty on made-jewellery items that enter India for commercial purposes may be hiked in order to protect the local goldsmiths and small-town jewellers.
- Licensing (Certificate holders) system may be brought into force in order to restrict entry of business persons who get down to doing jewellery business for profiteering, damaging the trust and ethical standards required in jewellery business.
- Hallmarking of gold jewellery items for ensuring the caratage of gold being sold should be enforced at the earliest in order to protect the consumers from being cheated with sub-standard quality. This would restore goldsmith in his original place in the society.
- The government should take action against misleading and deceiving advertisements (from business giants and mega showrooms) that play havoc with goldsmiths and small scale jewellers who are honest and trust worthy.
- Goldsmiths are not authorized to issue bills to the jewels they are dealing in. This necessitates the goldsmiths to be dependent on the jewellery shops and jewellery showrooms when it comes to issuing bills for the deal that take place. The bills issued by the goldsmiths may be recognized in order to protect the interests of the goldsmiths.
- Although fashion and branded jewellery seem to be zooming the market with a big bang, it is there in the back of the mind of every one of us 'the purity of the gold one is buying'. Our traditional jewellers instead of serving as agents of the branded jewellery should try to promote quality consciousness in buying gold ornaments and make a name for them as being dependable in terms of purity of the gold used. Similarly, the government should heavily tax the branded jewellery and the gold that comes from other states. The income generated that way can be made use of for allocating to the welfare of the traditional artisans.
- In the opinion of the artisans the Government-sponsored Handicrafts Board and SIPPO are nowhere near to help the

traditional artisans tide over the challenges they face. The artisans seek a separate 'Traditional Artisans Welfare and Industrial Development Board (TAWID)' at Central and State levels with structures to be of help at the grassroots level as well.

Conclusion

Gold jewellery making that was in the hands of the goldsmiths have to a considerable extent slipped into the hands of the business persons who rule capital and technology. The number of people who go to a local goldsmith for getting a jewel made has come down drastically. The trend is towards machine-cut fashion jewellery and branded jewellery displayed in the jewellery showrooms. The trend is such that the jewellery shops in the middle class towns also have to fall in line. The encroachment of North Indian business persons in Tamil Nadu who deal in gold bars is on the increase. The local jewellery shops and showrooms also have developed a new business strategy of doing business with the other's money. Providing showrooms for displaying branded jewellery items is another trend zooming. In the bargain, the goldsmiths are pushed from a stage of being a mere artisan to doing jewellery in business style. Then again the questions of capital for investment and technology pose a threat.

2. Traditional Blacksmiths of Tamil Nadu

Introduction

There was a time when Indian farmers used only a handful of tools such as plough, spade, sickle, and a pair of bullocks for agricultural operations. Blacksmiths and carpenters known as native engineers used to make all the tools and implements required for carrying out agriculture, which to contrast it from the mechanized agriculture is addressed as 'traditional agriculture'. A typical Tamil Nadu village generally has blacksmiths families involved in making these implements. As per the estimates available with Government of Tamil Nadu there are 35,695 blacksmiths in Tamil Nadu. Mechanization in agriculture has drastically brought down the tools and implements. Instead tractors and machineries are increasingly put to use. Making of agricultural implements that were in the artisan's hands are progressively slipping into the hands of big factories.

Marginalization of Tradition

This research team made a rapid appraisal of what is happening to blacksmiths who depended very much on agriculture – making spade and plough-shares, and sharpening sickles and crowbars. Blacksmiths face two different types of onslaughts. One is, due to shrinking agriculture, the quantum of work they used to get has come down tremendously; and the other is hi-tech factories have started taking over the production of spades, crowbar, plough-share and so on. They come branded such as Tata plough-share for example. Bullock carts have been replaced by tractors – that come with a cheap bank loan. Even those few bullock carts that are available for agricultural purposes or for sand-mining have been fitted on with tyre-wheels. They are called: *tyre-vandi* in local language. Gone are the days bullock carts used to have wooden wheel with an iron frame fabricated by a local blacksmith. The bullocks might silently thank this technical change, but the blacksmiths do not. The repair on the tyre-wheels is attended to by Automobile workshops and not by the traditional blacksmiths. Similarly, after the introduction of tractors, the use of animal energy in agriculture has almost become a thing of the past. If at all there are animals in villages, they are cows and buffaloes for milk; and sheep and goat for mutton and leather/hide. There are hardly any bullocks to pull carts. Neither are there bullock-carts nor are there bullocks to pull the carts. This has made the demand for horse-shoe nail die out which were a product supplied by traditional blacksmiths.

In sociological sense, blacksmiths are the original type of carpenters who used to deal in iron and wood works. Those involved mostly in wood works came to be called carpenters. For reasons such as:

(i) the drudgery of work involved in blacksmithy; and
(ii) poor wages that the blacksmiths make in a day, many blacksmiths have shifted to carpentry-exclusive, which still has demand.

Apart from the freedom from the drudgery in balcksmithy, those who shifted to carpentry talk of a few more advantages. They include:

(i) it gives them mobility to go around and carry out work wherever carpentry skills are required;
(ii) the tools required are much fewer when compared to those a blacksmith needs to possess; and

(iii) wages they get now, are comparatively higher. The recent generation is moving to work as rod benders in building construction works, and some even get technically qualified such as welders, fitters and go on to make grill works, car tinkering etc. This is a healthy shift noticed amidst the blacksmith community. The trend explained here can be generalized for all over Tamil Nadu, as these are the lessons that are drawn from several case studies conducted across five districts of Tamil Nadu.

Manamadurai — A Case in Point

A case in point is Manamadurai where about 60 families were involved in blacksmithy until late 1980s. There are hardly 20 families involved in this occupation. The others have either shifted to carpentry, migrated to places like Thirupur, Karur and Coimbatore or have left for the Middle East to work on errands. There are about 5-6 work-sheds that accommodate these twenty families to earn their livelihoods. They go to the work-shed every morning with no assurance of getting any job that day. If they get any work, they carry it out and divide the wages among themselves. Usually about three persons work in one shed – one main person, one helper, and a third person to blow air to keep the iron hot. The person who sits for blowing air is generally an aged person who retired from such work sheds after long years of hard work. On becoming aged, they have a saying in blacksmith's community: '*kollu muthina thuruththi*' meaning as you become aged as a blacksmith you glide from beating hot iron to blowing air to sustain the fire.

In Manamadurai, there was also a Blacksmith Co-operative Society functioning during MGR's regime which has become defunct and wound up now. The government used to grant loan to the farmers who wanted to make bullock-carts. The co-operative society used to provide cash advances to the blacksmiths who carry out such works. This is about the past. The situation that explains their condition now can be briefly put thus: *where you stand decides where you sit*. The blacksmiths who were owning their sheds in a row on a place owned by the Panchayat have been evicted from there and have been 'allowed to sit Vaigai', as there is no water flowing in the river. The Panchayat on the river-bed has constructed a shopping complex in the place vacated by the blacksmiths and has rented out the complex for earning income for the Panchayat.

They are unable to do anything else because they have been doing only iron and wood works since long. They have acquired this skill by hard work and practice. Working in a blacksmith's workshed requires a lot of muscle power and as one grows old it becomes difficult. Although there is hardly any new takers of this occupation, those already involved in this are lurking in darkness about what they would do to spend their old age, when they become physically weak. That the current generation from blacksmiths community does not get into blacksmithy is something that needs to be appreciated, as it is this occupation is already dying out. Factories have taken over the jobs that blacksmiths had been doing.

A Bird's Eye View

Although Manamadurai is cited as a case in point, wherever blacksmiths live in Tamil Nadu, the conditions they live with is almost the same. Emakkalapuram, near Sanarpatty in Dindigul district could be cited as another striking example. The village had about 200 families involved in blacksmithy. About ten years ago, there were about 25-30 worksheds with about 6-8 workers in each of them. Now, the total number of families involved in blacksmithy is hardly 20, with each workshed employing about 2-3 persons only.

In addition to making agricultural implements, there are blacksmiths involved in other types of works such as: making frying iron pan, *paniyara kal, Dosai kal,* Kitchen *Karandi* (spoon), *Sambirani karandi, arivamanai* (vegetable cutter), *Aruval* (saber), *katthi* (knife) and so on. These things still have demand in the rural market. Those blacksmiths who are involved in this kind of work do not take up other works such as mending of bullock-carts. Their market is weekly *shandy* and also they regularly supply to hardware shops known to them in the town. There are places in Tamil Nadu that are popular for certain kind of iron works. For example, Virupatchi near Manamadurai is known for the kind of saber they make. Dindigul was once known for locks.

In Dindigul there were several lock workers co-operative societies functioning and most of them are either dormant or have been wound up today. Dindigul gave in for competition from company-made locks that come branded. Godrej has become a popular brand for locks. The traditional lock workers had to give in for competition from big companies. This is another case of traditional workers being marginalized by the modernity. But, still some blacksmiths who could not think of an alternative employment are engaged in making locks. Reasons such as increase in the cost of iron and arrival of several equipments such as gas welding etc. that required capital handicapped them from expanding and challenging the modern company made locks flooding the market. Dindigul still enjoys the past nostalgia of having been popular for locks once upon a time.

Another category of the traditional artisan's occupation that is dying out is fenders. Fenders are locally known as *kannar*. These artisans are involved in making brass and copper vessels. The arrival of durable and elegant materials has brought down the demand for such brass vessels and copper utensils today. After earthen pots, aluminum, brass and copper vessels were the ones in use in Tamil Nadu. They were the ones in high demand before stainless steel and other non-stick cook-wares entered the market. Now that, for consumers, choice has become wide as far as alternative materials are concerned. The gifts given to a newly married couple as a matter of convention used to be brass vessels. It is not the case now.

People, today, have a wide variety of choices thrown before them for selecting vessels and domestic utensils. As 'the culture of wanting to have houses with the facilities of a hotel and hotels with the comforts of a house' people choose, a whole array of household utensils and serving vessels, where elegance, the esthetic looks and the presentability matter more than anything else. The brass vessels do not come anywhere near their choice of things. So, the demand for brass vessels has fallen sharply.

In Manamadurai, a person who employed about 14 persons in his brass vessel workshop is sitting alone, collecting and repairing old brass vessels. There are some who have shifted to stainless steel after brass vessels lost their demand. Manamadurai had about 80 persons employed both in brass vessel-making and in stainless steel-making. Now, there are hardly two or three work sheds. Those involved in trading of vessels are thriving. Some from traditional business community who deal in raw materials for this industry, and in buying and selling stainless steel utensils are growing. Only the artisans who are involved in actual production are losing out traders benefit. The artisans or the producers are degenerating.

Indicative of Post-Modernity

These are instances of modernity marginalizing the tradition. The post-modernity looks for a better world with less drudgery and more comforts. In the process, the occupations that bring with it certain drudgery get sidelined. Putting to use better technology and resources such as capital, modernity marginalizes the tradition. When a traditional and age-old occupation or practice is thought obsolete and when it is tossed out, one thing that bothers us as social scientists is: what should we do with the artisans or crafts persons who depend on it as the main source of livelihood. This is vital because many such occupations have been handed down from one generation to another. They never underwent any course modules to learn and acquire that skill. Moreover, they know nothing else so well as they do the as artisans'—blacksmiths, brass vessel-makers and lock-workers in this case.

One inevitable thing with post-modernity is that it evolves not with any intension of displacing any artisans or traditional occupations. But in the process, it does necessarily happen that some of the occupations get seen off silently. It is delighting to note that the contemporary generation from the artisans' families is able to understand the market realities. It is understandable from the fact that many youngsters from the artisan's families are either diversifying or have completely gone to take up a different occupation with willing consent of the family members.

The question is whether there would be anybody remaining after about 15-20 years from now to do a blacksmith's job in the same manner we see it today. The empirical evidences suggest that the response should be a definite 'No'. It does not mean that their services would not be required in the society. A blacksmith's work has already become part of the technical courses offered in Industrial Training Institutes, where many youths take up training in welding, grill works, lathe work, tinkering work and so on. This fills the technology-gap and the knowledge-gap that the blacksmiths are away from. Youth from blacksmith's families also undergo that training and get prepared to deliver the same kind of service his father had delivered, with a little more sophistication. This is a transition necessitated by the modernity which the society has automatically started responding to.

So, the demand for knowledge-gap, demand for technology-gap and the demand for capital investment-gap set in by the processes of globalization are being filled in by some means or the other in varied forms to face the future. Those marginalized by this modernity, such as the traditional artisans, the blacksmiths, brass vessel-makers, and lock-workers do require a social security while this transition is taking place triggered by the market forces. It is a vital function of the State to respond to such requirements in order to provide for the general welfare of the traditional artisans and uphold social justice.

3. Traditional Carpenters of Tamil Nadu

Introduction

Tamil Nadu is on the fast lanes in terms of urbanization. Construction industry is one that is booming. The paradox is that the carpenters—especially those with 'traditional carpentry skills'—are not in high demand. Whereas masons are in high demand, bar-benders, welders, and interior decorators are in high demand. What is this due to? Is it a problem of knowledge and awareness? Capability? Tools and technology? Competition? Or whether other factors have crept in? Estimates available shows that there are about 84,500 carpenters in Tamil Nadu. The way urbanization moves, there is plenty of work for those in similar kind of work such as brick-layers, construction workers and so on. Why is it that the carpenters do not seem to have been in the picture to the extent they could have been? We shall straight away get down to understanding the immediate plausible reasons.

One of the reasons stated for carpenters not being in high demand is the way modern construction plans are made, there is no much work for wood. During FGDs and informal conversations conducted with carpenters in several places across the five districts in Tamil Nadu, carpenters estimate that the use of wood has come down by 40 to 70 per cent in modern houses and buildings. The iron rods and iron grills have taken the place of wood in such constructions. The obvious reason could be in the past local masons and carpenters were primarily involved in constructing houses. Modern houses and office buildings are constructed principally by qualified engineers, whose training mostly imparts them the use of bricks, hallow blocks and cement mortar rather than wood works. The other reasons could be wood is costly because of competing demand from industries such as wood pulp industry, plywood industry and sports industry.

Secondly, the governmental restrictions on felling of trees for environmental reasons have also reduced the use of wood in building construction. In the bargain, the carpenters are required to modify their skills and add additional skills to remain relevant in the marketplace. This analysis shows the changes that have taken place in traditional carpentry, and the additional demands made from a carpenter's capability to carry out the occupation to suit the changing needs of the contemporary society.

Understanding the Tribe

Generally, carpenters are viewed as one class as wood workers. However, distinction can be made based on the nature of carpentry work one is involved in. They are:

(i) There are carpenters who usually engage themselves in making wood works relating to house construction, and they also engage in furniture making as an activity of earning during idle time;
(ii) There are carpenters who are primarily wood carvers. They make temple cars, and craft works especially for temples and art galleries. (By nature this is a sculptor's work and so they are included along with stone sculptors in this report); and
(iii) And the third category can be called blacksmiths who are primarily involved in iron darning works, and take up wood works that come along with it. (This is covered under blacksmiths in this report.)

All said and done, when one mentions about carpenters the immediate semantic interpretation goes to the first category only, unless specifically stated otherwise. Generally, carpenters work as individual entrepreneurs selling their capabilities with the use of the tools they own. Normally, a carpenter's tools box contains: saw, cold chisel, awl, drilling tool, a pair of hammers, and a file. The practice of getting employment usually is, one carpenter gets a contract work from a client and he mobilizes the number of carpenters and helpers required to carry out that work. They share the work and the principal carpenter decides the wages for the other carpenters and helpers based on the prevailing local rates. Efforts to organize them do not seem to have been very successful. However, there are carpenters organized into cooperative such as the *Manamadurai Iron and Wood Workers Industrial Cooperative Society.*

Wood Workers Cooperative

The Manamadurai Iron and Wood Workers Cooperative Society has been in existence since 1959. It has a membership of 110, including 45 women. Carpenters and those involved in occupations that are related to carpentry joined as members. But it is now dormant. There was a time, when carpentry work order used to come the society's way. The society used to divide and assign the work to the members and delivered chairs, tables and other furniture items to the clients. Getting carpentry works through cooperatives was easier a few years ago. The members used to get their wages from the cooperative based on the work executed. The society was busy and very much functional until 1987. There was a time (between 1977-1987) when the members would not be able to carry out any work order, if they accepted in personal. The transaction per year touched upto Rs. 15 lakhs when the members got annual bonus etc.

The government offices and schools felt comfortable placing order for their furniture requirements from the co-operative. There was also a G.O. in existence that government offices should procure furniture items from wood workers cooperative only. It has been done away with now. The bills issued by the cooperatives were also beyond questions by the external auditors. Things have changed in the last fifteen years.

Ten Reasons why Traditional Carpenters are not in High Demand

The following are the reasons empirically found why traditional carpenters are not in high demand. These are also the main factors that have resulted in dormancy of the Carpenters' Cooperative Society that were referred to:

(1) The protective nature of cooperatives was questioned after open-market and competition erupted calling for quotations.

(2) Arrival of alternative materials such as plastics, plywood, mica, glass sheets with aluminum frames, and iron materials started entering the market. Use of wooden materials have naturally started declining.

(3) Influx of plastic chairs and light-weight materials in market started side-lining the wooden furniture items.

(4) The comparative advantage that people have found out in terms of cost and handling in materials other than wood. One block of *neem* wood that sold for Rs. 70 about twenty years ago costs Rs. 400 today.

(5) The additional cost involved and time one has to wait for being able to get a wooden item decorated elegantly.

(6) The life of wooden furniture goes beyond a generation and so demand does not arise frequently.

(7) For private, office and commercial complexes, people who want to buy wooden furniture prefer to buy branded furniture

items from companies such as the Godrej after perusing designs in a design catalogue rather than placing an order with those local carpenters.

(8) Arrival ready-to-fix doors, ready-to-fix-windows, grill windows, false ceiling, and concrete roofing have considerably reduced the need for wood and wood works.

(9) The measure of the government to reduce felling of trees on environmental reasons also reduced the need for wood workers.

(10) At a time when chairs, tables and furniture items were completely being made of wood, a trend emerged to use iron pipes also in order to reduce the weight of the materials as well as the cost. This necessitated the carpenters to work get the pipe and iron works done from outside which took away a slice of the business.

The society has become dormant now, but it has not been liquidated because there are quite some assets in terms of buildings and land in the name of the society. The society when it was in its boom had acquired the assets that belonged to an Iron workers cooperative that was being liquidated at that time. Now, the society shows a loss of Rs. 1.5 lakhs as per the books of account. The society owes a wage balance of Rs. 8,000 to each of the 36 active members. Although the society has scarcely taken up any work in the past ten years or so, some of the members still keep in touch and wish to remain as members. They express hope that because it is a cooperative, some future government might look into it and revive it. As of now, all the members go out and procure individual works from clients they are in touch with and earn a living.

Cooperative form of organizations, in general, is a failure in Tamil Nadu, and carpenters, cooperatives have also proved that they are no exception to the general trend. Apart from being organized as cooperatives, there are carpenter-sangams. They are organized to have a common voice such as Thirupathur Block Carpenters association with a membership of 200 carpenters. Carpenters also form part of *viswakarma sangam* of Tamil Nadu with district wings. However, they rarely raise voice, and are seldom heard. An institution is a kind of protection that any occupational group can have. As of now, whatever organization that are available of carpenters, they are only in a loosely organized form. Carpenters work as individual carpenters only. Two or three of them join together in small teams, based on the demands of the job they take up, and divide the wages they earn.

Migration and Seasonality

It was found through a chain of interviews across several places viz. Karaikudi, Singampuanari, Thirupatthur, Kalapur, and Manamadurai where carpenters are located in large numbers that distress migration such as in agriculture cannot be found in carpentry. Carpenters do get employment either locally or in the vicinity, but for certain intermittent gap of two to four days in between one assignment (contract) and another. January-June is the season carpenters, more often than not, have continual employment. July-December is the season carpenters sometimes have to take up making furniture items at home for sale in order to earn a living. During off-season when carpenters tend to quote low rates in order to somehow get a job. It becomes a race towards the bottom among themselves.

Recent Trends

Contract Method: Earlier, the practice of assigning jobs to carpenters used to be daily-wages labour. The prevailing wage rates were paid. The trend-change that has taken place in the recent years in building construction is also an important factor that has caused the recession the traditional carpenters are undergoing. The trend is, give out the entire work on contract to a construction contractor and monitor intermittently if work is progressing as per schedule. The attitude of clients standing close by supervising their house being constructed has become unwholesome. So, the contract given to carpenters has gone to the engineers or the construction contractors who hire carpenters for a few days. That which was completed in three month's time, has to be completed in about one month's time as per the requirements of the construction contractors. This necessitates the carpenters to use improved tools and machineries.

Technology: Machineries for wood works especially to cater to the requirements of the carpenters are the new occupational avenue that has opened up now. Arrival of machineries in carpentry is interpreted as an opportunity, taking cue from the feelings of the carpenters themselves. In the opinion of almost all the carpenters interviewed by this team of researchers, arrival of the machineries in carpentry is a welcome step. They do not consider that the number of working days has come down because of the use of machineries. They think the drudgery in the work has come down which is an advantage. The machineries enable them to deliver goods within the time they promised. That which they used to manually do for one week could now be completed in two-three days. They think they get on with the next work instead of dragging on with a single work which is viewed distrustfully by the clients who assigned the work. They still earn Rs. 150 to Rs. 200 a day.

Mix of Challenges and Opportunities: The challenge actually faced by the carpenters is only because of the arrival of ready-made doors, ready-made windows, less use of wood in building construction, attitude of the people to go to furniture showroom to select household furniture and dining table and so on. Similarly, modern offices use all ready-to-use furniture, glass partitions with aluminium feeding, thermocol-false-sealing, ready-made cabins, cabinets, sideboards, racks, tables, chairs, and so on. This is a challenge because of the use of wood pulp materials, and imported *novapan* boards.

The demand of the modern society from the carpenters is entirely different from what the carpenter as a traditional artisan supplied. He needs to change to suit the modern demands. He requires equipping himself to give shape to a computer-aided office with all kinds of interior decorations. He needs to endow himself to be a sensible interior decorator also to survive in India today. These may be perceived as threats at the same time as opportunities. So, opportunities open up. It is for the carpenters to equip themselves and grab such opportunities in order to remain relevant and reap benefits.

Knowledge and Contact: Almost all the carpenters interviewed by this team of researchers, have the knowledge of recent trends in the industry, and the demands of the market forces from the abilities of a carpenter to remain in the market. It was encouraging also to note that some of them have almost equipped themselves and a few others are in the line of equipping themselves to cater to the new demands of the market. Therefore, knowledge of the market is not a constraint. What really is a constraint is the lack of contact — the contact that can get them the opportunity to try their hands in the modern carpentry. By modern carpentry is meant the setting up of a computer centre with cubicle type partitions for each user, using glass sheets with *aluminium* frames to erect office partitions, false ceiling works, computer tables with movable key-board trays, cots made of *novapan* boards and so on.

Conclusion

There is no family of the carpenters that is starving due to lack of employment. Some work keep sprouting one after another which enables them get a living wage. The modernity has brought about new opportunities to them. In order to make the best use of the opportunity, they need to equip themselves with additional capabilities, and be prepared to deliver to the requirements of the market. Even now, the practice of seeking employment in foreign countries (especially, gulf countries) is prevalent among the carpenter's families, as they possess technical skills. Opportunities are opening up even in the domestic market, if at all they watch out. The government has set up a Welfare Board for the Construction Workers. The government and technical institutions should take up the responsibility of facilitating the carpenters grab the new opportunities.

4. Traditional Potters of Tamil Nadu

Introduction

Potter is a tribe that should be associated with human civilization itself. By common sense one can gauge that the potters must have been the first tribe of artisans that existed in India. Technology that came from time-to-time has introduced a whole range of vessels and household utensils that pottery is gradually being marginalized from the mainframe utility items at the household level even in many of the villages. That a class of artisans being marginalized goes without saying that a section of the population is being left without the livelihood opportunity that they depended on for years. There is an unvoiced communication that puts across to them that their occupation is being wiped out – the only livelihood option they are aware of to make a living. The reason could be modernity, globalization or anything of the sort. But the fact remains that the place of pottery items from in-door (at the kitchen) have come out-door to gardens (to grow decorative plants).

Government of Tamil Nadu report on Rural Artisans states that there are 50,585 potters in Tamil Nadu. What is happening to the potters as a result of the influence of post-modernist attitudes and life-styles? What are they upto so as to make a living in this changing techno-social environment? Do globalization processes open up any new avenues for them or would it pose further threat to their existence? These are vital questions that this study attempts to understand. In order to understand the issues, a series of field observations were made (Sivagangai, Thirunelveli, Dindigul and Madurai districts) at the potters residences, FGDs were conducted with them, and a series of individual interviews were conducted with key informants who were producing and selling pottery articles for years.

Livelihood Pattern of Potters

Pottery was a family occupation and it still remains so. However, a snap-shot view of outsiders to potter's residential area makes one think if women are involved more in making the pottery articles. The role of men seems to be at the beginning by making arrangements for procuring the right kind of clay, and at the end arranging the made-pottery articles in the kiln for baking. Preparing the clay and giving shape to it seems to be with women, off and on joined by men.

These days, due to the improved awareness level on the importance of education, children from potters' families are also sent to school. But, many boys and girls before and after school-hours try their hands in making pottery articles and help their parents increase the quantity produced. That which these children start as a fun, dirtying their hands with wet-mud eventually results in picking up a livelihood skill. This is how pottery has been handed down from generation to generation. Similarly, even the elderly women in the house engage themselves during seasonal requirements such as making *karthic* lamps. There is an admirable family dynamics that operates in potters' families in the process of carrying out their work for earning a living. Potters usually locate themselves in a place that is away from the main village considering factors such as availability of water and spacious place to sun-dry their articles. This is also in a way keeping the main community away from the kiln smoke, which otherwise is a usual complaint of the mainstream community about the potters that the potters pollute the environment with kiln-smoke.

As far as sale of pottery articles is concerned, taking pottery articles to long distance for sales seems to be with the men, whereas taking articles to weekly *shandy* at the villages in the neighbourhood seems to be with the women. Where potters work on a cooperative basis the cooperative society makes arrangement for the sale of pottery articles, including the transport to the marketplace. In the recent years, there are also business persons who buy pottery articles from potters and send lorry loads to places such as Kerala. They also offer money in advance to help the production take place.

The Cooperatives and the Khadi Commission have tried to organize the potters to do collective work. In Thirunelveli alone, there are 34

Pottery Cooperative Societies. The tragedy about them is that most of them are dormant. There are a few societies that are functional like the one at Thenpothai in Thirunelveli district (3 km. from Sengottai) viz. Thenpothai Potters Cooperative Cottage Industrial Society Limited. A case of how potters have been organized and another case of how they have been potters being unorganized may give an idea of the recent trend in the pottery work.

Case 1: Thenpothai Potters Cooperative

Thenpothai Potters Cooperative Cottage Industrial Society Limited started functioning in December 1947. The society has a membership of 92, but only about 32 members regularly work for the society. When the society was in its boom period it had 52 men members, and 35 women members. Currently, putting together men and women, there are about 50 members on roll. This society was a profit making one. The society produces both red pottery (with red clay) and glazed pottery (with china clay). The glazed pottery unit commenced functioning in 1961. There were two workers and a few casual labourers usually employed in the glazed pottery unit.

The society owns the building it functions in, workshed, sheela potter's wheels, common kiln and so on. Potters in Thenpothai produce pots, *chula*, and small festival lamps. About ten members work at the shed in the society. The remaining members (about 25 of them) work at their home and bring the finished products to the society. The society, often, takes up works on the basis of orders, and also in anticipation of certain regular orders. Despite the fact that the members of the society belong to potters families, they have undergone technical training in places like Sevvaipettai (Tamil Nadu), Kanappur (Karnataka), and Bhadravati (U.P.) arranged by the society.

Pottery prodtucts are regularly sent to Kanyakumari, Thoothukudi, Thirunelveli and Kerala by a lorry that is owned by the society. But, Thenpothai society that used to send ten loads a month now sends hardly three loads of products to Kerala. The production has come down to that extent. The society usually fixes 10 per cent profit margin. The problem is not one of demand, because, though not in Tamil Nadu, there is considerable demand for pottery articles in Kerala. The society does not have funds to organize raw materials to be able to capture the market in full. This is more so in the case of glazed pottery section that the society manages with one person at the moment. It is almost at its last breath because of funds constraint. Here again, the problem is not one of demand.

Regarding the wages that the potters get from pottery, they state that earlier 90 per cent of the sale proceeds remained as profit, as the expenses were minimal. But, now due to increase in the cost of firewood, clay, transport costs etc. not even 50 per cent remains as profit to the potters. A cursory workout of costs is shown below. It details that a work of Rs. 100 requires an investment cost of almost Rs. 50 as follows:

	Rs.
Clay	10.00
Firewood	25.00
Red schre	5.00
Kiln charges	6.00
Straw	2.00
Damages	2.00
Total	**50.00**

The value of pottery articles produced in 2004-05 was Rs. 11,60,355 which was Rs. 5,49,279 in 1994-95. The value of glazed pottery produced in 1994-95 was Rs. 3,16,102 which has reduced to Rs. 2,31,607 in 2004-05. The society used to give 8-10 per cent bonus during festival seasons, which it has stopped giving now. The reason for not being able to maintain production levels is reportedly due to lack of funds with the society, and lack of support from the KVIC. The society requires working capital for transporting mud, buying firewood and fuel for the baking furnace, etc. This is the state a potters' cooperative that gets the government support off and on.

Making glazed pottery items using china clay was successful with the support of the KVIC. After KVIC minimized its support, the unit is facing severe financial crisis not being able to meet the working capital requirements to procure raw materials such as china clay, chemicals, stone-materials, firewood etc. If the government withdraws its support completely, the state of the society would become further deplorable.

Case 2: Independent Potters in Sundarapandiapuram

Sundrapandiapuram Town Panchayat in Thirunelveli district had seventy households involved in pottery. They were making exclusively *chula* (mud stove) for Kanyakumari, Nagarkoil, Thoothukudi, and also for the Kerala market. As the market for pots is more in Kerala, about 30 families have migrated near Kerala. They live in places such as Veeravanallur, Vadakkukarkurichi, Surandai, and Kooniyur. The *chulas* made here sell more in Kerala.

The working pattern of potters at Sundarapandiapuram is that about 30 of the 45 potters families work for wages (on piece-rate basis) with two local men who have invested in workshed, potters' wheel, kiln, etc. These 'master potters' or 'the owners' (as the potters call them) arrange for clay and firewood as well. The remaining 15 families carry out work independently and sell finished products in the local *shandy* or they have agents who buy from them in bulk and distribute to markets in the places known to them.

The master potter offers advance money to the potters, and he deducts when paying the wages. Wage is paid on piece-rate basis depending upon the size of the article. The master potter arranges for sale of them through sellers known to him in places like Kerala. Box type *chulas* sell well in Kerala and that is the item produced at Sundarapandiapuram in large number. There are two other types of *chulas* made—single *chula* and double *chula*. A potter produces about 15 *chulas* in one day. On an average he/she earns Rs. 60 a day. Often it is the wastage that reduces the wages of a potter.

It was found that hardly anybody comes to take up pottery as an occupational proposition in recent years. Even those working in pottery units go to work as masons (helpers), or to work in brick-kilns. The children of potters go to schools. The potters do not want their wards to take up pottery for making a living. Although for an outsider it might look as if being involved in pottery does not require investment. Only a close look at their work makes one understand that they need capital investment, especially, in the work shed, kiln, and potters' wheel; plus working capital requirements for buying clay, transporting clay to their work spots, buying firewood for the kiln, straw, provision for damages and so on. In addition, those working on glazed pottery need to buy china clay, ball clay, stony materials, chemicals etc. It is not customary among potters to seek jobs in foreign countries like the carpenters going to the gulf countries.

Analysis: Contrasting Where the Contemporary Society is Heading

"We cook with a mud-*Chula* in an earthen pot, the hand-pound rice; and the spoon we use for serving the food is made of coconut shell, with a long wooden handle. And actually the stony pounding-tool and the wooden pounding-poll we use for separating husk from the paddy and lying down here since almost we were born". How does this scenario sound? Though not primitive, for most of us, it does definitely sound an archaic statement. It gives an impression that this narrates a phenomenon that existed about 30-40 years ago.

The modern kitchen is almost like an executive's official cabin with branded non-stick cook-wares, LP gas stove, pressure cookers, stainless steel serving vessels, and water running down the sink as one opens the tap and so on.

Objectively talking, the scenario – two contains half-real situation and half-dream situation. The real-half is about the villages that are in the peripheries of urban centres; and the dream-half is about villages that are a little away and remote but with a few TVs to nurture this dream. This is an exercise of identifying the potters, in a way, ourselves through time. The artisans (specifically potters) found a livelihood making mud-*Chulas*, earthen pots, and other household-utensils from clay. This is a traditional skill they acquire by observation and practice. Time and technological innovation have introduced new household-utensils, which are considered durable, elegant and work out cheap in the long-run. This is modernity, and it is obvious.

This change in the mindset of the people has resulted in poor off-take of pottery articles and poor income to the potters, except in a few places where local cultures still remains undisturbed like in Kerala, and Kanyakumari that we noticed in the cases discussed above. One significant thing found in this research is that pottery articles from in-side the house have come out-side the house – meaning pottery articles are no more used as household utensils. In fact, the modern utensils made of stainless steel and other durable materials have shown pottery articles the way out. Today, earthen pots are purchased as flower vase to keep at the entrance of houses, in cinema theatres, and in some government offices such as the Collectorate. Two bulk buyers of flowerpots are the Forestry Department and Department of Agriculture for raising tree saplings. Otherwise, they find no utility at the kitchen. Perhaps, people seem to think that it would be odd to place an earthen pot on a stainless steel gas stove, or earthen utensils require care in handling, whereas the lifestyle today is carefree and cheerful.

Potters are not unaware of the change in demand and market trends. They also seem to be doing their best to cater to the demands such as making glazed pottery items and terracotta articles. Items that are in regular demand are flower vases, and terracotta type decorative pieces. Items that are in seasonal demand are *Karthick* lamps, *Chulas* and pongal pots for which potters plan well in advance. Certain pottery items that are in rare demand or almost have been removed from the list of items the potters make are: hen-house and big vessels for watering the cattle which are made only if someone places order. Household-utensils still sell in some of the villages and they are purchased mostly in local *shandy* or from the itinerant potters who sell on the move.

Potters are not completely blind to market trends as one assumes. Apart from producing glazed pottery and terracotta items, potters also introduce an innovation to remain in the market. They make certain items, which attract the attention when one passes by in an exhibition. They include: Magic lamp – a kerosene-lit lamp that does not leak when one holds it up-side down; Rural Fridge – double layered pot that keeps water cool; Lamps in a whole variety and shapes; Water storage containers in attractive shapes such as deer, lion, and horse and so on. There are also potters who have turned to making articles using paper pulp. But the time and effort one has to put in for making these items are demanding. Capital investment and working capital requirements to organize materials remain another challenge, with government support not forthcoming to the extent required.

As far as the technology is concerned, the only tool that the potters were identified with was "a *potters' wheel*". Support extended by agencies of the government such as the KVIC and international agencies such as the UNDP have helped introduce a whole range of improved tools, machineries, and technology in pottery. They include buck machine, ball mill, power-run potters' wheel, jigger machine, gas *Chula* and so on. These are, of course, acquired by organized potters only. In Tamil Nadu places such as Manamadurai in Sivagangai, and Thenpatthai in Thirunelveli potters work on cooperative basis. There are also potters unorganized and as non-members of cooperatives. They do not get such support. But among those unorganized, there is no regret about unavailability of machineries. They look forward only to have loan for the construction of work-shed or shed for the kiln where they bake the pottery articles in order to protect the articles from sudden rain, and an institutional arrangement to provide for working capital requirements.

The reason for not being disappointed about the non-availability of machinery could be: (a) the machineries are not user-friendly; (b) it appears even to a visitor that what an improved tool could have done is tried with a big machine, the maintenance of which is unknown to the potters. Some of the machineries have come to a grinding halt because of the unawareness of the potters to repair the defects. This is apparent when we notice many of the machineries remain unused for long, due to some repair or the other. Although pottery seems to be getting obsolete, it takes reincarnation (such as glazed pottery, terracotta items and paper pulp articles made using different moulds) due to the ingenuity of the potters and stays on. It may not be profitable. But it ensures a source of living for a handful of potters in the State.

Conclusion

Affluence or well-being has never been associated with potters—now or anytime in the past for that matter. Perhaps, this is true of all the traditional artisans dealt with in this study. They have always been mired in poverty struggling to make both ends meet. They could earn a living only if they dirty their hands with the wet-clay and keep steering the potters' wheel. They barely own any assets except the few tools they work with. Science and efforts of external agencies such as the KVIC and Handicrafts Board have provided them with certain new technologies. But the machines provided to them do not seem to be in full use at any of the potter's work sites due to problems of operation, and maintenance. Working capital has been another constraint, which the institutional agencies have not been able to lend a helping hand. Pottery survives to a considerable extent, in places like Kanyakumari and in some parts of Kerala where tradition and culture still remains in tact. In typical Tamil Nadu villages pottery articles are gradually becoming less and less as years go by. Stainless steel and other durable materials have increasingly started occupying the place of pottery articles.

The potters are not unaware of the fact that the market and modernity are marginalizing the pottery tradition and the demand for ethnic items. Institutional agencies of the government such as the Tamil Nadu Handicrafts Development Corporation, KVIC and the Department of Cooperation of the Government are not in a position to support the potters through finance and marketing assistance, to the extent required. The increasing role of fashion, trends and market dynamics keep silently communicating to the potters that they should turn to doing red pottery articles and terracotta items only for the antique shops in five star hotels, and not for any utilitarian value as it used to be with women in the old kitchens.

This culture of making the artisans' products to find place in antique shops as if they are museum pieces should be done away with. Certainly, this is an attempt to cash in on the ethnic expression that pottery is identified with. But, an antique shop usually associates with it the features of a museum and it is not a place of activity and life. Its a place for displaying things that do not have use value. Pottery can survive. It requires protection and support. Potters need to identify and cash in on, by propagating the science associated with using pottery articles in addition to communicating the ethnic value it stands for. By science is meant spreading facts about the harmful effects of storing water in plastic pots, and the toxicity associated with cooking in toflan-coated cook wares. Preserving water in earthen pot or cooking in earthen pot is safe and helps us out of harm's way. By organising community Diwali, like it is done in some places of Maharashtra, where the every household lights several earthen lamps in local temple. It promotes the sale of earthen lamps to the potters as well as promotes communal harmony.

5. Traditional Sculptors of Tamil Nadu

"One can find in the temple at Aavudyar Kovil, that the sun rays touch the stone statue of Sivaligam far inside the temple on a particular date. It is obvious that the *Sthapathi* (Viswakarma sculptor engaged in the construction of temple) who designed the construction of the temple was an expert in astronomy", claim the traditional sculptors of Tamil Nadu.

Introduction

Temples of Tamil Nadu are known specially for the amazing sculptural wonders house. Starting from the marvellous single stone *nandi* sculpture of Thanjore to astounding thousand-pillar *mandapam* of Madurai are all beyond belief today that they are all artistic expressions of a tribe called *sthapathis* — the sculptors. Thousands of temples with lofty towers are scattered all over the state carved out of stone, wood, metal casts etc. The persons involved in sculpture are commonly known as "*sirpi* or *sthapathi*". In general, there are three types of sculptors engaging viz. stone, wood, and metal casting. In Tamil Nadu, they work either as a *sthapathi* at a worksite with a master sculptor or manage their own unit. Making sculptures require blending of professional skills and creativity. Wonderful sculptures from Tamil Nadu are in good demand in foreign countries also.

In order to sustain and promote this age-old skill, the Government of Tamil Nadu has set up training institutes in places like Mahabalipuram.

There are trainees enrolled for imparting the skills of sculpture and temple architecture. They learn drawing and making variety of carving works in stone, wood and metal. In the opinion of the sculptors, being and practicing as a sculptor requires concentration, patience, dedication, and more significantly a spiritualistic approach, as mostly these deal with sculpting figures of deities. Almost everyone involved in this work is men. Of course, all the *sthapathis* rely on making deities. The *sthapathis* make not only idols to temples but also showcase materials. Moreover, they do subsidiary works, which provides them some supplementary income. For example, stone carvers are engaged in making fencing stone, grinding stone, pillar stones for worksheds/cow sheds etc.

Post-Modernity

Tamil Nadu is considered to be one of India's fast developing states. Modernity and urban-development are taking place rapidly in various spheres of activities. This general rapidity of development coupled with post-modern trends brought about by various influences, including globalization, pose challenges to many of the traditional occupations. So much so, it is viewed as opening up opportunities for certain sectors, which one should be alert enough to recognize and make use of. While studying the impact/influences of globalization processes on the rural artisans, it is in order that we study the changes, if any, that are taking place in the traditional sculptors of Tamil Nadu. Attempts are made to identify gaps, if any, in capital requirements, technology requirements, capabilities, resources, new challenges brought about by market forces or the emerging business environment, and so on.

Case 1: Stone Carvers

Stone carving as observed in places like Thiruparangundram, Pillayarpatty, Devakottai, Karaikudi, Pudhuvayal, Lhanavillakku is an exclusive male domain. No women are involved. Stone carving is one traditional skill handed down from generation to generation. This tiresome work requires a lot of vision, imagination and creativity, and above all patience. Although stone carving gives them only just enough to make both ends meet, the stone carvers find pride in saying: 'We create the god who creates man'.

There is a predominance of stone carvers in Mahabalipuram where one can witness plenty of stone carvers actually engaged in a variety of stone carving works. Both traditional stone carvers and stone workers who were trained at the Institute for Art and Sculptures in Mahabalipuram make stone carving works in many places of Tamil Nadu. Apart from Mahabalipuram, there are other places in Tamil Nadu where stone carving work is carried out. What is worth noting is that men belonging to communities other than *asari* community have also taken up this occupation and are trained of Mahabalipuram.

The quality of the material is one extremely important part of the sculptural process. The quality of stone, its maturity, texture and colour are important. Stone carvers of Karaikudi, Puduvayal, Sakkottai and Devakottai are getting raw-stones from Pannaikaranpatty near Nammakkal. Stone carvers of Thiruparamgundram get raw mateiral from T. Subbulapuram near Andipatty. Stone carvers work on a soft stone for carving deities while a hard stone is suitable for making temple top, pillars, roof, *mandapam* (hall) etc.

Some of the stone carvers own small worksheds where they make sculptures. Some of the stone carvers own big worksheds (master stone carvers) where stone carvers are employed for a wage. Of the three types of sculptural works described viz. stone, wood, and metal, stone carvers usually have a high demand. Now-a-days, people like showcase pieces such as fish, frog, dolphin, rabbit and creature of that variety. Stone grinder sets for crushing spices, garlic etc. is in high demand amongst the Karaikudi *chettinad* people for making *chettinad samayal*. They send stone grinder sets also to their relatives in foreign countries. They also make fencing stone, shed support stone (*kavakal*) etc.

The tools they cannot do without are awl (small chisel), and a hammer. They have them in many different sizes. In addition, they have a few other tools, which put together makes their asset and main investment to carry out the work—of course, apart from the skill they have imbibed since almost boyhood. In small worksheds sharpening of awl is usually done by shed owners themselves. In big worksheds—owned by master stone carvers—separate workers are employed especially for sharpening of awls. A sharp tool and an undivided mind bring out a stunning piece of sculpture. Now-a-days, machines have been introduced for cutting stones and polishing them. Use of machine for cutting is considered to be a drudgery—reducing measure. Although use of polishing machine saves on the time, one has to spend time in manual polishing, it generates a lot of dust which is hazardous to the lungs. Also, lines are drawn on idols and polish is applied by using carbon cells. When they make huge idol, there are smaller pieces available that are used for making little idols. There is no much knowledge gap or technology gap as far as stone carving works are concerned. Perhaps, capital investment could be a problem.

One can understand the volume of work being handled by stone carvers by looking up the frequency of procuring raw stones, and the frequency of sending across a truckload of finished products. Small workshed owners procure a truckload of raw stones once a year for which they need about Rs. 5,000 to Rs. 7,000. The big workshed owners procure a truckload of raw stones almost bi-monthly for which they spend on Rs. 30,000 to Rs. 50,000. Those who can manage to arrange the investment carry out own work in own sheds. Others who only have the skill but cannot provide for the investment work as wage-earners. The master stone carvers are able to get regular income. The workers who work under a master get wages.

Availing bank loan is a tedious and long-drawn process and so, sculptors avoid seeking financial assistance from the local banks. They pledge jewels and borrow from informal money-lenders to make investments on stones and to pay truck fare etc. So much so, stone carvers do not approach the banks with proposals of expanding or repairing their workshed. They reason out that they would not be able to produce the security the banks generally ask for. With own assets or by pledging of jewels, the big shed owners run the shed and invest their own money as far as possible.

They make stone sculptures from ½′ to 6′. Male and female deities are made. No women are engaged in stone carving works, perhaps because of the menstrual periods and the associated belief that a woman should not touch deities nor should be involved in performing *pooja* while she is undergoing the menstrual period.

There is always demand for Ganesha idol. Showcase materials made of stone carving are exported to foreign countries as well. The normal practice is to receive one-fourth of the amount as advance money to commence working on a sculpture. Normally, the price of one-foot idol ranges between Rs. 1,000 to Rs. 2,000. Two-feet idol ranges between Rs. 4,000 to Rs. 5,000. As height of the idol rises the price of making charges also go up. Quite presumably, the wage component constitutes the major share of the cost of making an idol. Perhaps, this is one of the factors that is holding them in doing sculptures as a livelihood proposition, however tiresome it is.

Normally, for one stone carver to make a single grinder stone of "11 × 8" size, three labour days (*thatsu*) are required. Wages calculated at Rs. 100 per day, comes to Rs. 300 for three days. The raw-material (stone) cost is Rs. 75. They spend about Rs. 50 for sharpening awl, purchasing polish pad and current charges. In total, the cost of making a grinder stone set works out to about Rs. 425 (Rs. 300 + Rs. 75 + Rs. 50). The small workshed stone carvers are generally prepared to sell it at the rate merely adding the wages for the person days spent on it without profit. They are satisfied with the wage amount for making the sculpture. Large size workshed owners (master stone carvers) seek to get income to be able to pay wages as well as a margin for his pocket.

On account of using polish pads and cutting machines, the electricity charges goes up. Polish pads such as 60 medium polish, 120 polish, and 200 fine polish have to be purchased often. Transport charges and charcoal rates are rising. So, they have to raise the cost of materials they produce. Sometimes, it happens that the party that placed the order might not turn up. The amount and time spent on such sculptures go waste and the sculpture remains with the sculptor. Being a hard work combined with injury to eye and fingers, youngsters are not willing to take up this art related occupation.

Case 2: Metal Casting

Metal casting workers are more in number in place like Swamimalai near Kumbakonam, where metal casting is done as a cottage industry. Plenty of worksheds are seen when one crosses this place. It is reported that there are about 5,000 families dependent on this cottage industry. Swamimalai has the reputation of being the place with splendid skills in making metal casting. Finished products would be given to the society supported by the Tamil Nadu Government. Private companies also buy the finished products and disburse the amount in full immediately. The co-operative society pays partial amount and then disburses the balance in due course.

The cost of metal casting items is cheaper in Swamimalai than in other places on account of easy availability of raw materials and the skilled labourers who are engaged in this occupation for three to five generations. Going by the status of members in the society, they earn their livelihood by engaging in various activities associated with metal casting. While there are workers in a few big worksheds who earn more, there are as many who continue to live on the margin. The cost involved in making such items is too expensive. The efforts to avail bank loan do not work out due to the insistence on the security by the institutional lending agencies. Such insistence pulls down the motivation level of the artisans. They manage to raise money through local money-lenders and set up their own workshed or expand the existing one. Mostly metal casting is undertaken with the traditional knowledge obtained through the family. There is a general view that the training institute produces more number of stone carving experts than metal casting experts. For example, free training is provided to the students for making metal and stone carving at Kovilur near Karaikudi. Only three students have enrolled to learn metal casting, while 20 students have enrolled as students in stone carving. This is perhaps, because the scope and variety of work a stone carver gets is several times when more compared to the scope of work a metal casting artisan gets.

Case 3: Wood Carvers

Karaikudi is known for making wood carving items such as temple car, vaganam, vimanam and artistic wooden works. It is reported that about two decades ago, there were 300-400 wood carvers in Karaikudi and in the neighbourhood. It has come down drastically in the recent years due to migration and decline in the number of new entrants to take up wood carving as a livelihood opportunity. Though the traditional artisans have a limited educational qualification, they are well equipped with professional skills in wood carving through received wisdom and talents.

The practice earlier was that the wood carvers used to go and stay in the places where wood works had to be done. Now, most of the works are done in workshed itself and they make a visit to the client's places for necessary finishing works only. It is pertinent to note that the employment opportunities in wood carving is erratic, and comes in plenty a little before temple festival seasons. Otherwise, the wood carvers will have to concentrate on doing articles for display at antique shops.

The tool box of a wood carver looks a little bigger. He has more tools compared to what the stone carvers or the metal casting workers have. Machines have not occupied the space of workmen, as yet in wood carving, whereas such encroachment has taken place, to a great extent, among the wood workers involved in furniture making. When a master wood carver gets an order, he employs the wood carvers from nearby villages. Finishing works would be done by the master wood carver who usually is a person with long years of work experience.

Such master wood carvers are very limited in number, whereas workers are more.

Being involved in wood carving requires financial investment on the shed, tools and in other paraphernalia. So, many wood carvers remain as employees with master wood carvers who are financially a little better off or has the potential to raise funds from money-lenders etc. Not being able to avail themselves of bank loan for taking up large works is a grievance expressed by many of the wood carvers. If they would make items for display sale which is not possible now due to paucity of funds. As the cost of the wood has increased many folds, very small size of wood carving item ranges from Rs. 50,000 to two lakhs. Hence, on behalf of temples, rich people only place orders for such a large-size wood carving items.

There are master wood carvers who employ many of the wood carvers in Tamil Nadu. The master wood carvers have big workshed by which they earn more, there are workers who continue to live on the margin. What they need is 'financial assistance'. Banks are ready to give small amount of Rs. 20,000 only with a view to see the repayment capacity of the wood carvers. They are informed by the bank managers that the loan amount would be increased slowly. The required amount is Rs. 1.00 lakh to Rs. 2.00 lakhs which is not obtained through the banks. The Handicraft Board is no way nearer to help the wood carvers in erecting their own workshed. Government says that Self-Help Group for wood carvers may be formed by which they would be able to get economic assistance. This concept has not been accepted by the wood carvers in Karaikudi area.

There is a predominance of wood carvers in Mahabalipuram, Karaikudi, Salem, Thanjavur, Chennai, Kallakurichi, Elavankottai and Arumbavar apart from a considerable number in other places of Tamil Nadu. The master wood carvers do not go in search of orders. It comes to their places because of their professional skills. The price of wood carving item depends upon the size and type of wood being used for making a sculpture. Rosewood and teakwood are costlier than Kombu and Athi (country fig tree) woods. In spiritual sense, people believe that Manjanethi wood is highly suitable for idol making. They are not only capable of making wood sculptures but also silver and golden sculptures. In general, 65-70 per cent of the amount goes as wage component in the total amount.

There are lot of temples in Tamil Nadu where temple cars and vaganams (Peacock, elephant etc.) are prestigious possessions.

Tamil Nadu Government has a policy that the repair works have to be undertaken by approved *sthapathis* only. But, normally such people do not have experience or training in making big temple cars or master pieces of *vaganams*. But they manage to get approval because they have a certificate issued by the Training Institute at Mahabalipuram. It is a grievance of the wood carvers. The institute with the virtue of being in access with government is able to get such sanctions from the government. But, they cannot impart technical training in making huge-size temple cars and master pieces. That is a limitation of any training centre that they cannot impart training in such big scales. Similarly, it is a limitation with traditional wood carvers with received wisdom and skill being denied from taking up a work from temple committee, because of the non-possession of a certificate issued by a government institution, states Mr. Thiyagarajan, a traditional wood carver in Karaikudi.

The traditional sthapathis (60% in Tamil Nadu) outnumber the approved wood carvers of the total wood carvers. i e., approximately 25,000 in Tamil Nadu. The traditional artisans do not get government works in repairing of temple cars and vaganams. This Government Order exists since 1972 but, the traditional wood carvers are unable to do anything about it. However, the traditional artisans have achieved renown individually by making many sculptures which are sent to many foreign countries including America, Newsland, Canada, Malaysia, and Singapore. The traditional artisans strongly feel that this discrimination made based on the G.O. should be done away with so that they get government order for making masterpieces of vaganams in Tamil Nadu.

Recently, Tamil Nadu Government has announced Karaikudi as tourism centre. Foreigners are brought to wood carving worksheds for showing traditional wood carving works on the spot. In the worksheds, there are no pieces on display. To arrange for a display, each workshed would require an investment of not less than Rs. 6 lakhs. They are in dire need of such a large amount of investment. They have good market for wood carving items in foreign countries also. There is a general feeling that the wood carving items are too costly. The wood carvers may be issued identity cards by which they may be allowed to procure wood at the prevailing market rates. Thus, they can reduce the cost of wood carving items. Even middle class people can afford to buy such items. All that they need is financial support and direct purchasing rate for woods.

Analysis

There is nothing that can be stated as influence of globalization processes as far as sculpture as a livelihood venture of a section of the population in Tamil Nadu. One of the main reasons is that there are no alternative or competitive materials available nor can one think of promoting one so easily merely by deploying funds and technology. Sculpture is a skill that has been handed down from generation to generation. Machine or technology, to a very limited extent, can come in handy for easing the work. It cannot supplant the sculptor completely. It cannot take over the work of a sculptor altogether. No machinery or technology can unseat or displace the traditional *sthapathis*. There is no influence of modernity either, as one sculptor rightly put it: "as long as faith in god stays alive and temples exist, sculptors have a means of living".

Man-made materials can be used as alternative materials produced through an up-graded technology. But the faith and belief that people have in certain materials for making idols cannot be erased. The materials that the sculptors produce and supply are not viewed merely as materials but as an embodiment of certain values, spirit and godly-faith. It is valued not for the material but for what it embodies. There can be no alternatives to such things. There are three types of sculptors viz. stone, wood, and metal. Of the three types of sculptors stone carvers usually have a high demand, as preference for stone sculptures is high-demand.

They keep doing their work as always and the problems stated are also very much internal and domestic. The *sthapathis* accept the order only if they get profit. Otherwise, they won't take up the work. Earlier they loved art and they did it at will. However, it is noticeable that among the sculptors, there is a new-found tendency of becoming commercial. This is perhaps because there are no new entrants to this occupation as it involves drudgery. This gives them an edge to ask for more in terms of wages and making charges. Moreover it is reported that people these days usually ask for idols and ready-made sculptures. But, making an idol takes not less than a fortnight. This tendency of the clients to go away with ready-made idols and sculpture pieces force the artisans to ask for higher price.

No women are engaged in stone carving works. Today's gender activists might oppose this discrimination. But the practice of not allowing women to take up idol-making is still continues.

Capital is one of the main constraints faced by sculptors. Availing bank loan is a tedious and long-drawn process and so, sculptors avoid seeking financial assistance from the local banks. They pledge jewels and borrow from informal money-lenders to make investments on stones and to pay for truck fare etc. So much so, stone carvers do not approach the banks with proposals of expanding or repairing their workshed. They reason out that they would not be able to produce the security the banks generally ask for. With own asset or by pledging of jewels, the big shed owners manage the shed and invest their own money as far as possible.

There are training institutes imparting training in fine arts such as the one in Mahabalipuram. They also issue certificates and diplomas after a trainee completes the course work. However, one inherent lacuna about the training, in the opinion of the traditional sculptors, is that no training institutes can impart the technical expertise in making huge temple cars and master-pieces. That is a limitation of any training centre that they cannot impart training in such big scales. Similarly, there is a hitch with traditional wood carvers with received wisdom are denied work from a temple committee because of the non-possession of a certificate issued by a government institution. As per the Government Order issued by the State Government in 1972 (GoTN), the traditional wood carvers are denied the opportunity of taking up carving works on the grounds that they do not possess a certificate for having undergone training. This is an absurdity that the traditional *sthapathis* make fun about.

Traditional Rural Artisans of Tamil Nadu: Fast Facts

The Context

"Distress departure" from agriculture is a commonplace occurrence in Tamil Nadu. One pertinent question at this juncture is: what is happening about the occupations, especially, traditional rural artisans that are dependent on agriculture? In other words, if agriculturists themselves are in grief, what is happening to the rural artisans who, most often, depended on agriculturists? This is relevant in the sense, among the 93 per cent of the workforce that is unorganized in India, most of them either farmers or rural artisans. This study has attempted to find out the status of the traditional artisans of Tamil Nadu including goldsmiths, blacksmiths, carpenters, potters, and sculptors.

1. *Goldsmiths*

- The number of people who approach the goldsmiths for making jewellery has drastically come down, and the trend to select ready-to-wear jewellery from showrooms is fast catching up. This is sending shock waves in the spinal cord of the goldsmiths.

- There used to be a small jewellery shop by the workplace of the goldsmiths. This arrangement changed when the goldsmiths sat by the side of small jewellery shops. In either way, the goldsmith had a place. In the former case goldsmiths assumed significance and in the later case it is the jewellery shop that assumed significance. After liberalization, jewellery showrooms have assumed the prime-place, where traditional goldsmiths go seeking employment.
- Small and medium-size jewellery shop owners needed either investment or finance to showcase ready-to-wear jewellery items, and so they started holding new business deals with gold traders and financiers from north India. In the bargain the goldsmiths who depended on local jewellery shops got sidelined.
- The goldsmiths as artisans who have hitherto been making a livelihood out of their capabilities suffer as they need money to invest in gold to supply to the customers or to the small jewellery shop owners.
- Business giants (such as the Tatas for example) who have never been in jewellery business are opening gigantic jewellery showrooms and showcase machine-cut designs, fashion jewellery and branded jewellery which sell like hot-cakes. The goldsmiths are mute spectators to these developments.
- There are also jewellery complexes opened in places like Chennai and Coimbatore which in reality, have confirmed that goldsmith have to find employment in such complexes and they are no more the main players in making jewellery items.
- Popular jewellery shops having their showcases for branded jewellery to be displayed. That is somebody else's product upon which the jewel shop-owner have made no investment on the displayed items in showroom. The strategy of: 'doing business with others money' is catching up even among the middleclass jewellery shop owners. You get a percentages of the profit. This is out and out trade mentality that has affected the local artisans.

2. *Blacksmiths*

- Blacksmiths face two different types of onslaughts. One is, due to shrinking agriculture, the quantum of work they used to get has come down tremendously; and the other is hi-tech factories have started taking over the production of spades, crowbars, plough-shares and so on.

- There are hardly any bullocks to pull carts. Neither are there bullock-carts nor are there bullocks to pull the carts. This has reduced the demand for horse-shoe nails which were supplied by the traditional blacksmiths.
- Working in a blacksmiths workshed requires a lot of muscle power and as the blacksmith grows old, he becomes unfit for the job. Although there is hardly any new takers of this occupation, those already involved in this are lurking in dark about what they would do to spend their old age, when they become physically weak.
- The younger generation is opting to work as rod benders in building construction works, and some even get technically qualified such as welders, fitters and join the companies making grills or car tinkering workshops. This is a healthy shift noticed amidst the blacksmith community.
- In Dindigul there were several lock-workers cooperative societies functioning and most of them are either dormant or have been wound up today. Dindigul lock-workers could not compete with company-made locks. Godrej has become a popular brand for locks. This is another case of tradition being marginalized modernity.
- People, today, have a wide variety of choices thrown before them for selecting vessels and domestic utensils. As 'the culture of wanting to have houses with the facilities of a hotel and hotels with the comforts of a house' people choose, a whole array of household utensils and serving vessels, where elegance, the esthetic look and the presentability matters more than anything else. The brass vessels do not come anywhere near their choice of things. So, the demand for brass vessels has fallen sharply.
- Those involved in trading of vessels are thriving. Some from traditional business community who deal in raw materials for this industry, and in buying and selling stainless steel utensils are growing. Only the artisans who are involved in actual production are losing out. Traders benefit. The artisans or the producers are declining.

3. *Carpenters*

- Tamil Nadu is on the fast-lane in terms of urbanization. Construction industry is one that is booming. The paradox is carpenters – especially those with 'traditional carpentry skills' – are not in high demand, while masons are in high demand, bar-benders, welders, and interior decorators are also in high demand.

- One of the reasons stated for carpenters not being in high demand is the way modern construction plans are made. There is not much work for wood. The other reasons could be that wood is costly because of the competing demand from industries such as wood pulp industry, plywood industry and sports industry.
- The main reasons for carpenters losing employment opportunities are:
  - Alternative materials such as plastics, plywood, mica, glass sheets with aluminium frames, and iron materials have started entering the market. Use of wooden materials have naturally started declining.
  - The influx of plastic chairs and light-weight materials in market has started side-lining the wooden furniture items.
  - The comparative advantage that people have found out in terms of cost and handling in materials other than wood. One block of *neem* wood that sold for Rs. 70 about twenty years ago costs Rs. 400 today.
  - The additional cost involved and time one has to wait for getting a wooden item decorated elegantly.
  - The life of a wooden furniture goes beyond a generation and so demand does not increase frequently.
  - For private, office and commercial complexes, people who want to buy wooden furniture go in for branded furniture items from companies such as the Godrej after perusing designs in a design catalogue rather than placing an order with the local carpenters.
  - Arrival ready-to-fix doors, ready-to-fix-windows, grill-windows, false ceiling, and concrete roofing have considerably reduced the need for wood and wood works.
  - The measure of the government to reduce felling of trees on environmental reasons also reduced the need for wood workers.
  - At a time when chairs, tables, and furniture items were completely being made of wood, a trend of using iron pipes has reduced the weight of the materials as well as the cost. This necessitated the carpenters to get the pipe and iron

works done from outside which took away a slice of the wood work and their share of profit.

4. *Potters*

- Technology that came from time-to-time has introduced a whole range of vessels and household utensils that pottery is gradually being marginalized from the mainframe utility items at the household level even in many of the villages.
- This change in the mindset of the people has resulted in poor off-take of pottery articles and poor income to the potters, except in a few places where local culture still remains in tact.
- One significant thing found in this research is that pottery articles from in-side the house have come out-side the house—meaning pottery articles are no more used as household utensils. In fact, the modern utensils made of stainless steel and other durable materials have shown pottery articles the way out.
- Potters are not completely blind to market trends as one thinks. Apart from producing glazed pottery and terracotta items, potters also introduce innovation to remain in the market. They make certain show piece items, which attract the attention when one passes by in an exhibition.
- As far as the technology is concerned, the only tool that the potters were identified with was "a *potters' wheel*". Support extended by agencies of the government such as the KVIC and international agencies such as the UNDP have helped introduce a whole range of improved tools, machineries and technology in pottery, which are made available to those organized into cooperatives or under KVIC. Those outside cooperative fold do not worry about not getting those machineries as these machineries have problems of operation and maintenance.

5. *Sculptors*

- There are three types of sculptors viz. stone, wood, and metal. Of the three types of sculptors stone carvers usually have a high demand, since demand for stone sculptures is in high.
- There is nothing that can be stated as influence of globalization processes as far as sculpture as a livelihood venture of a section of the population in Tamil Nadu. One of the main reasons is that there are no alternative or competitive materials available nor

can one think of promoting one so easily merely by deploying funds and technology. They keep doing their work as always and the problems they state are very much internal and domestic, which have nothing to do with globalization or modernity.

- Alternative materials produced through an up-graded technology could be used for sculptures. But the faith and belief that people have about certain things cannot be erased. The materials that the sculptors produce and supply are not viewed merely as materials but as an embodiment of certain values, spirit and godly-faith. It is valued not for the material but for what it embodies. There can be no alternatives to such things.
- It is noticeable that among the sculptors there is a new-found tendency of becoming commercial. This is perhaps because there are no new entrants to this occupation taking into account the drudgery involved. Moreover, it is reported that people these days usually ask for idols and ready-made sculptures. This gives them an edge to ask for more money to pay for the wages and making charges.
- No women are engaged in stone carving works, perhaps because of the periods of menses and the associated belief that a woman should not touch deities nor should be involved in performing *pooja* while she is undergoing the menstrual period. Today's gender activist might oppose this but, this is a custom that prevails even now among the sculptors.
- Capital is one of the main constraints faced by the sculptors. Availing bank loan is a tedious and long-drawn process and so, sculptors avoid seeking financial assistance from the local banks. They pledge jewels and borrow from informal money-lenders to make investments on proposals of expanding or repairing their workshed.
- The sculptors are not allowed to take up work from the temples because of the non-possession of a certificate issued by a government institution such as the Institute for Temple Architecture and Sculpture at Mahabalipuram. As per a Government Order issued by the State Government in 1972, the traditional wood carvers are denied the opportunity of taking up carving works on the grounds that they do not possess a certificate for having undergone training. This is an absurdity that the traditional *sthāpathis* make fun about.

Conclusion

Affluence or well-being has never been associated with artisans — now or anytime in the past for that matter. Poor income has been one of the characteristic features of rural artisans. This is true of all the traditional artisans dealt with in this study. They have always been mired in poverty struggling to make both ends meet, except in certain point of time goldsmiths have been to some extent led a affluent life. When a traditional and age old occupation or practice is thought obsolete and it requires to be tossed out, one thing that bothers us as social scientists is: what should we do with the artisans or crafts persons who depend on it as the main source of livelihood? Under a globalized economy as market takes the centre stage it tends to exclude such people as producers/artisans or sellers if their assets, technologies, capabilities, techniques, and way of doing business, become obsolete or old-fashioned. The ability to create and sustain demand are vital for today's market economy, even to earn one's livelihoods. However, traditional sculptors because of the unique nature of their job,—that of creating god that creates man—they cannot be dislodged unless the art of sculpture itself vanishes.

Epilogue

There are institutional agencies to support the activities and promote the welfare of artisans in Tamil Nadu such as KVIC, KVIB, Tamil Nadu Handicrafts Development Board with schemes such as Scheme for Regeneration of Traditional Industries (SFURTI) and PRODIP and so on. It is learnt from the Policy note for the 11th Five Year Plan (2006-07) of the Government of Tamil Nadu that the Tamil Nadu Handicrafts Development Board has made a proposal to conduct a survey of all the artisans and crafts persons in Tamil Nadu. This shows how equipped and interested the government machinery is in uplifting the lot of the rural artisans. It is a pity that no one knows, how many artisans are there in Tamil Nadu.

It is reported that the KVIB, Tamil Nadu has incurred a loss of Rs. 5.57 crores during 2004-05. The accumulated loss of the Board as on 31-3-2005 is 49.74 crores. Reportedly, the loss is mainly due to the increasing establishment expenditures. The accumulation of stock is also said to be a problem.

All uneconomical production units and sales outlets of the Khadi Craft and District Offices, are gradually being closed down by the KVIB.

The government is in the process of retrenching employees (97 of them) and announcing Voluntary Retirement Schemes (169 staff gone already in 2004), and redeploying 862 surplus staff to other departments and corporations of the government. These facts indicate how supportive can the KVIB or the Tamil Nadu Handicrafts Development Corporation be in promoting the welfare of the rural artisans. Unless the artisans themselves understand the market demands and respond, they have a bleak future. The market brings with it not only challenges but also opportunities as has been pointed in several places in this study. It is in the ingenuity of the artisans to equip themselves to tide over the challenges and use the opportunities.

10

Traditional Handloom Weavers: Market Forces that Draw Caricatures

The Premise

"Community Gruel Centres opened to feed handloom weavers' families of Srivilliputhur in Virudhunagar district, Tamil Nadu".

"On July 9, the Handloom Weavers Union organized a fast in Srivilliputhur. On the same day, members of Saliya community organized a fast in Rajapalayam".

"On July 22, weavers called for a total bandh in Srivilliputhur".

"Weavers organize hunger march to Chennai".

"Weavers in Distress"

"Weavers in a quandary"

"Silence of the Looms"

"Hard times for handloom 'kora' silk units"

"Despite Relief package problems of weavers remain".

Introduction

Textile is one of the sectors in which a lot of economic reform measures are taking place in India. The last few years have seen tremendous changes in the textile scenario. The regime of liberalization and free trade has initiated a process of integration of world textile market by world-wide phasing out of quantitative restrictions on imports. The change has created new opportunities for global market; at the same time, it has led to new challenges for the domestic industry as import barriers are considerably being reduced.

The National Textile Policy, 2000 announced by the Government on 2-11-2000 is said to be aimed at preparing the industry for successfully meeting the challenges of the barriers and taking advantage of the opportunities it holds. The Handloom Sector occupies an important place in the Indian Economy as it contributes significantly to employment generation. Its economic importance also lies in its low capital investment and high-value addition, increasing contribution to sustainable employment and economic growth of the country and competing with confidence for an increased share of global market. In order to put the handloom industry on a fast track, the government has introduced several measures for up-gradation in terms of technology and skills of the weavers and so on.

The reform measures initiated in India record mixed developments in textile industry—especially, in the handloom sector. There are also Government Orders passed withdrawing certain conventional schemes that were viewed as monstrously expensive. But again, they are withdrawn after protests from the weaving community. Similarly, the weaving sector, considered as one of the weakest links in the textile value chain, is witnessing a technology revolution, with the installation of thousands of imported shuttleless looms in the Western Tamil Nadu (GoI, Economic Survey, 2002-03).

In this context, understanding the implications of globalization for the livelihood security (Gurumurthy G. 2003) of the handloom weaving community through the mediated policies and programmes of the State Government becomes necessary. Broadly, this study was initiated in order to understand the impact of globalization process on the livelihoods of traditional handloom weavers in specific pockets of Tamil Nadu covering a range from weaving of cotton, coarse varieties to silk weaving. Specifically the study had put down the following objectives:

- Understanding the milieu and social dynamics that are taking place amidst the handloom weaving community in the wake of globalization and the associated competition that is on the mount in the textile industry.
- Studying the changes, if any, that is taking place in the traditional technology and, economics of production associated with handloom weaving in order to keep pace with the changing political economy of the country.

- Analyzing the mediated policies (including the schemes) of the government vis-à-vis the competitive business environment in which the handloom industry finds itself today.
- Identifying problems, coping strategies and path alternatives, if any, adopted by handloom weavers and tapping the suggestions offered by them in order to ensure sustenance of the handloom industry and survival of the handloom weavers from the view points of the weavers as well as those involved in handloom promotion.

Research Approach

This study basically adopted emprico-inductive methodology:

Sample Districts: Almost all the districts of Tamil Nadu, except the Nilgiris, have weavers who depend on handloom weaving as primary means of earning their livelihood. Therefore, minus, the Nilgiris, all the districts of Tamil Nadu were made into clusters based on 'the nature of weaving undertaken'. Accordingly, Tamil Nadu can be classified: (1) as areas that heavily depend on *Janatha* Cloth weaving; (2) areas that depend on bed sheets and heavy cotton material weaving; and (3) areas that are involved in silk weaving. Based on the intensity of critical voices reported three districts from category 1; and two districts from category 2; and one district from category 3 were selected for sample. It made the total number of selected districts six. Thus, the districts selected were: Theni, Madurai, Virudhunagar, Erode, Karur and Kancheepuram.

Unit of Analysis: Village has been taken as the unit of analysis. In order to select villages from among the districts, villages with certain 'critical incidences pertaining to weavers livelihoods' were again identified. Such villages were taken for study. These were not pre-set villages. Rather they were identified during the process of conducting the research, from the key informants and Assistant Director/Special Officers of Cooperatives. Qualitative research methods such as Focus Group Discussion and Key Informant Interviews enabled the researcher's team to identify those villages.

Sources of Data and Information: The study has made use of both primary and secondary sources of data and information. Primary data have been collected from the selected study villages. As far as secondary data were concerned, they have been mostly collected from the Office of the Assistant Director of Handlooms. The tool used for collecting primary data was an interview guide. Collection of primary data was made on two modes: viz. (1.a) Chain of interviews with weavers, (1.b) Focus Group Discussions with weavers in weaving colonies, and (1.c) Holding Key Informant interviews; and (2) Interactions with officials involved in handloom promotion.

Direct observation of various types of looms, their productivity difference and functional efficiency, were made in weavers' colonies in various places and in the industrial weavers' cooperative societies, and with independent weavers. Case studies were made and cross-case analysis have been made searching for similarities and differences in multiple cases studied across districts. Thus, going native, making direct observations and holding informal conversations with officials working for the sector helped bring about both *emic* and *etic* perspectives.

Secondary data were obtained from the Office of the Assistant Director of Handlooms in the respective circles/districts, and from the Primary level handloom weavers cooperative societies and from the industrial weavers cooperative societies as the case may be. Secondary data were collected from the annual reports/annual notes of AD Handlooms. Official websites of Government of Tamil Nadu, Ministry of Textiles of Government of India, Handloom Export Promotion Council, National Handloom Development Corporation and the Co-optex have been widely used. Government websites have been used to refer to the policy papers of the government. As this study involves studying the micro perspectives and looking up for the macro influences in the occurrences at micro level, various policies of the government pertaining to textiles and handlooms, and government performance documents have also been referred to. These analyses helped to understand the policy implications of certain realities the researchers were able to observe and listen to in the field.

Selection of Methods and Tools: This study, in a way, is about understanding and recording how (macro) policies interact with the stakeholders at the (micro) grassroots level. It required comparing and contrasting the responses from various groups and various study sites. Methodology-wise, this study has taken several features of a 'multi-method study' where Focus Group Discussion (FGD) has taken the prime seat and several other techniques like use of a Short Questionnaire, Semi-Structured Interviewing (SSI), and Individual interviews were there in the tools box used in the field. The prime considerations in the selection of research methods and tools were: (i) bringing in as many perspectives as possible, and (ii) validity of the information generated in a given village through triangulation and or cross-checking. Hence, the methods used were mostly qualitative and process-oriented in nature which served the purpose of exploration intended. Wherever possible quantitative data have been obtained from the villages and used in the analysis. Cross-case analysis has been made to understand the perspectives across districts.

Respondents: Active weavers were the primary respondents. In some of the FGDs weavers above 65 years also participated and aired their views. Interviews were held with Textile Committee officials, the Assistant Directors of Handlooms in the selected districts, Special Officers of weavers cooperatives, and the staff in the Primary Weavers Cooperative Societies in selected villages. Key informants were identified in villages and interviews held with them. Focus Group Discussions were held with community members who are affected or remain vulnerable to certain policy change of the government. Chain of interviews held in various hamlets of selected Village Panchayats, chance encounters made with community members during direct observation in the field. In order to cover the weavers outside cooperative fold, the officials of Tamil Nadu Handloom Development Corporation Limited were interviewed.

Data Analysis

Intending to be a study of the grassroots realities, the study has primarily depended on qualitative data and information. It enabled the researchers to obtain divergent views and experiences. Hunches emerged when the study was half-way through, which were tested for validity during the successive field visits in different settings and districts. The categories, relationship patterns and themes from such data were derived as the study progressed. They have been used along with chain of evidences. It required collecting data with thematic sensitivity and putting to use the reflexive consciousness of what is being discussed and observed. It could be noted from the description of situations, events, and experiences as revealed in the study. Internal validity of the information was confirmed through triangulation and cross-checking between various categories of stakeholders interviewed and through various methods used for data collection and analysis.

Scope of this Study

The coverage of this study is confined to handlooms sector only. Statistics show that the influence of powerloom sector on the growth of handloom sector has been substantial and so wherever necessary references are made to powerloom sector as well. Any policy relating to any employment generating sector cannot come in isolation, it has to be viewed from the social milieu from where it is originating; it has to take into account the technology and the economics associated with it. Hence, government policies on textiles and handlooms and schemes meant for the weavers have been discussed touching upon society, technology and economics. Weavers outside the cooperative fold such as the master weavers and the individual weavers who are under the care of master weavers have been studied through Tamil Nadu Handloom Development Corporation Limited (THDCL). THDCL works for weavers out side the cooperative fold.

Limitations of this Study

Competitiveness in the textile industry in the wake of globalization or even otherwise is quite obvious. But, the relationship the weavers have in the decentralized Panchayati Raj System is nothing unique. Even in the weavers cooperatives it is not democratically elected Board but government-appointed Special Officers who make all the decisions. Hence, this study tends to have taken a tilt more on the globalization side throwing little light on decentralization side. Another limitation was with regard to compiling data from various Offices of AD Handlooms due to non-computerization of data and inconsistency in formats.

I. HANDLOOM INDUSTRY IN TAMIL NADU : AN OVER VIEW

Handloom Sector

The Handloom Industry in India has a very long history, spanning over several centuries. As a traditional industry, handloom has been serving the basic cloth needs of the people. Today, in India handlooms industry holds a prime place for three obvious reasons viz., (i) it provides the largest employment among the traditional industries, next only to agriculture; (ii) handlooms have maintained one-fourth share (23%) of total textile production in the country; and (iii) the textile industry, including handlooms, is a major foreign exchange earner of the country. It earns more than 35 per cent of the total exports revenue made in our country (www.blonnet.com). The major handloom states in India are West Bengal, Tamil Nadu, Uttar Pradesh, Andhra Pradesh, Assam and Manipur. These 6 States account for 75 per cent of handloom weaving in the country.

Textile production in this country commenced with handlooms and the passage of time has not lessened the role of the industry completely. The industry continues as a partner with the mill sector and the khadi sector. Spinning, Handloom, Powerloom, and Garment are the four pillars of the Textile sector in the State. There are nearly 3.8 million handlooms in India giving direct employment to about 3.5 million people and indirect employment to another 3.1 million in various pre- and post-loom process.

The textile industry occupies a pivotal place in the economy of Tamil Nadu. Tamil Nadu has played a key role towards achieving the growth of Textile industry in India. Handloom industry in Tamil Nadu provides employment for more than 4.29 lakh weaver-households and about 11.64 lakh weavers. Weaving as an occupation is taken up only by specific communities in Tamil Nadu. They include: Saliyar, Sengunthamudaliyar, Devangarchettiyar, Sowrashtras and Muslims in some pockets. Tamil Nadu has several popular weaving centres. They include Erode (Bed sheets and furnishings), Karur (Made-up items and placemat), Chinnalapatty (Art silks and mixed fabrics), Sundarapandiam (gada for uniforms) and Andipatty (low-cost cotton sarees—FDS), Srivilliputhur (Ayyappa towels), T Kunnathur (Lungies), T Sublapuram (Polycotton sarees), Andipatty (*janatha* sarees) and the triple-ply silks of Kancheepuram (A list of Weaving centres and varieties of handloom products in Tamil Nadu is given at the end of this chapter). Handloom is still the most flexible, decentralized and the least capital— and energy requiring livelihood-option in India.

The handloom industry has been able to maintain its own identity. This is due to the fundamental fact that it has an organization and structure which is very different from the mill sector. It is unique in its individuality and in the production of quality goods which maintain their own identity. For example, the silk sarees, dhoties, towels, kodambakam sarees, pumper sarees have a uniqueness in terms of craftsmanship and finish which cannot be claimed by the mill sector. It may be pointed out that the handloom industry has a great potential for the utilization of human resources. It is necessarily a labour-intensive industry. In a country like India, with considerable man-power and a high rate of unemployment any investment that can utilize idle human resources is welcome, so it has a great role to play. It is a cost-effective mode of textile production primarily because of low-capital cost and more labour, with growing unemployment, this sector provides a great opportunity.

Organization of Handloom Industry in Tamil Nadu

The way handloom weavers operate is not uniform all over the state. They work in different modes and methods. The organization of handloom weavers can be brought under three categories. They are: (1) Co-operatives, (2) Master Weavers, and (3) Individual or Independent Owners. Cooperatives are found to work in two types: (a) Primary Weaver's Cooperative Societies; and (b) Industrial Weaving Cooperative Societies.

1. *Weavers Under Co-operative Fold*

Weaving cooperatives – be it Primary Weavers Cooperative or Industrial Weaving Cooperative—have been formed as governmental effort to relieve the weavers from the clutches of the master weavers. The private master weavers in several places of Tamil Nadu hired weavers for poor wages, made them work for long hours and were involved in production and marketing of handloom fabrics. The weavers had to completely depend on the master weavers to earn their livelihoods. It was almost a slavery practice. The government took initiatives and formed Primary weavers' cooperative societies and Industrial weavers' cooperative societies in 1950s.

In Tamil Nadu, 2.11 lakh handlooms are functioning in 1247 handloom weavers cooperative societies as on 28-02-2005 and the remaining looms are outside the cooperative fold. Out of 1247 handloom weaver's cooperative societies, 1169 are cotton weavers' co-operative societies and the remaining 78 are silk weavers' cooperative societies. The handloom weavers' cooperative societies mostly exist in rural and semi-urban area, where there is large concentration of handloom weavers. Almost 50 per cent of the weavers in Tamil Nadu are under cooperative fold.

(a) *Primary Weaver's Cooperative Societies*

This is one of the vital sectors of the industry in which the Government of Tamil Nadu is actively involved. The government has throughout tried to develop the sector through active support to the cooperative units. Thus, the cooperative societies have been formed with the explicit purpose of having members involved in handloom weaving. Each society has the share-capital subscribed both by the members and by the Government. Weavers with looms may enroll themselves as members of cooperative paying a share-capital of Rs. 500 and an admission fess of Rs. 10 a weaver needs to have at least one loom to become eligible. Nevertheless, with mere one loom in possession, one to three members from the same family are given admission as members.

Table 10.1: Performance of Handloom Weavers Cooperatives in Tamil Nadu

Year	*No. of WCS*	*No. of Handlooms (in lakh)*	*Production (in lakh metres)*
1995-96	1439	4.15	1240.86
1996-97	1439	3.45	1055.36
1997-98	1386	3.67	1006.40
1998-99	1382	3.44	948.34
1999-2000	1354	2.83	886.45
2002-03	1313	2.16	415.71
2003-04	1286	2.17	467.61
2004-05	1247	2.11	559.72

Source: Department of Handloom and Textiles, Government of Tamil Nadu.
Note: Data are not available for the years of 2000-01 and 2001-02.

The main activity of the Primary Weavers Cooperative Society (PWCS) is to procure yarn (either from co-optex godown or from other sources through NHDC with the permission of the Assistant Director of Handlooms) and supply to the weavers, and collect the finished handloom goods from weavers and send it across to the co-optex showrooms. Weaving takes place at the residence of the weavers where the weavers have their own looms. The society does not arrange for looms or other accessories required for weaving. Weavers Cooperatives are manned by paid staff and they work under the control of the Special Officers (also known as 'Handloom Officers') from the Office of the Assistant Director of Handlooms.

The number of Weavers' Cooperative Societies, number of handlooms, and production show a declining trend between the years 1995-96 and 1999-2000. Even though the number of Weavers' Co-operative Societies and number of handlooms showed a declining trend, the production seems to be picking up slowly from 2002-03 onwards. As of now, 1247 Weavers' Cooperative Societies are functioning in which 2.11 lakhs handlooms have been enrolled in Weavers' Cooperative Societies during the year 2004-05.

(b) *Industrial Weaver's Cooperative Society*

In Industrial Weaver's Cooperative Societies, the cooperative society owns and manages looms, tools and accessories in a common shed where the members are expected to work. The society arranges for yarn and other raw materials required. The society approves the plan of production[1]. All the members work in a common shed and prepare goods as approved by the society. Each member is paid in proportion to the work done by him/her in the workshop (piece-rate system). The society enrolls one or two members from one family. The members become eligible to obtain all government schemes meant for weavers, including insurance, housing and stipend for children's education etc.

2. *Master Weavers*

The term is actually misleading in the handloom industry because the master weavers do not necessarily weave cloth. On the contrary they are owner-operators. Generally speaking there are two types of master weavers. They are:

(a) Some of the master weavers may not own any looms at all but have contacts with traders dealing in cloths. They procure orders from such traders. In order to supply to the orders, they purchase

1. The society approves the plan of production (decides the type of cloth variety to be weaved) based on the requirements assessed at the open market, or as order placed by the co-optex or as desired by deemed exporters.

yarn in bulk quantities from private spinning mills at competitive price and gets them weaved by a handful of weavers who usually depend on them for livelihood. In other words, this group consists of master weavers who supply yarn and raw materials to weavers who have their own looms and after a time period receive the finished products. Wages are paid for the quantity produced.

BOX 10.1
Earnings of a Master Weaver

Mr. Appuswamy is one among the 100 master weavers in Karur. He has been in the field since 1965. He has 12 looms right from the beginning. In his firm 12 men and 5 women (pre-loom workers) are working. He is producing export varieties such as bed sheet, screen cloth, pillow cover but for the past ten years screen cloth only. The weavers can earn Rs. 60-80 per day. The master weaver is getting Rs. 8 per piece, from that he has to meet the expenses such as wages for pre-loom workers (Rs. 30/ worker/day), electricity charges, transport charges. So, per month on an average a master weaver is able to earn Rs. 7,500 to Rs. 10,000. It works out to an annual income of Rs. 90,000 to Rs. 1.2 lakhs whereas the weavers are earning hardly Rs. 1,500 to Rs. 2,000 a month which is five times less than what a master weaver earns.

(b) Another type is that the master weavers may install a few looms in a shed for which he is the owner. The number of looms the master weavers own may range from ten to fifty. They procure orders from traders who deal in cloths and hire weavers to weave in order to fulfil the order procured. In other words, the master weavers own looms in a private shed and hire weavers to weave for the order the master weaver has in hand. Yarn and other raw materials are provided by the master weavers and the weavers earn the wages according to the quantity produced. This type of master weavers usually concentrate in the production of coarse varieties. The business of master weavers is not only the dominant sector but also a very profitable sector in the industry. Still about 40 per cent of the weaving community work under master weavers only. Master weavers are still found in large numbers at Kancheepuram (around 250). Merits and limitations of working under cooperatives and under master weavers is presented below:

Merits and Limitations of Working under Cooperative Sector

Merits for the Weavers	*Limitations for the Weavers*
• Weavers get certain privileges and facilities from government side. In particular, old age pension scheme is available to the weavers.	• It is not possible to take policy decision by single member as management is not controlled by a single individual like master weaver.
• Profit is distributed among the members as dividend and/or bonus.	• Weavers are supposed to work for pre-loom preparation works by the members themselves.
• Very small amount as share is invested on the part of the members.	• Poor quality of yarn is supplied by the co-optex.
• Regular increase of wages is assured per year.	• A large amount of advance for urgency is not possible.
• Marketing is arranged for their products by the government through co-optex.	• Job security is not assured in this sector. So, life of the weavers depends upon the procurement of their products by the government. If government stops the procurement from the co-optex, the weavers will be jobless.
• Training on new design making is given with stipend.	• Due to mismanagement of the societies, the societies incur loss. As a result, the weavers who are in the society will be in distress.
• Since the cooperative societies are registered body, weavers can rely on their functions. These societies will not switch over to some other business as it is done by master weavers.	• In general, productivity is lower because of not ensuring continuity of supply of yarn.

Merits and Limitations of Working under Master Weavers

Merits for the Weavers	*Limitations for the Weavers*
• There is no need for paying share capital to master weaver.	• Profit is not divided among the members. The proprietor can enjoy the benefits from the hard work of the weavers.

(*Contd.*)

(Contd.)

Merits for the Weavers	*Limitations for the Weavers*
• A large amount of advance for urgency is possible.	• As master weavers are acutely conscious of their profits, the weavers can not expect any humanitarian aid.
• There is no delay in the payment of wages.	• No welfare schemes are provided to the weavers by the master weaver.
• It is possible to introduce new marketable designs immediately because of the management is controlled by a single person.	• No amount is spent on training purpose and up-gradation of skills to the weavers. Weavers have to learn by themselves.
• Good quality of yarn is supplied to the weavers from the private mills at a competitive price.	• There is no old-age pension scheme available to them.
• As the processed yarn is supplied to weavers, there is no necessity to do pre-loom work preparation.	• Wage and employment are highly fluctuated by the demand of products in the market.
• As master weaver looks after the marketing, there is no need to find out the marketing.	• There is no forum available to express their views.
• Productivity is higher because of ensuring continuity of supply of yarn.	• Life of the weavers depends on master weavers for their livelihood.

3. *Individual or Independent Owners*

This is the smallest group in the handloom industry. An independent weaver is one who weaves the cloth himself or by members of his family. He owns one to four looms and purchases yarn to be used for weaving. The finished products are sold in the market through his own effort. Sometimes they procure orders from some traders and weave for them. They get paid based on piece rate system. Only about 10 per cent of the weavers would fall in this category.

Duo-Weavers: A fourth group we could mention is 'Duo-Weavers' if we can call them so. These are members of cooperatives who are not completely dependent on the cooperatives alone. They weave for the cooperatives only when the society supplies yarn. During the time when the society is not able to supply yarn, they have some master weavers for whom they weave. Kancheepuram is a typical example for this phenomenon. When weavers in cooperatives face unemployment problem due to accumulated stocks and very minimal supply of yarn, the silk weavers have the master weavers to fall back upon. This practice although ensures continuous employment to the Silk Weavers of Kancheepuram, the efforts of the government in increasing the coverage of handloom weavers under cooperative fold, and chances of reducing the number of master weavers in the field become a unprofitable proposition.

4. *Weavers not Covered by Cooperative Sector*

The weavers who are not covered by the cooperative fold are served by a quasi-governmental organization known as Tamil Nadu Handloom Development Corporation Limited (THDCL). THDCL has five regional offices covering all the districts of Tamil Nadu. They are located in: Kancheepuram, Salem, Madurai, Kumbakonam, and Coimbatore. The main activity is financial assistance, through property mortgage, to weavers not covered under cooperative fold. Despite the fact that this organization is supposed to serve all the weavers who are outside the cooperative fold, THDCL provides financial assistance to the master weavers only. It is reported that the problems related to recovery of loans from individual weavers made THDCL to limit their lending only to master weavers.

At the moment THDCL is undergoing a financial crunch. The budgetary allocations have started shrinking, due to the general trend of the government trying to bring down allocation to industries and corporations that have been under protection thus far. Therefore, THDCL is getting cash credit from State Bank of India (SBI) and is involved in onward lending to the master weavers.

THDCL primarily serves as an organization that caters to the financial needs of master weavers. As the number of master weavers in any given district of Tamil Nadu ranges from 50-80, the number of members THDCL serves is not too big. The number of members (master weavers) in Salem region (covering five districts) is 350 only. The number of members in Madurai (covering 8 districts) is about 500 only. Although there are no official records available to ascertain the exact number of master weavers in the State, extrapolating from the data available for certain districts, it could be said that for entire Tamil Nadu, the number of master weavers could be somewhere between 2800-3500 only.

Similarly, the number of individual weavers working under each master weaver is not fixed at any point of time. This is because they keep shifting between master weavers and the cooperatives. There is no way these numbers could be accurately given. Although the number of master weavers in the State is not too big, they assume significance from the point of view of number of individual weaver families that depend on these master weavers. The number multiplies several fold viewed from that angle. An estimate is that the number of individual weavers (not covered under cooperative fold) all over Tamil Nadu could be between 8,000 and 12,000. Most of them are, perhaps, in Erode and Karur districts. The relationship between the master weavers and the individual weavers is, sort of, symbiotic. The master weavers need the individual weavers so as to carry out the orders they get from dealers. The individual weavers get festival advance, bonus etc. from master weavers which makes them keep working for them.

Contrasting with Cooperatives

If one asked which is better – working for *cooperatives* or working for *master weavers*? Or to put it in other words, given a choice which of these two options weavers would choose? From the insights, one tends to say that it is six of one and half a dozen of the other, meaning neither those working for cooperative nor those working for master weavers is better off. They are working either for one or for the other by chance and not by choice.

Pre-Loom Livelihoods

Weaving viewed as a livelihood option, should include those involved in pre-loom works as well. Before the yarn goes on-loom, there are several 'preparatory works' to be done with the raw yarn. They include winding, warping, warfing, sizing, tyeing etc. These are usually not carried out by the weavers themselves. They seek some one in each family/village who are usually involved in doing such preparatory works only. For example, winding is a simple but time consuming work. The weavers usually engage women or men over 60 years of age who have retired from weaving due to weakening eyesight to do the job for them. They are paid on the basis of the number of cones they have filled winding. There are some places where young school drop-out girls, who are not physically strong enough to get on a loom are engaged in such works. The wages for such works are paid by the weavers from the wages they would get for weaving on piece-rate system. One of the studies reveals that at least 30 per cent of the weavers are full-time workers in preparatory works. Another 3 per cent shift between being a weaver and being pre-loom wages earner.

Livelihood Assets

An attempt to understand the type of livelihood assets the weavers possess revealed the following:

Human Assets: Weaving is a special skill which only certain communities living in certain specific places in Tamil Nadu possess. It is traditional and usually handed down from parents to their wards. As human beings, they have certain special skills which can be considered as human asset. Where it is weaved at the household level, it is still viewed as a family occupation. In a weaver's family almost every one possesses the skill of weaving or some skill that is relevant to weaving. The skill level and the entrepreneurship vàry even within the weaving communities. Some are conventional and saturated into the same old tradition while others are enterprising and are on the look out for better designs that are market-worthy and technologies that are less-drudgery.

Physical Assets: Loom is the major productive physical asset with the handloom weavers. Some of them have it in their own residential houses, others depend on the ones made available to them either by the Industrial cooperative society or at the factory of the master weavers. For those who work at home, it requires a minimum space of 10 × 10 sq.ft. This is mostly their living place as well. There are at least five major types of looms in Tamil Nadu. They are: (1) Pit Looms, (2) Frame Looms, (3) Jacquard Looms, (4) Nepal Looms, (5) Nepal Looms semi-automated. The cost of fabricating each loom ranges from Rs. 6,000 to Rs. 15,000.

Financial Assets: Finance is a problem only for the individual weavers who are independent. They need money to buy yarns. They need money even to buy the second feed of yarn for initiating pre-loom processes, while the first lot is still on-loom. Moreover, they are usually indebted to traders and money-lenders. However, for those who work under cooperative fold and for those who work for master weavers, yarn supply would be taken care of by cooperative society and the master weavers respectively. Weavers have little financial asset as such. They seem to have more liabilities rather than assets, in the sense, for changing the design, every time they need to change the frames which cost money.

Social Assets: For 50 per cent of the weavers in Tamil Nadu State, cooperatives serve as a social asset in terms of giving employment, ensuring a fixed wages, implementing government schemes etc. However, even the cooperatives they belong to, is not managed by elected Board of Directors. Instead, government-appointed (but paid by the society) Special Officers manage the affairs. The Village Panchayat views them on par with any other citizen of the village. They have no associations to protect their interests except in some places like Aruppukottai where their association is identified as "Weavers Associations" and they are protected based on the party they belong to. It should be mentioned here that many of the cooperative societies are either making loss or are facing severe financial crisis. Some of the loss-making societies are in 'adoption' by another society which is to some extent making profit.

II. HANDLOOM WEAVING AND SOCIAL DYNAMICS IN TAMIL NADU

The Community, Spread and the Size: Weaving is an occupation for certain communities such as Saliyar, Sengunthamudaliyar, Sourastra and Devangarchettiyar, in Tamil Nadu. The places they live are Arani, Andipatty, Aruppukottai, Bhavani, Coimbatore, Chennimalai, Chinnalapatty, Erode, Kadayanallur, Kancheepuram, Karur, Kumbakonam, Madurai, Srivilliputhur, Sundarapandiam, and Thiruchenkodu etc. Although most of them are involved in handloom weaving, a fast shift to powerloom weaving is noticeable in most of the places visited. Studies by the Department of Handlooms and Textiles in the late 1991 have shown that there is a steady decrease in the number of handloom weavers at the rate of 2 per cent per year. Therefore, the working of handlooms has been steadily decreasing. The rate of fall reported is only moderate. Given the trend noticeable in actuality, the rate of decline might be higher than this estimate. Pending confirmation by another detailed survey, it is likely that the actual number of working handlooms may not exceed 2.5 lakhs as of 1998. With 2 per cent fall every year the number of working handlooms could be a little over 2 lakhs as of June 2005.

Analysis of average number of members perloom reveals that Madurai and Kancheepuram districts adhere to the condition that one can become a member only if he/she holds a loom, where as it is not followed very strictly in Erode and Virudhunagar. In Theni, the number of members is very low compared to the looms which implies that the members are shifting to other jobs due to low wages in handloom sector. The country's average is 1.81 workers per loom.

Youngsters do not prefer Handloom Weaving: It could be noticed in most of the places visited that a major chunk of population in handloom weaving are above 40 years. There are hardly any youngsters doing handloom weaving. Nor do the parents encourage them to take up handloom weaving. The youngsters, except in a few places like Erode, have not been much educated either, although they are better educated than their parents. The youngsters are after a work that involves less drudgery and more remuneration. They go to work straight away to powerlooms and not as refugees from handlooms. Some of them have also taken up cloth sales and working as salesmen in cloth stores. Some of them go to work in many of the private spinning mills that have proliferated after delicensing that took place in 1995. They have diversified their search for employment rather than searching from within the village.

However, young girls who dropped out of school or are not aged enough to be given in marriage usually engage themselves either in weaving or in pre-loom processing works. Girls also work in the weaving sheds of master weavers in tasks such as winding, where they earn Rs. 2 for winding five cones using a motorized wheel. On an average a girl earns Rs. 30 a day winding cones.

Men Gradually Leave the Sector: Over the years, the number of men involved in handloom weaving has come down drastically. In most weaver's households visited by this team of researchers, only women were found weaving. Men consider handloom weaving non-remunerative or the wages they get is not commensurate with the labour and time they put in. They are on the look out for greener pastures elsewhere. The alternative that attracts them immediately is powerloom sector. As the normal human psychology goes, they want to earn their livelihoods from what they are already familiar with instead of learning something a new. They go to work in powerloom sector in their own village or in the neighbourhood, while the wife at home still weaves at home. Withdrawal of membership by men are more than that of the women. The declining number of membership in all the societies visited by researchers of this study corroborates this statement.

Women Stick to Handloom Weaving: Women, although have loads of complaints about the sector, continue to do handloom weaving as an occupation. This is because they considers their income to be supplementary to what the husbands bring from powerloom sector or from other sources. One important advantage the female-worker relates with being in handloom weaving is that she works at home leisurely while at the same time performs her other domestic chores such as cooking and taking care of children and so on. If she earns Rs. 30 a day from handloom weaving and the husband earns Rs. 70 to Rs. 90 from powerloom, their life goes on. Such is their calculation.

Handloom Weaving Supports the Aged: Another important revelation of this study could be that almost all the aged men and women (those above 60 years of age) are engaged in pre-loom processing works. Hence, being aged is not considered as being a burden to a family in the weaver's community.

BOX 10.2

Age-wise Classification of Weavers in India

Age Group	*No. of Handloom Weavers in Percentage*
25 - 30	4
31 - 45	32
46 - 60	42
61 and above	22
Total	**100**

Source: K.D. Saksena, *Dynamics of Handloom Industry in India*, 2002.

Pre-loom processing or preparatory works as it is called is a series of simple but time consuming activities such as winding, sizing, tyeing etc. Those in weaving usually get it done by the aged ones in the family. By the time the man or woman in the family finishes weaving one lot of yarn, the aged person in that family is done with the pre-loom works and gives the yarn ready to go on-loom.

They also have the practice of calculating wage for such pre-loom works carried out by aged people. Hence, the elders seem to lead a life that is dignified. We should note here that in addition these elders are also getting Old Age Pension (OAP) for retired weavers of Rs. 200 per month from the government. OAP plus their earnings as wage would work out to not less than Rs. 450 a month. Hence the dignity.

Handlooms, by Nature, Supports only an Optimum Size Families: By nature, handloom weaving seems to be favourable only to women and the aged who would like to work in leisure, is a point made already. Given the technology and the productivity levels, it is not remunerative for men to take it up as an income-earning proposition, unless the whole family is engaged in it. But, again, it neither supports a nuclear type of family nor does it support a big joint family. It could support only an optimum-size family.

It does not support a nuclear type of family because in a nuclear family there would be no elders available to do the pre-loom processes. Out of necessity, if the husband does the weaving and the wife does the pre-loom processes, then they have to necessarily live in destitution and struggle to make both ends meet. It does not support a big joint family because, in a big joint-family, there would be many mouths to feed but the houses of weavers are not spacious enough to accommodate more than two looms that too are invariably installed in their living room—the only spacious room of the house. By sheer necessity of requiring to have extra house to accommodate additional looms, one joint-family has to break out to be able to install new looms and increase earnings.

Problem of Splitting up: Apart from handloom weaving being non-remunerative, another reason for skilled weavers leaving the sector is that when a young man of a weaving family gets married and that he has to split away from the main family and lead his own life, he needs a loom (the physical asset) to work with. Finding a house for rent to live separately is possible but finding Rs. 8,000 to Rs. 10,000 to set up a new loom for oneself is difficult. One of the prerequisites to become member of a weavers cooperative is that he/she should own a loom. Government schemes provide loan and other grants only for loom up-gradation and not for setting up a new loom. These circumstances necessitate him to find employment with a master weaver who owns several looms or seek employment in other related mill sectors or at the least he joins a cloth store as a sales person.

Changing Life-Styles: The mindset with regard to the standard of living keeps changing and weavers are no exception to this general trend of development in the society. Things that once they thought as comforts are becoming necessities. For example, kerosene stoves and earthen *chulas* are being fast replaced by gas stoves. FM radios are considered outmoded and they are being replaced by Televisions in weaver's households. These items and improved kitchen wares (such as grinder and mixie) that they are introduced to day-in and day-out in the TV are also slowly becoming essentials. Fulfilment of these desires requires an increase in household-income. These desires also eventually drive men out from the handloom sector.

Leading a Life of Penury: In the opinion of the weavers, handloom weaving is 'a sector that keeps them scarcely fed, barely dressed, and poorly housed for life-long'. Hence, they keep looking out for better wages elsewhere—either from a master weaver or in some power loom factory in the vicinity. However, women in every household do the weaving so as to remain a member of the cooperative society to be eligible for getting the benefits offered to weavers by the government.

Official Records that Support Field Observations

The following tables and analysis made of them give official substantiation to the direct observations made in the field. These cross-checkings come as administrative validation of the statements made in the foregoing pages, and to draw them appropriately wherever required in the subsequent sections of this report. These data from various Offices of the AD Handlooms in the selected districts speak with official sanction, the number of looms where cobwebs have developed over the years; falling membership in the cooperative weavers societies; stock piling up in godowns; amount due by co-optex and rebate due by the government to the weavers cooperative societies etc. in the selected districts.

Table 10.2 : Functional and Dormant Societies in the Selected Districts

Districts	*Functional Societies*	*Dormant Societies*	*Total Societies*
Madurai	23 (51.0)	22 (49.0)	45 (100)
Virudhunagar	75 (98.7)	1 (1.3)	76 (100)
Theni	26 (96.3)	1 (3.7)	27 (100)
Erode	150 (82.42)	32 (17.58)	182 (100)
Kancheepuram	69 (93.24)	5 (6.76)	74 (100)

Source: Short Notes obtained from the respective Offices of AD Handlooms.
Note: Figures in parentheses are percentages.

In Tamil Nadu the cooperative sector is afflicted by a plethora of problems which put the societies in a dormant condition. In the case of Madurai district 49 per cent of the societies are reported to be dormant. In the case of Erode district, 17.58 per cent of the societies are reported to be dormant. The economic condition of those weavers in dormant societies got worse and their livelihood causes are pathetic.

Table 10.3 : Number of Looms in Selected Districts

Districts	*Active*	*Idle*	*Total*
Madurai	2022 (20.1)	8029 (79.9)	10051 (100)
Virudhunagar	10210 (90.8)	1040 (9.2)	11250 (100)
Theni	1058 (20.2)	4182 (79.8)	5240 (100)
Erode	26232 (72.3)	10042 (27.7)	36274 (100)
Kancheepuram	13874 (41.2)	19839 (58.8)	33713 (100)

Source: Short Notes obtained from the respective Offices of AD Handlooms.
Note: Figures in parentheses are percentages.

Among the functioning societies some of the looms lay idle which do not provide employment to the handloom weavers. Even though dormant societies are low (3.7% in total societies), the idle looms in the society are reported to be very high in the case of Theni district. Idle looms are found in all the societies. The percentages of the idle loom in Madurai district is (79.9%), followed by Theni district (79.8%), Kancheepuram district (58.8%), Erode district (27.7%) and Virduhunagar district (9.2%).

Table 10.4 : Profit and Loss making Societies in Selected Districts

Districts	*Functional Societies*		*Total Functional Societies*
	Profit Making Societies	*Loss Incurring Societies*	
Madurai	13 (56.5)	10 (43.5)	23 (100)
Virudhunagar	15 (19.7)	61 (80.3)	76 (100)
Theni	15 (57.7)	11 (42.3)	26 (100)
Erode	141 (77.47)	41 (22.53)	182 (100)
Kancheepuram	18 (27.03)	51 (72.97)	69 (100)

Source: Short Notes obtained from the respective Offices of AD Handlooms.
Note: Figures in parentheses are percentages.

Despite the loss, the Primary Weavers Cooperative Societies are being protected by the government for the welfare of the handloom weavers. It is clear from Table 10.4 that the loss incurring societies are found in all the selected districts. The percentages of the loss making society is as high as it is in Virudhunagar district (80.3%) followed by Kancheepuram district (72.97%), Madurai district (43.5%) Theni district (42.3%) and Erode district (22.53%). The reason for the highest percentages of loss making societies in Virudhunagar district is that more number of societies are involved in FDS Scheme which completely depends on payment by Co-optex and rebate amount from the Government. While the reason for the lowest percentages of loss making societies in Erode district is that more number of societies are involved in producing goods for export.

Table 10.5 : Average Number of Weavers per-Loom

Districts	*Members*	*Total No. of Looms*	*Average Number of Weavers per-Loom*
Madurai	10051	10051	1.00
Virudhunagar	20642	11250	1.84
Theni	1100	5240	0.21
Erode	44613	36274	1.23
Kancheepuram	13874	13874	1.00

Source: Short notes obtained from the respective Offices of AD Handlooms.

It is obvious from Table 10.5 that the average number of weavers per-loom is found high in Virudhunagar district (1.84 persons). So, the condition of one weaver per-loom is not adhered to by the societies in Virudhunagar district. The condition of one weaver per-loom is adhered to by the societies in Madurai and Kancheepuram districts. The average number of weaver is above one loom that is 0.21 in Theni district which means the weavers have other occupations to pursue and they have weaving as an alternative to fall back on. The country's average is 1.81 weaver per-loom.

Productivity of an average Tamil Nadu handloom weaver is shown in Table 10.6 (along with wages earned). The highest productivity per-loom per day is in Delhi (14.29 metres). The country's average is 5.12 metres per-loom per day. An average Tamil Nadu weaver is a little above the national average in terms of productivity.

Wages for the production by the weaver is calculated including the cost incurred in pre-loom processes which requires the expenses from

17 per cent to 31 per cent in the total wages. However, it varies from the variety of products weaved by the weavers.

Table 10.6 : Net Wage of a Handloom Weaver

Sl. No.	Product Variety	Productivity by an Average Weaver	Wage per Unit (in Rs.)	Gross Wages (in Rs.)	A Day's (Net) Wages of a Hl Weaver (in Rs.)	Cost Incurred in Pre-Loom Processes
1.	Low Cost Sarees (FDS)	1.5 sarees	45.00	67.50	51.90	15.60
2.	*'Gada'* cloth for school uniforms	10 metres	8.85	88.50	70.50	18.00
3.	Cotton Lungi	3 lungies	20.80	62.40	52.20	10.20
4.	Cotton Dothi	2 Dothies	40.00	80.00	55.00	25.00

Source: Computed from the field data.

Note: By 'Net Wage' is meant the wage that a weaver can call his own after paying for 'pre-loom processes'.

It can be revealed from Table 10.6 that a day's net wages of a handloom weaver ranged from Rs. 51.90 to Rs. 70.50 only. In particular, weavers at Sundrapandiyam in Virudhunagar district preferred *'gada'* cloth as it gives higher wages when compared to sari weaving. The weavers have opined that wages should be calculated excluding the cost incurred in pre-loom processes.

Table 10.7 : Production, Sales and Stock of Handloom Products

(Rs. in Lakh)

Districts	Total Production	Total Sales	Total stock
Madurai	394.34 (1.05)	446.57 (0.97)	65.19 (4.00)
Virudhunagar	3370.42 (8.96)	3579.16 (7.80)	222.01 (13.64)
Theni	306.8 (0.82)	486.16 (1.06)	49.97 (3.07)
Erode	26345.00 (70.03)	32384.1 (70.56)	1290.7 (79.29)
Kancheepuram	7200.00 (19.14)	9000.0 (19.61)	NA

Source: Short notes obtained from the respective Offices of AD Handlooms.
Note: Figures in parentheses are percentages.

Piling up of unsold stock of handloom goods with the cooperative is one of the most serious problems confronted by the handloom weaving societies in Tamil Nadu. The handloom silk weavers' societies in Kancheepuram district, face the problem of unsold stock in the godowns. The value of total stock noticed in Erode district circle is (Rs. 1290.7 lakhs) followed by Virudhunagar district (Rs. 222.01 lakhs) during the year 2004-05. In addition to these stocks in various handloom weaving societies, Co-optex has a large stock of handloom goods. In order to reduce the stock of handloom goods, the government is forced to announce rebates and concessions to handloom goods.

Table 10.8 : Dues to Societies by Co-optex and Government

(Rs. in Lakh)

Districts	*Dues from Co-optex*	*Rebate Dues from Government*	*Total*
Madurai	46.57	79.08	125.65
Virudhunagar	893.05	228.53	1121.58
Theni	12.97	58.50	71.47
Erode	1700.55	3173.54	4873.54

Source: Short notes obtained from the respective Offices of AD Handlooms.

The State Government is providing financial assistance towards rebates to promote the sale of handloom cloth to help the handloom goods compete with powerloom and mill made cloths in the market. It enables the primary weaver's cooperative societies and co-optex in liquidating their stock. In general, rebate subsidy has been delayed to the primary weavers co-operative societies. Hence, dues to societies

Table 10.9 : Beneficiaries under Various Government Schemes (2004-05)

Sl. No.	*Schemes*	*Madurai*	*Theni*	*Erode*	*Virudhunagar*
1.	Saving and Security	21	1100	0	7772
2.	Family pension	10	13	165	77
3.	Old Age pension	368	183	1641	1601
4.	Bunker Beemer Yojana	0	0	1969	849
5.	House-*cum*-Work shed	42	0	2976	545
6.	Work shed alone	15	195	3801	453
7.	DDHPYS	265	130	8366	375

Source: Short notes obtained from the respective Offices of AP Handlooms.

by Co-optex and Government is considered as a serious problem as it affects the functioning of the handloom weaving societies in Tamil Nadu. It is found from Table 10.8 that each district is yet to get dues from Co-optex and Government. The total value of dues by Co-optex and Government is (Rs. 4873.54 lakhs) in high Erode district followed by Virudhunagar district (Rs. 1121.58 lakhs), Madurai district (Rs. 125.65 lakhs) and Theni district (Rs. 71.47 lakhs) respectively.

Tamil Nadu State is the first State to introduce the Cooperative Handloom Weavers Savings and Security Scheme (SSS) with effect from 15-12-1975 for encouraging the saving habits among the weavers and to ensure a secured future for the handloom weavers. Under the Bunker Beemer Yojana Scheme 1969 weavers were enrolled in Erode district followed by 849 weavers in Virudhunagar district. These schemes have also played a role in serving the interests of the weavers in the weavers' cooperative societies.

Factors that have Contributed to this Slide

The reasons for the deteriorating conditions of handloom weavers and their shifting to power loom are: (a) erratic supply of yarn to the handloom weavers by the cooperative; (b) higher wages offered in powerloom sector due to higher output per-loom per worker per day; and (c) less drudgery involved in powerloom sector compared to handloom operations. One of the highlights of this study is that those who continue in handloom sector are at an age above 40 years. Those less than 40 years of age have got employment in powerloom sector or at the least they have converted their looms into Nepal looms with ½ HP electric power motor attached to it. They have opted to join the clothes banners or have become salesman in that business.

The hardest hit are the handloom weavers in the cooperative fold. This is because the master weavers go for weaving only based on what the dealers demand. They keep changing the designs, patterns, and variety keeping in view the market trends and demand. Operating on thin margins the weavers' cooperative societies are unable to absorb shocks. Moreover, almost all the cooperatives dependent on the government machinery. Decentralization in governance that existed with the cooperatives has vanished.

The master weavers are able to sustain business and are able to mobilize the required resources and find market with their higher productivity and increased turn over. However, the condition of the individual weavers who serve the master weavers is no better either.

III. TECHNO-ECONOMICS OF HANDLOOM INDUSTRY

Technology, and the economic benefit a given technology offers are crucial aspects in studying any livelihood proposition. This is based on the premise that any livelihood endeavour involves technology application which is otherwise known as putting to use certain physical assets. Handloom weavers use very traditional technology – hand operated looms. They are applauded on three counts, viz., (i) zero use of electric power, (ii) rich in providing employment opportunity, and (iii) setting up of a loom does not require big financial investment. The main drawbacks are poor productivity and meagre production, and every thing associated with it such as high unit cost of production, high price, poor wages for labourers and so on.

Technology Description

In terms of technology there are at least five versions of looms available in Tamil Nadu which can be called 'technologies of handloom weaving'. They are: (1) Pit Looms, (2) Frame Looms, (3) Jacquard Looms, (4) Nepal Looms, and (5) Nepal Loom semi-automated.

Pit Loom: Wooden frame loom set up with a pit in the ground for the man to get down and do the pedaling operation. It requires pedaling by legs and pulling a string by hands. It is known for the balance it gives while weaving and it is still the least-cost-option.

Frame Loom: Wooden frame loom in set up above the ground level. It requires two parapet walls on either side where the weaver sits. The rampart walls are meant to hold the loom frames and accessories. This is also pedaled for carrying out weaving. It also requires pedaling by legs and pulling a string by hands. It is a little costlier when compared to the Pit looms because of the need to construct parapet walls. Its advantage is that there is no need to dig pits inside the house. It is suitable for rented houses.

Jacquard Loom: This is a modified form of Pit loom (or sometimes it is done in frame looms also). The extra fitting is at the top of the loom where design cards are held. The design cards (made from thick card boards or from plastic) serve to produce different designs. The design can be changed by changing the jacquard card/design card.

Nepal Loom: Perhaps, the birth place of this loom could be Nepal. This loom is made from iron rods and iron wheels. The structure is the same like that of the frame loom. But, there is little use of wooden frames. This looks almost a miniature model of a power loom minus the use of electric power.

Nepal Loom Semi-Automated: This is Nepal loom with a ¼ HP or ½ HP motor attached to it. Strictly speaking this cannot be brought under handloom (Baby Powerloom?). However, attaching electric motor to Nepal loom is a local fabrication by the weaver in order to ease the drudgery involved in handloom weaving. In terms of productivity no handloom would compare even 30 per cent of the performance/out put of this powerloom. It matches up 80 per cent with the powerloom. Some youngsters in places like T Subbulapuram have fabricated this type of looms.

Determinants of Survival

There are three things that determine the success prospects in weaving sector. They are:

(i) 'What variety' one weaves? i.e., material.
(ii) 'What technology' is used for weaving? i.e, technology.
(iii) And to which market does one weave? i.e, market.

And of course there is also policy environment that surrounds these factors.

Material: By 'what variety' is meant if the variety a weaver weaves is in demand in the marketplace. Is he producing something in response to market demands? To put it very specifically that is, market-responsiveness of the variety being put on-loom.

Technology: The second aspect, by 'what technology' is meant the use of higher productive technology – a technology that can produce more quantity (metres?) within a short period of time so that the cost per unit of production is low, price of product is low, movement of the product in the market is high, which can lead to continuous employment and reasonable wages. It is here the powerlooms leave behind the handlooms and keep growing.

Market: To which market is one producing, in the sense, is the varieties produced are to be supplied to the co-optex showrooms (government supply as they call it), one's own showroom, or to the open markets, to the textile traders who have already placed orders, or to the deemed exporters at Karur and other places who have registered themselves with the Handloom Export Promotion Council of India etc. The share one is able to consistently claim and catch up in these marketplaces is one of the vital aspects of survival.

Determinants of Survival Analyzed

Taking cue from the discussions the present researchers had with the handloom weaving community and drawing support from the secondary sources of data available, an attempt is made to figure out each one of these determinants with a little more elaboration.

(a) *Material (or 'Variety' as they call it)*

Based on the variety of handloom produced Tamil Nadu can be geographically divided into several segments. Broadly speaking, (a) there are areas in Tamil Nadu where silk weaving is predominant, e.g. Kancheepuram and Arani; (b) there are areas where gada, bed sheets and mixed fabrics are popular such as Karur and Erode; (c) and there are areas where only '*janatha* sarees, dothies and towels' are taken as main chunk for weaving, e.g. Theni, Virudhunagar etc. As wages for each of these varieties are different, the earnings of these weavers are also different. However, in terms of standard of living only a marginal difference could be noticed between and among the weaving communities in various regions of Tamil Nadu.

Although the living condition in general is deplorable, weavers in some districts (Karur/Erode) are a little better off than the others (Theni, Madurai, Virudhunagar). Those who depend on one source of yarn, only on conventional designs and one source of marketing are the ones most struggling for survival where as the others are able to cope with and make a living.

- *Weavers of Janatha Items*: Those who weave only *Janatha items*[2]

2. Items produced for free distribution to the people living below poverty line. The Government of Tamil Nadu places order for these items through co-optex and takes about 6-7 months for clearing the credit bills to the primary weavers cooperatives or industrial cooperative society as the case may be.

for the government and those who expect the co-optex to procure all that they weave are the ones in deep trouble. Many of the weavers cooperative societies reiterate that in fact, it was the government which made them let lose the open market share to private traders and master weavers by compelling them to take up weaving of *janatha* cloths to implement the Free Distribution of Sarees (FDS) scheme in Tamil Nadu. The weavers have come to a mindset in the past 20 odd years that they do not have to worry about what changes are taking place in the textile industry, and that no government would dare to withdraw FDS scheme. In the year 2002, as part of reform measures the State Government made an attempt to put the Handloom industry back into the open market by withdrawing FDS scheme, on the plea of a depleted exchequer.

- The State Government refused to lift stocks and delayed making payments for the materials purchased. Consequently, cooperative banks which provide loans to societies stopped releasing funds. This led to the societies stopping wage payments to the weavers. The weavers of Srivilliputhur and Rajapalayam in Virudhunagar district opened gruel centres to draw the attention of the State Government to their sad plight following the withdrawal of popular *Janatha* cloth scheme. Badly hit were the societies that produced only for the *janatha* cloth scheme on orders placed by co-optex.
- Recently, the government has introduced skill building training through NIFT, and is providing Technology Up-gradation Fund Scheme etc. The handloom weavers resist and refuse to buy the idea because in their opinion these schemes indirectly (i) make them agree to the government's decision of withdrawing the *Janatha* cloth scheme; and (ii) the technology up-gradation support extended after NIFT training is insufficient. These are statements from the handlooms weavers in areas such as Srivilliputhur, Jakkampatty, Andipatty, Aruppukottai, Sundarapandium (Uniforms), and Manampatthy (dothis). In Aruppukottai the FDS has been withdrawn since April 2005 after imparting NIFT Training. Nevertheless, weavers in general did not respond to the new type of looms despite the fact that the government has announced a partial subsidy.

BOX 10.3

***Janatha* Cloth Scheme**

Badly hit are societies that produce only for the *Janatha* cloth scheme on orders placed by co-optex. In the traditional handloom weaving districts of Vellore and Thiruvallur over 3.5 lakh sarees have piled up with the societies. Over half the 520-odd cooperative societies in Salem, Namakkal and Dharmapuri districts, with over 30,000 weavers, remain closed. In Cuddalore district, the number of handlooms have dropped from 12,000 to a mere 2,000 in the past two years, and over 80 per cent of the 50,000 weavers are jobless. About 35,000 families, primarily from the Saliya community are affected. Over two lakh looms are lying idle.

According to the societies, stocks worth over Rs. 300 crores lying unsold. Even the oldage-family pension given to poor weavers has been stopped by the government for the last 15 months.

Co-optex which provides yarn to societies for the production of *Janatha* cloth, and procures sarees and dhotis for distribution, lifted stocks until last December. (It has in its godown over 45 lakh sarees and 45 lakh dhoties). It put procurement on hold this year with the cash strapped government not allowing funds for the scheme in the 2002-03 Budget. As a consequence district level cooperative banks which provide loans to primary level societies stopped releasing funds. This led to the societies stopping wage payments to the weavers.

Source: *Frontline,* August 30, 2002 pp. 125-126.

- The reasons for the weavers desperately wanting to have FDS Scheme are: (i) weaving *Janatha* sarees and dothies are less labourious—even aged-people could also weave and get wage upto Rs. 50 a day; and (ii) when FDS scheme is on, the weavers would get continuous supply of yarn from co-optex godown, which ensures their continuous employment. In the absence of the FDS scheme, the weaver would have to look for breaking into markets which has grown very competitive in the past 20 years, since the time they started weaving FDS.
- *Bed Sheets and Coarse Varieties*: The weavers in places like Karur, Erode, and Chennimalai, Bhavani are engaged in producing coarse varieties such as bed covers, sofa throws, floor mats,

pillow covers and furnishing fabrics. These are produced mainly for the foreign markets. Even those in cooperatives societies do export under deemed export system[3]. The type of weaving involved is comparatively harder and labourious. However, the wages of these weavers are comparatively higher. These are enterprising and hard-working type of weavers and so their wages are also little higher. They earn anywhere between Rs. 70 to Rs. 120 a day. This is the condition of the Kora silk saree weavers of Chinnalapatty also. Although the fact remains that the traditional Chinnalapatty art silk sarees are no more known in the marketplace, the wage of the weavers involved in weaving Chinnalapatty Silk saree is not encouraging them to stick on to the tradition. They do not earn more than Rs. 45 a day. They are shifting to weave kora silk sarees and many youngsters have become cloth merchants.

- *Pure Silk Weaving*: The problem of silk weavers of Kancheepuram is unique. The wages paid for silk weavers are not meagre. During the days they get employment, they earn not less than Rs. 60 to Rs. 100 a day. Wages in silk weaving depends on the complexity involved in the design. Therefore (average), earning Rs. 80 a day is normal. Their main problem is piling up of stock and so being in a compelled state of reducing production. Due to higher wages in silk weaving, there has been 'internal shift of labour even within the sector'. This has repeatedly resulted in over-production and stocks piling up. So, on one side, those who were weaving cotton cloths have also come to weave silk saris. On the other hand, due to intense competition in the market, the market has been flooded with a whole variety of art silk saris at cheap price. The AD Handlooms, Kancheepuram reports that the value of stock of silk saris as of June 2005 in various societies is Rs. 77.65 crores. Hence, the need to reduce production. Weavers are not allowed to weave not more than three sarees a month. However, master weavers are relatively better off because they are linked to a better marketing structure.

---

3. Deemed Exporters are registered with the Handloom Export Promotion Council of India at Chennai. They hold export licenses. They place orders with handloom weavers, both with cooperative societies and with master weavers, and export handloom goods to various countries.

- Cutting down production and restricted supply of yarn for weaving create problems of employment, and problems of wages in pure-silk weaving as well. The silk weavers of Kancheepuram are shifting between working under cooperative society and working under Master Weavers. In fact, the silk weavers of Manampatty (near Chengalput) have shifted to weaving dothies for co-optex for distribution under Free Distribution of Dothies Schemes.
- Pure silk sarees, especially the Kancheepuram variety is in great threat after the introduction of cheaply priced art silk sarees and apoorva silk sarees. The stock of pure silk sarees with the cooperative societies at Kancheepuram is on the increase. The societies either have to advertise and expand markets or shrink production.

BOX 10.4

Powerloom Weavers in Tamil Nadu

Tamil Nadu accounts for one-fourth of the powerlooms in the country. Against 16.66 lakh powerlooms in India, Tamil Nadu has nearly 4.00 lakh powerlooms of which 3.20 are registered. This includes 132 powerloom weavers' cooperative societies functioning with 28,376 powerlooms. The powerloom weavers cooperative societies produce upto 75 per cent of the cloth required under the scheme for free supply of uniforms to school children and Free Distribution of Sarees and Dhoties Scheme.

GoTN Policy Note 2005–06

As indicated earlier, weaving involves several preparatory works (i.e., pre-loom processes such as warping, roll winding, reed lifting etc.) which usually the weavers do not do themselves. The weavers get the pre-loom processes done by some aged persons in the family or in the locality for which the society does not pay anything extra. The wages paid by the society is all inclusive. The weavers will have to pay a portion of the wages they receive from the society or master weaver, as the case may be, to the people engaged in pre-loom works. However, there are a few master weavers and cooperative societies that hand over yarn ready to go on loom after completing the pre-loom processes. But, in most places pre-loom works are left to the weavers themselves for which the weavers have to pay from their wages.

The highest paid weaver seen in the table above is one who weaves 'gada cloth for uniform'. Weaving gada cloth is considered laborious where as weaving FDS saree is less laborious, hence the difference in the wage. The data pertains to Sundarapandium where weavers are generally considered hard working and they work not less than ten hours a day. They earn about Rs. 70 a day. Even within Sundarapandium those who weave only FDS sarees get only around Rs. 50 a day. So, what variety one chooses to weave is also a determinant of wages. Not many people prefer to weave fabric items (variety) that is tiring and laborious. This is also a reason for poor wages in certain pockets. This is very much applicable to areas such as Sundarapandium, Srivilliputhur and Virudhunagar.

(b) *Technology*

There has not been much change in the use of technology adopted by the handloom weavers over the years. All the technologies mentioned above (Pit Loom, Frame Loom, Jacquard Loom etc.) are traditional except the Nepal loom which looks a little modern. The youngsters in some villages such as T Sublapuram, and Jakkampatty have fabricated the Nepal loom and have also attached a ½ HP electric motor to it. They call it "Automated Nepal Loom". Although in the opinion of the outsiders, it cannot be classified under 'handloom', those using it clearly state two advantages about using it. First, productivity-wise it matches upto 80 per cent with the powerloom. Secondly, it is less laborious that the weavers can be free of the drudgery involved in traditional handloom weaving.

Power Loom Technology — A Big Threat to Handloom Sector

Year after year, there is considerable encroachment of powerloom in the handloom sector. One of the worst forms of encroachment (or even a kind of misuse) is that certain orders meant specifically for handlooms are procured by master weavers of powerlooms. They execute the order carried out in powerloom with a tag attached to it as 'Handloom Product'. This is prevalent not only in domestic market sales, but also in export items. The deemed exporters although are aware of it, would not prevent it because the finish is even better than what is done in a handloom.

Table 10.10 : Sector-wise Production of Fabrics in India

Year	*Mills*	*Power Looms (Including Hosiery)*	*Handlooms*	*Others*	*Total*
1996-97	1957 (5.6)	24885 (71.4)	7456 (21.4)	540 (1.6)	34838 (100)
1997-98	1948 (5.2)	27345 (73.0)	7603 (20.3)	545 (1.5)	37441 (100)
1998-99	1785 (4.9)	26966 (74.7)	6792 (18.8)	584 (1.6)	36127 (100)
1999-2000	1714 (4.4)	29561 (75.3)	7352 (18.8)	581 (1.5)	39208 (100)
2000-2001	1670 (4.2)	30499 (75.7)	7506 (18.7)	558 (1.4)	40233 (100)
2001-2002	1546 (3.7)	32259 (76.8)	7585 (18.0)	644 (1.5)	42034 (100)

Source: Government of India, Ministry of Finance and Company Affairs, Economic Division 2003, Economic Survey, 2002-03, New Delhi, p. 136.
Note: Figures in parentheses represent the percentages of share of production.

It is the master weavers who are fast converting their handlooms into powerlooms. Some of them have left weaving altogether and have moved on to do cloth business. With the conversion of handlooms into powerlooms, the handloom weavers who work in those looms fall under the category of powerloom weavers. The wages paid (piece rate) by master weavers to the powerloom weavers is less than that of the handloom sector. However, in terms of number of pieces (metres) weaved per day, the weavers earn a little more than what they would get under handloom sector. This is one of the important ways in which the number of handloom weavers has come down in the State.

BOX 10.5
The Uneconomical Handlooms

According to Mr. Shanmugam, a major textile trader/master weaver engaged in 'Kora silk' saree production and marketing from Puliampatti, Erode, in the 15 years of his exposure, he has in this particular variety of saree weaving and marketing, the drop in the demand is becoming sharp. He felt that the vigorous inroads made by the powerloom weaving into handloom weaving this special variety of sarees in recent times has partly made the production of 'Kora silk cotton blended sarees' from handlooms uneconomical.

***The Hindu Business Line*, 16th September, 2003.**

The independent weavers who have one or two looms at home feel the need for up-grading the technology to be able to augment the income levels. But, they do not seem to think of converting to power looms. Instead, in some of the places like T Sublapuram, Jakampatty and Aundipatty, they go in for converting to 'Automated Nepal Loom'.

The major wholesalers and master weavers, who hire the handloom weavers on a regular basis for producing the artistic 'kora silk sarees' in Chinnalapatty, have effected a cut in the hire charges paid to weavers from 20 per cent to 30 per cent. The intrusion of power loom is partly responsible for the reduction in the hire charges offered for the handloom weavers.

(c) *Handloom Markets*

Unlike some of the north-eastern states where handloom weaving is done primarily for self-consumption, in Tamil Nadu weaving is taken up mostly for others who would sell the finished products—to co-optex, master weavers and owners of cloth stores and so on.

Handloom Weavers vs. *Co-optex and Government:* As per a standing instruction of the government, the cooperatives should supply 75 per cent of their products to co-optex. Only the remaining 25 per cent could go for open market. Co-optex has usually delayed payment to the cooperatives in clearing the dues. The government has also delayed clearing the rebate claims. These two realities (payment due by co-optex and rebate due by State Government) have pushed several weavers cooperatives into deperation. The members have developed disenchantment with the cooperatives and have kept their names with the cooperative for obtaining government benefits while occasionally working for cooperatives, otherwise, they work for the private master weavers or are involved in some other livelihood option that is available.

This state of affairs has necessitated some of the weavers cooperatives to reduce supply to co-optex and start finding open markets (e.g. Murugan) or open their own showrooms (like Chentex and Chenkumar in Chennimalai). Some of the successful weavers cooperatives even refuse to supply to co-optex, because of the problem of getting cash payment for the goods sold. However, at times they have to give in at least partially due to pressure from the AD Handlooms.

Complete Dependence on Government: The weavers of Theni, Virudhunagar, Srivilliputhur, and Sundarapandiam have depended more on *Janatha* Cloth Scheme (otherwise known as 'FDS Scheme'). Many of them prefer to weave FDS sarees rather than school uniforms because weaving sarees is less laborious. When the government indicates that the scheme might be abolished, it sends shock waves down across their spinal cords.

Circumstances that necessitated the Opening of Gruel Centres: Weavers have moved from one crisis to another, surviving on the strength of their resilience. (1) The emergence of powerloom made handlooms unable to compete. (2) The increment of wage-rate has not increased for the last four and half years and also pension. (3) The scheme of Free Distribution of dhoties and sarees to the rural landless agricultural labourers, those living below the poverty line in urban and rural areas, rural artisans and fishermen has been implemented from the year 1991-92 to 2000-01. Government have discontinued the scheme from 2002-03, meanwhile expecting continuance of the scheme, 18 lakh sarees and 9 lakh dhoties were produced from January 2002 to April 2002 for distribution in the year 2002-03. The government refused to buy them because the government wanted stop the FDS Scheme. This rendered the weavers jobless. Moreover, the payment due to them from cooperatives did not get released. With a view to showing their plight, in some parts of Tamil Nadu where they had too much depended on FDS Scheme, the weavers opened 'gruel centres (Kanji Thotti)'. Then the Government reintroduced the scheme and started again to procure the products. This is a matter of wanting to have a little more political mileage by the ruling government. Any future government, if it withdrew the scheme, the left weavers would again be in the lurch.

Market and Export Orientation: Some prominent reasons that could be spelt out for the survival of handloom weavers in Karur, Erode and Coimbatore area are: (i) the textile market in Karur, Erode and Coimbatore is vibrant due to the presence of export segments and often they need to change design and variety to survive in the market; (ii) they have over the years trained themselves to respond to changing market dynamics; and (iii) the existence of Deemed Export System comes in handy for them to have continuous employment and reasonable wages all through the year. They did not depend on government to supply yarn or the co-optex to lift their stocks. They weave for the open market and are constantly getting orders from the deemed export system as well. They execute government order also for supplying school uniforms.

Management Models

In fabric production, there are two main segments—weaving and knitting. The weaving sector spans the handlooms units which produces around 5 metres a day. It can be compared to the State of the art loom in mills which produces 250-300 metres in an eight hour shift. The non-mill sector is sometimes referred to as the Decentralized Sector and includes powerlooms, handlooms, and the knitting or the hosiery sector. In terms of management there are several models could trace out in weaving sector. They are briefly described below:

- *Special Officer-Managed:* The cooperative-types are generally managed by Special Officers or Handloom Officers who have been appointed in the place of 'Elected Board of Directors'. This has demeaned the democratic character of the cooperative movement. The pattern of governance is one that supports bureaucracy, and the linear decision-making rather than being in favour of participatory and democratic process. The members at the village level have more affiliation with the weavers' cooperatives rather than the Village Panchayats. Although most of the development works pertaining to village centre around the Village Panchayats, the weavers have to be members of the cooperative and depend only on the cooperatives for obtaining government benefits and not the elected body—the Village Panchayat. So, neither the cooperatively elected board nor the Village Gram Sabha, but the Special Officers under the direction of AD Handlooms of the respective districts who control and manage the affairs of the handloom weavers.
- *Adoption:* Not withstanding the place a weaver cooperative society is located, there are some that run on profit and there are a few others that run on loss. One of the management models noticed was the practice of 'Adoption'. It means that a society that runs on profit adopts a society that is 'sick'. This happens, especially when the societies mentioned in the second place have almost lost their entitlement to receive cash credit from the Central Cooperative Bank, and it is likely that the weavers would lose job unless they are assisted to buy yarn. For example, Murugan Industrial Weaver Cooperative Society in T Kunnathur has adopted another near-defunct society in Chellur, Madurai. The All Women Primary Weavers Cooperative Society in T Subblapuram has adopted two more societies in the locality. Continuous supply of yarn and periodical lifting of finished goods are the lifeline of weaver's cooperatives. The society that

adopts supplies yarn to the near-defunct society and so that the members do not remain unemployed. It also procures the finished products. But, this arrangement only means helping a bed-ridden patience breath, using an oxygen cylinder. No society seems to have recovered from loss or revived its life through this arrangement. It has only temporarily provided employment to members and has deferred the closure of the society by a few more months or years.

- *Project Type Support*: Although 'Project Type Support' is not seen as a common practice, it has become a very successful model especially in Erode area. Originally, the idea of project based support has come about as part of 20 Point Programme. The objective was to bring those weavers who are not members of cooperatives under the fold of cooperatives. Later, in October 1979s they have been registered as cooperatives. Under 'Project Type Support' production centres have been constructed where members weave and supply to the cooperative for sale. Supply of yarn, procurement of finished products and accounting are all centralized. The support is independent of DCCB support. Such a project-mode support can also be thought of as a model to support the societies in the grip of financial crisis and those nearing dormancy. The support can be extended for a fixed period of time in a phased manner leading to its autonomous functioning.
- *Privately Managed:* Several different kinds of management models could be noticed as far as managing handloom units by private people are concerned. Managed by individuals, and family managed; Master weavers managed and so on.
- *Deemed Export:* Deemed Exporters have themselves registered with Handlooms Export Promotion Council of India[4]. Deemed

4. This Handloom Export Promotion Council (HEPC) is a statutory body constituted under the Ministry of Textiles, Government of India to promote exports of all handloom products like fabrics, home furnishings, carpets and floor coverings, etc. HEPC was constituted in 1965 with 65 members and its present membership is around 2000 spread all over the country. The handloom industry mainly exports fabrics, bed linen, table linen, toilet and kitchen linen, towels, curtains, cushions and pads, tapestries and upholsteries, carpets and floor coverings, etc. The basic objective of HEPC is to provide all support and guidance to the Indian Handloom exporters and International buyers for trade promotion and International marketing. HEPC has its head office at Chennai and regional offices at New Delhi and Mumbai.

Exporters establish contacts with foreign buyers and procure orders from them. They enter into business deals with foreign buyers in agreed quantity, quality, and colour etc. and place order locally with the private handloom master weavers and cooperatives (as sub-contracts) to supply to them. Deemed Exporters never reveal to the handloom weavers to which country or which buyer he would export them to. He supplies the yarn, determines the price for the items, and decides the delivery date etc. All that the cooperative or the private weavers have to do is weave, deliver it to the exporter and get the wages as agreed.

Intricacies of Going in for Export

The expressive thrust of the Government of Tamil Nadu with regard to handloom marketing is to go in for exports. Weavers' cooperatives are being encouraged to go in for exports, at times even without depending on Deemed Exporters. All said and done, as of now, the handloom export depends on the 'deemed export system' only. These deemed exporters are private investors who are long-time players in textile business. They have very clear ways of working with the weavers and with buyers. Often, they work as middlemen without letting the producer know the buyer. However, there are several advantages in deemed export system. It has its risk factors too.

(a) *Advantages*

- The Deemed Exporter 'supplies the yarn' in the quality the buyer wants it. This saves the weavers from investing in purchasing of yarn or for the cooperative to get cash credit from DCCB to purchase yarn. This is an ideal business proposition for PWCS that have lost CC facility with the DCCBs. The society does not require working capital for purchasing yarn.
- The Deemed Exporter 'decides which items are to be produced'. The weaver need not worry about what the market demands. He can be contented if he could weave and supply the items demanded by the Deemed Exporter.
- There is no chance of Deemed Exporters delaying payment to the weavers. They seem to be sending Demand Drafts within a fortnight's time.

- There is no problem of marketing because the Deemed Exporter procures the entire lot he placed order for.
- The wages paid are also comparatively better, although it is on a declining trend over the years.

(b) *Limitations*

- The quality of work and finishing have to match cent per cent with the prescription given. Otherwise, the exporters tend to reject which will be a heavy blow on smaller societies.
- An order placed should be executed on time. Delayed delivery would not be accepted. Once a delay is made, the prospects of getting next order would be bleak.
- As more and more weavers approach the Deemed Exporters for orders, the wages paid is on a declining trend year after year.
- As the international markets are open for textiles also, the competition for Indian textile goods in foreign countries have also become too intense. This has resulted in cost-cut by the Deemed Exporter, and it is reflected in the wages paid to the weavers as well.

IV. POLICY ENVIRONMENT OF HANDLOOM INDUSTRY

Effective policies, institutions and processes (PIP) are recognized as essential in sustaining livelihoods. These three essentials form the context within which individuals and households construct and adapt livelihood strategies—whether they are handloom weaving or any other livelihood venture for that matter. This includes complex issues such as participation, authority, governance, policies, service delivery, and public relations. In effect, they determine the freedom that people have to transform their assets into livelihood outcomes. Handloom weaving provides livelihood to millions of weavers and crafts persons. The sector has not only survived but also grown over the decades due to its inherent strengths like flexibility of production in small quantities, openness to innovation, low level of capital investment and so on.

Nevertheless, the sector is facing problems like (i) obsolete technology and traditional production techniques; (ii) dependence on in-put subsidy, price support and rebate; (iii) high price of hank yarn; (iv) inadequate availability of inputs like standard dyes and chemicals in small pockets, new designs etc.; and (v) inadequate market intelligence and feedback. In addition, the handlooms have certain inherent disadvantages like (i) unorganized structures and its dispersal throughout the country, (ii) weak financial base of the weavers, (iii) bureaucratization/politicization of cooperatives, etc. However, the government, taking into consideration the high employment potential involved and amount of appreciation Indian handloom products have in foreign markets is making efforts to support the sector through changes in trade policy, tax systems and other regulatory arrangements, in addition to the schemes announced for the handloom weavers.

The Textile Policy, 2000 has come about with measures to put the textile sector, and specifically the handloom sector in a global-business mode. The change has created new opportunities for growth as global market has now become available to the trade; at the same time, it has led to new challenges for the domestic industry as import barriers are considerably reduced, if not totally removed. The policy statement of the government states that the policy aims at preparing the industry for successfully meeting the challenges of the barriers-free-era and taking advantage of the opportunities it holds. The policy has incorporated a series of measures in the form of schemes for technology up-gradation of handlooms, skill up-gradation of handloom weavers, design developments and so on. The thrust is towards going to open market and in favour of exports. Organizations such as National Institute of Fashion Technology (NIFT), Indian Institute of Handloom Technology (IIHT), Weaver's Service Centres, and National Institute of Designs (NID) have been brought into action to facilitate the process of going global and going open.

Issues and Concerns

The issues and concerns of the handloom industry empirically recognized and culled from the analysis of secondary data received from various official sources are presented in two distinct heads in a way they address the research questions raised at the outset of this study. They are:

(*a*) *General Issues*: Issues and conditions that are generally persistent and long-standing with the handloom sector that trying to get an expression.

(*b*) *Specific Issues that Point at Reform Measures*: Certain issues point at reform measures or the globalization processes as the causative factors for their occurrence.

(A) *General Issues*

- *Membership in Cooperatives:* The number of members covered by cooperatives are said to be 80 per cent. But in actuality the chances are that hardly 50 per cent of them are weavers with looms. Others while they are engaged in other jobs, get the yarn from the society and give it to someone who weaves, so that the former can maintain his membership with the society to be eligible for obtaining the schemes of the government implemented through the cooperatives. There needs to be a head count enumeration of weavers vis-à-vis looms to be able to state authoritatively members per loom and actual number of active handloom weavers, covered especially under the cooperative fold. Otherwise, there would be many handloom weavers on record, while actually they have quit the sector or have shifted to power loom weaving. Weavers not covered under the cooperative fold are said to be covered by an organization called Tamil Nadu Handloom Development Corporation Limited (THDC Ltd.). It provides financial assistance to improve the socio-economic conditions of the handloom and powerloom weavers outside the cooperative fold. But, no handloom weaver seems to be aware of what THDC is doing.
- *HL Weavers Swinging between Cooperatives and Master Weavers:* Even those members who are under the cooperative fold are not completely away from master weavers. They go to weave for the master weavers on and off. In some places like Kancheepuram even the cooperative society allows the members to take work from master weavers and earn their living because the society is unable to give employment all the days due to the problem of poor sales turn over and accumulation of stocks. So, the purpose that was stated for the establishment of weaver's cooperatives—relieving the weavers from the clutches of master weavers—remains in letter—neither in practice nor in spirit.
- *Supply of Yarn*: Uninterrupted supply of yarn to the weavers is a *sine qua non* for ensuring continuous employment to the

weavers. There are several modes in which yarn is supplied to the weavers or weavers procure yarn for weaving. Some of the problems are stated below:

(a) *Co-optex Yarn Godown:* The yarn godown of the co-optex is the main source of yarn for those who work under the cooperative fold. In the event of non-availability of yarn at co-optex godown, the societies are expected to procure yarn from Government/Cooperative Spinning Mills at various places in Tamil Nadu with the permission of the AD Handlooms. There are problems relates to the quality of yarn supplied by the co-optex and cooperative spinning mills. This reflects in the quality of finished products and productivity also.

(b) *NHDC:* Another option is that individual societies, in the event of co-optex not being able to supply yarn, can approach the National Handloom Development Corporation (NHDC, Coimbatore) and procure yarn with the prior permission of the AD Handlooms. NHDC approaches various sources including private spinning mills and procures yarn for the weavers. The weavers state that in practice weaving is also seasonal. When there is interruption in yarn supply, it leads to problems of unemployment. It is reported (*The Hindu* dated June 18, 2006) that of late, the Government is considering the need to increase the number of yarn supply depots of the National Handloom Development Corporation (from 65 to 230 in the country).

- *Wage Fixation and Wage Revision:* The wages for the handloom weavers are fixed by the government and implemented through the cooperatives and co-optex. The members complain that wage revision has not taken place for handloom weavers for quite some years now. The basic wages is too minimal (it is Rs. 25 for saree) and so the DA is paid upto 80 per cent. Similarly, even for export items, the wages are fixed by the Deemed Exporters or the master weavers concerned. Neither the society nor the members have a say in the wage fixation.
- *Payment Due by Co-optex:* As per a standing instruction of the government, the weavers cooperatives should supply 75 per cent

of their products to co-optex. Only the remaining 25 per cent could go for open market, although this is variable from time-to-time. Co-optex usually delays payment to the cooperatives in clearing the dues. At times, it takes even years to clear the dues by co-optex. This has necessitated some of the cooperative to reduce supply to the cooperatives and start finding open markets. Some of the successful cooperatives (such as Murugan Industrial Cooperatives of T Kunnathur that produces quality lungies) who think they have sufficient open market even refuse supply of products (fabrics, lungies, etc.) to co-optex, because of the problem of obtaining payment from co-optex for goods sold. The only time they have to give in is when the AD Handlooms intervenes and officially instructs them to supply to co-optex.

- *Rebate Claim from Government:* Owing to productivity differences, the price of handloom products are usually higher when compared to the same variety weaved in powerlooms. So, price-wise powerloom varieties have a competitive edge over handloom varities. In order to offset this, and to lend a helping hand to the weavers, the Government of India and Government of Tamil Nadu provide rebate subsidy as 'marketing incentive'. Accordingly, the primary cooperatives and co-optex may allow 20 per cent rebate throughout the year and there are also special rebates during festival seasons. The Government takes several months to release the rebate subsidy amount to the weavers cooperatives. This has pushed some of the cooperatives to become financially weak and not being able to supply yarn to the weavers for further weaving.
- *Lose of Cash Credit Facility with Central Cooperative Banks:* The money locked up with the co-optex and the rebate claim due by the government to the weaver's cooperative societies together make up a huge sum of money. This results in PWCS becoming unable to settle the Cash Credit Facility (CC Facility) availed from with the District Central Cooperative Banks (DCCBs). In addition to this, the interest amount payable by the PWCS gets compounded month after month. This results in District Central Cooperative Banks (DCCBs) disqualifying the primary-level cooperatives from obtaining cash credit (CC) facility from the DCCBs. This crumbles the working capital requirements to purchase yarn, and money for payment of

wages for the HL weavers. There are several societies that pay to the DCCB a lump sum amount by way of interest. But, this remains only as book profit for the DCCB concerned until it is realized from PWCS.

- Another facet of this issue is that the failure of DCCBs in repaying the CC facility they (DCCBs) availed from the NABARD makes the NABARD deny further loan assistance to DCCBs. As a result, the DCCBs have to lend only its borrowed funds (i.e., deposits collected from various types of customers) to PWCS. The difference is that the loan availed from NABARD can be lent to PWCS for 9 per cent rate of interest whereas the depositor's money can be lent for not less than 12 per cent rate of interest. This means further financial stress on PWCS when they are already in the grip of financial crisis.
- *Stock piling:* Piling up of unsold stock of handloom goods with the cooperative is another serious problem faced by the handloom weavers. It is more so in the case of silk weavers. The cooperatives are expected to supply upto 75 per cent of their production to co-optex. The co-optex delays procurement because their showrooms have sufficient stock of unsold goods. Delay in procurement results in the funds of cooperatives locked up in the form of finished goods. This affects the operating cycle of the weaver's cooperatives. This leads to a situation where the primary-level societies delay giving yarn to the weavers for production, as a result the weavers face the problem of unemployment and giving in to the master weavers and work for very poor wages. Or some of the HL weavers leave the sector not being able to put up with the grind all the time.
- *Privatization of Spinning Mills:* Spinning mills supply yarn to the handloom weavers cooperatives and to master weavers through co-optex and NHDC. The number of cooperative spinning mills in the State which were 18 a few years ago, have come down to 14 in the year 2002, and today there are only 4 cooperative spinning mills existing. Where as under private sector, in Aruppukottai area only that which was just 4 spinning mills (Jeya Vilas Group's) have become 14 spinning mills in the same period. This is a very clear indication for spinning sector being taken away by the process of privatization. The reasons for

cooperative spinning mills being closed one after another are: (i) problems of quality with regard to the yarn supplied, and (ii) labour unrest and frequent lock outs.

- *Cooperatives Losing out to Privatization of Looms:* The society that is not able to offer continuous employment to the weavers is indifferent when the weavers go to work for private master weavers. Going to the master weaver in due course would lead to the member becoming inactive with the cooperative and becoming active with the master weavers. The name of the member remains in the Membership Register of the cooperative society so as not to miss the benefits of government schemes implemented through the cooperatives, whereas the member works most of the time for the master weaver and occasionally for the cooperative society. The officials of the cooperatives keep quiet about it, because it involves their personal survival as well.
- *Preference to Industrial Cooperatives*: Handloom weavers prefer to work in industrial type of cooperatives because it is almost like going to office. They start work at 9.00 in the morning and close at about 5.30 in the evening. The wages paid is only based on pieces rate system. The weavers need not do the pre-loom processes. The society gets it done through some aged-members and gives the yarn that is ready to go on loom. The members enjoy the benefits of all the government schemes meant for weavers including housing. But, setting up an industrial cooperative requires a lot of investment for the government such as finding a place to house about 100 to 200 looms in one place, the shed, the looms and other accessories, and yarn supply for all the looms and so on.
- *Corrupt Practices:* Those working for cooperative showrooms and co-optex seem to have developed a mentality that they can relax for 10½ months in a year because they can sell off the goods during the rebate period of 45 days. Regarding rebate claims from the government, one of the officials sneaked out unofficially that in some of the cooperatives neither production would have taken place, nor would it have been sold to another party. But, documents and papers are prepared to claim rebate amount from the government.
- Another interesting practice is that when cooperatives offer 30 per cent rebate, the powerloom weavers and master weavers

stop production, procure in bulk from cooperatives and keep them as stock. They sell them later at a higher price when cooperatives stop offering rebates.

- *Decentralization:* The weavers' cooperatives function under the control of AD Handlooms at the District and of the Special Officers at the Primary and Industrial Cooperative levels. There is no elected Board of Directors. The relationship of weavers (whether they work under cooperative, or under master weavers, or as independent weavers) to the local bodies is nothing unique. One opinion that constantly kept coming in all the societies was that the Board that existed was corrupt. But the appointment of Special Officers in the place of Board is no good either. It is because in terms of payment of salary to special officers each society pays handsome money every month, which aggravates the situation with regard to financial position of the societies, most of which are already incurring losses. As far as management models are concerned, there is no viable model found yet, although some experiments such as adoption, Project-type support, and Deemed Export System have helped recover some of the sick societies.
- *Poor Market Orientation:* The weavers under cooperative have very poor market orientation. They keep producing the same design and variety for years. One of the reasons for their not changing the design is that change of every design involves loom modification with a capital investment of anywhere between Rs. 1,500 to Rs. 4,000 which they cannot afford. Unless there is a guarantee by the cooperative that a given design would last in the market at least for one year, they do not make this investment on loom modification.

(b) Specific Issues that Point at Reform Measures

There are certain issues that point at reform measures or the globalization processes as the causative factors for their presence.

A WTO study on textile trade in India after liberalization points out (*The Hindu*, May 21, 2006) that the Indian textile and apparel sector was all set to become the second largest beneficiary following the dismantling of quotas. This might be true of large textile mills and giant garment industries in Thirupur, Karur and Erode. Handloom weaving has historically been favoured by government action, receiving input subsidies and price supports. The Government is coming out with policies and schemes to protect the handloom weavers from the blitz of globalization. The Handlooms and Textiles Policy Note of the Government of Tamil Nadu – 2002-03 states that in the back drop of globalization and to compete in the global market, the weavers Cooperative Societies need to equip themselves to the level of International Standards. To sustain in the global market and to make them aware of the WTO impact, the department is taking all efforts to face the future with full confidence. These include Technological up-gradation; Introduction of new designs; Handloom Cluster Development Scheme, Enhancement of Productivity; Quality Consciousness; Product Diversification; Social Security Net for Weavers, Development of Handloom mark, Increase in exports and innovative marketing strategies; Financing arrangements, welfare schemes to weavers etc.

In spite of special patronage by both Central and State Governments, the handloom industry has remained mostly tiny, traditional and lacking the competitive spirit. In the era of liberalization and globalization, government protection for the industry is getting reduced. Therefore, strengthening and encouraging the handloom industry to produce value-added items are essential, and it would assist the industry to forge joint ventures to secure global markets. The Policy of the Government of India till recently has been a fascination with employment generation. The aspects of efficiency, quality, market-orientation and growth did not matter much until the government started finding ways to introduce reform measures in India as a mark of globalizing the economy. In other words, government policies on handloom industry depict a sort of shift from 'protection-led growth' to 'competition-led growth'. It is time handloom weaving firms (both cooperative and private) reorganize themselves from capturing quotas to capturing markets.

This section presents some of the policies of the government that obviously expresses going global, along with the reactions of the handloom weavers regarding these steps. The over all policy on handlooms on the part of the Government of India had four centres of attention. They are:

(a) Focus on forming and strengthening weavers' cooperatives as part of a rather complex organizational structure that also included 'apex bodies' such as District Central Cooperative

Banks, and co-optex and is supposed to provide inputs, and credit and marketing channels to the weavers.

(b) Improving productivity and quality through improved looms, imparting new skills, designs and technology to the weavers.

(c) Provision of subsidies, including assured supply of cotton yarn and credit at subsidized rates; and other forms of protection including reservation of certain items for the handloom sector. Under the Hank Yarn Obligation Order of 1985, fifty per cent of yarn production by spinning mills has to be in the form of hanks for handlooms.

(d) Setting up of welfare schemes to help weavers improve their livelihood and working conditions.

The primary objective of the government's policy on handlooms since Independence was the production of cloth for the masses and providing employment. A range of varieties[5] of cloth was reserved for production in the handloom sector, especially controlled or *Janatha* cloth (that is cheap cloth for poor rural households to be sold at subsidized rate through PDS or distributed as free). The Textile Policy of 1985 was a continuation of the earlier policies of protection to handlooms in the form of reservations and hank yarn obligations, while the Textile Policy of 2000 was much more of a departure. It has put down things to state 'Survival of the Fittest' or let those with competitive spirit at a global pace thrive.

---

5. In order to protect Handloom weavers and the Handloom Industry from the onslaught of powerlooms, the Government of India have enacted Handlooms (Reservation of Articles) for Production Act, 1985 for implementation by all States in the country. The Government of India have reserved 11 items exclusively for handlooms and the 11 items are as follows:

   (1) Sarees, (2) Dhoties, (3) Towel, Gamcha and Angavastram, (4) Lungi, (5) Khes, Bedsheet, Bed cover, Counterpane, Furnishing (including tapestery), (6) Jamakkalam Durry or Durret, (7) Dress Materials, (8) Barrack Blankets, Kambal or Kamblies, (9) Shawl, Loi, Muffler, Pankhi, (10) Woollen Tweed, (11) Chaddar, Mekhala/Phanek.

   A separate Enforcement Machinery in Tamil Nadu had been formed with a Deputy Director/Enforcement Officer at Headquarters, Chennai and five subsidiary Officers at Salem, Tiruchengodu, Erode, Tiruppur and Madurai each headed by an Assistant Enforcement Officer in order to implement the Handloom Reservation Act, 1985. This would take criminal action against erring powerloom owners.

For instance, it recommended that the least skilled weavers should be shifted to semi-automatic powerlooms,. and that the Hank Yarn Obligation Order be reviewed. It only shows that the recommendations of the Sathyam Committee[6] are being introduced slowly through the New Textile Policy. Changes recommended in legislation include doing away with Handloom Reservation Act and shifting textile industry out of the purview of the Essential Commodities Act (ECA).

An analysis of the policy and practice of handloom weaving sector in Tamil Nadu reveals that the governments — both at the Centre and at the State—have taken several steps to face reforms in a competitive spirit while at the same time allowing certain provisions for social safety net. It has retained the weavers in the sector. But, one of the negative attempts, in the view of the weavers, that was made by the government in order to promote economic reform was the attempt made to withdraw *Janatha* Cloth Scheme in December 2002. The sign of revolt shown by a section of weavers by opening 'gruel centres' could also be a reason for the government to be cautious in introducing reform measures as far as handling handloom weavers are concerned. The government shortly reintroduced the scheme and the scheme goes on as usual.

Janatha Cloth Items: The policy of the State Government to withdraw *Janatha* cloth items in the year 2002 sent across shock waves amidst the handloom weaving community, especially in Theni, Srivilliputhur, Rajapalayam, and Aruppukottai areas — a scheme that they depended on for over 20 years being withdrawn. They have almost physically and mentally got set to weave such items only. Co-optex, which provided yarn to societies for the production of *Janatha* cloth, and procured sarees and dhoties for distribution, refused to lift stocks after December 2002. It had in its godown over 45 lakh sarees and 45 lakh dhoties. It put procurement on hold with the cash-strapped government not allocating funds for the scheme in the 2002-03 Budget. As a consequence district level cooperative banks, which provide loans to primary level societies, stopped releasing funds. This led to the societies stopping wage payments and employment to the weavers. These developments have led the handloom weavers in some parts of Tamil Nadu (Srivilliputhur) to open gruel centres (Kanji Thotti) to

---

6. To study and make recommendations for a new textile policy, the government constituted a committee in July 1998 under the Chairmanship of Mr. S.R. Sathyam, a former Secretary in the Ministry of Textiles. The Committee submitted its report to the government in early 2002.

communicate to the State Government the plight of handloom weavers consequent to the withdrawal of the *Janatha* Cloth Scheme.

Table 10.11 : Free Dhoti – Saree Scheme – Tamil Nadu

Year	*No. of Sarees and Dhotis Produced*		*Expenditure (Rs. in Crores)*
	Sarees (in lakhs)	*Dhotis (in lakhs)*	
1991-92	60.00	59.85	41.20
1992-93	60.71	61.23	44.64
1993-94	74.99	74.99	59.54
1994-95	62.25	61.72	49.85
1995-96	72.00	68.00	76.25
1996-97	72.70	68.00	88.49
1997-98	71.54	68.28	92.32
1998-99	76.66	69.92	102.08
1999-2000	77.10	70.42	101.92
2000-01	80.96	73.94	110.95
2001-02 2002-03	Scheme not implemented		
2003-04	108.00	108.00	187.48
2004-05	111.52	110.00	179.00
2005-06	164.00	164.00	263.00
2006-07	164.00	164.00	273.00

Source: *The Hindu*, August 26, 2006, p. 5, Madurai.

The scheme continues even now. For the year 2006-07, Tamil Nadu has earmarked Rs. 273 crores for this scheme. The points given in favour are: one, sustained employment is provided to handloom weavers, and secondly, clothing needs of the people living below poverty line (BPL) are addressed. The scheme benefits 19,200 handloom weavers and 3.28 BPL people.

Level of Absorption: There are certain protective measures and schemes specially introduced in order to enable the handloom weavers face the challenges and become competitive. But, the pace of absorption or utilization of such policy facilitations by the handloom weavers is not at the required level due to:

- the mental make-up weavers have developed over the years that they can go on with *Janatha* Cloth weaving;
- low levels of market responsiveness;

- poor understanding of the need to be market responsive when the economy is globalized.

This has resulted in, the powerloom weavers, disguising themselves as handloom weavers, grabbing these opportunities. Even the authorities in-charge of promoting handloom weaving seem to turn a blind eye to this state of affairs due to the need to be cost-effective and effect timely delivery. This has gone to the extent that powerloom cloths going for export camouflaged as handloom cloths—boldly stamped "A HANDLOOM PRODUCT FROM INDIA". As the quotas (reservations) remain undone from January 2005, the plight of the handloom weavers is going to be still tougher in the days to come. This is first of the substantiation to state that policies of the economic reforms *per se* cannot be attributed as reasons for the problems of the handloom weavers. But the slow-take-off of the handloom weavers to respond to changing market situations; the opportunistic attitude of the powerloom weavers; and the lack of concern of the authorities in-charge of promoting handloom products also play equally attributable roles.

BOX 10.6
Procurement Price for Saree and Dhoti by the Government of Tamil Nadu

Sl. No.	*Variety (per unit)*	*Procurement (Price in Rs.)*
1.	Handloom Saree	105.00
2.	Handloom Dhoti	88.63
3.	Powerloom Saree	79.44
4.	Powerloom Dhoti	64.00
5.	Gada Cloth (Uniform cloth) per metre	24.25

Source: Tamil Government G.O.Ms.No. 47 dated 31.07.2003

Subsidies: Due to low value-addition, low productivity and increasing costs of raw materials and labour, handloom fabrics have traditionally suffered a cost handicap in the market compared to similar products by powerlooms. This is particularly true in the case of simple, plain weave fabrics like dhoties, lungies, towels, plain sheeting and plain sarees. Conscious of the problems faced by the handloom sector in marketing its products, the Union Government also comes up with schemes that offer 10 per cent rebate on sale and so on. As of now, this scheme is expected to be active until March 2009. In order to offset the inherent handicap faced by handloom sector, subsidies have traditionally been given to the handloom sector. Direct subsidies include rebate on sale of finished products, modernization of showrooms, interest subsidy on working capital, margin money assistance and so on. Indirect subsidies include training for skill up-gradation, welfare measures like group insurance, housing and health care, purchase of handloom fabrics for free distribution under various Government schemes etc. Similarly, to clear the heavy stock of silk varieties and provide continuous employment to the silk weavers, the Central Government provides 10 per cent special rebate (in addition to what the State gives) without ceiling. Rebate sale is active for 128 days in a year (*The Hindu*, September 24, 2006).

The Give-Aways: The Government of Tamil Nadu is procuring sarees and dhoties for free distribution to the people living below poverty line and 'gada' cloth for providing free uniforms to poor children in schools. This is done with dual purposes: First, helping those below poverty line and secondly, providing employment to handloom and powerloom weavers in the State who depend on weaving for a livelihood – in the same order of importance as stated first and second. Now that over twenty years have run down the line since the introduction of the scheme, the purpose stated as 'second important' has assumed the place of 'first important' purpose. The expenses to the State Government for the free distribution of sarees scheme for the year 2005-06 amounted to Rs. 175 crores and the expenses for providing free uniforms to school children for the same year was to the tune of Rs. 42 crores. Apart from these expenses, it is estimated that the annual subsidy in Tamil Nadu is of the order of Rs. 70 crores for implementing various welfare schemes for the weavers[7].

As one of the important statements of the New Economic Policy is to reduce/cut down subsidies and give-aways, the government seems to be taking steps to reduce schemes that stand on subsidy, instead the government shows interest in spending on capacity-building training for weavers, technology up-gradation and market-promotion activities with a tag attached to it that those who avail such schemes should get away from weaving *Janatha* Cloth items.

7. Budget 2005-06 Government of Tamil Nadu.

This shows that the government, perhaps after the incident of 'opening of gruel centres' following the withdrawal of the popular *Janatha* Cloth Scheme, has realized that skill building, technology up-gradation and market-promotion assistance should be gradually strengthened while *Janatha* Cloth Scheme and other monstrous subsidies schemes are strategically withdrawn in a gradual phase. One such attempt is NIFT training.

NIFT Training: The government, through NIFT is imparting technology up-gradation training for weavers from areas where there was heavy concentration of *Janatha* cloth weaving. The idea is to convert them to weave commercial varieties that have demand in the market rather than keeping them dependent on weaving for co-optex or for government supply. In the opinion of the weavers the NIFT training was useful, but it did not sufficiently clarify the aspect of financial support to up-grade technology or assurance for marketing of the items advocated in the NIFT training. The concentration is on training with a condition that those who undergo NIFT training should be prepared to go for weaving commercial items and should not ask yarn for *Janatha* cloth weaving. Weavers are not in favour of this idea and so there seems to be no sufficient cooperation for NIFT training from handloom weavers.

Technology Up-gradation: The government has announced Technology Up-gradation Fund Scheme (TUFS) for up-grading the looms. The type of looms being recommended is said to be inappropriate to accommodate in the weaver's houses. It is said that the space required for housing such looms is 10 × 25 sq.ft. But, no weaver house has that much space to accommodate those looms. Instead, the weavers prefer to use the Nepal looms. But, they also seem to have a clandestine idea of fixing a ½ HP motor to it and convert it to 'Automated Nepal Loom'. In the opinion of the handloom weavers, the proposals of the government to implement a 'Cluster-based Loom Up-gradation Scheme' where weavers and master weavers can go in for modernization of looms by establishing a cluster of automatic or shuttleless looms; and 'Composite Textile Park' at a cost of Rs. 60 crore in one place would not be of any use to the household-based handloom weavers.

Government modernization schemes have included the promotion of frame looms and jacquard looms, and training to weavers in new techniques. Several drawbacks with frame looms that weavers have identified themselves such as less flexibility, having to weave in worksheds as opposed to in the house, more physically difficult, and substantial additional investment expenses which weavers cannot afford. These are proposed not understanding the family or household-based nature of weaving occupation, opine the weavers of Sundarapandium in Virudunagar, and T Subbulapuram in Theni district.

Deemed Export: There is one major advantage in taking up order for deemed exporters. That is the coloured yarn is supplied by the Deemed Exporter (merchant exporters), and the type of fabric or material required is clearly stated by the Deemed Exporters. All that the weavers have to do is execute a quality work and keep up the time schedule. This is applicable for members of cooperatives as well. The problems of procuring yarn, getting Cash Credit from District Central Cooperative Banks and all that hullabaloo are avoided when a society is able to procure export orders under the deemed export system. The societies can fix profit upto a maximum of 21 per cent for export varieties.

"Go Export": The Government of Tamil Nadu is pro-active and is fully supportive of the idea of individual weavers societies/or a consortium of weavers cooperative society, if they get down to export instead of being dependent on/making export supplies to deemed exporters (who are actually private people). But, the weaver's societies have a feeling that given the managerial and technical expertise available with the weavers cooperatives getting down to export is no small plan. Rejection from a foreign buyer on quality or on delivery schedule grounds would be a fatal blow for the cooperative[8]. It might even paralyze the functioning of the cooperative leading to closure.

Export by Cooperatives: The Commissioner of Handlooms, Government of Tamil Nadu seems to encourage some of the successful cooperatives such as Chentex, Kumartex, Ero-tex etc., to involve themselves in direct export with the assistance of Handloom Export Promotion Council of India. But, these cooperatives are not confident enough about exporting because these societies feel they do not have the wherewithal to take up exports. They are scared that two subsequent

8. The government has announced there would be Export Guidance Cell established in almost all the textile towns of Tamil Nadu. This is yet to get materialized.

rejections against poor quality work, not keeping up the schedule with foreign buyers would quake even the very survival of the cooperatives. Although they do export business through private deemed exporters at Karur, they are not aware which country the handloom products are exported to, and in what form (cloth or made-up) and so on. This is a corollary of globalizing the economy and competition that is prevalent in textile sector.

BOX 10.7
Falling wage rate

Falling wage rate is a normal phenomenon in Handloom industry. In Karur, two years back, there was a complete shut down of looms due to reduction in the wage-rate for export varieties. Mr. N. Palaniswamy, President of Handloom Weavers Association and the members held a procession twice to the District Collector's Office and gave petition explaining their plight. There has not been any improvement in wage structures, it tends to fall down year after year. In Karur, A.D Handlooms Office also weavers showed their agitation. The wage rate has fallen more than 15 per cent recently per piece (i.e., from Rs. 24 to Rs. 20).

Source: From a discussion with the members of Handloom Weavers Association, Karur.

Wages Revised Downwards: One of the reasons for some of the societies being successful in Erode and Karur areas are that they often take export orders under deemed export system. The deemed exporters place orders with the society and fix the wages as well. The HL weavers do not have the bargaining power to claim certain wages. Often, the deemed exporters revise the wages downwards on the pretext that there is hectic competition in the international cloth market and so the prices spiral downwards. Consequently they have to reduce the wages.

Agreement on Textiles and Clothing: The US and EU markets would do away with the textile "Quota Raj" that protected Indian Textile industry since the day the Agreement on Textile and Clothing (ATC), a modified version of the Multi-Fibre Agreement was signed as per the WTP guidelines. The MFA under which India's exports of textiles and clothing have been subject to quotas as per bilateral agreements signed separately with each trading country got completely phased out in December, 2004. The international trade in textiles has become totally free, non-discriminatory and non-protective from the beginning of

January, 2005 onwards. Considering the economies of scale, this trend encourages only the mill sector in global competition while handlooms would have to stand away and watch because of the tiny nature of production and high costs.

Handloom Mark: The Government of India has launched a quality mark for handloom products that will help buyers distinguish between genuine items diligently crafted by artisans and the poor imitations mass-produced by powerlooms. The marks are in two forms—one for the domestic market and the other for the international market. The scheme is expected to not only help the buyers in getting guaranteed products, but also help the weavers, who are facing myriad threats to their very survival with the advent of the powerlooms. With technological developments, powerlooms are able to flood the markets with imitations of handloom articles at a much faster pace and at a much lower cost.

Safety Net: In India, Safety Nets are in the form of food subsidy (PDS), Primary Health Care, Clothing, Free Education or educational scholarship given to weaver's children, health insurance, Savings and Security Scheme, Old-Age Pension Scheme, livelihood support and welfare. These are some of the social safety net the government has introduced in the wake of the liberalization of the economy since 1991. But, these aim at providing welfare and not prepare the handloom weavers face global competition.

SWOT Analysis

Handloom forms a part of the heritage of Tamil Nadu and exemplifies the richness and diversity of the State. Taking into account the present status of handloom industry in Tamil Nadu, an attempt is made to analyse the problems and prospects of this traditional industry by using SWOT Analysis.

Strengths

- Its rural base, low-capital investment, and employment, intensive nature of production not only help in providing livelihood to large number of people in the rural non-farm sector but also in strengthening its survival in the age of computerized weaving technology.
- It is eco-friendly in nature and inflicts no harm to health.

- It prevents distress migration of rural artisans to the cities by providing work in the village itself.
- It provides productive employment to the women, old and destitute in their households (in the preparatory work) and thus serves an important social purpose, at virtually no cost to the government.

Weaknesses

- The inherent weakness of handloom industry is low productivity.
- The sector is weak and needs protection from the government by giving rebate/concessions periodically during festive seasons.
- It is relatively higher wage component of handloom products as compared to the powerloom products which affects their commercial viability.
- It grapples with problems like non-availability of good quality yarn, low technology, lack of market intelligence and poor marketing facilities.
- Another important weakness of the handloom industry is related to poor capacity of the weavers to switch over to new products and designs according to consumers' tastes and preferences on the short notice in comparison with powerloom products.

Opportunities

- Good design and colour combination in the products are done in accordance with the customer's satisfaction.
- The products made by the handloom weaving are durable for long life.
- Diversification of products like sarees, dhothi, bedsheet, pillow cover, sudithar material and window cover will have wide scope for marketing within the country as well as foreign countries.
- It gives employment opportunities to the livelihood of lowly-skilled and semi-skilled workers in rural areas.
- Export-oriented items made by the handloom weaving will fetch foreign money.

Threats

- In a free-market economy, the handloom products will have to compete with foreign made goods even in the domestic market.
- Encouraging the big capital type industry in textile sector by the government policy is not helpful to increase the long-term growth opportunities in handloom weaving sector.
- In spite of having excellent skills, the handloom weavers are languishing in poverty and they are not able to exploit the market in their favour.
- In general, the handloom products are not superior to the powerloom products and mill products on price, quality and design.
- Marketing of the handloom products is much more difficult when government cuts the subsidy and rebate for the handloom products.
- Phasing out of the multi-fibre arrangement (MFA) and functioning of the World Trade Organizations (WTO) are likely to pose new challenges for the handloom industry. Removal of controls required under MFA and WTO will increase competition among developing economies.

V. REMARKS AND SUGGESTIONS FROM THE FIELD

Referring to the handloom weavers in Tamil Nadu, one can say that there seems to be only 'ringing out the old', there seems to be 'no ringing in the new' taking place. This means that the rate of new entrants in handloom weaving taking it up as a livelihood venture/ occupation is almost zero, where as retirement from the sector is taking place in the normal pace. Even those who are already there in the occupation leave it to their wives and look for employment in powerlooms, mills, and cloth stores etc. This one observation could speak volumes about the state of the handloom-weaving sector in the state.

Enumeration Required: Initiative should be taken to make a complete enumeration of 'active handloom weavers' in Tamil Nadu. This can also be classified as 'Full-time weavers' and 'Part-time weavers (including those involved in pre-loom processes)'. Otherwise, we have a tendency to count active full time weavers, idle-members who keep their name with cooperatives merely for obtaining the benefits of government schemes, or in brief anybody who is born in a weaver's family or daughter-in-law of weaver's families being counted as active weavers. A situation assessment survey similar to that carried out by the National Sample Survey Organization is essential. As per the 1987 Handloom Census, there were 4.27 lakh Handlooms in Tamil Nadu. As on March 31, 2002 there are only 2.83 lakh handlooms functioning. As of now, available estimates show that there are 2 lakh active weavers in Tamil Nadu, and this study has taken this as a fact for granted.

An Irony that Reveals a Fact: One of the interesting observations made during the data analysis was that the number of looms keeps reducing year after year, the membership in cooperatives keeps falling; and the number of societies becoming dormant or non-functional is increasing where as the handloom production and sales show an increasing trend. This irony stands testimony to the fact that powerlooms encroach the handloom sector and the practice of disguised sales of powerloom goods as handlooms products are prevalent.

No Reservation of Items for Handlooms: In order to protect the handloom industry from the modern mills and powerloom sectors, the Textile Policy, 1985 had reserved certain 22 items for exclusive weaving by the handloom weavers. The Textile Policy of 2000 reduced the number of items reserved for handlooms to mere 11. The Agreement on Textiles and Clothing (ATC) – a WTO agreement – made the domestic reforms necessary and has put forward complete integration of textile sector into a world trading system from January 1, 2005 onwards. This means that there would be no quotas or reservations for handloom sector any more. They have to compete in the open market along with the mill sector and powerlooms. Not only is the handloom industry desparate, but it also has to fight for market space with the mills and powerlooms. The impact of the globalization policy on handloom sector needs to be watched.

Textiles and Apparel Park: The predominant theory after globalization is that small units are unviable and that big clusters needed to be encouraged. Even among handloom and powerloom weavers those with more than 4 to 6 looms are to be encouraged is the trend. In line with this, the government has proposed to set up textile parks to produce cloth using high power jet looms, in places like Karur (at a budget of Rs. 60 crores) and also in Aundipatty. The apprehension of some of the handloom weavers and traditional powerloom weavers is that this move may leave the weavers without even the little work they now get. While about 1000 weavers may get jobs in the textile park, lakhs will be rendered jobless outside. This apprehension stems from similar attempts made in Andhra Pradesh[9].

NIFT Training: In order to equip the handloom weavers to weave items for open markets and to enable them to come out with innovative designs, the government has introduced skill building schemes and technology up-gradation arrangement for the handloom weavers. There are two aspects to discuss: (i) most weavers in Tamil Nadu are in the age group of 40-60 years, and so they have least interest in learning anything new. They seem to be attending the training with a closed mind; (ii) the NIFT training introduces weaving export items and items for open market motivating the handloom weavers to come away from *Janatha* cloth weaving. The looms and other technology related accessories are not viewed as livelihood enhancing effort (Manampathy, for example) because the weavers need to change the size of their looms at home to be able to weave items for export and open market. The space available in their houses do not accommodate the looms recommended after NIFT Training (for example, Andipatty).

Technology Up-gradation: The technology up-gradation recommended should take into account the existing technology, space availability in weavers' houses and the ergonomics. The space available in most weavers' houses can accommodate 10 × 10 sq. ft. looms and the recommendation after the NIFT training (Andipatty) is to convert them as 12 × 12 sq. ft. or 12 × 25 sq. ft. looms. The handloom weavers consider them to be non-pragmatic propositions. However, some weavers in Theni district have got special permission from the AD Handlooms to set up such looms on the terrace of their houses.

NID Design Cards: To get the handloom weavers in a competitive mode another attempt made by the government is introduction of design cards done by the National Institute of Designs (NID). While these cards are really useful, the change of each design requires an additional capital investment of anywhere between Rs. 1,500 to Rs. 4,000 which the weavers find it difficult to find. Moreover, if there is a market-guarantee that a given design sarees or any cloth material would be taken by a particular buyer (or deemed exporter) for at least one year, it would be an intelligible proposition to invest in design. Otherwise, the weavers feel it to be a little unwise to make such investments.

---

9. 'Weavers in a Quandary – A Frontline Investigation of four districts in Andhra Pradesh' *Frontline*, October 22, 2004. Vol. 21 No. 21, p. 100.

Potentiality of Domestic Market: The government seems to think that preparing handlooms for export is one of the viable solutions to sustain the handloom sector. But, given the sheer size of textile consumers in India, one can say that leading textile exporters around the world might find India as a global hub for textile trade. Therefore, preparing for competitions within India and securing and sustaining a share of market even within the domestic market is essential. Gone are the days when handloom products were viewed as cloths for the poor. Now, it is viewed more as cloths for the rich and there is a special class of consumers who ought to use handloom products to be able to quietly communicate and build a '*swadeshi*' image to the kind of clientele they deal with. Wearing handloom products is viewed as a portrayal of positive image of patriotism and conviction for being truthful to India, and a show of feeling proud in being an Indian. Handloom sector needs to work on this positive image and secure and sustain a standard class of hard-core handloom consumers who would not fall for cheap imports. Therefore, any strategy designed to meet this objective will have to start with the markets and work backwards.

The Government of Kerala, for example, has finalized a proposal (*Indian Express* November 12, 2006) for weaving khadi/handloom uniforms mandatorily once a week for all the schools including the ones at the higher secondary levels. This is for the first time in the country that such a pogramme is being introduced in schools. Similar attempts in Tamil Nadu would do well too.

Wage Structure for Handloom Weavers: Falling wage rates, high costs, shrinking market and duplication by powerlooms have pushed the traditional handloom weavers into crisis. It is well known that the wage structure in the handloom industry is very disparate, and depends on factors such as the product and the production channel (cooperative or master weaver). A coherent wage policy is essential if successful marketing practices are to translate into stable livelihoods for the primary producers. Wage revisions should take place periodically to match in proportion to the price-rise. There are silk weavers in Tamil Nadu whose wages have not been raised for more than four years.

FDS and Free Uniforms: Under FDS, instead of giving sarees and dhoties free, it may be sold for half the price (with 50% subsidy), which can ensure employment for weavers. Similarly, the government, instead of giving one free uniform to school children when actually they need a minimum two sets, can supply two uniform sets at subsidized rate. But, the quality and variety in varied price ranges need to be ensured.

Amount Due by Co-optex and Government: The amount due by co-optex and government to the primary weaver's cooperative societies should be cleared as and when stocks are lifted. Co-optex should work out market-promotion measures to be able to clear up dues in time.

Weavers Outside Cooperative Fold: The Tamil Nadu Handloom Development Corporation Limited does not seem to be in a healthy state to be able to support the activities of those not covered under the cooperative fold. Although the THDCL seems to be working for the master weavers, each master weaver has employed anywhere between 7 and 20 individual weavers. These individual weavers need to be taken into account when the impact of globalization on weavers is studied. Their livelihoods also should be protected.

Potentiality of Panchayati Raj Institution: The government is withdrawing systematically itself from the responsibility of providing the weavers market guarantee or access to inputs at reasonable prices. The economy is left open for market factors and competition to take over. The welfare state characteristic of India is losing out to globalization. In India, over 72 per cent of the handloom weavers are rural-based and the remaining 28 per cent are urban-based. The State has the responsibility to rope in peoples' participation in making decisions that affect a given sector. Similarly, the State is accountable for its policies on various sectors of the economy. Development models can be evolved for each weaving region only through an engagement with the realities of the field. The potentiality of the Panchayati Raj System can be given a serious thought while thinking of sustaining the livelihoods of weavers' community.

Areas Affected

All said and done, the weavers under cooperative fold suffer more due to irregularity in supply of yarn, and irregularity in payments made to the cooperatives which in turn delay payment of wages to the weavers. The following are some of the study villages that have suffered due to their dependence on cooperatives. The weavers of these villages are mentally conditioned that they would weave *Janatha* cloth variety for the government to distribute free during *Diwali* and *Pongal*. If the government makes a decision to withdraw *Janatha* cloth scheme or withdraw support to cooperatives, it sends shock waves across the spinal cord of the weavers in several villages across Tamil Nadu where people depend on handloom weaving as the only means of earning their livelihoods for years.

As far as Tamil Nadu is concerned there could be many villages in this category. But the villages mentioned in this study are the ones visited by this team of researchers. Those who weave for open market and those who procure orders from deemed export system go on, although they also have a feeling that their products are challenged by the lot from the mills and powerlooms. However, but for the higher price, they have trained themselves and under various schemes to stand up to the competition.

11

Changing Waves of Fisheries: The State of Fisheries Sector in Tamil Nadu

Introduction

Fishing and fishery related activities play a crucial role in the economic profile of the coastal villages in Tamil Nadu. Livelihoods that were directly or indirectly dependent on fishing activities, such as working as crew members on the boat, head load fish vendors, dry fish sellers on the seashore, fish merchants, fish commission agents, workers involved in loading and unloading of fish in trucks, ice plant workers and owners and so on. There are so many dimensions in understanding coastal livelihoods. It involves society, culture, economics and environment and so on. Investigations of livelihoods mean attempting to 'understand the working of human society on the coast' which is so complex and diverse. While fishing is the most obvious and noticeable livelihood on the coast, all the other livelihoods put together could actually be employing a number equal to that of fishing. Further, these other livelihoods employ a wider mix of persons including women from the fishing communities and persons from non-fishing communities that live or work near the coast.

Fisheries, in India, have been relatively open even before 1991—meaning even before the current round of globalization. Owing to this fact, which set of policies can be considered as globalization is still tricky so as to put down categorically, the aftermath of globalization in the fisheries sector. But, the kind of market changes that are taking place, policy changes that appear to reflect market-friendly approaches, technological invasion, and trade liberalization are issues to discuss as far as fisheries sector is concerned.

Tamil Nadu has the highest number of fisher population (7,90,408) among the states in India, report Marine Fisheries Census for India 2005. It accounts for 22.11 per cent of fisher population in India. So, Tamil Nadu has the highest total working fishers i.e 2,06,908 among the states in India. In Tamil Nadu, marine fisheries account for 82 per cent of all active fishermen, who are responsible for 76 per cent of the total fish production in the State and 8 per cent of the total marine catch for India. Majority of the (89.70 per cent) fishers in marine fishing sector have taken up as a full-time occupation.

The traditional fishing community and particularly the artisanal fishworkers have been under varied pressure of marginalization right from the dawn of industrial fishery development since the mid-sixties. The fishing community in Tamil Nadu, with their traditional knowledge of the sea and its environment harvested the resources in a moderate scale. The craft and gear deployed were the most appropriate to suit the environment and these were developed by the fishermen themselves over centuries of experience and skill. The catamarans, small canoes, big canoes, and different gears were all results of traditional innovations to meet the dynamics of tropical waters, multi-species, fish behaviour and seasonal changes. The traditional fishermen never over fish the resources which they recognize as their common property. For the fishing communities fishing is a way of life, not just a source of income. Traditionally, small scale or artisan fishers have provided fish for local consumption, but as fish becomes scarce, its value increases. The opening up of the economy to private companies has led to rapid sitting of mega projects along the coast leading to destruction of the coast and livelihood system. Industrial fishing fleets are dominating the world's fisheries at the expense of the vast majority of the fishing communities.

The focus of Tamil Nadu Government fisheries development policies was on development and exploitation of fisheries resources, both for domestic consumption and export. These policies were pursued more aggressively post-1980 period. This to a greater or lesser extent went in for liberalization, privatization and deregulation, with an emphasis on increasing trade and foreign exchange earnings. The consequences of these policies are clear that there is strong evidence of over-fishing in coastal waters. The emphasis has clearly been on economic growth, trade and revenue generation. While the importance of management was recognized to ensure sustainability of the fisheries resources, in practice, this was not a priority. In the past two decades, there was a trend of motorization of traditional craft. This was possible through liberalization of imports and subsidies to promote marine fisheries. The capacity of fishing has rapidly expanded even in the small-scale sector which has also adopted many of the gear earlier used by the mechanized sector.

I

Fishing, which was a simple occupation on the coast with a *kattumaram* and net, has grown exponentially today. The livelihoods that are dependent on fishing are so many including on-shore fishing, deep-sea fishing, sun drying of fish, fish processing and packing, marketing, export and so on. As the scope for occupation in fisheries—including export—expands, the complexity associated with it also expands. Complexity comes in the form of technology used for sailing, the type of motors used, technology (or the type of net) used for catching fish, on-board and off-board handling of fish, cleanliness of the fish landing centres, sanitary measures adopted in delivering fish to the consumers, packaging when it is exported and so on. Although, in practice, many of these are adhered to more in fish-export rather than in domestic market, the point is that the complexity of fishing as an occupation has become long-drawn-out. Reportedly, many of the inputs for fisheries sector such as nets, Out Board Motors etc. are imported from other countries only. Capital investment to build boats, and cost of operation have gone up along with advanced technologies introduced in fishery.

Fisheries sector has undergone a significant structural change in which capitalists from outside the fisher folk community began investing directly in fish production. These financiers first invested in processing and export trade. Later, they started directly investing in production by purchasing trawl boats and hiring crews on wage to operate. Moreover, the capital investment in mechanized boats and gear, and their maintenance, became well beyond the reach of most artisanal fishers. What once was a small-scale livelihood centered occupation, became a modern export-oriented industry, organized along capitalist lines.

Trawling for shrimp, for example, was promoted since the early 1980s, given the high demand for shrimp in the world market. Unregulated exploitation of shrimp for exports has led to higher pressure on resources. There is a clear link between high export demand and over-exploitation of resources, particularly in the absence of effective management and regulation. The market signals, often in many sectors unless they are moderated and countered by collective decision-making, leads to disaster. One technology is introduced and it gives good catch (fish) then, everybody invests in that of net or type of fishing, then everyone starts facing the problem of over exploitation of fishery resources; or the prices crash. One thing that is very clear is if one goes by market signals one would end up over exploiting the resources. Globalization gives the technology to do this.

Analyzing in terms of opportunities or the challenges the fishers have to face in the contemporary global business, there are certain issues that stand on the top. The prime of them include: variety of fish that is targeted, method or technology used for catching fish (tuna, prawn or whatever), handling of fish after the catch and while processing. The rapidity of spread of new technology in fishing villages is reported to be very high. Practically if one boat used a technology and has seen a good catch, all the other boats in that area adopt that technology until it reaches a point of saturation. Year after year, newer technologies are used for ensuring higher targets of catch, and to identify newer fishing grounds. But, in deed, very little is done as regulation to ensure that the fishes and other resources in the sea do not get depleted. Three important concerns of those who are working for the welfare of the fishermen are: (a) fast depleting fish resources, (b) the ecological damage caused by some of the technologies, and (c) the developments in other sectors, such as industrial development and consequent pollution, that affects the fishery. Another interesting dimension about this is that it is more the environmentalist groups and activists rather than the governments that make noise about this indiscriminate netting.

Fishing, when it was a simple livelihood venture, remained in the hands of the fishermen. Technology-dynamics and market-signals have changed the face of fishery from a simple livelihood domain to a technology-and-market-driven activity. By modernizing the sector, it has adopted technologies like trawling and purse seining, and expanded the industrial fleet. It left many without a livelihood. Traditionally fishing nets were woven locally using cotton yarn or other natural fibre. But this has changed now. The introduction of synthetic yarns and net making machines has led to the displacement of thousands of people traditionally involved in these activities, many of whom were women. In Kanyakumari district of Tamil Nadu, the introduction of net making machines reportedly led to the displacement of 20,000 women employed in this work.

Referring to technology one can say, for example, that the type of fishnet recommended for use by fishermen are such that they do not catch smaller fish, and do not damage coral reefs and precious weeds in the sea. But, the fishermen are often indiscriminate and so they tend to use nets that would catch the smaller fishes also or use trawling nets. The environmentalists complain that the fishermen are, often, unconcerned about the damages caused to the resources at the sea-bottom. This is becoming a challenge in the wake of globalization where the conditions are that if the method of catch or the technology used for catching fish had damaged the ecology of the sea such consignment would not be imported into some of the western countries. Often, this is used as a non-tariff barrier to reduce import from other countries, where tariff barriers would not work out to the favour of the importing nation.

What has really changed in recent years with the liberalization of the Indian economy and the quest for economic growth, is the higher pressure on the coasts. While earlier fisheries was perhaps the main user of coastal and marine resources, today there is pressure from tourism, urban growth, ports and harbours and the oil industry, on the one hand, and from conservation imperatives on the other.

II

Standards and Regulations

The rational for liberalization of tariffs and quota in the fisheries sector is to facilitate more trade and also benefit from increased access to market, increased production and employment opportunities. However, there is a growing concern that liberalization of trade could be undermined by the new protectionist use of regulatory barriers such as food safety regulations, quality and composition standards, and labelling requirements..

The denial of market access for fish and fish products from developing countries could be under the mantle of environmental concerns, hygiene, quality and food safety standards. This is one of the main issues of the recent globalization process. A number of regulations for fishery products have been introduced to upgrade and improve the overall hygienic and sanitary conditions of existing fishing harbours and fishing landing centres. Failure to adopt this could result in exclusion from international markets and marginalization of competitiveness in export of marine products. The government needs to develop realistic and practical sustainability criteria so as to help the fishermen community. Moreover, as markets for fishery products become ever more globalized, it is required that the fisher folk must understand and meet international product quality and certification standards which are so weak in many places in Tamil Nadu.

Hygienic handling of fish should start even while the fish is still at the vessel in the sea, off-board at fish landing centres and in fish processing centres where it is packed for export. The sanitary and phyto-sanitary measures are used so effectively by some of the western countries as non-tariff barrier. This is considered as a fencing or barricade that some of the developing countries with poor infrastructure for sanitary handling of fish find very difficult to make a break through. In South India places like Kollam and Tuticorin have developed infrastructure, to some extent, comparable to international requirements. Kollam is reported to have the opportunity of emerging as one of the vital fish processing export centres in India. One opportunity here is that if infrastructures were developed, there is potential for export. Who would develop these infrastructures and in whose interest is another question. Either the government should take it up or some kind of Public Private Partnership arrangement can work if the private players should not be allowed to take upper hand. Whatever be the arrangement it should not completely turn into a business mode where the fishermen are marginalized in getting the benefits of the business. One of the recent technologies that have come in handy for the fishermen is 'mobile phones'. The fishermen report that it works upto 7-10 km. in the sea. They are able to communicate to the fishermen in the vessel that is fishing a few kilometres away and also with their family members at the shore.

The contention of many of the fishermen is that ports are coming up and port developments are taken up as mega projects. But, little is done to construct harbours or fish landing centres that would really benefit the fishermen. Their version is ports are, by nature, for commercial purposes and not for the fishermen. Rather port development is a process that would dislocate the fishermen – the area being guarded by the coast guards. Whereas a harbour is more a fish-landing centre that would benefit the fishermen. As ports come up more and more in number or existing ports are expanded, the space left for fishermen keeps becoming less and less is a strife raised by fishermen across coast.

The Micro Financing Mechanism

Apart from technology and sanitation aspects, another important dimension that comes on the surface is the financial requirements and intuitional support for fishermen. It is an old story that many of the fisheries cooperatives are either defunct or liquidated. The merchant–fishermen tie-up which most often works in favour of the merchants is the one that is taking care of the operational expenses or working capital requirements of the fishermen. Advancement in terms of technology, and inputs required for actual fishing operation are inevitable. But the irksome thing about it is when the costs grow up almost to measure equally with returns. The traditional fishermen who used to venture into the sea with the aid of a *kattumaram* did not require motors, diesel, or huge bars of ice etc. Today for a crew of fishermen to go for fishing, they require anywhere between Rs. 3,000 and Rs. 5,000 to make the fishing operation possible. Fishery is becoming technology-driven. Fishery has become an operation that can be carried out only if you have certain working capital. Most of these technologies and in-puts are imported. The finance comes from the hands of the local merchants or fish traders, except a few who are members of some organized intuition that is capable of helping with both finance and technology. Fishery has fishermen as working partner, along with several other sleeping partners who claim share in the profit. The profit from fishery goes in the hands of several people involved including the motor supplier, diesel supplier, technology supplier, engine repairing man, ice-plant owner and so on. The actual fishermen who ventured into the sea for catching fish also get a share, if they are alert enough!

III

Involuntary Resettlement

Fishermen community is one that is at once the most cohesive and the most combatant. The solidity of this community is such that although the government has brought about constitutional amendment to set up elected Village Panchayats, in many of the fishermen villages, Traditional Panchayats are said to be more powerful and highly influential of decisions. Although in some places it is being questioned by the youth who want to break the tradition, the community, in general, has the tradition of respecting and abiding by the traditional leader. Many of them have not even bothered to obtain a land patta from the government for the land they are living in. Perhaps, talking in legal terms it is possible that the court can issue an order in favour of evicting them from their settlements, if the place is required by the government for some kind of development activity. Apparently, this is not a far-stretched imagination when the government is very much after developing infrastructure on various fronts. But, executing such a court order to evict the fishermen from their settlements, flouting the traditional Panchayat and the cohesiveness of the community is really a Himalayan task.

The then government in the year 2003 as part of a larger plan initiated a move to evict the fishermen families in some of the villages (Nochikuppam, Nochinagar, Thideernagar, Dumeengkupam, Selvarajapuram, Rajiv Gandhinagar, Mullikuppam, Bhavanikuppam and Srinivasapuram) on Marina beach. The fishermen leaders state that it was not new. Similar attempts had been made during Rajai's period, Kamarajar's period and also during MGR's period. It did not succeed. The government had to withdraw. In that respect it was not new. The Government of Tamil Nadu signed an MoU with Malaysian Government to improve the Marina beachfront in Chennai, and for building an 'administrative city' providing accommodation for multi-nationals and embassies relocating the local fisher folk. The hitch was relocating the fisher folk. Another problem was the policy decision to go ahead with the project was taken without bringing it for discussion in political or public arena. It was massively opposed by several fishermen union and fishing community and so the project was withdrawn.

Similarly, after tsunami one of the important lessons that the government thought sensible enough was that no settlement—fishermen's or whose so ever it is—should not be located within the high tide line of the sea (1000-500 metres depending upon elevation). This has found place in the Coastal Regulation Zone, now modified as Coastal Management Zone also. The fishermen have it that they should live close to the sea, because they are not working with a laptop and parker pen to bring them home everyday. They sail by boat which has to be anchored in the sea, at a distance that the fisherman can keep an eye on. Unconfirmed information across the coast is floating around that beach is to be given to tourism industry for the promotion of hotels, and resort etc. Some activists also state that this is likely to take place in areas where the fishermen have vacated due to regulations imposed through CMZ. But, this is only a hearsay that goes around. The ground that makes people to take it serious or believe is their earlier experience with the government on attempts such as Marina Beautification, where government attempted to evict people for the sake of MNCs, foreign embassies and with the proposal of constructing some government buildings on the Marina.

IV

Pollution—The Negative Externality

The negative externality caused by polluting industries that results in environmental and social costs to which these industries turn a blind eye, can be witnessed in *Pazhaverkadu near Chennai*. The dismal thing about this is that the traditional fishermen from seven villages around who used to make a living by fishing and catching prawns from the lagoon of Pazhaverkadu have lost a substantial amount of income they used to get a few years ago. In fact, the situation has landed the fishers from these seven villages to go for fishing on rotation-basis so that all of them survive.

Pazhaverkadu lagoon is reported to be the second biggest lagoon in India. This lagoon is known for prawns and fish that traverse between the sea and the lagoon alternately during high-tide and low-tide. The locals report that the fish like to be in the sea during low-tide and go over to lagoon during high-tide at sea. They return to the sea when the tide becomes low again. This traversing time is the time the fishermen make use of for catching them. The price the white-prawns fetch both in the domestic as well as in the international market is very high. The wider the traversing area, larger is the amount of fish and prawns that traverse between the sea and the lagoon. During rainy season as there would be a lot of water passing through, when the movement of fish would also be high, making good catch possible for the fishermen. The fishermen in Pazhaverkadu report that the fishermen from seven villages who are dependent on fishing in the Pazhaverkadu lagoon have invested upto Rs. 2 lakhs widening the passage to lagoon so that fish traverse in large numbers.

The challenges that have emerged: (i) industrial wastes that are let into the sea and lagoon, and (ii) development of prawn culture farms in the neighbourhood. The third threat is that the government's announcement that Special Economic Zone (SEZ) would be set up near Pazhaverkadu. That the fishermen and their union shouting slogans against the polluting industries, and the industries reducing the discharge of effluents when there is revolting, and take it easy after the fishermen become calm, is a normal tug of war in Pazhaverkadu. Power Plant at North Chennai, Ennore Port, and a series of chemical plants and industries that let their effluents, often hot, run into sea killing fish and prawns is a big danger to the livelihoods of the fishermen. Besides this, a kind of ash is also deposited in the lagoon area that is filling the depth of the lagoon reducing the chances of fish and prawn traversing. It has also made the danger of sea erosion easier. Be it SIPCOT at Cuddalore or these plants in Chennai, they all do not find difficulty in disposing their effluents. They have this easy solution of letting it run into the sea unmindful of the consequences it causes to the species in the sea and the livelihoods of the fishermen in the neighbourhood villages who are dependent on sea. The fishermen and their union are not much worried about challenges brought about by globalization in terms of technology or sanitary measures etc. rather they are worried more about the havoc caused by these polluting industries in places such as Pazhaverkadu and Cuddalore.

Fish catch has considerably come down over the years, report the fishermen. One clear evidence to this is that the seven neighbourhood Panchayats have passed a joint resolution that the fishermen from these villages would go for fishing into the lagoon or in the sea water close by only on designated days so that everyone gets something to make a living. A local Panchayat Committee monitors this and reports to Panchayats.

Another related development that has amounted to rubbing salt into the wounds of the fishermen is prawn culture farms being promoted in areas close to Pazhaverkadu lagoon. These prawn farms promoted by private commercial interests are: (a) cutting into the business share of fishermen who used to make a living catching and selling natural prawns from the lagoon; (b) they also let out waste-water from prawn farms into the sea.

Perhaps, for a country like India with vast coastal-line, it might be difficult to put in place strong regulatory mechanisms. But, in the interest of coastal ecology and livelihood of the fishermen it is vital that regulatory mechanisms are developed and implemented effectively. All said and done, deregulation should not be at the cost of devastating a natural resource such as sea, water or land. Nor should it be at the cost of livelihoods of a section of traditional population who depended on it for years. Perhaps, the fishermen in Pazhaverkadu would be able to still make good money stating the difference between prawn caught from the sea and the ones cultured in an artificial setting. But, they should know how to communicate this message to the consuming public. Moreover, if the private prawn farms were asked to pay for the negative externality they cause calculating the environmental and social costs, then, most probably, the price of natural prawn brought to the market by traditional fishermen would be cheaper. Similarly, the polluting industries should be directed to set up effluent treatment plants to the 'level required' and not as an eye-wash to the inspecting officials or as an excuse for the rebelling fishermen. In the event of failing to do this the 'polluters pay' principle should be applied to the extent that it adequately compensates the fishermen, and the resources the effluents are destroying in the sea.

The state of affairs in Pazhaverkadu has aggravated in the past five years. The talk about Special Economic Zone (SEZ) in Pazhaverkadu area is becoming another threat to the traditional fishermen. SEZs are essentially industrial complexes such as the SIPCOTs that the government provides a lot of concessions to start and turn a blind eye to aspects such as pollution which causes loss of livelihood to the community that originally belongs to that area.

V

Infrastructure Development *versus* Coastal Ecology

Among the major infrastructure development projects of the Government of India are Golden Quadrangular roads, development and modernization of airports in various cities, and Sethusamudram Channel Project. Although almost all these three projects are being criticized by environmentalists, activists groups, and a section of the population on various counts, one of the most criticized projects is Sethusamudram Ship Channel Project. The project idea, as put across by the Sethusamudram Corporation Limited—a 'special purpose vehicle' set up for the purpose of this project located in Rameshwaram, is: In order to reduce the steaming distances between the East and West Coast of India and to improve the navigation within territorial water of India, a navigation channel connecting the Gulf of Mannar and Palk Bay through Adam's Bridge has been envisaged so that the ships moving between the East and West Coasts of India need not go around Sri Lanka. Tuticorin Port Trust is the nodal agency for this

Rs. 2,427 crore project. The work has been commenced and dredging of a ship channel across the Palk strait between India and Sri Lanka is taking shape.

According to Sethusamudram Corporation Limited some of the vital benefits the project envisages are: (i) This will lead to a saving of upto 424 nautical miles (780 km.) and upto 30 hours of sailing time; (ii) It will provide shorter navigation route between Kanyakumari, Tuticorin, Chennai, Ennore, Kakinada, Vishakapatnam, Paradip, Haidia and Kolkata and ports in neighbouring countries such as Chittagong; (iii) Substantial saving can be had in ship time and bunkering costs. This will directly benefit the shipping industry and EXIM trade; (iv) Greater employment generation in the Ports and the industries in the vicinity; (v) It will become an invaluable asset from national defence and security point of view enabling quicker access between coasts; (vi) Fishermen will benefit due to the potential for development of fishing harbours with proper landing and storage facilities; (vii) Trade will benefit from reduction in maritime transport cost; and (viii) Domestic consumers will benefit with industries producing cheaper goods for the domestic market due to cost of raw material imports.

There are NGOs, and campaign committees spreading information protesting the implementation of the project. The points of contention raised by the dissenters (range from social, ecological, and engineering) are:

- It is proposed to dump a large quantity (1 lakh million cubic metre) of sand and sediments on the seashore and in deep sea. What will be the effect of the water currents on the disposed materials? Will the dredged materials remain idle? Won't the water currents carry them away or back into dredged area again?
- Viewed from any stand point—be it engineering, economic, ecological, environmental, and social—it is unviable and unintelligible.
- The mass of earth excavated so large that depositing it somewhere in the deep sea will definitely affect the microorganism of deep seabed, which is the birthplace of all biological activity of the marine life forms.
- The restrictions in the fishing activity during construction and operation periods. That the fishermen would be given 'timings' to go for fishing is not a logical argument, as fishing is like

hunting which they cannot surely say within a given time they would be able to catch fish and clear out of the sea. We shall provide drinking water, health and recreation facilities, community hall etc., but you should stop going into the sea for fishing is irrational argument.

- The social cost of displacement and resettlement of fishermen from Dhanushkodi.
- What is the guarantee that dredging would not affect coral reef, precious sea-grasses and sea-weeds to protect which the government is spending several crores through Gulf of Mannar Biosphere Reserve Project.
- There are complaints that mechanized boats spill oil in the sea. But, now it is planned that 3055 ships will transit through the channel in a year. Wouldn't they all spill oil, and discharge all unwanted plastic materials into the sea.
- The disturbance caused by the movement of ships and coast guard vessels would make this area an uninhabitable place for the fishes, resulting in very poor catch for the fishermen.

The dissenters keep doing their campaigning on one hand, and the Project is making progress on the other side. All that the dissenters state cannot be brushed aside, because it has happened earlier while constructing Chennai/Ennore Port that the government had promised that setting up of port would not affect the fishermen or their livelihoods. Later, after the port came up the fishermen were not allowed entry into any of those areas. They are tightly guarded by the coast guard. One can talk the neo-liberal language that in the long run everybody including the poor fishermen would also benefit. Or put in other words, for the sake of trade through ships, which might benefit the country and eventually the poor fishermen also, we need to do this, is a logical argument. Taking it and continuing to fighting against it is upto the people who are likely to be affected. But, one cannot deny the fact that dredging would disturb the sea-ecology, the normal life of fishermen, and hence their livelihoods. Browsing the website of Sethusamudram uploaded by the government, one can say that the government is trying to be transparent. The website is also showing the progress made. But, NGOs, fishermen trade unions, social and environmental activists in Rameswaram and Coastal Action Network uniting several NGOs in Tamil Nadu, have several questions still be answered.

VI

Concerns in the Recent Globalization Process

In fact, the fishery sector has derived benefits which include improved quality and better access of fishery products to markets, increased export earnings, greater exchange of technology, increased productivity and efficiency and better supply of fish products to local populations through liberalization of imports. At the same time, there are some negative effects of globalization on fisheries which are given below:

- The fish production has been stagnating in Tamil Nadu while pressure on coastal resources has been increasing.
- Even the artisanal fishery has become increasingly capitalized and fossil fuel dependent. This makes the fishery unsustainable.
- Investors and government have been targeting coastal resources disregarding fishermen's livelihoods and security in gross violation of the Coastal Regulation Zone (CRZ) norms. For example, as per the 1996 Tamil Nadu Coastal Zone Management Plan the entire Pulicat Lake is classified as Coastal Regulation Zone I and which means a fragile area and no development zone.
- The growing dependence on these marine resources due to over population and more number of mechanized crafts leads to over exploitation due to more number and conflicts among users.
- There is a serious concern that the increased market competition between the small-scale fisheries sector products.
- Another main issue of the recent globalization process is the greatest denial of market access for fish and fish products from developing countries indicating sanitary norms could be under the mantle of environmental concerns, hygiene, quality and food safety standard.
- As markets for fishery products become ever more globalized, it is required that the fisher folk must understand and meet international product quality and certification standards which are so weak in many places in Tamil Nadu.

VII

Women in the Fishery Sector

Women are an integral part of the fishery sector, especially in traditional fishery sector. Women, as everywhere else, are almost entirely responsible for the care and nature of the family. They take on a range of work within the fisheries and within fishing communities. They are very active in the processing sector, as either part-time or full-time workers in processing plants, or workers under sub-contracting systems, working on a piece-rate basis. A sizable number of women are engaged in fish vending in almost all the fishing habitations. They are mostly itinerant sales woman in their 40s. Some of them sell fish on the sea shore itself while others sell door to door or at fish markets in the neighbourhood villages. Their asset includes an aluminium vessel or bamboo basket, a weighing scale and a wooden piece to sit on. In addition to this fixed asset, they need to have some working capital also. Some women who generally sell door to door invest a working capital of Rs. 300 to Rs. 600. Other women who sell in the fish market invest anywhere between Rs. 2,000 to Rs. 5,000. In general, in each of the fishing village there will be some number of middle and old age women involved in dry dish making and selling. They buy fish from the beach during gluts, dry and sell it later.

Tamil Nadu fisheries display an assortment of fishing techniques and women too engage in a variety of fish related tasks. In the districts of Ramnad, Tirunelveli, Kanyakumari and Thanjavur, they are more engaged in drying, curing and vending, whereas the dominant activity in the northern districts of Chennai, Chingelpat and South Arcot are marketing including auctioning and purchasing at big fish landing centres. In the northern districts, the women had earlier auctioned the fish their husbands brought back. Today, they have been completely marginalized in this work because of the centralized landing and bulk purchase for export marketing. Today, hundreds of young women and girls from the fishing villages are migrating for work as wage labour in the fish processing plants. Earlier, young women worked in the saltpans. Today, these are being displaced by the shrimp farms.

Women's role in pre-harvest activities is largely eliminated as net making is mechanized, though some mending work remains. With increase in industrial fishing and long distance fishing, the women become 'housewives' or work in other jobs. With trade becoming long distance and export oriented, women are marginalized in the marketing. With fisheries becoming more export oriented and industrialized, women lose more and more control over resources as innovations are aimed at men. Where women work in industrial processing, their link with the fisheries sector as a whole tends to be weak.

Women in Kasimadeu and Pulicat, the women are also involved in the work of auctioneering for which they are paid by the owners. Mainly, girls are working as labourers in the fish processing centres. They do the cleaning, peeling and processing work in the centres. Some of the women belong to Self-Help Groups. They are involved in thrift and self-help credit. The existence of these SHGs has not grown to the extent to lend all the credit requirements for making direct marketing without depending on agents. After the tsunami, the concept has picked up in many of the tsunami affected areas (Kottaikuppam Panchayat near Pulicat in Ponnari block of Thiruvalluvar district).

VIII

Impact of Globalization Processes on Fisheries in Tamil Nadu

The fishery sector is being affected by various factors, both from within and outside fisheries. These could be enumerated thus:

- Modernization of the fishery sector, including, adoption of efficient technologies like trawling and purse seining, expansion of the industrial fleet, and the rapid development of technologies related to refrigeration, transportation and processing.
- Increasing export-orientation as fishery is seen as an important exchange earner by the government.
- Expansion of export-oriented fish species.
- Growing competition for coastal resources for, among other things, urbanization, industrialization and tourism.
- Degradation and destruction of coastal resources.
- Adoption of policies by State Government to attract foreign investment, including tax incentives and policies facilitating joint venture agreements.
- Adoption of policies linked to privatization and liberalization by state, reducing the role of the state in service delivery.

We live in a complex world where change is happening at ever increasing speeds. Increasing globalization has meant that what happens in one place of the world affects other parts far away. It may have a number of positive or negative effects on the fisheries sector in Tamil Nadu. The fishery sector has derived certain benefits from globalization, and some obnoxious as well. These benefits include improved quality and better access of fishery products to markets; increased export earnings; greater exchange of technology; increased productivity and efficiency and better supply of fish products to local people through liberalization of imports. Negative effects of globalization on fishery sector in Tamil Nadu have been noticed in the form of increased market competition between the small-scale fishery sector products and imported low priced fish products; increased production costs to meet quality and sanitation standards applicable in main foreign markets; higher prices for tradable fish products in domestic markets and potential reduction of fish supply from local fisheries to domestic markets; and increased pressure on fully or over-exploited fish stocks and potential risk of depletion.

Major Changes after Globalization Processes

Fishery has always, in a sense, been a globalized sector, as there has always been the imperative to sell. Unregulated exploitation for exports has led to higher pressure on resources. There is a clear link between high export demand and over-exploitation of resources, particularly in the absence of effective management and regulation. As competition over and pressure on resources has increased, fishing operations have tended to become more capital-and technology-intensive. To some extent this trend has been supported by the State, such as through schemes promoting motorization and mechanizations. This has also meant that there is a trend towards centralization of landings and bigger catches. This has also, in a way, disrupted some of the traditional patterns. There are harbours, large landings, merchants, traders, exporters etc. instead of small and diversified landings.

Higher volumes and values are reported to be more in the hands of the merchants, traders and exporters now, which are controlling the dynamics at the harbours and fish landing centres. This whole pattern of development requires review. If women are ousted from the sector, the well-being of the community is affected, even if the incomes of the fishermen go up marginally.

What has really changed in recent years with the liberalization of the Indian economy and the quest for economic growth is the higher pressure on the coasts. While earlier fisheries was perhaps the main user of coastal and marine resources, today there is pressure from tourism, urban growth, ports and harbours and the oil industry, on the one hand, and from conservation imperatives on the other. The fisheries sector is also being affected by decisions taken at the international level agreements and decisions under various international conventions. Fishing operations have, over time, become more capital-and technology-intensive. However, there is need to review this pattern of growth in order to find out who is actually benefiting. It appears that it benefits the input suppliers, oil companies, engine manufacturers, and exporters, more rather than the fishing community or fish workers. The fishing community as organized forums nee to be alert enough to understand at what stage it affects the local markets and the ordinary fishers.

Developments in Other Sectors

Developments in other sectors are increasingly impacting the fisheries sector. Today, on the coast there is large industry, urban growth, tourism, ports, the oil industry, intensive aquaculture being set up. The space left for fisheries and for fishing communities is being squeezed—at one level there are the pressures of economic growth, and at the other level, there are conservationists fighting for protected areas. So, coasts are increasingly becoming contested territories. Earlier fishing communities were the only ones on the coast, now there are so many others and communities have to compete with each one of them for space for housing and for fishing and related activities. At the same time the relative power of the fisheries sector vis-à-vis all these other high-profile economic activities is certainly low, especially with the emphasis on liberalizing the economy and promoting economic growth.

The contention of many of the fishermen is that ports are coming up and port developments are taken up as mega projects. But, little is done to construct harbours or fish landing centres that would really benefit the fishermen. Their version is ports are, by nature, commercial domains and not a domain for the fishermen to operate or benefit from. Rather port development is a process that would dislocate the fishermen—the area being guarded by the coast guards. Whereas a harbour is more a fish-landing centre that would benefit the fishermen. As ports come up more and more in number or existing ports are expanded, the space left for fishermen keeps becoming less and less is a strife raised by fishermen across coast.

Conclusion

Complexity to fisheries sector comes in the form of technology used for sailing, the type of motors used, technology (or the type of net) used for catching fish, on-board and off-board handling of fish, cleanliness of the fish landing centres, sanitary measures adopted in delivering fish to the consumers, packaging when it is exported and so on. Although, in practice, many of these are adhered to more in fish-export rather than in domestic market, the point is that the complexity of fishing as an occupation has become long-drawn-out. Reportedly, many of the inputs for fisheries sector such as nets, Out Board Motors etc. are imported from other countries only. Capital investment to build boats, and cost of operation have gone up along with advanced technologies introduced in fishery, as a result it is the small-scale fish-workers, who are in rough waters.

12

Globalization and Grassroots Action

That the subject globalization is divisive and that the issues it brings forth are contentious is not new. It becomes still more controversial when it is spoken concurrently with decentralization. No two social scientists interpret a phenomenon or a set of data exactly similarly. This variation in interpretations, counter-interpretations, and 'interpretations of interpretations' apparently stem from the disciplinary choice one has made, the ideology one grows up with, or the kind of theoretical framework one deliberately chooses to appraise a phenomenon with.

All social scientists, political scientists or economists look at any phenomenon with his/her own 'viewfinder' on. Therefore, consciously or unconsciously, one tends to understand and interpret things the way one has learnt to develop a world view. This gives them a standpoint from which to view and appraise things. Based on standpoints, perceptions and reasoning change, views differ and the details one assembles to put up an argument vary. For a researcher, the more the standpoints, the more are the perspectives developed. Multiple perspectives result in better comprehension of a given phenomenon and more light on the range of issues associated with it.

At the beginning of this research exercise at the grassroot level, the Research Team was clear about one thing and uncertain about another. The thing that we were clear about was our standpoint: from which standpoint do we view globalization? Being a Gandhian institution known for its work on governance at the grassroots level, obviously, our standpoint was: Panchayati Raj and grassroot level changes. The thing that we were uncertain about was: how to distinguish and put down in writing whether a globalizing act was appreciable or obnoxious. But uncertainly vanished when we applied the following talisman of M.K. Gandhi:

> "Whenever you are in doubt or when the self becomes too much with you, apply the following test.
> Recall the face of the poorest and the weakest man whom you may have seen and ask yourself if the step you contemplate is going to be of any use to him. Will he gain anything by it? Will it restore him a control over his own life and destiny? In other words, will it lead to *Swaraj* for the hungry and spiritually starving millions?
> Then you will find your doubts and yourself melting away".

India is reported to be one of the fastest adopters of globalization policies and is fast emerging as a market economy, spreading the culture of consumerism. It is also reported of India that it is here that most of the world's poor live. Among the states of India, Tamil Nadu is reported to be on the fast track of adopting globalization policies and is found to be a favourable destination for FDI in India. Much in the same vein, the process of decentralization is also promoted for devolving powers at the grassroot level. So, we have globalization concepts operating and, at the same time, decentralization being encouraged as well.

One can argue here that market culture and decentralization are two different extremes, and that they cannot go together. Markets serve by providing incentives to produce and they strengthen democracy by providing means of sustenance outside government structures, and by including excluded groups such as women and the poor. This is what is expected of globalization, or in the process of responsible globalization. Globalization should be fair, inclusive and democratically governed. It should provide opportunities and tangible benefits to all people. One of the plausible reasons why decentralization needs to be supported is that companies are accountable only to the shareholders, whereas a democratic institution is accountable to every citizen.

In Tamil Nadu sectors and industries such as Information and Communication Technology (ICT), road transport and airways, telecom, insurance, banking, automobile, construction and those associated with such industries and sectors have benefited significantly. That is primarily the service sector and some of the industries have benefited. These sectors have generated considerable employment opportunities as well. But, the areas such industries and projects benefit and the type of people who get employed in such places need to be analysed. It has generally benefited the villages on the fringes of cities and urban centres, and those they employ are mostly skilled professionals. Only a few local people who are unskilled are employed in such industries.

The issues that globalization has thrown up in Tamil Nadu relate to increasing ecological and environmental damage which results in loss of livelihoods for those especially in the primary sector. Sometimes the wealth of the State goes to individuals within Tamil Nadu rather than to an MNC; still wealth slips away that ought to belong to the State as a whole. Examples can be cited commodification of water, and selling water as a branded product; boom in the construction industry leading to rivers being used as sand mines; acquiring lands for construction of industrial complexes; paying attention to setting up industries unmindful of the damage that effluents are likely to cause to the environment, and to the lives and livelihoods of the rural poor; the problems of displacement and rehabilitation of long-established communities; increasing profit mentality that reduces ethics in business, leading to problems such as casualization of labour.

Specifically the change in the livelihoods of artisans such as handloom weavers, potters, goldsmiths, ironsmiths and carpenters has been analysed. For the rural artisans who were once addressed as native engineers, the toughest thing today is remaining contemporarily relevant in the ever changing global market environment. There are new machines, new technologies, and professionally trained manpower entering all spheres of work. Trade zones and trade oriented capabilities and skills thrive; and traditional skills with primitive kinds of tools that used to provide livelihoods to a section of the population are at peril. The analysis of many of the rural sectors clearly tells us that globalization is grabbing the resources in rural areas. It is fast depleting or diverting resources for commercial benefits, caring little for societal benefits.

Those few people in the rural areas who have learnt to fall in line and exploit natural resources for private profits thrive as well. They are those who are moneyed, knowledgeable and who have easy access to bank credit etc. The percentages of such people in villages is miniscule. So, the way globalization has behaved so far, it is favourable to the moneyed and the knowledgeable. It is exploitative of the natural resources that the poor depend on for their livelihoods. This is so because the rich and the knowledgeable have easy access to information, credit, and technology, which many of the rural producers do not have any access to.

The Gangaikondan incident (discussed in Chapter 3) clearly tells us that economic rules and institutions prevail over social rules and social institutions. It also shows that capital has the power to influence official decisions, get Gram Sabha meetings postponed, or cancelled, if the resolution(s) passed are not likely to favour entry of an MNC to draw water from within the jurisdiction of a Village Panchayat. The present process of globalization has no means to keep the balance between democracy and markets. That globalization should have a social dimension that sustains human values and enhances the well-being of people in terms of their freedom, prosperity and security remains a request for consideration by the business behemoths.

As mentioned already those in rural sectors do not have easy access to information or financial and technological resources to benefit from globalization. It can be channelized to benefit the large section of the rural community as well, provided we are alert enough to understand the market dynamics and respond appropriately to market changes. The risk difficulty for the poor in doing this are: (i) market-signals are not always dependable or predictable; and, (ii) mobilizing the capital and accessing the right kind of information and technology to remain competitive in the market.

All that many of the Civil Society Organizations have been doing so far is to raise slogans that globalization is no good. The fact is that it is water under the bridge a flood gate that has been let open. The wise thing to do now is it to understand and devise ways to govern or manage the course it takes so that benefits are more, and damages—in terms of social and environmental costs—are less.

Responding to globalization moves at the grassroot level is partly in the hands of local bodies and partly in the hands of the rural community as producers and consumers. Our farmers, floriculturists, horticulturists, weavers, potters, carpenters, blacksmiths, goldsmiths and rural entrepreneurs should equip themselves to cater to what the market demands rather than keep producing what they have learnt to produce over the years. The market demands efficiency. Efficiency is not always contained in what one delivers, but also in how it is delivered, at what cost and at what speed. This might require new technology, credit facilities etc. for which they may have to be organized into SHGs, and other occupation related groups. For one to be alert and change the direction globalization processes take, in the case of rural sectors, it is not slogans that are required, but actionable learning, and learning that can relevantly serve to contemporary demands.

One obvious thing to note from the current trends is, there is very little the rural sectors gain from globalization. There is much they require to protect themselves from being exploited by profiteering interests. Being alert and making right decisions through democratic bodies and preserving the supremacy of democratic bodies rather than giving in to private commercial interests in themselves can constitute appropriate action.

As for facing globalization at the grassroot level, undoubtedly Village Panchayats can play a significant role and give the leadership required to face the challenges, protect resources and use them for societal interests, and make way for using opportunities. The following are some of the suggestions that emerged in a national workshop conducted for validating the research findings on globalization and decentralization.

(a) *Being Aware*: The Panchayat functionaries, first of all, need to be aware of what is globalization, what are the concepts it spreads and the issues it throws-up at the grassroot level and potentially what role can Panchayats play in handling the outcome of globalization processes at the Panchayat level.

(b) *Be Indian by Values and Culture*: In India the first thing that the Panchayats should be aware of is that products are not the real issues. It is the psychology or the submissive mentality that anything indigenous (ideas, technology, etc.) might not be good enough and that what comes from abroad in always better. This psyche must go. The first requisite is cultivating an attitude of respect for indigenous ideas, knowledge, technology, goods and services. In the process of empowerment there has to be an underlying identity of our being Indians, of belonging to this culture, and this environment—that is, identifying a strong self-sustaining footing in this very country of ours.

(c) *Resource-Base of Village Panchayats*: Every Panchayat should know what its assets are: land area, rivers, water, ponds, sand, stone, cattle, wood, agricultural products etc. Then they must go into planning to make the best use of these resources without allowing others to exploit them for making private profits. The Tamil Nadu Panchayat Act, 1994 provides for that. The State Planning Commission has also provided detailed guidelines on how to go about doing the planning exercise at the grassroot level.

(d) *Weighing Benefits vis-à-vis Social and Environmental Costs*: Panchayats need to assess—with help from outside, if required—if the opportunities and the benefits of globalization outweigh the risks. The local bodies have the authority to decide if they should let a given industry be set up in their Panchayat jurisdiction or not. Do a cost benefit analysis in terms of the employment it would generate, the tax payable to the Panchayat and mode of tax collection, and the kind of resources, especially land and water it would require to run, the quantum of effluents the plant would generate, the effluent treatment arrangement and the adequacy of the effluent treatment plant with reference to the overall production capacity planned etc. The Panchayats may seek the help of universities and technical institutions to do this for them.

(e) *Developing Linkage and not Working in Isolation*: The Panchayats today are working in isolation, in coordination with the government machinery at the best. Panchayats should develop linkage with neighbouring Panchayats, NGOs, SHGs, *Dalit* movements, women's movements, workers' movements and other civil society organizations to be able to put across to governments and private profiteering interests that the consent of the Panchayat matters.

Conclusion

Globalizing is good rather than remaining a closed economy. Being closed obviously means stagnating. Globalizing without adequately preparing the domestic sectors on various fronts will throw the economy out of gear. What matters is that, if a development model is likely to leave behind a vast section of population in penury, benefiting only a few, it is obnoxious. The market and technology might leave the common man behind. But, a state cannot make decisions that make some blissful and leave others distressed. Whichever is the level of government—Central, State or Local—public (and private) actors at all levels with power to influence the outcome of globalization must be democratically accountable for the policies they pursue and the actions they take. The need to protect or guard the resources at the village level seems to be more than the benefits that villages might get out of globalization processes. Village Panchayats have an important role in planning to make use of the local resources for the benefit of the society.

Although Tamil Nadu is fast developing in several of the sectors, especially on the service and industry fronts, when it comes to the primary sector, distress departure from agriculture and abandoning rural livelihoods for casual employment in urban centres is becoming the trend of the day. Reinventing the rural culture, regenerating agriculture and rejuvenating rural livelihoods is largely in the hands of the local bodies actively supported by the State.

Annexure

Weaving Centres and Varieties of Weaving Products in Tamil Nadu

Manufacturing Centres		*Products*
Anakaputhur	:	Lungies, shirtings, Real Madras handkerchiefs
Arani	:	Lungies, kerchiefs, saris, silk/cotton saris, mixed fabrics
Arakonam (Area)	:	Lungies, shirtings
Ayyampettai	:	Cotton/Silk saris, mixed fabrics
Andipatti	:	Saris, shirtings, dhoties
Arupukottai	:	Saris, lungies, matty cloth shirting, towels
Bhuvanagiri	:	Shirtings, coatings, lungies, kerchiefs, Madras fabrics
Bhavani	:	Carpets, jamakkalams, bedsheets, furnishings
Cheyyar	:	Cotton/Art silk saris, mixed fabrics
Coimbatore	:	Saris, lungies
Chennimalai	:	Bedsheets, furnishings, towels, dhoties, shirtings, matty cloth
Chinnalapatti	:	Saris, shirtings, mixed fabrics, art silk
Dharmpuri	:	Long cloth, shirtings, towels, dhoties, saris, mixed fabrics, bed sheets
Erode	:	Bedsheets, furnishings, towels, dhoties, shirtings, matty cloth
Emaneswaram	:	Saris, shirtings, mixed fabrics
Gudiyatham	:	Lungies

Manufacturing Centres		*Products*
Jayankondam	:	Shirtings, saris, dhoties, kerchiefs, saris, silk, gada
Jakkampatti	:	Saris, shirtings, dhoties
Kadayanallur	:	Lungies, shirtings, dhoties
Kallidaikurichi	:	Bedsheets, towels, dhoties, saris
Karaikudi	:	Chettinad saris, lungies, dhoties, towels
Kunnathur	:	Cotton/Silk saris, pavadais, lungies, shirtings, kerchiefs, dhoties
Kancheepuram	:	Cotton/Silk saris, pavadais, lungies, shirtings, kerchiefs, dhoties
Kilkodungalur	:	Dhoties, towels, shirtings, kerchiefs
Kurinjipadi	:	Shirtings, coatings, lungies, kerchiefs, Madras fabrics
Karur	:	Made-up items, bedsheets, home furnishings, upholsteries, towels, Turkish towels, shirtings, coatings, casement, saris, dhoties
Kodlikaruppur	:	Saris, mulls, mixed fabrics
Kumbakonam	:	Cotton/Silk saris, mixed fabrics
Koorainadu	:	Cotton/Silk saris, mixed fabrics
Madras/Chennai	:	Lungies, shirting, Real Madras handkerchiefs,
Manampatty	:	dhoties, angavastram, saris, dress materials, lungies
Mokshakulam	:	Saris, mixed fabrics
Mallasamudram	:	Gada, dhoties, towels
Madurai	:	Saris, towels, Turkish towels, dhoties, made-up items, furnishings, shirtings
Naduveerapattu	:	Shirtings, coatings, lungies, kerchiefs, Madras fabrics
Nagercoil	:	Turkish towels, made-up items, towels, furnishings
Palani	:	Saris, shirtings, mixed fabrics, Art silk
Rasipuram	:	Towels, saris (korval), shirtings
Rajapalayam	:	Gada, shirtings, lungies
Saidapet	:	Lungies, shirtings, Real Madras handkerchiefs
Srimushnam	:	Shirtings, coatings, lungies, kerchiefs, Madras fabrics

Manufacturing Centres		*Products*
Salem	:	Saris, dhoties, mixed fabrics
Satyamangalam	:	Saris, mulls cotton/silk, dress materials, silk yardages, shirtings
Srivilliputhur	:	Shirtings, lungies, towels, dhoties, mixed fabrics
Sundarapandium	:	Shirtings, lungies, towels, dhoties, mixed fabrics
Thirumazhisai	:	Lungies, shirtings, kerchiefs
Tiruthani	:	RMHK, lungies
Thirukkazhukun-dram	:	RMHK, lungies
Tindivanam	:	Towels, lungies, shirtings
Tirukoilur	:	Cotton/Silk saris, mixed fabrics
Thanjavur	:	Cotton/Silk saris, mixed fabrics
Tiruchengodu	:	Gada, long cloth (white and solids) shirtings, coatings, dhoties
Taramangalm	:	Saris, shirtings, lungies, mixed fabrics, T. Kunnathur dhoties, lungies
Thirunelveli	:	Lungies, saris, dhoties, shirtings, bedsheets towels
Vellore (Area)	:	Saris, lungies
Woriyur	:	Muslins, fine mulls, saris, dhoties, mixed fabrics.

Source: http://www.hometextilesonline.com/tamilnadu.htm

Notes and References

Chapter One

Ann Majchrzak, "*Methods for Policy Research*", (New Delhi: Sage Publications, 1984).

Biplab Das Gupta, "*Globalization: India's Adjustment Experience*", New Delhi: Sage Publications, 2005.

Business Line, "Tamil Nadu Plans to Move IT into Small Cities and Towns", July 29, 2006.

Deepak Nayar (Ed.), "*Governing Globalization: Issues and Institutions*", (New Delhi: OUP, 2002).

Government of Tamil Nadu, "*Human Development Index – 2001*", (Chennai: 2001).

Jagdish Bhagwati, "*In Defence of Globalization*" (New Delhi: OUP, 2004).

Joseph, E. Stiglitz, "*Globalization and its Discontents*", (New Delhi: Penguin Books, 2002).

Joseph, E. Stiglitz, "*Making Globalization Work*", (New Delhi: Penguin Books, 2006).

Krishna Kant (Vice-President of India), [inaugural address] "*Impact of Liberalization and Globalization on Rural Livelihoods: Proceedings of a National Seminar*", (Hyderabad: NIRD, 2003).

Nayan Chanda, Yale Global Online (ppt), Nov. 2002.

OECD, "*Measuring Globalization: OECD Handbook on Economic Globalization Indicators*", OECD, 2005.

Palanithurai, G., "*Towards Decentralization of Power*", (Gandhigram: Rajiv Gandhi Chair, 2001).

Ramakrishnan, T., "Promoting Tier-II Cities for IT Growth", *The Hindu*, November 19, 2006.

Wikipedia – the Free Encyclopaedia Online, 2002.

Chapter Two

Agarwal, A. and Narayan, S., "*Making Water Everybody's Business*", (New Delhi: Centre for Science and Environment, 2002).

Anitha Sampath *et al.* "*Water Privatization and Implications in India*", Association for India's Development, USA.

Ballaha Vishwa, "Governance Issues in Water Sector in India", Paper presented at IRMA, Anand at a Symposium held by Institute of Rural Management, Anand,

Governance in Development: Issues, Challenges and Strategies, December 14-19, 2004.

Lennart Nilsson, *"Making Rural Water Supply Schemes work"*, Government of Tamil Nadu/Danida, 2002.

Maude Barlow, *"Blue Gold – The Fight to Stop the Corporate Theft of the World's Water"*, (New Delhi: New Press, April 2003).

Mehta, M.A., *"Review of Public Private-Partnerships in Water and Environmental Sanitation in India"*, (New Delhi: DFID, 1999).

NAAS, "Emerging Issues in Water Management – The Question of Ownership", *Policy Paper 32*, National Academy of Agricultural Sciences, New Delhi: June 2005.

Policy Paper, *"Sector Reform Programmes"*, Rajiv Gandhi Drinking Water Mission, (New Delhi: GoI, 2000).

Raghav, Narsalay, *"Who Controls Rights over Water in an Unfolding GATS Regime?"* (June 2003).

Ramasamy, R. Iyer, "Water: Changing a Course for the Future – 1", *Economic and Political Weekly* (Special Article) March 31, 2001.

Statement by Dr. Prodipto Ghosh, Secretary, Ministry of Environment and Forests on Water Issues at the Twelfth Session of the Commission on Sustainable Development, April 2004 (published by: *Permanent Mission of India to the UN* e-mail:india@un.int)

The Hindu, December 9, 2005.

Water and Sanitation Programme South Asia, (New Delhi: World Bank, 2000).

Chapter Three

Dina Malar (Tamil Daily) January 27, 2006, "Suspicions over Panchayat President's Death".

Dina Malar (Tamil Daily) January 27, 2006 reports that the wife of the former Village Panchayat President, Kamsan has filed a case against the South India Bottling Company that the company people took Kamsan to a tourist resort in Coutralam and gave him a lethal cocktail of drinks so as to get the no objection certificate. Mr. Kamsan who recently recovered from jaundice died after returning from the cocktail party.

Institute of Water Studies, *"State Framework Resources Plan for Tamil Nadu"*, Government of Tamil Nadu, 1998.

Jagdish Bhagwati, *"In Defense of Globalization"* (New Delhi: Oxford, 2004).

Kasi S. Viswanathan, *"Thamiraparani Thanneer Kollai"*, July 2005.

Krishna Iyer V.R., *The Hindu*, dated 28.01.2004.

Nityanand Jayaraman, *"Water Wars and Bottle Battles"*, India Resource Centre, May 24, 2005 www.IndiaResource.org.

Public Works Department (1994) *"Groundwater Resources of Tamil Nadu – Present Status of Development"*, GoTN.

Raja J. Chelliah, *Global and Local,* News Letter Jan. 2006, RGC-GRI, Gandhigram.

Rajagopalan, M.R., *Global and Local,* Newsletter Nov. 2005, RGC-GRI, Gandhigram.

SIPCOT, Allotment Order for Plots addressed to South India Bottling Co.(P) Ltd. Ref: N. P-1/GKN/SIBCPL/04 dated 21.10.2004.

Soumyen Sikdar, "*Contemporary Issues in Globalization: An Introduction to Theory and Policy in India*", (New Delhi: Oxford, 2005).

Stephen Cullenberg *et al.* "*Globalization, Culture, and the Limits of the Market: Essays in Economics and Philosophy*", (New Delhi: Oxford, 2004).

The Hindu, Thursday, September 29, 2005.

The Hindu, May 10, 2005 "Cancel License of Soft Drink Unit".

The Hindu, August 31, 2005. "Gangaikondan Panchayat President dies in Hospital".

The Hindu, February 11, 2006, "Panchayat Union gives nod to Soft Drink Unit".

William Nordhaus *et al.* Nature's Numbers: Expanding the National Economic Accounts to Include the Environment (Washington, D.C.: National Academy Press, 1999).

www.hinduonnet.com Viswanathan S. Bottling, Thamiraparani (*Frontline,* Vol. 22, Issue 21: October 8-21, 2001).

www.IndiaResource.org Coca-cola Linked to Bribery Scandal.

Chapter Four

Advocacy Internet, Stealing Our Water — Implicaitons of GATS for Global Water Resources.

Anitha Sampath *et al.*, "*Water Privatization and Implications in India*".

Ashim Goyal, "Getting Water from Public-Private Partnership", *India Infrastructure Report, 2004.*

DFID, "A Review of Public-Private Partnership in Water and Environmental Sanitation in India", (New Delhi: DFID, 1999).

Gleick, H. Peter *et al.*, "*The New Economy of Water – The Risks and Benefits of Globalization and Privatization of Fresh Water*", California: Pacific Institute for Studies in Development, Environment and Security.

Government of Tamil Nadu G.O. Ms No. 260 RD (WSI) dated December 9, 1998.

Government of Tamil Nadu, New Thiruppur Area Development Corporation Limited, Minister for Information, Publicity and Local Administration, 2005.

Government of Tamil Nadu, "Policy Note 2005-2006" NTADCL Demand No. 33.

Government of Tamil Nadu, "Tamil Nadu Panchayats Act 1994".

Jishnu, Latha, "Getting Ready for a Big Splash", *Business World,* 18 (10), pp. 32-34.

Kaushik, Dab, "*Reforms in Drinking Water and Sanitation*", (New Delhi: NDP/TERI, 2004).

Keith Gaunlett, "Water — Life Before Profit", *Integral Liberation,* Vol. 9, No. 9, No. 2, June 2005.

Lyla Mehta and Birgit Ia Cour Madsen, "Poor People's Access to Water", *IDS Bulletin* 35.1.

Saikrishna N. and Vishwa Ballabh, "Entangled Dimensions of Water Privatization: Some Theoretical Underpinings", paper presented at the NIRD Foundation Day Seminar on Democratization of Water, 10-11 November, 2006.

Vishal Narain, "*Making Every Drop Count*", New Delhi: TERI—The Energy and Resource Institute, 2004).

www.psiru.org The Relative Efficiency of Public and Private Sector Water, 2005.

Chapter Five

Farmers Conference held on 9.2.2004; Federation for Protection of Water and Livelihood Resources, Karur.

GoTN, "Rural Development Policy Note 2001-02".

GoTN, "Season and Crop Report of Tamil Nadu 2003-04", (Chennai: Department of Economics and Statistics, 2004).

Janakarajan S, "Avala Nilaiyil Thamizhaga Arugal", (Tamil) (Chennai: MIDS and Kalachuvadi Publications, 2003).

Jeevanantham, "Pannattu Niruvanagalin Tanneer Kollai" (Tamil) (Erode:Tamil Nadu Green Movement, 2004).

Nityanand Jayaraman, "Water Wars and Bottle Battles", India Resource Centre, May 24, 2005.

Polaris Institute, "How Corporations are Planning to Take Control of Local Water Services", *Thirst for Water* (Chennai: Puthiya Kalacharam, 2005).

Raghav Narsalay, "*Who Controls Rights Over Water in an Unfolding GATS Regime: A Case Study of India*", June 2003.

SANDEE *Policy Brief*: "Tank Degradation and Poverty Reduction". www.sandeeonline.org.

Sethu, "Thanneerai Thaniyar mayamakkathe" (Tamil), (Madurai: SIRD, 2003).

The Hindu, December 9, 2005.

Vaidyanathan, A., "*Tanks of South India*", (New Delhi: CSE, 2001).

Vandana Shiva, "The First and Last Commons", *Yojana*, June 2005, Vol. 49.

Viswanathan, S., "Taking on the Sand Lobby", *Frontline*, November 7, 2003, pp. 38-40.

Chapter Six

A country's ability to develop competitive advantage is determined by quickness with which systems and institutions in the value chain adjust international markets.

Ability to develop comparative advantage is determined by the quickness with which the production systems adopt and adjust to new technological advances so as to improve comparative advantage.

Batra G.S. and Dangwal R.C. (Eds), "*Globalization and Liberalization: New Developments*", Deep and Deep Publications Pvt., New Delhi, 2004, p. 101.

Bunsha Dionne, "Villages for Sale in Vidarbha", *Frontline*, Vol. 23 (5), March 11-24, 2006, p. 43.

Comparative advantage refers to the resource positions of a country, which enable it to produce goods cost effectively. A country's resource endowments in terms of soil, agro-climatic conditions, and human resources may enable it to produce certain crops at comparatively lower costs than other countries.

Contract farming is a system designed to obtain desired quantity of quality products as per mutually agreed and pre-determined prices between the farmers and the company.

Dorin Bruno and Jullien Thomas (Eds), "*Agricultural Incentives in India*", Manohar Publishers, New Delhi, 2005.

GoTN, "Season and Crop Report of Tamil Nadu 2003-04", Department of Economics and Statistics, Chennai, 2004, p. 17.

Government of Tamil Nadu, "Policy Note 2005-06", Agriculture Department, Tamil Nadu, Chennai.

Government of Tamil Nadu, "*Report of the Committee on Agricultural Labourers*", Chennai, 1998, p. 12.

Government of Tamil Nadu, "Tamil Nadu—An Economic Appraisal 2002-03, Evaluation and Applied Research Department", Chennai, August 2004, p. 17.

Planning Commission, "*Tamil Nadu Development Report*", Academic Foundation, New Delhi, 2005, pp. 71-72.

Planning Commission, Tamil Nadu Development Report, Academic Foundation, New Delhi, 2005, p. 74.

Planning Commission, "Tenth Five Year Plan-Volume I", Government of India, New Delhi, 2002, p. 121.

Salam Abdul A.: "*Agricultural Input Subsidies in India: Quantum of Subsidies of SC/ ST Farmers in Tamil Nadu*", Agro-Economic Research Centre, University of Madras, Chennai, 2004, pp. 43-44.

Shiva Vandana, "Sowing the Seeds of Dictatorship", *Advocacy Internet*, Vol. 7 (1), January-February 2005, pp. 21-25.

The Hindu, dated September 10, 2005, p. 12.

www.dsharma.org.

www.wto.org/wto/online/ddf.htm.

Yadav, R.L. *et al.*, "Need for New Technologies", *The Hindu, Survey of Indian Agriculture 2005*, Chennai, 2005, p. 99.

Chapter Seven

Debshis Chakraborthy, "*Food Security in India: Policy Challenges and Responses,* (Briefing Paper)" Rajiv Gandhi Institute for Contemporary Studies, New Delhi, February 2005.

GoI, "*Tamil Nadu Development Report*", 2005, Planning Commission, GoI and Academic Foundation.

GoTN, "Policy Note – 2005-06", Government of Tamil Nadu, Department of Cooperation, Food and Consumer Protection Department, p. 2.

GoTN, "Policy Note–2005-06", Government of Tamil Nadu, Department of Cooperation, Food and Consumer Protection Department, p. 5.

GoTN, "Tamil Nadu Development Report", 2005 Planning Commission, GoI, L.P. Singh, *Employment News*, Vol. XXIX, No. 22 28, Aug.-3 Sep. 2004.

Madhura Swaminathan, "Strategies Towards Food Security", *Social Scientist*, Vol. 31/Nos. 9-10 Sept.-Oct. 2003.

Madhura Swaminathan, "Targeted Food Stamps", *The Hindu*, 3, August 3, 2004.

Nakkiran, S., "A Study on the Effectiveness of PDS in Rural Tamil Nadu", Planning Commission, GoI, 2004.

Stephen Jackson, *"Food Security: An Agenda for Global and Local Change"*, (Ireland: The International Famine Centre, 2002).

Surinder Sud, Issues of Food Security, *Yojana*, Vol. 48, No. 4, April 2004. p. 12.

Chapter Eight

A. Tea

– –, "Price Trends", *UPASI UPDATE*, Vol. 5, No. 1 & 2, April 2006.

– –, "Primary Marketing of Tea in India – A Perspective", *Commodity India*, Vol. 6, Issue 2, (February, 2006).

– –, "Tamil Nadu Planters Blame Free Trade for Decline in Tea Price", *Business Line*, June 4, 2001.

– –, "Tamil Nadu Tea Estates to Defer DA Revision", *Financial Daily*, November 25, 2000.

– –, "TN Planters, TUs Talks End in Stalemate", *Financial Daily*, December 2, 2000.

Boriah, G., "Substantial Forex Earnings", *The Hindu Survey of Indian Agriculture*, 2006.

Das, N.K., "The Outlook on Indian Tea-2005", *Commodity India*, Vol. 5, Issue 10, October 2005.

Indian Tea Planters Association, "Why This Problem of Common Tea for India", West Bengal: 1958.

Jaganathan Venkatachari, "Valparai Going Down the Hill With the Stagnation of the Local Tea Industry, Valparai Has Gone into Decline. Can Tourism Revive It?", *Financial Daily*, April 23, 2004.

Sundar, P.S., "Tea Exports Set to Fall Well below Target", *Financial Daily*, November 2006.

The UPASI, "Tea Situation", Nilgiris: May 2006.

B. Coffee

– – "Big Coffee Growers left out in K'taka's Sop Opera", *Economic Times*, February 2004.

— —, "Bail-out Package for Coffee, Tea Growers", *Business Line*, May 26, 2005.

— —, "Coffee Farmers Send SoS to Centre", *Economic Times*, April 24, 2005.

— —, "*Coffee Producers told to Recognize Structural Changes*", *Business Line*, April 16, 2004.

— —, "Modalities on Implementation of Scheme on Support to Small Grower Sector", *Indian Coffee*, July 2003.

— —, "Plea to Pare Borrowing Cost for Coffee Sector", *Business Line*, February 18, 2004.

— —, "Rise in Coffee Prices Not Enough, Feel Growers", *Business Line*, November 4, 2004.

Coffee Board, "Pulney Zone — Self Contained Note", Batlagundu, Senior Liaison Officer, 2006.

Coffee Board, Database on Coffee, Bangalore: Economic & Market Intelligent Unit, March 2006.

Krishna Gopal, "Coffee — A Boon to the Tribals of Shevaroys', *Indian Coffee*, Vol. LXVIII, No. 11, November 2004.

Krishnan Ragu, "Coffee Growers Seek Govt. Aid to Bridge Rs. 170 crores Loss", *Economic Times*, February 15, 2004.

Kulkarni Vishwanath & Kurian Boby, "Tata Coffee to Focus More on Value-Added Segment", *Business Line*, February 18, 2004.

Kullan, T.M., Toxic Tea Market in the Nilgiris, Nilgiris Profusely Bleeds, Save Nilgiris Classic Tea, Coimbatore: Hill Tea Printers, April, 2006.

Kumar Priya, "Indian Tea — The Challenges Ahead", *Commodity India*, Vol. 5, Issue 1, January 2005.

Marketwire Crisil, "Coffee Board Pulls Up Firm for Fake Exports", *Business Line*, May 15, 2005.

Narasimhaswamy, "Glimpses of Shevaroys Coffee", *Indian Coffee*, Vol. LXVIII, No. 11, November 2004.

Phadnis Chitra, "Bitter Coffee", *Financial Express*, August 22, 2004.

Radhakrishnan & Hunasikatti Mahesh, "Global Coffee Market Share: Who Gains and Who Loses?", *Indian Coffee*, Vol. LXIX, No. 11, November 2005.

Rajes Mohan, "The History of Shevaroys", *Indian Coffee*, Vol. LXVIII, No. 11, November, 2004.

Rossillian Florence, "Devotion to the Indian Coffee — A Travelogue", *Indian Coffee*, Vol. LXVIII, No. 4. April, 2004.

Shan Milan & Jayanthi Harris, "A promising Open for Coffee Markets in 2005: An Analysis of Current Trends in Coffee Market", *Commodity India*, Vol. 5, Issue 1, January, 2005.

Subramani M.R., "Coffee Exports Come to a Standstill", *Business Line*, May 3, 2004.

Thomas Abraham, "Coffee Regions of India: Anamalais", *Indian Coffee*, Vol. LXVII, No. 10, October, 2003.

Venkatarmanan *et al.*, "Package of Practices for Coffee, Tamil Nadu Region", *Coffee Board*, December, 2001.

Chapter Nine

Abbe J.A. Dubois, "*Hindu Manners, Customs and Ceremonies*", OUP, New Delhi, 1897.

Amar Kothari, "Jewellery Costs and Carats", The LBMA Precious Metal Conference 2002, Sanfrancisco.

Andre Beteille, Sociology: Essays on Approach and Methods, Oxford, 2004.

Bharti Patel, "Special Agricultural Zones are the need of the hour", *Splash Newsletter*, October 2006.

Financial Express dated Tuesday October 17, 2006.

GoTN "Policy Note 2006-07", Department of Sericulture www.hhkt_demand16.pdf

Himadri Bhattacharya, "Deregulation of Gold in India", World Gold Council (Research Study No. 27), London.

Jaya Jaitly, Visvakarma's *Children: Stories from India's Crafts people*, Institute of Social Sciences, Concept Publishing Company,

Joseph, E. Stiglitz, "Globalization, Technology and Asian Development", *Asian Development Review*, Vol. 20, No. 2.

Letter dt. 14.03.2005 of K.P. Subbayan, Patron, Tamil Nadu Viswakarma Artisan's Sangam to Thiru P. Chidambaram, Finance Minister, GoI.

Letter dt. 23.2.2001 of K.P. Subbayan, Patron, Tamil Nadu Viswakarma Artisan's Sangam to Shri Ruban Hobday, Regional Officer, The Gems & Jewellery Export Promotion Council.

Lyon, *Post-modernity*, Viva Books, Chennai, 2005.

M. Francis Abraham, *Contemporary Sociology: An introduction to Concepts and Theorie*, Oxford, 2006.

Rhona O'Connell, "India: Exciting Advances in the Local Gold Market" http:www.gold.org.

Srinivasan S. and Deenadayalan R., "Rural Artisans in Tamil Nadu", MIDS Working Paper.

Stephen Cullinberg & Prasanta K. Pattanaik, *Globalization, Culture, and the Limits of the Market*, Oxford, 2004.

Y.V. Reddy, "Gold in the Indian Economic System", paper presented at the Gold Economic Conference, New Delhi, November 28, 1996.

Chapter Ten

Government of India (2003), Ministry of Finance and Company Affairs, Economic Division (2003), Economic Survey, 2002-2003, New Delhi, p. 136.

Government of Tamil Nadu (2005), "Policy Note 2005-2006". Handlooms Handicrafts, Textile and Khadi Department, Chennai.

Gurumurthy, G. (2003), "Hard Times for Handloom Kora Silk Units", *Business Line*, Sept. 16.

http://www.blonnet.com/2002/07/30/stories/2002073001141700.htm

http://www.equitymaster.com/buget0506/sectors/textile.asp
http://www.sipcot.com/policies_tn_1a.htm
http://www.tn.gov.in/gorders/hhtk_e-127_2002.htm
http://www.tn.gov.in/gorders/hhtk114_e.htm
http://www.tn.gov.in/gorders/hhtk153_e.htm
http://www.tn.gov.in/gorders/hhtk79_e.htm
http://www.tn.gov.in/gorders/hhtk92_e.htm
http://www.tn.gov.in/gorders/hhtke-74_2002.htm

Krishnakumar, Asha (2002), "Livelihood Issues: Weavers in Distress", *Frontline*, 19 (17), 125 & 126.

Krishnakumar, Asha (2004), "Weavers in Quandary", *Frontline*, 21 (21).

Lakshmipathi, T. and K.M. Dayashankar (2001), "Relief for the Weavers", *Frontline*, 18 (9), 124 & 125.

Muruganandan, "Financial Performance of Handloom Weavers' Cooperative Societies in Dindigul Districts. Ph.D Thesis submitted on October 2004 on Department of Rural Industries and Management, Gandhigram Rural Institute-Deemed University, Gandhigram.

Nagaraj, B. and Narayana S.C. (2003), "Impact of Reforms on Handlooms and Powerlooms: A Case Study of Chittoor District, Andhra Pradesh", *Journal of Rural Development*, 22 (3), pp. 345-62.

Performance Budget 2004-2005 – Department of Handlooms and Textiles – Government of Tamil Nadu.

Policy Note 2005-2006 – Handlooms and Textiles – Government of Tamil Nadu.

Roy, Tirthankar (1998), "Economic Reforms and Textile Industry in India", *Economic and Political Weekly*, August 8, pp. 2173-82.

Saksena, K.D. (2002), *Dynamics of Indian Textile Economy Towards a Pragmatic Textile Policy*, Shipra Publications, New Delhi.

Sharma, Sameer (2004), "The Experience of Providing Innovative Business Development Services in the Handloom Clusters of Andhra Pradesh", *Journal of Rural Development*.

Sundar Sing D.K., John (1980), *The Handloom Industry in Madurai City*, Publication Division of Madurai Kamaraj University, Madurai.

Sustainable Livelihoods Guidance Sheets – Department for International Development.

Chapter Eleven

Antony, Samy L., *Status of Tamil Nadu's Environment* 2005, Tamil Nadu Environment Council (TNEC), Dindigul, April 22, 2005.

Ayyappan, S., "Inland Fisheries: Enhancing Global Competition", *The Hindu – Survey of Indian Agriculture* 2004, pp. 97-99.

Bavinck Maarten and Karunaharan, K., "*Legal Pluralism in the Marine Fisheries of Ramnad District, Tamil Nadu*", IDPAD, Working Papers Series 2006, Number.

Coastal Action Network (CAN), *Protection of Coastal Ecology and Coastal Communities: Issues and Concerns*, January 2004, Nagapattinam.

Department for International Development, *Small-Scale Fish Marketing in Tamil Nadu – An Alternate Fish Container for Women Petty Fish Traders*, Information Bulletin 13, Post-Harvest Fisheries Project, Chennai.

Ganz Katharina, "Social, Political and Environmental Aspects of Micro Finance after the Tsunami: The Case of Tamil Nadu", *Micro Finance Matters*, Issue 9, February 2005.

Gomathy N.B., "The Role of Traditional Panchayats in Coastal Fishing Communities in Tamil Nadu", *ICSF Post-Tsunami Rehabilitation Workshop Proceedings*, January 2006.

Grain, "Fishing profits, farming disaster: The cost of liberalizing Asia's fisheries", *Seedling*, July 2006, pp. 29-33.

Ramesh R., *Impact of Tsunami on the Livelihoods of Coastal Communities*, NGO Coordination and Resource Centre, Nagapattinam, June 2005.

Jose Sunny and Rodrigo Gilbert, *Bioethics in India: Proceedings of the International Bioethics Workshop in Madras*, Bio-management of Bio-geo Resources, 16-19, January 1997.

Pillai, V.N., "Marine Fisheries: Waiting for the next leap", *The Hindu Survey of Indian Agriculture* 2000, pp. 121-23.

ICF, *Report on Coastal Fisheries and Poverty: The Case of India*, International Collective in Support of Fish Workers (ICSF), October 2003.

Special Correspondent, "Coastal Regulation Zone Notification amended to suit Industrial lobby", *The Hindu*, June 16, 2005, Madurai.

Special Correspondent, "Women Fish Workers' Plea: Give Concession on a par with men", *The Hindu*, January 10, 2007, p. 5, Madurai.

Sridhar, V., "Living on the Edge", *Frontline*, Vol. 22, Issue 03, January 29 — February 11, 2005.

Staff Reporter, "FRP Boat boom in Tamil Nadu", *Bay of Bengal News*, Vol. IV No. 9, September 2006, pp. 10-12.

Tamil Nadu Government, *Policy Note* 2006-07, Fisheries Department, Chennai, 2006.

Weber Eberhard, *Globalization and the Human Right to Feed Oneself: The Impact of the Blue Revolution on the Food Security of Small-scale Fisher People in Tamil Nadu*, South Asia Institute, University of Heidelberg, Germany.

Whittingham Emma *et al.*, *Poverty and Reefs: A Global Overview*, Vol. I IMM Ltd., Exeter, UK, 2003.

— —, *Workshop on Globalization and Fisheries*, National Federation of Fisher Folk Organisations in the Philippines, Kualalumpur, Malaysia, November 1998.

— —, *Workshop Report on Fishing Communities of Tamil Nadu*: Traditional Governance and Post-Tsunami Responses, February 15, 2006, Chennai.

Yadava, Y.S., "Improving Safety and Health among Fishers: A Major Challenge in Small-Scale Fishers", *Bay of Bengal News*, Vol. IV, No. 7, March 2006, pp. 2-4.

Yadava, Y.S., *The Impact of Tsunami on the Livelihoods of Coastal Fisher Communities in Tamil Nadu, India – A Preliminary Damage and Needs Assessment*, Bay of Bengal Programme Inter-Governmental Organisation (BoBP-IGO), Chennai.

Index

Above poverty line, 140
Advancement in public water for private profit, 23
AEZs, 92-93
Agrarian families, 106, 132
Agreement on
  agriculture, 87-89, 95, 99, 101, 113, 122, 133, 145
  textiles and clothing, 326, 330
Agri export zones, 92
Agricultural
  activities, 103-5, 110, 112, 120, 129
  costs, 90
  credit, 109
  export zones, 92 , 93
  globalization of, 132
  income tax, 182, 192, 201
  modernization of, 111
  Produce Marketing Committee, 91
  tariff, 98
  workers, 102-03, 124
Agriculturists, 73, 147, 173, 220, 262
Amaravathi River Basin Farmers Association, 70
Annammakoil lake, 78
Antyodaya Anna Yojana, 139, 143
Athoor village panchayat, 60
Auction
  centres, 176, 180, 184, 189, 195, 197, 217
  system, 180, 195-96, 216-17

Bank loan, 110, 120, 130, 257, 259
Bank of India, 231
Below poverty line, 139, 140, 142, 321
Bhavani river, 46
Bio-fertilizer, 111
Blacksmithy, 150, 162-63, 220, 222-23, 233-36, 238, 240, 262-64, 357
Bonus Act, 198
Bore-wells, 26, 78-81, 83
Bottled water, 59-60
Bottling company, 19, 31, 63
Brass vessel-makers, 238
Bunker Beemer Yojana, 295
Bureau of Indian Standards, 229
Bureaucracy, 30, 32, 307

Campaign committee, 27, 36
Carpenters work, 220, 222-23, 233-34, 239-45, 249, 262, 264-65, 356-57
Cash credit facility, 314
Cash income, 148-52, 161-62, 168-69, 171-73
Central Cooperative Bank, 307, 314
Central Institute for Cotton Research, 116
Central Water Commission, 33
Chennai Corporation, 61
Civil society organizations, 16, 19, 20, 24, 32, 37-38, 41, 45, 54, 134, 146, 357, 359
Coastal
  action network, 347, 373
  ecology, 344-45
  management zone, 342
  regulation zone, 342, 348, 373
Coffee
  Board, 175-76, 200, 202-05, 207-11, 216-17, 370
  cultivation, 203-04

estates, 203, 205, 218
industries, 177, 201, 207, 213, 216-17
market, 209
plantations, 177, 201, 203, 207, 217
planters, 203, 217-18
producers, 201, 207, 212, 217
Coke, 23, 25-26, 30, 41, 61, 215
Combined water supply scheme, 72
Commercialization of agriculture, 101
Commission on agricultural costs and prices, 90
Commission on sustainable development, 15, 365
Commissioner of handlooms, 325
Commissioner of land administration, 83
Commissionerate of agriculture, 116-17
Committee on agricultural labourers, 368
Common property resources, 2
Communist Parties of India, 24, 27
Community Grain Banks, 152
Community Gruel Centres, 270
Comparative statement of tax liability, 191
Competitiveness, 89, 95, 98, 132, 182, 275, 340
Composite Textile Park, 324
Computer-aided design, 230
Constitution of India, 137
Construction contractors, 243
Consumer Civil Supply Corporation, 109
Consumer protection, 140-41, 229
Contamination, 15, 117, 121, 129
Contract farmers, 117-21, 128, 130
Contract farming, 87-88, 115-21, 127-30, 133, 212
new management model, 120
Cooperative handloom weavers savings and security scheme, 295
Cooperative societies, 141, 235-36, 257, 294
Cooperatives and master weavers, 312
Cooperatives and the Khadi Commission, 246
Cost-price relationship, 105
Cotton Corporation of India, 117, 121
Cotton cultivation, 115-16, 118-20, 127-28, 130
Cotton farmers, 116-17, 120-21, 128-29, 131
Countervailing measures agreement, 94
Crop
foodgrain, 100, 122-23, 138, 153, 173
horticultural, 87, 147
insurance scheme, 113, 126
non-food, 84, 100-01, 123, 137-38
plantation, 176, 182
Cropping pattern, 79, 85, 95, 100
Cross-case analysis, 273-74
Customs authority, 201

Decentralised procurement system, 143
Decentralization of powers, 1, 4-5, 7
Deemed export system, 306, 317
Department of
Agriculture, 111, 115-16, 118, 122, 126-27, 130, 147, 250
Economics and Statistics, 101-02, 368
Handloom and Textiles, 278
Rural Development, 50
Rural Industries and Management, 372
Sericulture, 371
Direct government interventions, 90
Direct Procurement Centre, 110
Disparity, 16, 207, 218
District administration, 37
District Central Cooperative Banks, 314, 325
Drinking water scheme, 40
Drudgery, 159, 163, 234, 237-38, 243, 255, 261, 267, 287, 295, 297, 303
Dry-fodder, 155
Duo-weavers, 282
Duty exemption scheme, 92

East and West Coasts of India, 345
E-auction, 180, 186, 216-17
E-Banks, 314
Economic and market intelligence unit, 202-05, 209
Economic policy, 3
Election identity card, 165, 174
Electricity board, 52
Employment assurance scheme, 139
Encroachment, 76-79, 81-83, 86, 233, 258, 303
Entrepreneurs protection committee, 31
Environmental damages, 17, 36, 41, 356
Essential Commodities Act, 91, 145, 320
European Union, 99, 115, 131
Evaluation and Applied Research Department, 368
EXIM policy, 91-93
Exploitation, 3, 23, 36, 41, 59, 336, 338, 348

Export credits, 93-94
Export promotion capital goods scheme, 92
Externalities, 38

Fair price shops, 136, 138, 141, 145, 151, 153, 164, 168, 174
Family cards, 140-41
Farm
 exports, 92
 families, 106, 114
 science centres, 194
Farmers
 conference, 70
 Scheme, 112
FDS Scheme, 276, 292-93, 299, 300, 305-06, 332
Fine Cup of India Award, 208
Fish markets, 349
Fish processing export centre, 340
Fishermen community, 340-41
Fishermen trade Unions, 347
Five Year Plan, 87, 268, 368
Focus group discussion, 20, 39, 88, 136, 148, 165, 177, 187, 223, 272-74
Fodder, 153, 155-56
Food and consumer protection, 140-41
Food Corporation of India, 90-91, 113, 126, 146, 172
Food distribution component, 139
Food security programme, 144
Food security, 33, 134-38, 143-53, 155, 157-69, 171-73
Food self-sufficiency, 138
Food stamp programme, 145, 172-73
Food subsidy bill, 135, 164-66, 173-74
Foreign Direct Investment, 2, 6, 16, 33-35, 181, 355
Forestry Department, 250
Free *dhoti*, saree scheme, 321

Gandhigram Rural University, 221
GATS, 16-18, 21, 33, 44, 365, 366, 367
General Merchants Association, 189
Geographical indication system, 212
Globalization
 cultural, 8, 10
 economic, 4, 8
 implications of, 5-8, 271
 policies, 221, 330, 355
Goldsmiths, 150, 222-33, 262-63, 356-57
 local, 226-27, 231-33
 traditional, 225, 228, 263
Government
 buildings, 343
 canals, 102, 111, 123, 126
 failure, 48
 funds, 93
 grant, 52
 incentives, 82
 local, 8
 machinery, 69, 268, 295, 359
 schemes, 279, 289, 316, 323, 330
 sponsored Handicrafts Board, 232
Gram Panchayats, 4, 15
Grassroots action, 354
Green-fodder, 155
Gross area irrigated, 101
Groundwater, 17, 19, 21-22, 25, 28, 35, 37, 54, 57, 61, 63-69, 75-76, 80, 82, 101
Groundwater (Regulation) Act, 64, 68-69
Gruel centres, 306, 320, 324
Gulf of Mannar Biosphere Reserve Project, 347

Handicrafts Board, 222-23, 252
Handloom Cluster Development Scheme, 318
Handloom Export Promotion Council, 273, 308
Handloom Reservation Act, 319-20
Handloom weavers union, 270
Handlooms Export Promotion Council of India, 308
Hank Yarn Obligation Order, 319-20
Harvesting season, 152, 168, 170, 204
Hindu Survey of Agriculture, 185
Hindustan Construction Corporation, 46
House service connections, 49-51, 55
Household grain storage system, 152
Hunger free programme, 144

ICDP, 111
IMF, 18, 44
Indian Bank, 231
Indian Institute of Handloom Technology, 311
Indo-Sri Lanka Agreement, 179
Industrial Dispute Act, 198
Industrial Training Institutes, 238

Industrial Water, 44
Industrial Weaver, 273, 277, 279
Industries
  construction, 4, 197, 239, 264, 356
  cottage, 92, 225, 257
  domestic, 270, 311
  employment-abundant, 199
  hosiery, 57, 160
  oil, 339, 351-52
  plywood, 239, 265
  polluting, 343-45
  private seed, 113, 126
  sports, 239, 265
  sugar, 92, 122
  water-intensive, 67
  wood pulp, 239, 265
Infrastructure Development *Versus* Coastal Ecology, 345
Institutional agencies, 222, 252, 268
Institutional credit, 109-10, 125
Insurance agencies, 116
Integrated pest management, 119
Intensive Cereal Development Programme, 111
Inter-governmental organization, 206
International Coffee Organisation, 200, 217
Irrigation, 12, 13, 39, 57, 68, 75-76, 81-82, 84, 111

Jacquard Loom, 285, 296, 303, 324
Janatha cloth scheme, 299-300, 305, 320-21, 324, 333
Jewellers Consortium Development, 231
Jewellery complexes, 226, 230, 263
Jeya Vilas Group, 315
Joint Commissioner of Labour, 197

Khadi and Village Industries Commission, 222
Kinley brand of water, 60-61, 63, 69
Kokulam water, 61
Kora silk saree weavers of Chinnalapatty, 301

Larsen and Toubro Limited, 46
Leaf factories, 182, 184, 186, 194, 214
Liberalization policy, 179, 187, 190, 213

Maanur Panchayat Union, 31
Macro-level changes, 178, 200
Madras metropolitan area groundwater, 65-66
Management models, 120-21, 212, 306-08, 317
Marginal farmers category, 109
Marketable commodities, 18, 207, 218
Marketing costs, 108
Marketing function, 175, 216-17
Mathur Village Residents General Welfare Association, 66
Maximum cost advantage, 179, 190
Method of distribution of essential commodities, 141
Metro water, 61, 65, 67
Migration, 159, 161-62, 170-71, 243, 258
Milch animal rearing, 151, 170
Mineral water market, 61
Minerals and Metal Trading Corporation, 231
Minimum Wages Act, 112, 126
Ministry of Commerce, 92, 200, 205
Ministry of Environment and Forests, 15, 365
Ministry of Textiles, 273, 308, 320
Money-lenders, 109-10, 125, 150, 170, 259, 285
Mud-chulas, 249-50
Multi-crop village, 158
Multi-fibre agreement, 326
Municipalities and Corporations, 83
Murugan Industrial Weaver Cooperative Society, 307

National Agriculture Policy, 116
National Bank for Agriculture and Rural Development, 110, 315
National Handloom Development Corporation, 273, 313
National Institute of Designs, 311, 331
National Institute of Fashion Technology, 311
National Pulses Development Programme, 111
National Sample Survey Organisation, 106, 330
National Textile Policy, 271
National Water Policy, 13, 15-17, 21, 57, 92
Neighbourhood villages, 38, 344, 349
Nepal looms, 285, 295-97, 303, 324
Nestle India Ltd., 209

Net area sown, 85, 101
New Economic Policy, 89, 323
New EXIM Policy, 92
New Panchayat Act, 4
New Thiruppur Area Development Corporation Limited, 43, 46, 366
Non-tariff barriers, 99, 339-40
Notified villages, 65
Nuclear type of families, 289

Oil seeds production programme, 111
Old-Age Pension Scheme, 327
Organisation for Economic Co-operation and Development, 95
Organisation of Handloom Industry, 277
Out Board Motors, 337, 353

Paddy cultivation, 102-3, 107, 123-24
Panchayat committee, 344
Panchayat leaders, 3-4, 8
Panchayat union, 75
Panchayati Raj System, 275, 333
Panchayats Act, 25, 366
Parry Group of Estates, 189
Patent Ordinance, 113
Pesticides, 85, 95, 109, 120, 129
Planning Commission, 368, 369
Plantation crisis, 175
Plantation Labour Act, 182, 184, 198
Planters associations, 175, 177, 182, 185, 190-92, 198
Pollution Control Board, 41, 42, 63
Pottery articles, 246-48, 250-53, 266
Pottery Cooperative Societies, 247
Powerloom weavers, 302, 304, 312, 316, 322-23, 330
Prawn farms, 344
Prescribed distribution centre, 145
Price Stabilization Fund, 201
Primary Agricultural Co-operatives Society, 110, 125
Primary Weavers Cooperative, 277, 298
Private milk procurement centre, 153
Privatization, 2, 14, 17, 18, 44, 47, 54, 55, 87, 145, 147, 315, 336, 350
Procurement
  centre, 123
  price, 109, 113, 120, 125-26, 130, 143-44
Project type-support, 308
Promoters-cum-rule setters, 185
Public Distribution System, 135-40, 142-43, 146, 148, 151-53, 155, 163-65, 167-69, 172-74, 319, 327, 329
Public Works Department, 83, 365
Public-Private Partnership, 48, 366

Quality up-gradation scheme, 195
Quasi-governmental organizations, 194, 283
Questionnaire survey, 153

Ragi, 152, 164, 167, 169
Ration card, 164-65, 174
Rationalization, 198, 201
Recent policy initiatives, 91
Reforms in domestic agriculture, 90
Relief package problems of weavers, 270
Reserve Bank of India, 110
Revenue village, 141
Rice farmers, 107
Riparian rights, 33
River adjacent cultivators, 71
Riverbeds, 69, 73
Rural
  artisans, 3, 149, 220-22, 245, 254, 262, 268-69, 306, 328, 356
  families, 152, 163, 167-68
  water supply, 13

Sales Tax, 180, 196
Sand mining, 19, 21, 63, 69-70, 72, 74
SANDEE Policy, 82
Sathyam Committee, 320
Savings and Security Scheme, 295, 327
Sculptures, 253-57, 259-61, 266-68
Season and crop report, 88, 102, 115, 138, 367, 368
Seasonal
  dimensions, 135, 137, 148
  employment, 104
Sector reform initiatives, 15
Seed Act, 113, 126
Self-help groups, 150, 170, 350
Sethusamudram Corporation Limited, 345, 346
SGRY, 139
Single crop village, 158
SIPCOT Entrepreneurs Protection Committee, 26, 37, 39
Slum dwellers, 46, 51, 57

Social assets, 150, 170, 286
Social security scheme, 112, 126, 132
Special Economic Zones, 2, 91-93, 343, 345
Specialty coffee association, 212
Spinning mills, 315, 319
Starvation, 134, 148, 153
State Backward Community Welfare Board, 224
State Bank of India, 283
State Planning Commission, 358
State Trading Corporation, 91
Stone carving, 221-22, 254, 256, 258
SWOT Analysis, 327

Tamil Nadu Agricultural University, 116
Tamil Nadu coastal zone management plan, 348
Tamil Nadu Encroachment Act, 83
Tamil Nadu Handicrafts Development Corporation, 252, 269
Tamil Nadu Handloom Development Corporation Limited, 274-75, 283, 333
Tamil Nadu Panchayat Act, 358
Tamil Nadu Small Industries Promotion. Corporation, 55
Tank operators, 52, 54
Tariff escalation, 97, 99
Tea
- auction centres, 180
- board, 180, 182-83, 185, 193-95
- Development Directorate, 193
- estates, 176, 183, 198
- leaf, 188-89
- Planters Association, 369
- trade, 186, 190
- green, 184, 186, 193

Technical know-how, 120, 122, 127
Technology Mission on Cotton, 119-20, 130
Technology Up-gradation Fund Scheme, 299, 324
Technology-gap, 238
Terracotta items, 251-52, 266
Textile and Khadi Department, 371
Textile Committee, 274
Textiles and apparel park, 330
Thiruppur Area Development Project, 46
Thiruppur Local Planning Area, 46
Trade liberalization, 97-98, 100, 113, 126, 132, 146, 335, 339
Trade mentality, 226-27, 263
Traditional artisans, 149, 220-22, 230, 232, 237-39, 244, 252, 258, 260, 262, 268
Triangulation, 20, 136, 274
Tribal
- settlements, 135
- villages, 148

Tsunami, 145, 342, 350
Tuticorin Port Trust, 345
TWAD Board, 50-52, 54-56, 72, 79, 83

Union budget, 180, 182
Union Government, 322
Universal Declaration of Human Rights, 135, 137
Universal Public Distribution, 140
Urban slums, 135, 137, 148, 161, 163, 165, 168
Urbanization, 60, 64, 239, 264, 350
Uruguay round agreements, 91

Various government schemes, 294
Vessels, 237, 245, 250-51, 264, 266, 340
- brass, 237, 264
- copper, 237

Village Industries Commission, 222
Village shop programme, 138
Voluntary retirement scheme, 175-76, 198, 200, 269
Vulnerable panchayats, 39-40

Wage earners, 86, 104, 106, 124
Wage rate controversy, 36
Waste-water, 344
Water
- analysts report, 82
- bills, 47
- charging, 49
- conservation, 28, 44
- contamination, 25
- crisis, 12-13, 43, 56, 64-65
- crunch, 51
- governance, 14, 44
- industry, 15
- level, 62
- lifting devices, 75
- plant waste, 25
- policy, 15, 45
- pouches, 69
- privatization, 16, 44, 55

resources, 12-15, 17-19, 24, 32-33, 44-45, 77, 78
scarcity, 25, 57, 63, 66, 70, 150
schemes, 13
security, 63
service provision, 43
shortage, 46, 75-76
tanker operations, 59, 64, 66
users associations, 15
Weave fabric items, 303
Weavers
associations, 286
outside cooperative fold, 333
service centres, 311
Weaving centres, 361
Welfare schemes, 282, 318-19, 323
Women fair price shops, 141
Worksheds, 236, 254-55, 257, 260, 325
World Bank, 13, 18, 44, 46, 48, 135, 146, 166, 172-73, 365
World Food Programme, 152
World Trade Organisation (WTO), 2, 44, 87, 88-89, 92-94, 97-101, 113, 126, 132, 133-34, 145, 146, 166, 172, 178, 216, 217, 317, 329-30
demand from, 99
impact of, 95
World Water Council, 15

Yarn, 279-82, 284-85, 288, 295, 298, 300, 302, 307-09, 312-13, 315-16, 320, 324, 333
Yield, 107, 119-21, 128-31, 133, 153, 194